The COMPLETE HANDBOOK of
ATHLETIC
FOOTWEAR

The COMPLETE HANDBOOK of
ATHLETIC FOOTWEAR

MELVYN P. CHESKIN

with KEL J. SHERKIN, D.P.M. • PODIATRIST

and BARRY T. BATES, Ph.D. • BIOMECHANIST

FAIRCHILD PUBLICATIONS
NEW YORK

Melissa Makris, Designer

Copyright © 1987 by Mellon, Cheskin Associates, Inc.

Produced by Fairchild Publications

Standard Book Number: 87005-548-8

Library of Congress Catalog Card Number: 86-82186

Printed in the United States of America

To Ray M. Schiele (former Adidas Director):
Who took me from the running track and put me on the road to the athletic shoe business.

P R E F A C E

The growth in the popularity of athletic footwear has been so meteoric over the past two decades that one need be neither participant, shoemaker, coach or sportsmedicine specialist to recognize and appreciate it. A quick glance would suffice. On the streets as well as on the playing fields, magnified by the ever growing reach of television, sports shoes are everywhere.

Indeed, the athletic footwear business has boomed so rapidly that there has been little or no time for anyone to chronicle its historical roots and the reasons for its rise. The new marketing techniques, the technological advances, the opening of societies to accept new sports—these have all occurred almost more quickly than they could be recorded.

More than 20 years ago I began keeping loose scrapbooks full of the shoemaking information I found most helpful and fascinating in my then-young career. At first I was fueled largely by curiosity. Gradually, as my work in the shoe industry evolved to include at one time or another almost every area of the business, I began to realize that my bulging scrapbooks might provide insight and value to many others beyond myself. Talking with my professional peers, I learned that they, like me, were struck by the lack of a comprehensive handbook covering the athletic footwear industry.

Suddenly I recognized that my scrapbooks could provide the grist for just such a book.

In developing the one into the other, I decided that the book should be complete enough to have appeal outside the immediate shoe trade. Given the astonishing growth of sports shoes, many other professionals also need the best advice available about the equipment they wear daily. They also need to know how this equipment affects the athletes and patients they work with.

At this point I hasten to make one emphatic comment: This book was never intended to, nor does it, recommend one shoe brand over another. Throughout the book I have focussed on how the demands of human biomechanics and each particular sport has an impact on the design of the shoes for that sport. Then I discuss how various shoe components can meet the given demands.

I leave it to the reader, however, to decide if the shoes in front of him (in the store) or on his feet can successfully meet the demands. Finally, don't ever forget the axiom that the shoe designed to excel at one function will almost surely fail at another. In this business, you can't have your basketball shoe and run in it, too.

But you can find wonderful shoes for almost every use. Today's athletic footwear is without question far superior to what existed just a few years ago. The shoemaker's craft has been well integrated with the scientist's explorations. The resulting shoe may be more complex to evaluate, but it's definitely better suited to its specialized function. Where once the identifying logo was all-important (it still is important to many buyers), now design and construction have grown more critical, diversified and sophisticated.

Due to the large number of sport shoes available, I had to establish some criterion concerning which shoes would and wouldn't be included in this book. The operant definition I settled on for sport shoes is "a functional piece of footwear designed for sports use." Obviously, then I haven't included sports such as swimming and karate that do not require foot-wear. Likewise, I haven't dealt with skis but certainly have included ski boots.

The case of water-skiing proved most interesting. Until re-cently, the binding or latex rubber foot harness would not have been considered footwear; however, the latest developments in this sport have transformed the original harness into a "detach-able boot." When I discussed this situation with Joel McLintock (1979 world water ski champion), he insisted that his foot support was in fact a boot.

In this case I followed the same rule that has guided true athletic shoemakers from the beginning: If it's good enough for a world championship athlete, it's good enough for us.

Melvyn P. Cheskin
Braintree, Massachusetts

A C K N O W L E D G M E N T S

The idea for the conception of this book derived from a genuine quest for knowledge. After writing several articles for sporting goods publications in 1978–79 I began to sense a requirement from both within the trade and on behalf of the consumer for more complete knowledge of sport shoes. The idea for the format of the book was almost instantaneous, it has never changed from my original concepts.

Although I have always been encouraged by my industry colleagues in completing this work, many people felt I was building a boat in the basement. With a traditional family shoemaking background and the dedication known to all true athletes I never gave up hope of publication.

Through my association with Quabaug Corporation an opportunity for them to review the book and offer assistance came in 1985.

An arrangement was made with Fairchild Publications to finally give the industry and the sport shoe enthusiast their own book. I should like here to give them thanks for their confidence in this project.

SPECIAL CONSULTANTS AND CONTRIBUTORS:

Michel Bonhomme, Jim Bryant, Robert Chasen, D.P.M., James Clancy, Steve Cohen, Armin Dassler, Horst Dassler, Jim Davis, Charles Eaton, Jr., Tom Erich, Leonard Fisher, Joe Foster, Phil Knight, Horst Lachmayer, Carl Levi, Grady Lewis, Edward Manning, Peter Martin, Roberto Muller, Tom Nease, John O'Neil, Sr., Kihachiro Onitsuka, Ken Orton, John Overlock, Doug Roosa, Art Simburg, Jerry Turner.

MANUSCRIPT EDITORS, READERS AND TYPISTS:
Amby Burfoot, Joseph Miranda, Angus Cranston, Eddie Chen,
Vickie Harris, Janet Anderson, Jean Bouzan, Georgina McCaw.

CONTRIBUTING ILLUSTRATIONS AND PHOTO-
GRAPHS FROM: Adidas, ASICS Tiger, Avia, Bata, Bjorksten
Research Laboratories, Brooks (Div. of Wolverine), Brütting, Con-
verse, Danner, Etonic, Greb (Bauer Skate Div.), Hyde Inds.,
Koflach, Kukje (Div. of Hanil), Lotto, New Balance, Nike, Nordica,
Pony, Puma, Reebok, Rockport, Rocky Boots (Wm. Brooks),
Spalding, Turntec.

C O N T E N T S

PART 1

• COMMERCIAL ASPECTS •

"Our future lies at our feet."

HISTORY OF
SPORTS FOOTWEAR

There exists prehistoric proof that shoes were among the first implements early man tried to invent to improve his hunting of animals and birds. Early Homo Erectus, the first man to walk and run in an upright position, dates back some 500,000 years. From caveman drawings we can see that Homo Erectus experimented with crude forms of footwear. The primary purpose of these shoes was to protect the wearer's feet as he ran over rocky surfaces and other rough ground.

Initially, Homo Erectus strapped leaves to his feet for protection. Later he switched to tree bark and then animal hides. Sandals of yucca leaf with corn husk linings, which were tied to the feet with twine, have been found in Arizona in the United States. Some artifacts from these early eras—such as stone tools and bones for scraping leather, and needles and awles for stitching the leather—have survived to the present. No doubt some of these leather-working tools were used for shoemaking. The earliest known footwear dates back some 10,000 years. Sandals of this age were found in 1932 by archaeologist Luther Cressman as he explored a cave in Oregon in the United States.

The Pharoahs of ancient Egypt, dating from around 4,500 B.C., wore shoes made from plaited papyrus. A pair of royal calf leather sandals have been preserved from the tomb of Tutankhamun from 1,325 B.C. The Chinese, dating back to the Tang dynasty, wore shoes of cloth, wood and animal furs. These represent history's first record of footwear from colder climates. Other reports indicate that fishermen from the western part of Ireland wore hide or braided grass held to the foot by leather strips, which they called a "pampootie." In Central Europe as well as in China, wooden clogs were the norm.

1-1. Fossilized fish preserved in rock and cut into foot shapes.

1-2. Early sandals of rope and leather.

More sophisticated early civilizations from around 4,000 B.C.—including the Nile Egyptians, Assyrians and Babylonians—invented early forms of sandals and thongs as a practical solution to protect their feet from the burning sands of their native habitats. However, for specific sports purposes such as running, athletes preferred going barefoot, as vase paintings of 1,300 B.C. show us.

Greek and Roman soldiers wore leather sandals. The Romans might also have been originators of the first spiked shoe, called "caliga," from which Caius Ceasar derived his personal title, "Caligula." It was also during Roman times that shoemaking derived its religious connection with the Saints Anianus, Crispianus and his brother, the popular patron saint of shoemakers, St. Crispin, who preached by day and made shoes by night. Although there are two conflicting stories of their lives, both in Rome and Soissons, France and an English account relating to Canterbury and Feversham, it is generally agreed that St. Crispin was martyred in Briton under Roman rule in 287 A.D.

Wherever they came from and during whatever age, early shoes were often regarded as having magical qualities, since they seemed to make rough terrain smoother and a redhot sand tolerable. Because early man often ascribed supernatural powers to such characteristics, many legends and stories evolved around the miraculous properties of shoes. Among these are: the winged sandals of Mercury, Seven-league boots, Puss-in boots, Cinderella's glass slippers, and Goody two-shoes. Horseshoe and clover-leaf designs both ancient mystic symbols, were advertised as "magic treads" on sneakers as recently as 1934.

THE EARLIEST SPORT SHOES

From the earliest times shoemaking has been known as "the Gentle Craft." Ironically, this presents rather a contrast to man's first shoe needs related to sports, which developed from hunting and combat activities.

The origins of sport date to the days when man finally began to meet his needs for water, food, shelter and warmth. The advent of competition probably begins with the notion of the fastest, most skilled hunter. Archery, for example, was certainly recognized as a hunting skill in mesolithic times some 8,000 years before Christ. However, it did not become an organized sport among the Genoese until circa 300 A.D. According to the *Guinness Book of Sports Records*, the earliest sports records date to 2,450 B.C. in the sport of fowling, which involved throwing sticks for distance, similar to our modern javelin.

Sports relating to hunting and warfare—such as archery, boxing, equestrian events, fencing, track and wrestling—all have origins that date to before the first century. We don't have an exact date, however, to mark the time when man began to transfer the benefits of protection and superior traction from his early shoes to specialty footwear. It was probably in Roman times when spiked shoes were used as weapons against opponents. Mention of running shoes called "gallica" occurs in an edict issued by Roman Emperor Diocletian (248–313 A.D.). These types of sandals with a single sole were probably of Roman/French design. In Egypt shoes used in a bowling game have been found in a child's grave dating back to 3,000 years B.C. Egyptian murals from about 2,050 B.C. depict players of ball games who are wearing sandals.

In early Greek footraces, dating back to the religious festivals held by the first tribes of the Peloponnesus in Olympia, contestants ran unclothed. Kings and commoners alike competed on an equal basis. In tracing the development of sports footwear, as of sport itself, the Olympic Games serve as the best chronological guide. At the first Olympics in Greece in 776 B.C. the winner of the Dolichos (5,000 meters), Coroebus of Elis, ran barefoot. By the end of the first Olympic era, however, the Greek athletes were wearing a type of sandal shoe called "ligula" or "krepis." The Romans later called these "crepida" or "soccus" (sock). By 480 B.C. a Vatican vase painting showed the introduction of sandals on female runners. Today, it seems symbolic that "Nike," the Greek goddess of victory, was chosen the brand name of what has become one of the world's largest athletic shoe companies.

EARLY SHOEMAKING

Early forms of shoes developed from two basic types, the sandal (or platform type) and the moccasin (or wrapped-under type). The earliest boot resulted from joining the original moccasin with a sandal bottom. Little additional modification was made until the Egyptians developed an inward-curving shoe for greater comfort. Early shoemaking emphasized style and function rather than comfort; shoes were straight or symmetrical (no rights or lefts) until the Egyptian idea was readopted in the 1860s.

Manual welted constructions, such as Norwegian welts, lock-stitching and tack construction came into existence during the twelfth to fourteenth centuries. Although there was little direct sport shoe application for such basically traditional shoe constructions, it's interesting to note that the use of metal work, such as the outside iron studs and heel plates as well as the equestrian use of spurs on boots, dates back to the fourteenth century.

Golf can be traced directly back to the Roman empire. In the open country fields the Romans played a game that they called "Paganica" (from "paganus" or "countryman") that involved use of a club and a ball stuffed with feathers. As the Roman legions advanced over Europe and into Britain they probably took Paganica with them. If so, that would account for the development of similar games in several European countries: Cambuca in England, Jeu de Mail in France and Het Kolven in the Netherlands. All these games involved striking a ball cross-country with a club. Cambuca (also the name of the club) was played in the thirteenth and fourteenth centuries and was described in 1363 in Thomas Rymers' *Fredera* as "a game with a crooked stick or curved club or playing mallet with which a small wooden ball is propelled forward." This explanation ties directly into the "official" origin of the game in Scotland in 1474.

Many shoe features, such as lightness and flexibility, are related to sporting developments dating back many centuries. Underfoot shoe cushioning was born several thousand years ago when hikers and travelers first placed layers of soft wool or moss in their shoes to cushion their feet. In the sixteenth century a French monk, St. Feutre, invented a compressed-hair-and-wool mixture for a "felted" insole to assist long distance travelers.

Prior to the white man's arrival in the Americas, natives of the South American jungles learned how to form crude rubber shoes by pouring milky latex fluid obtained from the hevea tree, over a clay cast on an open fire. François Fresnau and Charles Marie de la Condamine reported the discoveries of the unique properties of rubber to Europe in 1751.

Exclusivity of the rubber tree was precluded by the British of the Victorian era by clandestinely removing hevea tree seeds and growing them into plants at London's tropical greenhouses at Kew Gardens; later to be shipped to parts of the Empire such as India and Malaysia.

At the end of the sixteenth century, boots, when worn at all, were used entirely for hunting, fighting and riding, giving rise to their military namesakes—Wellinton and Blucher—as boot styles of the day.

"Pumps" were among the earliest lightweight footwear developed for jugglers and dancers in the courts of European monarchs in the sixteenth century. These turn-shoe constructions became popular in France and England for indoor games such as tennis, and became the forerunner in England of the rubber "Plimsoll" shoe. This shoe was named after Sir Samuel Plimsoll's 1876 regulation governing the loading of ships with merchandise. The shoe itself was developed as a canvas pump with a rubber foxing and calendered sole. Later, this type of shoe was modified into the first popular sport shoe, which became a fashionable street item. In England it was known as the "Plimsoll," in America as the "sneaker," "gym shoe" or "tenny," and by various other names—including "gutty," "sand shoe," and "kaki" in other parts of the world.

The leather industry in America's new world was started by Samuel First Settler in 1629. The first American shoemaker, who came on the second voyage of the Mayflower, was reported to be Thomas Beard of Salem, Massachusetts in 1629. Philemon Dickerson, of Salem, is credited with opening the first tannery.

Prior to 1800, very few recreational sports, other than those already mentioned, originated from war games. Among them were golf (1474), cricket (1550) and soccer (1672). The evolution of athletic footwear continues with sports such as these, which introduced some of the earliest forms of specialized footwear.

The next sport shoe era takes us into the mid-1800s when, along with the growth of shoe industry mechanization, a number of new recreational sports gained in popularity, including almost all of our modern-day favorites. Among these were: baseball (1786), tennis (1793), bowling (1845), hockey (1855), badminton (1863), roller skating (1866), football (1873) and volleyball (1895). Of course, not all these sports gained instant acceptance. When an Englishman named Joseph Merlin invented roller skates to help actors simulate ice skating on the theater stage, he demonstrated his invention at a London party. The preview ended abruptly when Merlin crashed into a mirror.

MODERNIZATION OF THE SHOE INDUSTRY: NINETEENTH CENTURY

It wasn't until the invention of the sewing machine and equipment to roll sole-leather and sew soles to uppers that the shoe industry entered the age of mechanization. As early as 1790, the first patentee of a machine resembling a sewing machine for boots and shoes was Thomas Saint in England. Three other attempts were made before John Nichols of Lynn, Massachusetts successfully adopted Elias Howe's 1846 sewing machine patent in 1851. Shoes built prior to the 1860s were totally hand-cut and stitched, such as in the early turn-shoe constructions. Isaac Merritt Singer's further modification of the sewing machine was in popular mass production by 1863.

Wait Webster of New York was granted a U.S. patent for his process of "attaching India Rubber soles to shoes" in 1832.

In 1839 Charles Goodyear discovered the vulcanized process of curing rubber, which was to have a significant impact on the shoe industry. But it was not until 1868 that the first flat-soled rubber canvas shoes were manufactured. These were principally used as running and court shoes.

Not until the early part of the twentieth century did mass production of shoes make specialty footwear readily available to the general public. Prior to this time, specialty shoes, such as those used for cricket in England, and for ice skating, skiing and baseball in America, were accessible only to a small number of consumers. One of the first large companies to specialize in running shoes was the A.G. Spalding Co. in the United States. Spalding produced shoes for the marathon, high jumping, hurdling and cross-country running in 1909.

Rubber soles, as well as the traditional leather soles, were tried at this time. Spalding even sent members of its staff to the 1908 Olympic Games in London to help develop running footwear. Since tennis (in those days) and cricket were played on lawn, the shoes were hand-sewn, highcut leather boots. Kangaroo leather was used for uppers, along with such other soft, light leathers as russet and buckskin. The lacing patterns were normally a derby or bal cut with brogue. Decorated vamp and toecaps were very popular. The shoe soles were made of leather with blunt spikes and raised heels. The first patent for a spiked shoe was recorded in England in 1861 for cricket shoes. Four years later spikes were produced on a running shoe for Lord Spencer, one year after the first recorded track dual meet between Oxford and Cambridge. Golf shoes of the time were identical to regular streetwear—sturdy leather heeled boots with spikes added later. Soccer shoes were fashioned from a thick natural oil tanned, hide boot with a reinforced hard toecap. These boots had leather soles and heels, and sometimes included leather bars across the sole for traction.

Of particular importance in the newly developed court games of the era was the vulcanized canvas rubber tennis type shoe (sneaker) that was produced around 1868. These shoes were the forerunner of the first flat-soled sport shoes. Originally, these sneakers were designed for the sport of croquet. Later they were adapted as running and tennis shoes. The term sneaker was first used in 1873.

Sometime between 1850 and 1900 the sport shoe look for the first time began to play an important role in the fashion of the day, thanks to the growing popularity of sports for women as well as for men. Boating, tennis and bicycling led the way with a rubber sole shoe with sateen, canvas or buckskin uppers, banded with black or brown elkskin leather. The highcut Victo-

1-3. Early Adidas track spike with leather sole, McKay stitching and permanent metal spikes.

rian style street boot with blades added was adapted for ice and roller skating. Outdoorsmen interested in hunting or fishing wore a leather gaiter with boot. This was similar to a long textile spat covering the shoe, only in leather. Another important breakthrough in shoemaking coincided with the period when Lyman Blake invented a machine to sew soles to uppers in 1858. Blake's patents were bought and improved by Gordon McKay whose name still adorns the McKay stitching process. McKay, Littleway and Goodyear (son of Charles Goodyear, inventor of the vulcanizing process) were the founders of the stitching and welting constructions that bear their names. Machinery such as Jan Ernst Matzelinger's lasting machine (invented in 1882) were being developed in this period to make possible rapid duplication of the operations previously performed by hand. This made more shoes available for the escalating public demand.

In the year 1863 the English Football (soccer) Association issued its first footwear ruling. (#14—"No player shall be allowed to wear projecting nails, iron plates or gutta percha on the soles or heels of his boots") (Gutta percha was a brittle pre-rubber like substance.)

During the same period in the United States, football and baseball players were using identical shoes. In 1870 these were highcut leather uppers fashioned after the styles of the period. After 1900 the three-quarter, or semi-cut, boot became more fashionable, and shortly afterwards the low-quarter shoe came into vogue. Heel and toe plates, sold unattached at first, became a basic part of the shoe by 1890. Changes in materials along with the introduction of better construction methods, such as the Goodyear welt and asymmetric lasts (right and left versions) helped to improve fit and comfort. Whereas football players started out with plain-soled baseball shoes, by 1887 they were wearing strips of leather across the soles to improve traction. In the 1890s cleats were introduced, consisting at first of pieces of sole leather glued together and nailed to both the heel and the sole of the shoe.

The one-piece fiber cleat was introduced in 1915, adding extra traction, and interchangeable cleats followed in 1921.

The rubber heel, discovered by accident as an added underfoot cushion, was first used in 1896 by Humphrey O'Sullivan, an immigrant Irishman from Lowell, Massachusetts.

When Joe Hall, one of ice hockey's most colorful figures, walked into George E. Tackaberry's bootshop in 1903, he didn't realize he was starting an industry that would mushroom in Brandon, Manitoba. Hall ordered a special pair of hockey boots that would later develop into C.C.M.'s world famous "Tacks" brand. As with other early sport shoe designs, it took a dedi-

1-4. Clarence DeMar (wearing shoes with leather uppers, rubber soles, and leather heels) running in the Boston Marathon back in the good old days (from 1911 to 1930). He won the Marathon more times than anyone else, seven.

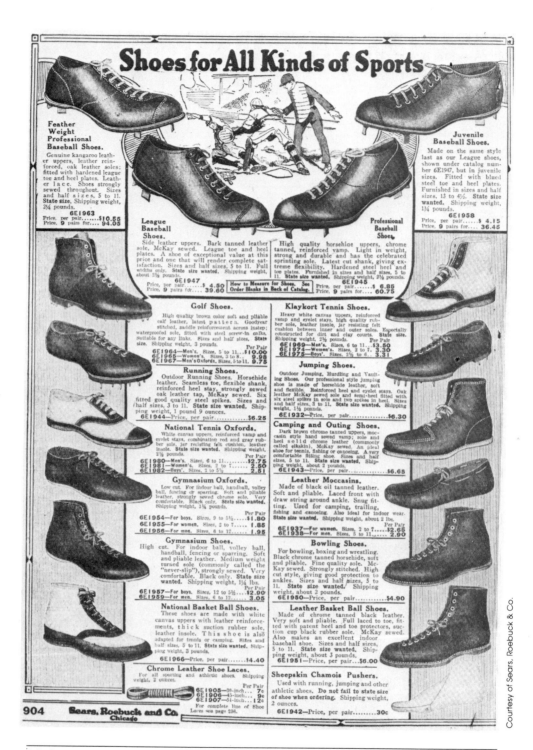

1-5. Specialization in sport shoes appeared in a 1921 version of a Sears, Roebuck Spring Catalogue.

1-6. The beginning of the "Sneaker Era" from a 1935 Sears, Roebuck Spring Catalogue.

cated shoemaker who was willing to listen to a great athlete's request to create what would become ice hockey's most famous skates for over 70 years.

Soccer shoes were progressing at about the same rate throughout Europe, with the rubber-soled canvas Plimsoll, originally called a "pump" or "croquet sandal" gaining popularity in tennis and court circles. Both leather shoes with small spikes or light fabric pumps were used by leading tennis players of this era. Americans such as Tilden and Vines preferring leather while the famous "Musketeers" from France, Lacoste, Borotra and Cochet wore hemp soled sandals. By the early 1900s some of the first name brand "sneaker" manufacturers were selling basketball shoes—these included Goodrich (P.F. Flyers and Red Ball), Converse, Spalding, U.S. Rubber (Keds), and Hood Rubber (Arrow Brand). Even the world's largest catalogue retailer, Sears Roebuck, listed specialized running shoes as early as 1897. The previous year, Spiridon Louis, the Greek winner of the first Olympic Games marathon, had worn lightweight, flat-soled shoes. Obviously influenced by the attention focussed on this event, the Boston Marathon was run for the first time in April, 1897.

Ski boots developed from the original solid leather mountaineering boots used in the Alps in the later part of the nineteenth century. Skating boots for ice and roller skating were just adaptations of street boots which, with little change, proved functional in those sports demanding firm ankle support. Elegant recreational wooden skates with acorn-tipped blades date from around 1780 but more functional designs were not introduced until 1850 when Blondin patented a skate with an ankle support device. The first spikes for track shoes were made by inserting hand wrought nails through leather soles, backed with a metal plate to prevent injury. These date back to England and Germany in the mid-1800s.

The "pedestrian" or marathon era that created headlines beginning in the mid-1860s also influenced the development of flat soled sport shoes. By the end of the century pedestrianism was the rage on both sides of the Atlantic. Most renderings of these contests that often covered six days show participants wearing highcut leather boots that were probably designed to support the athletes on their feet through the long, grueling run-walks. The maximum distance covered in a six-day race involving 144 hours of running, walking or resting at will was 623¾ miles (some 1,004 km) in 1888 by George Littlewood from England round a small indoor track. If there was a historic lowpoint in athletic shoe development, the pedestrian era would probably qualify. At a time when human endurance was being pushed to

1-7. James Foster, son of the founder of J.W. Foster & Sons, at work on running shoes at his factory in Bolton, England in the 1930s.

the limit, the shoe industry was contributing little or no aid or knowledge to further the participant's efforts. Accounts of the races are full of horror stories of blisters, taped toes, blood stained shoes and the pickling of feet (to toughen the skin).

After this time, the quest to find softer, more comfortable flat-soled running shoes accelerated. Entrants in the 1927 Redwood Highway All Indian Marathon (that covered 482 miles of Northern California) reportedly wore double-soled, highcut leather boxing shoes.

There could be no doubting the huge contrast between the flat-soled canvas rubber Plimsoll or sneaker and the highcut leather shoes used by the pedestrians, yet both were used for long distance running in the early parts of this century. This contrast seems to have lasted right up until the new era of biomechanical footwear that began developing in the 1960s and has continued since. As a young sprinter in England in the late 1950s I vividly recall my puzzlement over why all the track runners wore very similar spiked shoes. The marathon runners and long distance walkers, on the other hand, sported a variety of shoes, ranging from one extreme to the other in terms of weight, style and support.

The first great athletic shoemakers began to appear simultaneously in several different countries around the turn of the century. The founders of these great sport-shoe brands were George E. Tackaberry of C.C.M. in Canada, Joseph W. Foster (Reebok) in England, the Dassler family in Germany and Marquis Converse in the United States.

Two family owned shoemaking businesses with a special interest in sports followed remarkably similar paths up until the mid 1960s. Adidas, founded as Dassler Bros. in the early part of this century, can claim such early and great athlete-users as Uli Jonath (Bronze medal, 100m) in the 1932 Los Angeles Olympics and the incomparable Jesse Owens, who won four Gold Medals in the 1936 Berlin Olympics. Adidas first gained soccer pre-eminence in 1954 when West Germany captured a surprising World Championship. Six years earlier the Dassler Bros., Rudi and Adi had split over a family argument. Today Adidas is the world's largest athletic shoe company, while Puma, founded by brother Rudi, ranks number three in size.

In 1924 an Englishman and a Scotsman, Harold Abrahams and Eric Liddell, shocked the world with victories in the 100 and 400 meters at the Paris Olympics. The stories of Abrahams and Liddell were retold in the film "Chariots of Fire," authentic in every detail even to the Foster's shoes the runners wore.

Joseph W. Foster's Reebok company, founded in England in 1900, attracted such early track stars as Alf Shrubb, Arthur

1-8. Boxing shoes with leather stitched soles from 1949. This type of shoe was previously used by runners.

1-9. Adidas' first Olympic medal shoe used by Uli Jonath, Bronze medal winner (Los Angeles, 1932). Weight—215 grams.

1-10. One of the shoes used by Jesse Owens when he won four medals in the Berlin 1936 Olympics.

1-11. The legendary Alf Shrubb who broke world records for six miles, ten miles and one-hour running in the same race in Glasgow in 1904. Here he is wearing Foster's running pumps. J.W. Foster & Sons evolved into the present-day Reebok brand.

Postle and Lord Burghley in the 1928 Olympics. J.E. Lovelock wore Fosters to his 1500 meter Gold Medal win in 1936. During the 1950s members of the famous Moscow Dynamo soccer team made sure they had Foster boots with them upon returning from their first ever trip to the West. In 1958 the winning goal in the F.A. Cup final was scored by a Bolton player, Nat Lofthouse, who was wearing locally-made Foster shoes. The same year Joseph and Jeffrey Foster left Foster Bros. to form Reebok in the U.K. Reebok has remained Britain's largest indigenous brand and now number four in worldwide sales volume.

Typical of the innovators of this period is the fitting story of Leon Leonwood Bean's entry into sports footwear. Vexed by 18 years of chronically wet feet on deer hunting expeditions in his native state of Maine, L.L. Bean hit on the notion of sewing lightweight comfortable leather uppers to the vulcanized rubber bottoms of ordinary galoshes in 1911.

Stressing the importance of performance features such as width fittings, traction and lightness his aim was to give the hunters every advantage for successful deer hunting. Relying on a local shoemaker L.L. Bean quickly found out these ideal features were not so easily translated into a successful product. Early failures to hold together the upper and rubber vamp resulted in 90 of the first 100 boots sold being returned for credit.

Turning this challenge into an opportunity to stress the quality guarantee to every customer Mr. Bean persuaded the U.S. Rubber Co. of Boston to manufacture soles that he could successfully stitch to uppers. By 1913 the famous Maine hunting boot was on its way to destiny. L.L. Bean was probably one of the first companies to offer a resoling service and replace eyelets and high-grade, hand tested, leather laces on his shoes.

By the 1930s the foundation had been laid for most categories of specialized footwear. The major founding brands and their respective shoe companies were already becoming internationally recognized in sporting circles. These included J.E. Sullivan and G.L. Pearce of the Spalding Company, the Dassler brothers, Richings of the Riley Company (later renamed New Balance), Chuck Taylor of Converse and J. Law of England (who made Roger Bannister's famous four-minute-mile spiked shoes).

Vulcanized tennis and basketball shoes were now in production with features that included non-slip and suction cup soles, arch cushions "shock proof insoles" and a variety of colors, which represented a major departure from the traditional black and white shades. Interchangeable cleats as well as nailed-on studs were being used for field sports and in winter sports; skating boots for hockey and figure skating had basically found a

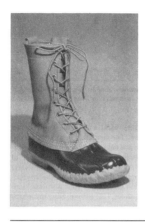

1-12. *Left:* Maine hunting shoes—new (left) and a vintage model (right) turned out by L.L. Bean in 1918.   1-13. *Right:* L.L. Bean in 1912. Harvard Business School has conducted a three-time case study on the success his company has had transforming a greatly antiquated business into a sizable modern corporation with the same image.

functional format. Colors were black or brown, until Hyde introduced the white figure skate for ladies in the late 1930s. The Nordic norm pin binding was first invented in 1928 by the Norwegian Rottefella Company (Rottefella means "rat trap" in Norwegian). Golf shoes, although identical to streetwear, had cleats in the sole and heel, and track spikes had become lighter and more functional. Companies such as Dassler Brothers, Converse, Spalding and others were already beginning to acquire a reputation for "specialized sports footwear."

In at least one case, specialization occurred through necessity. It is believed that the large U.S. rubber manufacturers in the 1930s deliberately confined the smaller Converse Company's distribution to sporting goods stores. None of the others realized it at the time but they were merely helping Converse to become known as the leading rubber sports shoe brand.

Even the most famous outsole for sports use had an inspired functional performance origin. The development of the Vibram lug sole resulted from a fatal mountain climbing expedition in 1935. That expedition was lead by the Italian alpinist, Vitale Bramani, who gave the first syllables of his two names to the lug sole.

Until the invention of Vibram, alpinists had been forced to use two separate pairs of boots. The approach climbing required a heavy, stiff, waterproof boot with a hobnailed sole. For steep rocks, climbers changed to an unlined, lightweight boot with thin, flexible sole of rope or crepe rubber. As was commonplace at the time, the 1935 Rasica climbers discarded their warm, heavyweight boots midway up the mountain, continuing in their

1-14. Vitale Bramani (1900–1970).

rock boots. Unfortunately, bad weather conditions and poor protective footwear forced them to bivouac for the night. Six died of frostbite and exposure.

Vitale Bramani immediately set to work on an effort to create a multi-purpose sole suitable for both the rugged approach climb and the safe, sure-footed traction needed on rocky surfaces. After exhaustive research, he found the optimum formula for his Vibram sole and established his company near Milan, Italy.

Similarly in the United States, Paul Sperry's narrow escape from death in a boating accident caused by a slippery deck surface inspired him to invent the famous "siped" non-slip sole for boating use in 1935.

The fledgling sport shoe industry in the United States was sharply divided into two camps by the mid-1930s—the leather footwear makers and the fast-growing vulcanized rubber/canvas manufacturers. Names such as Hyde, Riddell and Brooks were the major brands in leather, with the rubber/canvas business belonging primarily to Converse, Pro Keds, Red Ball and P.F. Flyers. Many of the rubber shoe makers were divisions of tire companies like Uniroyal, Dunlop and Goodrich.

The 1920s and 1930s saw increasing usage of sponge rubber heel cushions, insole inserts and loose linings in vulcanized and leather footwear. However, it wasn't until the late 1940s that the first modern polymer (plastic) open and closed cell foam cushions were introduced as a shock absorbing feature in wedges, midsoles and insoles. The first cushioned outsole design, invented in the 1940s by the U.S.'s Nathan Hack, took the form of a ripple sole.

Another introduction of the 1940s was the side-laced running shoe with elasticated gore top for snug fit. By this date lowercut athletic footwear was beginning to dominate the market. Shoes of this era weighed about 1.5 pounds (680 gms) each.

It was also during this period that the Japanese sporting goods industry began paying more attention to footwear. K.J. Sohn (actually a Korean) stimulated great interest in long distance running in the Orient with his 1936 Berlin Olympic Marathon victory in Japanese colors. As an historical sidelight, it's worth noting that Japanese soldiers wore athletic type footwear, specifically canvas-vulcanized shoes, during military combat in World War II.

1-15. While the "World Cup '78" (right) weighs only 240 grams, the "1954 World Cup" shoe tipped the scales at 350 grams (on the left). In comparison, English shoes of the early 50s, as the one shown in the middle of the picture, weighed around 500 grams.

THE SNEAKER ERA

In the 1940s with most of the world at war, the American domestic market experienced its first major boom among the specialized sport shoe companies. The famous "sneaker" basketball shoe led the way in comfort, durability and low price. Soon both the highcut models, and later the lowcuts, became the American post-war youth symbols of the era, along with blue jeans. Companies such as Converse and Keds became increasingly important, not just among serious athletes whom they had been serving for years, but also in the mass market that now accepted and copied the style of canvas shoes with vulcanized rubber bottoms as one of the fashion looks of the 1940s and 1950s.

1-16. One of the original Converse "All-Star" models. Hightop basketball, 1917.

As the quality of life had dictated the origins of early sports like fishing, boxing and archery, so did lifestyle play a key role in establishing the athletic footwear industry over the past 50 years. Before the twentieth century, the masses concentrated their energy on the work ethic and economic survival. The overriding necessity of earning a living made leisure time a rarity. Most people worked long hours, six days a week in an industrial or agricultural setting. Sport played only a limited role as an off-work activity. Consider the limited means of communication and transportation, the lack of athletic facilities (outdoor and particularly indoor), and it's easy to understand why sport was enjoyed mainly by the few and rich.

Many of these factors have changed since the 1920s. The work week has steadily decreased, giving the laborer more leisure time. Household appliances have made the woman's job easier and less time-consuming. Automobiles and public transportation have become a way of life, along with radio, television and newspapers. The standard of living has improved tremendously throughout the Western World, giving the average family more money to spend on their increased amount of leisure time.

Numerous studies have shown that most people will buy good quality sports equipment not only because it tends to be more durable but also because it performs better. This fulfills the individual's natural sporting instinct to perform at the top of his/her ability. In a sense, we have even tamed the climatic limits on sports with the construction of more and more indoor sports facilities. Now enthusiasts can enjoy tennis and other court sports, ice-skating and swimming, to name just a few, on a year-around basis. Another emerging influence on sports has been the birth of professionalism. This and the commercialization of sports have drawn heavy financing, advertising and mass exposure to the sports world. Television, through the major role it plays in influencing people's lifestyles, has dramatically increased the public's interest in sports.

1-17. Tiger's first entry into sports shoes. Basketball model from 1951.

It's almost ironic when you consider that television viewing, among the most sedentary of activities, has moved many to begin participating in sports to improve their health. Television has focussed attention on the healthy body, which can only be attained through a vigorous exercise regimen. In beginning to exercise, many people have found the routine pleasurable and meaningful in addition to health-enhancing.

With this upsurge in sports participation, it immediately followed that the demand for athletic footwear would swell. No matter what sports activity the individual chooses to pursue, there is almost certainly a specific sport shoe made for that activity. Following the economic laws of supply and demand, the growing need for athletic shoes produced greater availability, more specialization and a better quality of sport shoes.

MODERNIZATION OF ATHLETIC FOOTWEAR

Thus the stage was set in the 1950s for a small industry to leapfrog into a major segment of the footwear business. The major shoe manufacturers had always considered the specialized sport shoe category too small to merit their attention and had never attempted to fill this market niche. The specialists, spearheaded by Adidas and Puma (formerly Dassler Brothers until their 1948 split) in Europe and Tiger in Japan, not only gave birth to centralized sport shoe marketing, but also brought "testimonial advertising" and early biomechanical shoe designing to the shoe world.

First they conquered soccer, then they turned to track and field, then they used their expertise to make new inroads into most of the world's major sports markets. Spot Bilt, the U.S. brand, had at this time the lion's share of the track shoe market. Tiger, formed in 1949, concentrated strongly on their chosen area—long distance running and track and field. Their efforts in introducing new materials, such as nylon uppers and blown rubber wedges and midsoles, carved out an historical place for Tiger in the 1960s. The same efforts also laid the foundation for an off-shoot company, Nike, destined to play a major role in the 1970s.

By then most of the world's great sport shoe makers had been attracted by the huge success of the big three. In 1968, after the Mexico City Olympics had been televised world-wide, Adidas was able to claim that over 80 percent of all the Olympians had been wearing its shoes. This type of advertising, coupled with the already discussed increases in leisure time and health awareness, triggered a sports shoe boom that took athletic shoes out of the gym and off the track and landed them on the streets in the middle of the booming athletic fashion look.

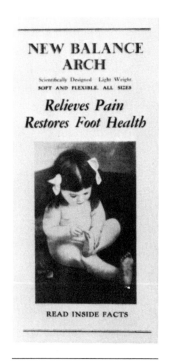

1-18. New Balance started as an Orthotics producer in 1912.

The new leather training flats (originally adapted from soccer training shoes in the 1950s and used as training flats by track and field athletes) swept the Western World just as the sneaker explosion had spread across the U.S. 20 years earlier.

Economically, the time between 1968–1971 was an opportune one for the West German sport shoe companies to attack the traditional U.S. market. The U.S. had just abandoned the gold standard and prices of European imports were extremely competitive during this period. This economic factor, along with the new styling and better function of the European brands, led to the domination of the U.S. sport shoe market for the next decade. The U.S.'s domestic leather sport shoe manufacturers were slow to adjust to new constructions like direct vulcanized rubber soling on cleated footwear. They preferred to remain with the traditional welted types of construction, which they considered safer and cheaper than experimenting with the lighter, more functional new materials. The shell sole basketball shoe, introduced by Adidas in 1968, and the direct attached bottom of PVC and PU introduced in the early 1970s, were two more examples of more modern constructions.

If any single event marked the beginning of the "European dominance" era in athletic footwear in the U.S. it was one that occurred on a pleasant warm evening in Houston, Texas in 1968. On the eve of the National Sporting Goods Show at Houston's Astrodome, a major collegiate basketball rivalry was coming to a head with the confrontation between John Wooden's famed UCLA Bruins, undefeated for the season, and the local Houston Cougars, also undefeated.

As an integral part of the U.S. canvas vulcanized sneaker era of the 1940s and 1950s Converse had reigned supreme on the basketball court over all other brands, including Pro-Keds, P.F. Flyers and Red Ball. For the previous year, however, Adidas had been working quietly on a new leather basketball shoe construction, now known as the stitched shell sole construction.

With its famed trademark everywhere in evidence, Adidas launched their new shoe in true Adidas style. About half the UCLA and Houston players wore it in their national championship contest. Members of the professional San Diego Rockets of the National Basketball Association also soon broke the old basketball shoe tradition. The message was clear that U.S. manufacturers had lost the lead in product innovation and visual identification. The Europeans had established superiority. The U.S. brands would face a long, difficult struggle before they could again call themselves equals.

With modern communication and promotion aiding the world-wide athletic shoe brand message, Adidas and Puma soon

1-19. Bill Bowerman, the athletic coach who loved shoes.

1-20. Nike's outstanding contribution to athletic footwear started in the early 1970s, after its founders broke from Tiger.

1-21. Early Nike models of training shoes from 1972.

1-22. New Balance's "Trackster" running shoe from 1967, warns of "look alikes."

cornered the market in such international sports as soccer, tennis and track and field. U.S. manufacturers, meanwhile, continued to stick to traditional American sports like baseball, football and basketball. It was not until the running boom of the late 1970s that the traditional U.S. firms and some notable newcomers began to compete on a more international basis with the Europeans and Japanese. During those years, the U.S. sport scene changed dramatically from its previous focus on high school and college team sports to the more general pursuit of individual fitness.

The traditional shoe companies responded to this new market by joining in, if not in function at least in appearance with the "pseudo-athletic" look. However, at the same time dozens of new functional sport shoe manufacturers like Nike and Pony started to bring out new ideas. A number of revitalized companies, including Brooks, Hyde and Converse, also joined the push to product innovation. In 1960 Bill Bowerman started tinkering with track shoes and to his joy world class runners from his University of Oregon team broke records in shoes he made.

During an association with Tiger shoes in Japan, Bill Bowerman introduced his concepts and specifications for running shoes. In 1965 in collaboration with another Oregon runner Jeff Johnson, major innovations such as nylon uppers and full-length cushioned midsoles were introduced onto running shoes. After forming Nike in 1971 this team along with founder Phil Knight continued major innovations over the next decade by introducing the waffle sole, air cushioning and variable width lacing system.

From 1975 onward other companies namely Etonic, Brooks and Saucony joined Nike to introduce such features as EVA material, rearfoot motion control devices and removable molded insoles.

In 1961 another small, specialized company, known for its orthopedic inserts and shoes since 1906, started to take a serious look at the types of shoes worn by long distance runners. No one outside the immediate Boston area was aware of the company's early experimentation with ripple soles for added traction and heel wedges for added shock absorption. This company was also the first to introduce width fittings to athletic shoes, bringing an even greater specialization to sports shoes (and a certain aggravation to retailers, who were hounded by runners to stock them). This company, New Balance, founded appropriately close to the Boston Marathon, also deserves its place in athletic shoe history.

Many relics of sport shoes and shoemaking equipment from the past, dating back to 1914, can be viewed at the Adidas

1-23. *Left:* Shoe making equipment and machinery from the 1920s, at Adidas' Museum in Herzogenaurach, West Germany.   1-24. *Right:* Factory photo of Converse's Malden production. Early 1900s.

museum in Herzogenaurach, West Germany. The museum features the first multi-studded soccer boot (made in 1949), the first four-spiked track shoe (1951), the first screw-studded soccer shoe (1953), the first track shoe with lateral ball reinforcements (1955), the first nylon-soled soccer shoe (1957) and early nylon-soled track shoes. Finally the American football boots and baseball shoes from the late 1950s and early 1960s give ample testimony to the Adidas creativity that reached fruition in the 1960s, springboarding the company to the forefront position in the minds of sports enthusiasts everywhere.

Not to be overlooked in the development of advanced sports shoes is the mono-bloc polyurethane injected downhill ski boot pioneered in the United States by Lange in the 1960s. A decade later this revolutionary boot was voted the most innovative shoe construction of the century by a group of prominent international shoemakers. In 1948 when most skiers were trying to conquer the linkage problem by lashing their leather boots to skis with long thongs, Harvard student Bob Lange had a different idea. Lange first experimented with applying polyester resin to stiffen leather boots. Although this did harden the boots it did not solve the problem of easy forward flex with lateral rigidity. Entering the plastic business in his home in Dubuque, Iowa he worked at night with an ABS plastic compound to make a boot that would ski.

Finally, in 1957 Lange made his first successful plastic boots. In true athletic shoe tradition, using himself as a wear tester on the slopes, he quickly added a hinge to gain forward flex and switched to a Du-Pont plastic. At the same time in Europe Fritz

1-25. Early Adidas track shoe in white leather with leather sole worn by Rudolf Harbig when setting his 800 m. world record in 1939.

1-26. Adidas' sport shoe. The Museum's earliest remaining track shoe model from 1930.

Henke put an end to lacing frustration when he introduced buckles to ski boots in 1955. By 1966 these two innovations were appearing together on a ski boot and at the Grenoble Winter Olympics in 1968 many of the world's top racers were in Lange's. Lange sales took off in Europe as well as North America, and ski-boot factories everywhere switched from leather to plastic overnight. Custom-fitting the skiers through innerboot injection of polyurethane foam began in the early 70s. By the early 1980s compufit offered to marry custom fitting with computer analysis to recommend the most suitable boot for the skier's foot shape.

By this date polyurethane was the most widely used material for ski boot shells and a whole mold and injection center had developed in Monte Belluna, Italy.

In the late 1960s changes in cross-country skiing started to effect the traditional Nordic Norm standards of 75mm and 50mm/12mm binding for touring and 50mm/7mm for racing. Norwegian surgeon Dr. Nils Eie was one of the first iconoclasts. He developed a bail-less binding, appropriately named the EIE system. Other experimenters tried to improve upon a combination boot-to-binding link but little progress was made until Adidas entered the cross-country ski market in 1976 with its 38 mm system.

Another important landmark in sports shoe history was reached in 1975 but this time not by a shoe manufacturer. A running magazine named *Runner's World* (founded in 1966) that year published the first of its controversial ratings of running shoes found in the U.S. The effect of these early shoe comparisons by doctors, runners and other running experts intensified product development improvements in all areas of athletic footwear. At the same time the ratings made public a knowledge of shoe features and constructions long regarded as secrets of the trade. In 1977 when *Runner's World* introduced independent biomechanical laboratory testing of running shoes, the age-old craft of shoemaking found itself suddenly thrust into scientific and medical areas that included chemistry, kinesiology, biomechanics and podiatry.

Specialization continued in sport shoe manufacturing throughout the 1970s and 1980s, as you will read in this book. Almost every sport in the world now has developed its own type of shoe, specifically suited for the functions required by each individual sport. Even obscure sports such as parachuting and luge have their own unique footwear.

At the retail level the demand for sport shoes in the last two decades has even created its own chains of specialty stores. In addition, shoe sales have climbed to the point where they represent about 30 percent of overall sales in the retail sporting goods trade. According to the best available estimates, about one in every 12 pairs of shoes sold today are functional sports shoes. One in nine are of sports appearance.

The 1980s saw the athletic shoe industry reach full maturity. The biomechanical era had arrived. Industry sales increased from the millions to the billions and previously tiny companies became household words. Every category of sport shoe became more specialized, more functional, more technical and more expensive.

Spearheaded by the running boom in the U.S., sport shoes became less traditionally crafted with natural materials and more scientific, calling into use man-made upper and soling components. Emphasis was placed on product protection, foot support and injury risk reduction through use of expanded rubbers and plastics as cushioning materials. Biomechanical, electronic and computer testing were added to the decades old practice of wear testing. Specialized companies from different countries all began moving in the same direction—trying to improve their shoes' biomechanical performance. If a company met with success in one sport, it quickly moved into others, hoping to capitalize on the booming athletic market. Older, established sport shoe manufacturers expanded into clothing and software. Some like Adidas even produced hard goods, inflatables and luggage.

The 1980s have already seen additional technological advances, particularly in the area of computer aided design-computer aided manufacturing (CADCAM). Combination sole materials have also proliferated, among them PU/rubber, replaceable outsoles, custom molded sporthotic inserts and Nike's air-filled midsoles. Personal endorsements for sport shoes have helped make certain star performers the first athletic shoe millionaires, while Adidas became the first billion dollar sport shoe company in the early years of the decade.

1-27. Two American institutions team up for an early 1930s promotion for children's shoes—Converse and Mickey Mouse.

"What profits now to understand, a dapper boot, a
little hand." Alfred, Lord Tennyson, 1846

C H A P T E R $\quad$ 2

MARKETING OF ATHLETIC FOOTWEAR

Considering the universal success athletic footwear has enjoyed in both shoe and sports industries, surprisingly little has been written on the subject of sports shoe marketing. Recent years, however, have seen many articles on running shoes and their impact on the sports market in terms of sales and shoe technology.

Many observers consider athletic footwear a phenomenon that has come to symbolize the modern-day fitness look. Waves of faddish enthusiasts turn from one sport to another every couple of years, taking their court, running, deck or aerobic shoes with them onto the streets. Although the street use of functional athletic shoes has no doubt been responsible for huge volume sales, the world-wide industry has grown from a true dedication to sports performance and innovation in shoemaking.

The business schools at Harvard, Wharton and Stanford have already recognized the marketing successes of a few sports footswear companies. This chapter likewise records the coming-of-age of the industry, presenting a comprehensive report on a much discussed, but little understood subject.

In 1962 Phil Knight, a keen runner and former student at the University of Oregon, completed his Stanford University thesis on a method to develop a new business in athletic footwear. His theory, based on Japanese successes in the camera business, could be applied to foreign competition from European sport shoes. In 1964, with the help and product guidance of his former track coach, Knight went into business importing Japanese made "Tiger" running shoes to the U.S. Eight years later, after breaking with the Japanese firm, he decided to create his own brand name

(a) NIKE: BILL BOWERMAN/PHIL KNIGHT

(b) ADIDAS: ADI DASSLER

(c) CONVERSE: MARQUIS CONVERSE

(d) PUMA: RUDI DASSLER

(e) TIGER: KIHACHIRO ONITSUKA

2-1. The international sport shoe champions: (a) the sportsmen who loved shoes; (b) the shoemaker who loved sports; (c) father of the "sneaker"; (d) turned athletic footwear into a business; (e) the greatest sport shoe maker in the "Eastern" world.

shoes. The name of the new company was Nike and over the next 10 years Knight implemented his business strategy to take Nike to the top of the U.S. market in running shoes.

Nike, like many of the other top athletic shoe companies, started out as a specialized producer of shoes for one sport. In Nike's case, the sport was cross-country and road running. In the 1920s Adidas had specialized in soccer and track shoes. Puma followed the same pattern in the 1940s, and Tiger specialized in running shoes in the 1950s. Converse, almost from its inception in 1908, concentrated on basketball. Reebok, after following the traditional specialized marketing pattern in the United Kingdom for over half a century, catapulted into the world's top 5 brands in 1985 by capitalizing on the aerobics exercise market in the U.S.

Whether by design and timing, as in the case of Nike, or by dedication and tradition as with Adidas, successful sports shoe marketing begins with functional, innovative products. The development and ultimate superiority of a product starts with scientific testing and acceptance among leading world class

MAJOR INTERNATIONAL ATHLETIC SHOE BRANDS 1985–1986

BRANDS AND MAJOR MANUFACTURERS OVER $100,000,000							
1. ADIDAS	2. NIKE	3. PUMA	4. REEBOK	5. TIGER	6. CONVERSE	7. PONY	8. NEW BALANCE
BATA INT.	KUKJE (ICC) KOREA		H.S. CORP. KOREA				POU CHEN (P.C.C.) TAIWAN
ADIDAS	DUNLOP		REEBOK				N.B.
POWER	NIKE		CONVERSE				REEBOK
NORTH STAR	SPALDING		TIGER				ADIDAS
BELMAR	PRO-SPECS		SPALDING				AVIA
SPARX	PONY						WILSON
							PONY

EXAMPLES OF OTHER IMPORTANT NATIONAL BRANDS							
U.S.A	GERMANY	U.K.	ITALY	FRANCE	JAPAN	CANADA	OTHERS
ETONIC	(E.B.) BRUTTING	MITRE	LOTTO	LE COQ	MIZUNO	BAUER	KARHU—FINLAND
HYDE INDS.	ROMIKA	GOLA	DIADORA	PATRICK	ASAHI	C.C.M.	KOFLACH—AUSTRIA
FOOTJOY	DACHSTEIN	STYLO	NORDICA	NOEL	YONEX	MICRON	KASTINGER—AUSTRIA
TIMBERLAND	PHOENIX	HI TEC	SUPERGA	HUNGRA	HARRIMAYA	POWER	TYROL—RUMANIA
ROCKPORT	LICO	DUNLOP	CABER	T.B.S.	YAMAHA	DAOUST	INTER—HOLLAND
KANGAROOS	GUTE		TECHNICA	TRAPPEUR			RAICHLE—SWITZERLAND
BROOKS	GEPARD		MUNARI	AIGLE			TRETORN—SWEDEN
AVIA							PRO-SPECS—KOREA
SPERRY							
K-SWISS							
KAEPA							
AUTRY							
DEXTER							
PRO-KEDS							

2-2. Major international athletic shoe brands—1985–1986.

athletes. This leads to the next and most important part of sport shoe marketing, the creation of an image in the marketplace.

Once a company has established sales expertise in one sport, it generally moves into another sport or category. New Balance, for example, established its reputation in running shoes, and then planned to position its brand with innovative features in a selected segment of another sports market. True to its image creating pattern, New Balance made its entry into tennis at the high end of the market, where top calibre players demand the best in performance footwear.

WITHIN THE SHOE TRADE

The regular shoe industry has traditionally enjoyed sales volumes far higher than the athletic shoe segment. This explains why many countries, such as Canada, which produce significant quantities of their own regular footwear requirements (40 percent), have developed only a few areas of domestic athletic shoes, namely, ice skates, cross-country and curling shoes. Only in the latter part of the 1970s was an attempt made in Canada to produce shoes for the higher volume areas, including running shoes, field shoes and court shoes.

In larger sports market countries like Germany, Japan and the United States, small traditional sports footwear manufacturers have expanded their original areas of specialization to encompass many of the other major volume sports categories. The largest sport shoe manufacturer today, Adidas, produces specialized shoes for more than 60 different sports categories. Other leading companies have also made large increases in their range of shoes in recent years.

Some athletic shoe company executives believe their companies have simply done a better job of providing a comfortable product at a reasonable price than either the traditional dress shoe or casual shoe manufacturers. With dress and work shoe costs averaging around $45 and casuals around $35 (U.S. prices, 1984, *Footwear News*), the average athletic shoe cost of $25 certainly seems to give this argument some credibility.

Comparing the world's shoe producers to farmers, if you will, it seems reasonable to compare the regular shoe manufacturers to grain farmers and the sport shoemakers to dairy farmers. Both share the same basic rudiments of farming. However, the dairy farmer, like the sport shoe company, produces a more complex product that serves a smaller percentage of the population than the grain farmer.

Like its counterpart, the larger shoe industry, the athletic footwear producers make many varied constructions of shoes. It is said that there is as much diversity in athletic shoe production as there are in all the areas of regular footwear. Certainly there are as many different categories, including the following:

MAJOR SHOE STYLES
    Moccasin
    Ladies' Dress
    Slippers
    Clogs
    Casuals
    Joggers
    Men's Dress
    Work boots
    Espadrilles
    Sandals
    Rubber Waterproof

MAJOR SPORT SHOE STYLES
    General Trainer
    L.D. Trainer
    Track

Soccer Shoes
Tennis Shoes
Cross Country Ski
Ski Boots
Golf
Skates
Outdoor
Gymnastic Slippers

MULTI-NATIONAL VS. INTERNATIONAL

It is an enigma, of course, that the larger established trade has allowed a major and technically innovative area of its business to develop into a separate trade. Few of the large shoe companies have made an impression with a branded athletic shoe line even though one of every 12 shoes sold in the Western World is now from the athletic category.

Among the largest manufacturers and distributors of regular footwear (other than branded athletic shoes), we find the following companies: Bata of Canada (originally of Czechoslovakia), Clarks of England, Brown Shoe of the U.S., US Shoe Corp., International Shoe Co. of the U.S., I.C.C. Korea, Genesco U.S.A., C. Itoh & Co. of Japan and Stride Rite Corp of the U.S.

Bata, which ranks as the world's largest shoe organization with over 100 companies in almost as many countries, has made a token, and largely unsuccessful, effort to establish a brand identity of its own. Only Kangaroos, among larger U.S. shoe companies is now attempting to alter its marketing orientation from popular family brand to core athletic.

Many of the biggest companies, including Brown Shoe, U.S. Shoe Corp., International Shoe, Clarks and British Shoe Corp., have not involved themselves to any degree in sports footwear, preferring to manufacture and market in their traditional fashion area. Other large organizations like Mitsubishi (Pony), Romika of Germany, Bally of Switzerland, Stride Rite (Pro Keds), Wolverine (Brooks and Kaepa) of the U.S. and I.C.C. (Pro Specs) of Korea have either invested in their own name brand (for example, Bata Power brand in North America) or made sport shoes under license for other major brands. Some of these companies have also bought existing or troubled brands, hoping to revitalize them and capture a portion of the expanding sport shoe market.

Once a shoe company has established expertise in one sport area in one country, where the sport is especially popular, the company generally tries to export to other countries where the sport is played. The product development and marketing is first centralized in one country. Then distribution or manufacture under license is set up in other international markets. The head office normally appoints distributors, who have exclusive rights to sell the brand in the selected country. If the market is particularly large, more than one geographical distributor might be appointed.

It is also common for parent companies to launch joint venture businesses with distributors, or to set up separate companies to handle distribution on a direct basis. Then a distributor makes purchases from a parent owned factory at a trade discount (normally not allowed to exceed the maximum trade discount given customers in the producing country, so as not to contravene anti-developing regulation). If purchases are made from a licensed factory, a royalty is usually paid to the parent company. Centralized marketing and product development work effectively in sports footwear because the requirements for each sport shoe do not vary much from country to country. For example, a good tennis shoe designed and made in the United States can be used around the world.

In the traditional shoe trade, by contrast, fashion and climate conditions dictate shoe styling in each part of the world. Buoyed by mass purchases of everyday shoes, traditional shoemakers have tended to become national rather than international firms. If a regular shoe company does decide to go multi-national, it will allow each national branch to design and market shoes best suited for its locale.

Athletic shoe companies, having established a centralized approach to marketing (product research and development, a centralized logo, name and advertising) can use these tools throughout the world. The number one ranked tennis player not only plays the same game in every country; he or she wears the same shoes, advertising the brand name. If the shoes are good enough for the world's best, one assumes they're good enough to be sold around the world.

BRAND IMAGE: THE KEY TO SUCCESS

Marketers are fond of saying: "The product makes the brand; the brand doesn't make the product." In sports footwear this adage although true certainly has a different meaning when applied to sales success. If there has ever been a stronger marketing image than the visually endorsed "testimonial" sport shoe brand it would be hard to find. Given an unknown product at an equal price, it is obvious that a well publicized brand will gain market preference over a lesser or unknown brand.

The power of a strong brand name as a status symbol has never been more dominant than in athletic footwear today. People want to associate with winners, particularly in the sporting world. Intermediate level tennis players might guess that it isn't the shoe he's wearing that elevates the champion to the number one position, but why take a chance? If the champion's shoe is readily available in the marketplace, buy it. Oftentimes price isn't a major factor. A 1981 survey in the U.S. showed that consumers weren't discouraged by expensive shoes as long as they perceived the shoes to be of unusually high quality. Shortly thereafter, the New Balance Company smashed the psychological $100 retail barrier with its 990 running shoe model.

BRAND NAMES

The selection of brand names for athletic shoes hasn't followed the usual marketing adage: "Support the product's image with an easily pronounced, distinctive word or phrase that matches its marketing concept and positioning." Instead, older athletic shoemakers have mostly adhered to family brand names or named the product after animals, usually fast and graceful ones. More recently, some companies have turned to scientific names or names associated with a high degree of comfort. One major exception is the name Nike, plucked from the realms of Greek mythology, which seems to suggest that just about any name can fit in a given category.

The following chart gives the derivation of some of the biggest shoe company names:

FAMILY NAMES
    Adidas (Adi Dassler)
    Converse (Marquis Converse)
    Etonic (Charles Eaton)
    Hyde (Max Hyde)
    Brooks (founder's wife's maiden name)
    Lotto (Giovanni Caberlotto)
    Lowa (from founder's name Lorenz Wagner, also German for "lion")
ANIMALS
    Puma
    Pony
    Tiger
    Cobra
    Reebok

Kangaroos
Ram Golf
SCIENTIFIC
Avia (Greek for "to fly")
Technica
New Balance
Pro Specs
Lazer
MARKETING
Power
Foot-Joy
Spring-Court
Ice Master
Road King
Pro-shu
HISTORICAL
Nike (Greek mythological goddess of victory)
Osaga (U.S. Indian tribe)

THE MANUFACTURING LEVEL

Every successful major athletic shoe company has stressed innovation and function in its initial marketing thrust. Firms that leaned heavily on cosmetics, or advertising or gimmicky approaches either failed or quickly changed their emphasis to that of high quality and strong performance.

To produce footwear that functioned better, the companies did not look to the world's shoemakers. First they turned to athletes, coaches, and trainers, and then to sportsmedicine specialists, podiatrists and biomechanics engineers. The prime focus of the whole industry has been and remains the attempt to maximize functional efficiency of both the foot and the shoe. Traditional shoe companies have been involved only in the areas of shoe productivity and shoe technology.

Having established their sport shoe expertise, many athletic shoe companies have chosen to expand their production capability by looking to countries with low wage scales and proven shoe facilities. A model might be developed and perfected in the U.S. or Germany, but then production is moved to Korea, Taiwan, Czechoslovakia, Yugoslavia and other countries for mass production at lower costs. Otherwise the amount of product development necessary to develop a new sport shoe, coupled with the smaller production runs of the shoes, would lead to prohibitive costs. Companies that have not adhered to these principles or who have suffered quality control problems have paid the price.

By 1980 Korea and Taiwan produced 23 percent and 21 percent, respectively, of the world's athletic shoes. Yet neither of these countries has an internationally recognized brand. The largest Korean facility, Kukje (ICC) Korea in Pusan, has the staggering production capacity of approximately 300,000 pairs daily. The traditional market leading countries—the United States, Germany, Japan, Italy and France—now account for about 45 percent of the world's athletic shoe production, with the remaining 9 percent scattered around the globe.

ESTIMATED ATHLETIC SHOE PRODUCTION BY COUNTRY
Korea: 24%
Taiwan: 22%
U.S.: 12%
Germany: 12%
Japan: 9%
Italy: 7%
France: 5%
Others: 9%

Others include: Philippines, Malaysia, Thailand, Yugoslavia, Canada, Spain, Finland, Sweden, England, Czechoslovakia, China and various South American countries.

MARKETING MANAGEMENT
A few years ago marketing management was little more than a function of available financing to expand production, there being little competition and limited consumer demand for sports footwear. Nowadays market research and analysis concerns itself with distribution and supply, consumer information and competitive market share (see below).

DISTRIBUTION AND SUPPLY FACTORS
1. Dealer and salesmen incentive programs
2. Advertising image, target and launch
3. Profit margins and mark-ups
4. Store displays and service (technical assistance)
5. Seasonal supply and backup stock
6. Booking, dating terms and discounts
7. Product range and pricing structure
8. Locations and target group
9. Distribution channels and exclusiveness
10. Sales force targets, surveys and reports

CONSUMER INFORMATION FACTORS
1. Consumer publications, media advertising, consumer surveys and reports (demographics)
2. Sports Associations
3. Sporting good store owners/shoe store owners
4. Government participation statistics
5. Active athletes and coaches' advisory panels
6. Major sports events (i.e., Olympic Games)
7. New sports
8. New markets
9. Credibility and brand acceptance

COMPETITIVE MARKET FACTORS
1. Dealer shelf space and share
2. Sales force information
3. Trade show analysis
4. Trade publications: editorial and advertising
5. Professional player endorsements
6. Market share, position and analysis (smart reports)
7. Sourcing and international economic factors
8. Innovative, performance product

BUYING PATTERNS

As one would expect after 20 years of sport shoe growth, buying patterns have become more sophisticated. The volume businesses of large retail chains and department stores have changed the seasonal buying habits of smaller, independent dealers to a year-around readout of computerized SKU's (Stock Keeping Units) and weekly sales reports per model, per shoe.

Of course, many shoes, such as ski boots and baseball shoes to name but two, still remain largely seasonal in appeal. However, the introduction of more indoor facilities and the general increase of active sports participants have made many categories of athletic shoes year-around sales items. Thus, sport shoes are not as susceptible to market trends and changes as fashion footwear.

When a sport shoe transcends its original purpose and becomes a popular street item, as has happened with nylon upper running shoes, canvas rubber court shoes or leather boating dock-sider models, the buyer must be aware of these trends to purchase sufficient quantities. With fast moving items, brand name often becomes all-important. At the same time, there will be great competition among stores to sell the popular items with lower prices and margins. In such cases, the best buyers will have anticipated the sales patterns, negotiated supplies, booked discounts and firmed up business relations with manufacturers and distributors well ahead of the peak selling season.

One major retail chain in the U.S. reported selling 15,000 pairs of one brand during a special promotion week. Good buying will often make the difference between securing a profit or merely breaking even on a popular model in heavy demand. Many buyers and retail selling organizations will attempt to capitalize on big sales trends by developing their own version of a popular shoe but at a slightly lower retail price and a higher margin for the store.

A third party influencing factor can affect the sales of sports footwear at the retail level. One form of third party factor is the governing body of the sport itself. Over the years sports associations and governing bodies have often, and quite arbitrarily, placed a ban on previously acceptable shoes, such as when a baseball cleat is banned from future use. In another variation of this influence a governing body may actually specify the legal type of shoe for age group play, such as in junior league soccer or football, "outlawing" other types. Generally, this sort of ruling is adopted after a panel researches injuries related to footwear. The ruling can catch both manufacturer and retailer by surprise. In the extreme case, it can render a particular shoe obsolete almost literally overnight.

Another major third party influence on buying patterns has resulted when consumer magazines like *Runner's World* publish an annual shoe rating. The *Runner's World* survey in particular, introduced in 1967 and modified several times since then, has spiked demand for models that receive the top, five-star rating. However, numerous controversies have surrounded the survey over the years. A major complaint from retailers was that the tremendous immediate influence the survey had on buying habits. During 1978 to 1980 in particular, every running shoe retailer in the U.S. had to adjust his purchases according to the results of the October survey.

PACKAGING AND MERCHANDISING

In contrast with buying patterns, packaging and merchandising has followed more normal marketing practices. Sport shoe packaging today is little changed from the pre-boom years of the 1960s and 1970s, and have continued to follow closely practices of the regular shoe industry. Probably the only major improvement has been the inclusion of comparative shoe sizes and equivalent charts on shoe boxes (see "Fitting" chapter). Most of the larger brands, such as Adidas and Nike, have included messages on tongue labels or boxes warning of imitators and

stressing the design features of each specific model. However, even this has been copied or emulated by other, less technically oriented brands, with statements on tongue labels such as, "This shoe has been designed to meet the exact specifications and standards of leading professional players." This might mean no more than that several lesser known National Basketball Association players have looked the model over and suggested a couple of changes.

Merchandising has improved significantly, thanks to specialized athletic shoe stores and separate departments for sports footwear and clothing in larger department stores. As sport shoes have become more technical in the past decade, it has become more difficult for mass merchandisers and self-help outlets to do justice to the leading models. Some of the principles behind the success of such chains as "The Athlete's Foot" and "Footlocker" are worth noting. In addition to creating an atmosphere for the athlete, the successful chains have brought athletic footwear to the masses by maintaining small area stores in high-traffic malls. Add this combination to the advantages of group buying and a centralized stock, from which individual stores can draw without maintaining a large inventory at each location, and you have the basic success formula of a new creation in sports retail merchandising.

SPORT SHOES AT THE RETAIL LEVEL

It is estimated that athletic footwear has a market share of about 15 to 20 percent of all footwear sold in the West while functional athletic shoes represent eight percent of sales. Specialized athletic footwear started as part of the sporting goods trade. Since the early 1970s, however, there has been considerable overlap with the regular retail shoe trade. Originally the athletic footwear industry grew up outside the regular trade. Some 25 years ago, large volumes of "sneakers" used for tennis and basketball were sold through the shoe trade, leaving the sporting goods trade with the specialized, lower volume shoes for soccer, track, skiing and so on. When the high tech new brands of the 1960s appeared, they first found their way almost exclusively to the sporting goods stores.

Then, with more leisure time available, sports participation began to grow. Field sports such as soccer, long a mass participation sport, were followed by general training programs and health trends that led to more tennis, downhill skiing and cross country skiing. More recently, we've witnessed the running and aerobics booms.

The sport shoe industry itself was booming by the mid-1970s. Since it had started with and remained closely tied to the sporting goods retailers, it tended to stay there rather than to move to the regular shoe stores. New industries create their own growth subsidiaries, and soon athletic shoe retailing expanded into specialized athletic shoe stores. Later it came full circle when regular stores created special sport shoe departments. Interestingly, some of today's larger specialty chains, such as Footlocker and Athletes' World, are operated by the shoe trade giants, Kinney and Bata.

Some larger sport shoe manufacturers have also moved vertically to become directly or indirectly associated with "showpiece retail stores." Mizuno, for example, has a large chain of retail stores in Japan. Many of the world's largest airports contain "Adidas Only" stores; similar Adidas stores are franchised in certain countries.

Nike, from its inception in 1972, always had retail outlets since taking over from their founding company Blue Ribbon Sports (1966). These outlets traditionally sold only Nike shoes and were regarded as valuable training centers.

The "Open Concept Shop" or boutique within department stores featuring merchandise displays, demonstrations and celebrity shows and appearances, has recently been introduced in order to promote and popularize a single brand identity.

In one regard sports footwear is not affected by the same trends that drive fashion footwear. However, magazines have had a significant impact on retail selling patterns in the 1980s.

THE EMERGENCE OF THE SPECIALTY ATHLETIC SHOE STORE
(FROM SPORTING GOODS, SHOE AND DEPARTMENT STORES)

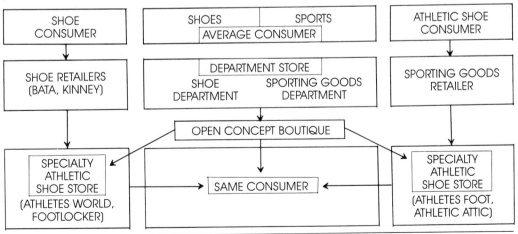

2-3. The emergence of the specialty athletic shoe store (from sporting goods, shoe and department stores).

SUCCESSFUL RETAIL MARKETING GUIDE

To substantiate the importance attached to brand identity at the retail level, a retail dealer survey in 1982 listed the six most important dealer services offered by athletic shoe retailers rated as follows:

1. Brand names
2. Co-operative advertising
3. Broad style selection
4. In-store clinics
5. Point-of-sale purchase material
6. Sport star endorsements

All other dealer aids or services combined only rank between 5. and 6. on the scale.

The following points are crucial to the success of a sport shoe retailer:

1. The more specialized and expensive the athletic footwear category, the greater the need for genuine, in-depth retail sales specialists.
2. Consumer expertise in sports footwear creates a special set of priorities, problems and potentialities for the sport shoe retailer.
3. The retailer must understand how endorsements and use by local celebrities affects the sales of certain models and brands.
4. Be sure to listen to experienced athletes in the sport to tell you what brands and models are now in vogue, and which have passed peak popularity.
5. Keep on top of survey ratings in consumer magazines.
6. Be aware of current national and local media advertising on brands and models in your market area.
7. Study inventory records and stock movement.
8. Don't ever forget that much athletic footwear is still seasonal.
9. Understand the types of clientele attracted to different retail outlets, i.e. department stores, sporting goods stores and specialty athletic shoe stores.

RETAIL SALES ASSISTANCE

The interaction between the potential purchaser and the store assistant is one of the most important areas of shoe sales. With the meteoric rise in popularity of athletic shoe sales in the past decade, the athlete has had few places to turn for specific knowledge about shoes. An exception was the pioneer work of

Bob Anderson, the first publisher of *Runner's World* and *Soccer World* magazines. Peter Cavanaugh's book, *The Running Shoe*, published by Anderson, added a detailed history and analysis to the consumer's tools. Nevertheless, sport shoe buyers attend carefully to the store salespeople and are often influenced by their advice. This has forced the retail trade to recognize that a well-trained, knowledgeable staff is essential to maintaining credibility and sales.

In the 30 years I've worn athletic shoes and the 20 years I've worked with and talked to hundreds of sport shoe retailers, I've found that the knowledge being passed along to the consumer varies tremendously. The best advice I've heard or given is: Never underestimate the consumer or fellow users of sport shoes. Yet the retail assistance being offered consumers generally leaves much to be desired, especially for those who have passed beyond the rank beginning points of a particular sport.

Granted, with the sophistication of today's shoes, including all the high tech advances, it's not easy to get shoe knowledge down to the level of the sales clerk. Still, when a sales assistant unwittingly sells a pair of speed skates without attached blades as wrestling boots, or when a store manager has never heard of Adi Dassler, something isn't working quite right.

Now that the athletic shoe industry is reaching maturity, we can hope that manufacturers will devote more energy than ever before to educating their retailers and the sales forces. The information learned can then be passed along to consumers to help them choose the correct pair of shoes, which should add to their enjoyment of sport, decrease injuries and improve performance.

PRICING

In today's mature sporting goods market, athletic footwear has largely settled into a three-tier price structure:

1. High, priced professional, top quality products with technical and innovative performance features. This category involves a considerable amount of research and product development to produce limited quantities, such as air soles shoes, which add considerably to the cost of the product. It's prestigious for the manufacturer to offer the most elaborate, expensive shoe of its kind on the market.

2. Medium priced, functional, quality products that contain as many basic performance features as possible. The objective is to meet a specific price point.

3. Lower priced models that contain basic features and less expensive materials. The best athletic shoe companies

strive to keep even their least expensive models well above a certain quality and functional standard.

In their original domestic formats, sports footwear companies were not greatly affected by such factors as international currency fluctuations, government footwear quotas and duties or alternative supply sources. Prior to the 1960s the few specialized makers of performance footwear were either satisfied with supplying their own markets or weren't large enough to market their products effectively to the limited international markets around the world.

To be competitive today the athletic shoe maker must contend with supplies of raw materials, advances in shoe making technology and even political connections. Government economic policies may protect domestic shoemakers with quotas or duty rates and may influence investment by a large, established athletic shoe company to protect its homegrown companies. Finally, a government might insist on the development of new technology through a licensed domestic manufacturer. This in turn affects the traditional sources of supply in other countries, possibly restricting growth in more highly developed, established factories.

2-4. *Left:* When governments threaten duty or quota protection for domestic producers—imported brands fight back.   2-5. *Right:* The importance of the brand name image.

THE STREET SHOE PHENOMENON

High performance shoes have never been explicitly designed for streetwear. However, just as the canvas "basketball sneaker" became all the rage from the 1930s to the 1950s, new style training shoes enjoyed a meteoric rise in popularity from about 1968 onward. Actually, the original canvas, rubber-soled, vulcanized-construction shoe—known as a tennis, basketball or gym shoe, and often called the "sneaker," "tenny," "Plimsoll," "gutty" or "skippy"—had been on the market since the 1850s. But it was companies like U.S. Royal, Spalding and B.F. Goodrich, and later Keds, P.F. Flyers, Dunlop and Converse—that carried the footwear to the mark of 200 million pairs-per-year sales by the mid-twentieth century.

Developed mainly by Adidas and Puma after the second World War, flat-soled leather training shoes started to become popular with athletes around 1960. They gained acceptance as a regular piece of equipment and grew into a status symbol among the better athletes. As training shoes evolved into lighter, softer and more comfortable forms by the mid 1960s, sportsmen and women started wearing their comfortable flats outside the training arena. The stylish new training shoes felt good on the feet; moreover, the addition of side striping added a "visual endorsement" to the shoe. By the end of the decade, this visual endorsement had established training shoes as a status symbol among sports enthusiasts and active athletes themselves.

In the 1970s and 80s we have witnessed reoccurring waves of flat-soled sport shoes dominating the marketplace. The two most prominent being the nylon running shoe category led by Nike and more recently the garment leather aerobics models which have elevated Reebok to fame and fortune.

By 1980 the athletic footwear industry, without accessories and clothing programs, accounted for approximately 30 percent of all sporting goods and department store (sports departments) sales, which were estimated at about $12 billion in the U.S. in calendar year 1981 alone. It had created its own retail chains of specialty stores and separate sections or identity within many major shoe stores.

The most popular sport shoe categories used as common leisure footwear have continued to be basketball, running, training flats and tennis. However, any flat-soled sport shoe has the potential to encroach on the huge casual market, as has been seen with deck, aerobic, hiking and even football astro-turf models.

The largest category of sport shoe production is in the area of general training shoes. This category of athletic footwear has

2-6. After successfully capturing a large portion of the casual shoe market with training shoes, athletic shoe companies really went after the leisure market with street shoes of their own.

2-7. *Left:* High-tech takes to the high seas as another "wave" of functional sport shoes goes onto the street.
2-8. *Right:* The street use of athletic footwear is climbing to unprecedented heights.

evolved from different sports; but, regardless of styling and the originally intended function, these shoes have been adopted for street use by young trend setters, which has contributed greatly to the sale of sports footwear throughout the world. The court shoe category, influenced by the basketball and tennis sneaker, experienced prodigious growth in sales in the U.S. market in the 1930s, 1940s and 1950s.

Next came the leather training shoe in the mid-1960s. This category was first introduced in the 1920s as training footwear for soccer players. Sports-minded European shoemakers, in conjunction with leading players, identified the need for a more comfortable shoe in addition to the cleated soccer shoes of the day. By the 1950s, soccer players who trained long hours on hard grounds had helped establish the original leather upper with rubber wedge sole. The color was either brown or black.

Another specialized sport that quickly adopted "training flats" was track and field. Warmup shoes for jogging before and after the training session were added to the normal equipment bag filled with spiked shoes. With the running boom of the

1970s the next generation of training shoes, with their nylon uppers, flared heels and soft prefabricated soles, took on brighter colors. In the early 1980s a higher quality version of the original vulcanized canvas court shoe returned the training shoe full cycle to the "sneaker" look of 40 years earlier.

The "dock sider" boating shoe with leather moccasin style uppers (introduced by Sebago in 1948) also enjoyed increased popularity in the early 1980s. This shoe, a standard in the "outdoor" sport shoe range for many years in the United States, was originally popularized by the Sperry "Topsider" model (designed by yachtsman Paul Sperry in 1935.)

2-9. Sperry Topsider's famous boating shoe model. The original sole was designed by Paul Sperry in 1935.

In addition to the trend toward "sporty" comfortable shoes with an "athletic look", the last 40 years have seen the fashion market occasionally select a true athletic shoe for massive appeal. The next sport shoe to make a big impression on street sales could be an aerobics shoe, an astro-turf shoe or even a windsurfing boot. Only the vagaries of fashion and the impulses of certain trend setters will determine the market direction. After the running boom established itself in the late 1970s, sport shoe makers attempted to create a demand for walking shoes, but this effort wasn't considered a success. However, by the mid-1980s it appeared that walking shoes were on the verge of a major breakthrough. These trends are nearly impossible to manipulate or control.

Nonetheless the athletic footwear industry has certainly been successful. A 1983 shoe survey in the U.S. found the 36.9 percent of men's footwear purchases were sport shoes. Around the world, the sales of sport shoes by major categories is approximately the following:

TRAINING SHOES (flats)	40%	(running, aerobics/fitness, pseudo athletic)
COURT SHOES	28%	(tennis, basketball, etc.)
FIELD SHOES	12%	(soccer, basketball, etc.)
WINTER SHOES	8%	(alpine and cross-country)
OUTDOOR	8%	(hiking, boating, etc.)
SPECIALTY	4%	(all other)

THE "PSEUDO" ATHLETIC SHOE

After the sporting goods trade had controlled the booming sports footwear trade from about 1966–1976, the larger shoe trade began to take notice of the new look, which they interpreted as the latest fashion craze. The traditional shoe trade enjoyed larger margins than what they saw in the sports shoe segment and consequently were reluctant to compete. At the same time, specialized sport shoe retailers had grown loyal to their suppliers and did not want to fill their shelves with models from the regular shoe trade. The shoe trade, strongly price and style conscious, but not wanting involvement in the specialized sport shoe business, turned to their suppliers for "look alike" models that mimicked the popular functional athletic shoe models.

These pseudo athletic shoes varied greatly—some copies were good, some terrible—but results at the retail level were exciting. The huge retail trade with its vastly superior store locations and numbers of outlets was hungry for the product. Some of the "knockoffs" became so well known as streetwear that their companies decided to switch to the production of serious athletic footwear. This isn't an easy transition to make. As early as 1911 the A.G. Spalding Company, one of the first to specialize in high performance sport footwear, warned in their catalog: "Beware of pretty athletic shoes and just-as-good makes offered to athletes."

A 1978 national consumer survey sponsored by *Footwear News* magazine and conducted by the Home Testing Institute in the U.S. outlined a consumer preference list when purchasing regular footwear. The most sought after features were:
1. Comfort/Fit
2. Style
3. Quality
4. Price
5. Brand
6. Store

Fit also ranked number one in a French footwear survey conducted by the Leather Technical Center in Lyon, France in 1974. According to Clarks of England's *Manual of Shoemaking* book, the main consumer needs are:
1. Appearance and Fashion Content
2. Fit and Comfort
3. Performance in Wear
4. Price

Similar surveys, if applied to athletic footwear, would be more likely to read as follows for sport shoe customers:
1. Function and Style
2. Brand
3. Comfort and Fit
4. Price
5. Quality
6. Store

Function has always been the main consideration for those contemplating the purchase of performance sport shoes. Without question, the better a shoe functions on the wearer during a particular sport, the better he or she should perform. Since all athletes strive to perform better, which also helps them enjoy the game more, function is the crucial element.

Another major consideration when dealing with athletic shoes is brand recognition. With regular shoes, by contrast, this ranks only fifth on a scale of six customer preferences. A 1982 sporting goods business survey found that the number one reason (54.2 percent) young people bought a sneaker was the logo. Color was the number two reason (42.5 percent) and peer pressure the third (40 percent).

These estimates are more than adequately substantiated by 1981 high school surveys that showed the following:

BASKETBALL:

> 70 percent of basketball shoe wearers chose the shoe for comfort as well as looks.
>
> 80 percent chose the shoe for looks as well as comfort.
>
> 30 percent chose the shoe for looks only.
>
> 80 percent chose the same brand.

RUNNING:

> 75 percent of high school users chose the same brand.

These surveys and their success in the marketplace account for the tremendous upsurge in the past decade of branded athletic footwear and their subsequent copies.

ATHLETIC SHOE CATEGORIES

Due to the climatic and regional factors affecting participation in sports, the major sales categories of athletic footwear vary from country to country. However, the large volume categories of athletic shoe production worldwide provide us with an accurate overall analysis of sport shoe sales.

These are as follows:

1. **Running, Training and Walking Shoes** This category covers most of the flat-soled shoes used for running and walking, and includes the large general training shoe areas that have been termed "athleisure," "fitness" and "aerobics."
2. **Court Sport Shoes** As the category implies, it covers all flat-soled shoes used for major and minor court sports, from tennis to Jai Ali.
3. **Field Sport Shoes** This category covers the cleated, studded and spiked shoes used in most field sports such as soccer, rugby, etc.
4. **Winter Sport Shoes** All winter sport activities, such as

skiing, skating and other specialized ice and snow-related sports.

5. **Outdoor Sport Shoes** Outdoor sport shoes cover the large recreational sports, such as hunting, boating and fishing, with numerous outdoor applications to leisure footwear.

6. **Track and Field Shoes** Due to the numerous diverse and specialized shoes produced under the heading "Track and Field," these shoes have a category of their own.

7. **Specialty Sport Shoes** All the minor, unrelated, specialized sports or major categories, such as golf or aerobics not covered under the other groups.

GROWTH OF THE RUNNING SHOE

Synonomous with its true international image and participation, the evolution of the running shoe has had contributions from many parts of the world. Many nations, including Finland, New Zealand, Great Britain and Russia, have long traditions in producing top distance running athletes. However, technical progress in running shoes has been largely confined to the three countries that monopolize sports footwear at the present—West Germany, Japan and the United States. Progress in running shoe development and technology has taken runners through the vulcanized rubber flat-soled era of the mid-1800s, to the leather training shoes of the 1950s and 1960s, to our presentday nylon, rubber and polyolefin combinations.

Today's running shoes are not just the product of shoemaking but of thousands of hours of research and development by experienced runners, podiatrists, and exercise physiologists and biomechanical experts, all of whose ideas have been incorporated into the shoes. Nylon uppers, for example, were introduced in the late 1960s by the Japanese Onitsuka Tiger Company based on an original concept by Bill Bowerman, later a co-founder of Nike. Designs and modifications were largely influenced by the two huge German firms, Adidas and Puma. Soling innovations—such as the one-piece midsole, the flared heel and protective materials for improved shock absorbency—resulted in the 1970s largely from the work of U.S. companies like Nike, Brooks, New Balance and Saucony (Hyde).

When *Runner's World* magazine began its shoe ratings in 1967 and eventually progressed to the point of having shoes analyzed in Penn State University's biomechanical labs, shoe companies roared ahead to try to excel at the stringent testing. Many new improvements quickly followed: air-soles, orthotics, traction and wear bars, cantilever outsoles, lacing modifications, adjustable density midsoles and interchangeable component parts.

In this way the popularization in the late 1970s of the ancient and fanatically traditional sport of running led naturally to the commercialization of a formerly small, craft-oriented athletic shoe industry.

GROWTH IN COURT SHOES

Although running and training shoes have accounted for most of the phenomenal increase in sport shoe sales in the past decade, certain other categories have also experienced meteoric success. Tennis, basketball and volleyball are major sports in many parts of the world, and court shoe sales have grown tremendously. The fact that women participate in most court sports has been a positive factor.

The court shoe category, encompassing all racquet and team court sports, has long been a major sport shoe category. In the 1940s and 1950s alone, millions of pairs of canvas vulcanized tennis and basketball shoes were sold. The "Plimsoll" tennis shoe was also a worldwide sales winner. Like its U.S. counterpart, the "sneaker," the "Plimsoll" was a lowcost shoe that could also be worn for street use. The Pro-Keds and Converse sport shoes were the first U.S. large volume sellers, reaching multi-million dollar sales figures by 1950.

Although Adi Dassler produced his first tennis shoe in 1931, Adidas didn't turn its attention to this category until the late 1960s. He reacted because the better tennis and basketball players began demanding improved support, comfort and lightness in their competitive shoes. They had noticed the development of these qualities in leather training shoes and wanted the same for their own specific use.

Following the proven principles of dedicated innovation, testing and, of course, branding, new court shoes with a rubber shell sole were soon developed for tennis and basketball. First produced in leather, later in nylon mesh combinations, these new shoes offered three big advantages over the old canvas vulcanized product: 1.) upper support; 2.) upper comfort; and 3.) lightness.

The 1970s saw a fascinating marketplace battle develop among the new rubber shell sole shoes, the more traditional canvas vulcanized varieties and the most recent introduction, the direct injected polyurethane soled shoes. In basketball the newer upper materials and soles have gained strong market acceptance because of their obvious advantages. Shoes with polyurethane soles have not been well accepted for use on wooden floors as they tend to slip, particularly if the surface is dusty.

In tennis, leading players prefer the latest leather or nylon mesh uppers, or shell or PU soled shoes. However, these shoes are expensive and tennis shoes have a relatively short life, due mainly to toe drag. Hence sales are somewhat restricted to players from upper income brackets. By contrast, the canvas, builtup type shoe has a much lower price tag and offers many functional features, such as the gum/rubber grip and the breathability of canvas.

Today the market is evenly divided between the functional old and functional new court shoes, so the category remains one of continued growth for athletic footwear makers.

FIELD SPORTS

Field shoes were once, before the training shoe boom of the 1960s and 1970s, regarded as the largest sales area in sports footwear. Unlike training and court shoes, this category is "pure"—that is, the shoes are only worn for their intended athletic purpose. There is no secondary, or street shoe, use (although some multi-studded, astro-turf models have found their way onto the street in the 1980s). As a general category, field sports now rank third. Field sports are predominantly male-dominated, with women's field sport participation generally restricted to field hockey and far lower levels of softball and soccer.

Soccer is the world's most popular sport. Although more youngsters try athletics (track and field) at some point in their early years, soccer is the sport that regularly attracts millions of participants world-wide. It's no surprise, then, that soccer shoe sales have greatly affected the new athletic shoe boom. In fact, they were the first major growth category of the new era.

Soccer shoe styling changed drastically in the early 1950s from highcut to Oxford lowcut for better ankle flexibility. A major innovation of the 1960s was the elimination of nail-on studs; they were replaced by the multi-studded sole. These were originally glued and stitched to the upper. Now most are directly injected in either PU or PVC materials. Screw-in and molded-in cleat systems have been perfected in the past decade, using such soling compounds as nylon solid PU and other synthetic materials. Leather uppers are still predominant, due to their resilience, scuff-proofing and durability. However, uppers of man-made materials are making some inroads, particularly in baseball and American football.

Otherwise baseball, rugby, American football and field hockey have mainly followed the innovations started in soccer. Riveted interchangeable metal cleats for baseball and the female screw-in stud system used in American football were developed in the United States in the 1920s and 30s.

WINTER SPORTS

Although largely restricted to mountainous regions and colder climates, winter sports have enjoyed a considerable increase in popularity over the past 15 years. Participation in downhill and cross-country skiing has been most notable, due largely to the development of large, recreational ski areas. Since ski boots are a specialized area of sporting footwear, new boot developments have tended to come from within the industry and from established specialists rather than from other areas of athletic footwear.

Alpine skiing sales are concentrated around the Alpine and Scandinavian regions of Europe, certain regions of North America, Japan, and select mountain regions of other countries. The leading manufacturing center of this small industry is located in the small town of Monte Belluna, Italy. World-wide downhill ski boot sales are estimated at less than 10 percent of the combined total sales of all other performance footwear (and considerably less if pseudo sports footwear totals are included.) Many of the larger downhill ski boot companies have risen to their current position in the marketplace with the now predominant direct injection polyurethane construction boots. As injection molding equipment represents a costly capital investment, ammortization can be realized quickly only if production is geared to large quantities from a limited number of suppliers. This explains why few downhill ski boots are manufactured outside the area of the Alps.

The direct injection molded process has had more influence on skates and downhill ski boot manufacturing than on any other area of athletic footwear. In a 1978 discussion the owners of the leading shoe companies agreed that the direct injection molded boot process has been the most innovative contribution to the footwear industry as a whole in the last 50 years. From the former construction (a basic stitched hiking boot), the ski boot industry has converted entirely to the complete plastic molded boot, made in two pieces—a boot and a shaft, which are hinged together for forward flex.

The first cross-country ski boots came from Scandinavia. Until the early 1970s, most production and development was based in Norway. Since the ski boot was traditionally manufactured, it was relatively easy for athletic shoe makers from other wintry countries to mimic the Scandinavian boots. Cross-country ski boots are still largely made with leather uppers, although the soling has graduated from Goodyear Welt (or lockstitch) to cement and stitch or rivet. More recently, direct injected attached thermal rubber or polyurethane have been introduced. Boot binding systems are gradually changing from the standard 75mm bail binding to narrower toe attachment bindings for weight saving and higher efficiency.

In North America, cross-country skiing wasn't adopted by large numbers of enthusiastic, recreational skiiers until the early 1970s. While the sport took many decades to become popularly recognized in the U.S., it was an almost "instant" success in Canada, meeting with great success in just five years.

Figure skating and ice hockey skates complete the other large segment of winter sport shoes. These sports account for substantial numbers of more expensive types of sport footwear that traditionally had leather stitched uppers and later added a ballistic nylon mesh with leather reinforcement. In recent years the skate market has gone to injection molded plastic outer shells with considerable success. As with Alpine ski boots, skate manufacturing has largely stayed in the countries where the sport enjoys its greatest popularity. Eastern Europe and Canada, therefore, account for most of the world's skate production.

OUTDOOR SPORTS

As with winter sports, the outdoor recreational or "rugged" shoe market is a regionalized, specialty area of performance footwear, encompassing some of the world's largest participation sports. Outdoor sports, including such recreational activities as hunting, fishing, hiking and water related sports are popular mainly in the affluent countries of the world where the great outdoors is a lure and contrast for the businessman and outdoor type. This category of footwear, with its steady growth over the years, has been one of the less volatile areas of performance footwear. Except for the inexpensive canvas boating type shoes, leather outdoor boots and shoes are among the highest priced footwear available today.

Traditionally sold through specialized sporting goods and outdoors stores, this area of footwear has seen increasing growth in the regular retail shoe trade, where less expensive versions, as well as higher priced performance models are sold for everyday wear.

Although no single company has been able to dominate this market, there are a number of sizeable outdoor footwear companies in Europe and North America. Among them are: Sperry and Romika in the boating area; and Red Wing (Vasque), Wolverine, Timberland, Herman Survivors, Chippewa, Trappeur, Dachstein, Raichle, Koflach, Dolomite, Kastinger and Falkenschuh in the hiking, mountain climbing and hunting areas. Many of Europe's larger boot makers, while changing to molded ski boots, have continued their original leather factories in the still largely traditional climbing and hiking boot areas.

SPECIALTY SPORTS

Under the heading of "Specialty Sports" is a roundup of all other sports not included in separate categories. It is not however without importance. Even though many sports included in this section are destined to never play a major role in terms of sales volume, others have enjoyed considerable market success. The most notable ones being golf, a continual worldwide favorite, and roller skates that enjoy huge peaks of popularity, especially among western youngsters each generation.

Golf shoes have only recently made progress in terms of biomechanical and constructional features whereas roller skates are continuously being improved in both materials and mechanical function.

Any flat-soled sport shoe has the potential to become part of the "street shoe phenomenon." Current proof of this can be seen only too clearly in the new category of athletic footwear that has evolved in the 1980s—aerobics for women and fitness for men. North America at least has witnessed a sea of white garment leather move out of the health clubs and fitness studios onto the street.

Within the category classed as specialty footwear we have such diverse sports as cycle touring models, equestrian sports, boxing, weightlifting, motor racing and bowling. Although none of these sports have major market appeal in terms of participation there is as much specialized research and expertise in each area as any of the larger sports. In fact cycling rates alongside downhill and cross-country skiing as one of the most technical areas of sport shoe manufacturing and design.

If sport shoes are true to form one might yet see an obscure segment leader such as Lind's in bowling or Sidi in cycling become the next street shoe giant.

FOOTWEAR CLASSICS—SHOES WITH A HISTORY

While fashion footwear must meet constantly changing demand, classical sport shoes have enjoyed life cycles of up to 50 years with little change. Most major athletic shoe companies have at least one shoe in this category. The following are some of the most famous:

COMPANY	MODEL	TYPE	INTRODUCED
Adidas	Rom	Training	1961
Adidas	La Plata	Soccer	1963
Adidas	University	Football	1964
Adidas	Samba	Soccer	1962
Adidas	Robert Haillet Rod Laver Stan Smith	Tennis	1963
Asics Tiger	Corsair	Running	1966
Asics Tiger	Spiker	Volleyball	1964
Asics Tiger	Wrestling/ nylon	Wrestling	1963
Bata	Polymatch	Tennis	1972
Bean L.L.	Main Hunting Boot	Hunting	1911
Brooks	Vantage	Running	1975
CCM	Tackaberry	Skate	1927
Chicago Roller	Black Leather	Skate	1920
Converse	Chuck Taylor	Basketball	1920
Dexter	Stanford	Golf	1963
Dunlop	Green Flash	Tennis	1935
Hyde/Spot Bilt	Coaches Shoe	Coach	1959
Karhu Titan	Norwegian Welt	X-C Ski	1920
Keds/ Uniroyal	Blue Flash (Label)	Basketball	1929
Lange	Moulded Boot	Alpine Ski	1965
Linds	Goodyear Welt	Bowling	1936
Nike	Waffle	Running	1972
Nike	Cortez	Training	1976

Nike	All Court	Tennis	1977
Patrick	Copenhagen	Indoor Court	1976
Puma	Clyde	Basketball	1973
Puma	Velcro	Track	1976
Raichle	Goodyear Welt	Hiking	1909
Sperry	Topsider	Boating	1935
Tretorn	Canvas	Tennis	1966

2-10. Nike's classic waffle trainer from 1972.

SHOE LOGOS ON THE MOVE

As with sport shoes, the use of shoe brand names on clothing and bags had humble beginnings. The practice began as support advertising on items for athletes who were already receiving free shoes. Soon companies decided this support advertising could be extended to create a marketplace need for high quality, functional clothing. Adidas, in 1967, was the first to move into these "accessory" items. In the 1970s, as the popularity of branded sport shoes grew, so too did the association of these brand names of apparel.

It must have come as quite a pleasant surprise to companies like Adidas and Puma to find that consumers would actually pay for t-shirts that advertised their brand names. By 1983, according to a survey conducted by *Sporting Goods Business* Magazine, almost half the athletic footwear companies produced at least one clothing item bearing the shoe's brand name. Adidas, in fact, owes approximately half of its sales turnover to non-shoe items.

SPORT SHOE BRAND SUCCESSES IN OTHER AREAS

Patrick, France's largest indigenous brand, won the 1983 "Prestige de la France" award; given every year to the French Corporation which through its expansion and dynamism represents the best product from France.

Adidas was awarded the German marketing prize for 1985 for successfully opening up the leisurewear market. As a trend and transition from sport, it marked an important step for traditional sport shoe companies. After exhausting the brand's potential in the sports segment, Adidas, Nike and Puma particularly have set their marketing sights in other areas.

The two West German giants have established a major share of the world sportball (Inflatable) business. Joined by Nike from the U.S.A., all three companies have captured large portions of

VERTICAL GROWTH OF SPORT SHOE CATEGORIES

20th CENTURY	AEROBICS/FITNESS WIND SURFING MOTOR RACING SKYDIVING WEIGHTLIFTING SQUASH CYCLING LONG DISTANCE RUNNING TRAINING WRESTLING
BEFORE 19th CENTURY	BASKETBALL FOOTBALL TENNIS BOXING SKI BOOTS BASEBALL
BEFORE 16th CENTURY	X-COUNTRY SOCCER CRICKET GOLF
BEFORE 14th CENTURY	TRACK RIDING (EQUESTRIAN) SKATING HIKING

HORIZONTAL GROWTH OF SPORT SHOE COMPANIES INTO ACCESSORY ITEMS

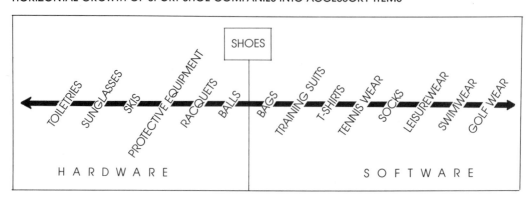

2-11. *Top:* The growth of sport shoe categories through the ages and; *bottom:* the growth of sport shoe companies into accessory items.

the activewear market. In addition, Arena, one of the top two swimwear brands is owned by Horst Dassler of Adidas.

Both Adidas and Puma have entered the sport hardware business in skis as well as tennis, squash and badminton racquets. It is an auspious note to add that both brands have already made their presence felt. In addition to numerous World and Olympic championships won in their cross-country ski products, the tennis world noticed three major grand slam events won with "shoe brand" racquets in 1985.

Having flirted with huge leisure and casualwear markets since 1980, the major sport shoe brands are now actively pursuing the casual clothing and shoe business with great success. In addition to its huge apparel lines, accounting for over a reported 50 percent of sales turnover, Adidas also devoted 20 percent of its international shoe catalogue to items other than shoes including their latest entry into toiletries; while Puma has launched an extensive range of sunglasses.

Following a logically consistent marketing course, as they did with sport bags in the 1960s, the original sport shoe brands seem destined to gain an ever increasing market share into areas they have been led by popular demand.

Emphasizing its strong political as well as business connections with the European communist nations, Adidas has signed a 51 percent ownership arrangement in a new Hungarian company. Covering both trading as well as retail shops this type of accord has previously only been granted to such Parisian fashion houses as Pierre Cardin and Christian Dior. The 1985 arrangement in addition to established licensing and subcontractural manufacturing arrangements in the Soviet Union will ensure permanent technological transfer in the fields of athletic shoes, activewear and soccer balls. The new Hungarian company as a trading partner will act as import and export licensee for Adidas products, mostly within the Eastern Bloc.

Perhaps an even greater political achievement has been attained by Nike in becoming the exclusive licensee manufacturer with the Peoples Republic of China. Some national sports teams are already wearing Chinese produced Nike shoes to say nothing of the potential to supply the world's largest single national population.

"They sold the righteous for silver, and the poor for a pair of shoes."
                                                    Amos 2:6

3

ADVERTISING AND PUBLIC RELATIONS

The fact that athletic footwear today has emerged from its roots as an enterprise of a few humble but specialized cobblers into a multi-billion dollar business is alone remarkable, especially when you consider that it has all happened in less than 25 years. True, the world's population explosion and the trend towards healthful sports activities have helped escalate the sport shoe business. However, it's still unusual that some specialized sport shoemakers could become household brand names along with the likes of Kleenex, Xerox and Coke, and do it without a major consumer advertising push. The secret behind this is a classic public relations and image creation story we shall call "The Visually Endorsed Product."

As early as 1908 the A.G. Spalding (formerly "Spaulding") Company recognized the possibility of making a commercial success by connecting the shoes worn by Olympic champions with those of the everyday runner. Spalding sent Mr. G. L. Pearce, a shoe manufacturer, to the 1908 London Olympics with the U.S. team to give his advice on footwear. The sharing of knowledge between Pearce and Olympic athletes has been documented in a book James E. Sullivan published in 1909. Even earlier—in the latter part of the nineteenth century—a trade publication called *The Sporting Goods Dealer* carried the news that track stars Arthur Duffey, M. W. Long, Charles Kilpatrick and John Cregan wore Spalding running shoes.

Well known collegiate basketball coaches were recruited as shoe endorsees as early as 1926. Chuck Taylor's endorsement of Converse shoes was easily the best known and longest running of these agreements. Taylor was also the first to take to the road and conduct celebrity clinics on behalf of a product.

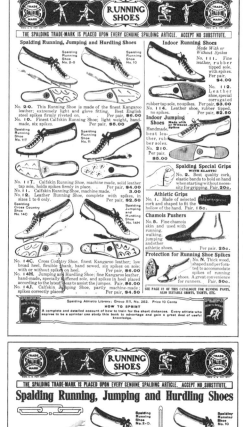

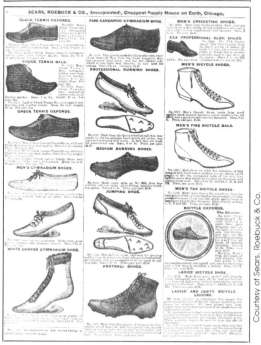

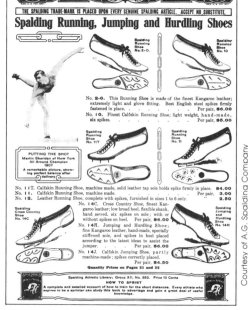

3-1. Examples of early athletic footwear advertising emphasizing such selling points as endorsements by the experts and specialization and variety of shoes.

Spalding LONG-DISTANCE

MARATHON "Μαραθών" RUNNING SHOES

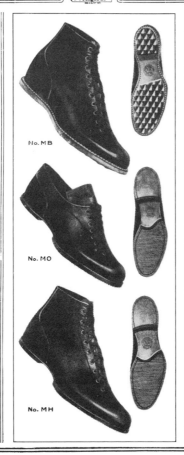

No. MB

No. MO

No. MH

SPALDING RUNNING SHOES were worn by many of the American Team at the Olympic Games, London, and the news of the unparalleled success of the men from these shores came to us with the added knowledge that we had contributed in at least some small degree to make their victory so conclusive. We had been building for just this result for over twenty years, or since our shoes have been made in the Spalding Factory, sparing no pains or expense in our endeavor to turn out absolutely perfect athletic shoes, and when the importance of having a shoe expert on the ground with the American athletes at the Olympic Games, London, was borne to us, our expert went to give whatever aid, counsel and encouragement he could to the sterling athletes who competed for the glory of America and the Stars and Stripes.

BUILT TO WIN.

The same models as used by many of the competitors in the famous **Marathon "Μαραθών"** race at the 1908 Olympic Games, London.

No. **MB.** High cut. Made with special pure gum "diamond point" rubber soles and special quality black leather uppers. Full finished inside so as not to hurt the feet in a long race. Hand sewed. This is a special shoe, **not** carried in stock, and made to order only. We cannot guarantee the soles on these shoes as they are pure gum, which, while the best and most costly material for the purpose, is not, unfortunately, the most durable. Pair, **$8.00**

No. **MO.** Low cut. Made with corrugated tap rubber sole and cushioned leather heel; special quality .black leather uppers. Full finished inside so as not to hurt the feet in a long race. Hand sewed. Per pair, **$5.00**

No. **MH.** High cut. Made with corrugated tap rubber sole and cushioned leather heel; special quality black leather uppers. Full finished inside so as not to hurt the feet in a long race. Hand sewed. Pair, **$5.00**

The above represent the three styles most popular among American distance runners.

Spalding Athletic Library; Group XII, No. 174. Price 10 Cents
DISTANCE AND CROSS-COUNTRY RUNNING
By George Orton, the famous University of Pennsylvania runner. Tells how to become proficient at the quarter, half, mile, the long distance and cross-country running and steeplechasing, with instructions for training and schedules to follow when preparing for a contest

Courtesy of A.G. Spalding Company

3-2. Early A.G. Spalding advertisement connecting the shoes worn by Olympic champions with those of the everyday runner.

Prior to the 1950s, except for the U.S.'s basketball sneaker, most Western industrial nations had a few small specialized shoemakers who would either custom make or produce small numbers of sport shoes for various sports such as soccer, baseball, ice skating and track. That is not to say that one company made all types. In fact, this was rare. While one company might be making a reputation locally, or at best nationally, for track shoes in England, another was becoming well known for ski boots in Austria or ice skates in Canada.

The following list shows some of the more famous early names in athletic footwear prior to 1930, along with their country of origin and original specialty.

SPECIALTY	NAME	ORIGIN	INTRO- DUCED
American Football	Riddell/Hyde	USA	1910/1896
Basketball	Converse	USA	1908
Baseball	Brooks	USA	1923
Bowling	Linds	USA	1919
Cross-Country Ski Boots	Karhu	Finland	1916
Downhill Ski Boot	Dolomite	Italy	1897
Hiking	Dachstein	Austria	1925
Hunting	Dunham	USA	1885
Skates	CCM	Canada	1905
Soccer	Lawrence	England	1908
Tennis and Cricket	Spalding	USA	1897
Track/Soccer	Dassler Bros.	Germany	1920
Track	Reebok (Fosters)	England	1900

3-3. Early Adidas design, before the three-stripe trademark.

3-4. The evolution of the three-stripe trademark from 1930–1941.

EARLY BRANDING

Prior to the new era of internationally recognized name brands, certain early brands, though not classified as "specialized athletic footwear," enjoyed considerable success. Probably the biggest success was that enjoyed in North America by the all-purpose "sneaker." This canvas, vulcanized rubber combination became the standard not only for tennis and basketball but also as an everyday shoe that signified the athletic look. Several brands such as Converse and Keds, who were using the ankle patch identity and heel label, fought the same battle of "utility or brand mark" that Adidas was to encounter in the 1960s with its stripes. Another predecessor of the modernday logo with a utilitarian function was the white tab or spot used by Spot-Bilt. The white spot was originally devised as a trainer's aid for marking names or sizes on all-black leather baseball and football shoes as early as 1896.

In the 1940s it was ankle patches that identified the product and raised a key question: Were they a trademark of a functional part of the shoe (utility patent)? The courts ruled in favor of function, which opened the way for Converse, P.F. Flyers and Keds to fight it out in the huge sneaker market.

THREE STRIPES

Adidas originally designed its shoes to have many different stripe combinations finally settling on three, as a functional feature. However, the company soon realized that this feature wouldn't make a good utility patent, as the three stripes quickly became known in West Germany and around the world as a trademark, while a functional patentable feature cannot be trademarked.

3-5. The three-stripe logo design.

Naturally, Adidas chose the trademark as the superior marketing route to follow. Although the company still advertised the three-stripe feature as a functional part of the shoe, all references to this feature were dropped by 1967. Thus, in the true tradition of performance athletic footwear, the most famous sport shoe trademark—the three stripes—was originally designed as a functional support system.

Adi Dassler, in his quest to develop the best shoe for each sport inadvertently elevated visual promotions to world-wide fame. As recently as 1981, Asics-Tiger showed the function of the Tiger stripes in conjunction with a recognized registered trademark in a U.S. catalogue, again opening this issue to debate (see Figure 3-7).

3-6. The four-stripe logo design.

Adidas was long admired for its visual brand identification, and in the 1950s others began to emulate them. Years later the failure of Adidas to register its trademark in the U.S. caused an interesting compromise in the U.S. law courts. It was decided that any U.S. domestic shoe manufacturer that has used three stripes on its shoes prior to the Adidas trademark application in the mid-1960s would be allowed to continue using three stripes, despite the undeniable confusion with the Adidas trademark. This is the reason that some non-Adidas shoes with three stripes are still allowed to be marketed in the U.S. today.

Adidas entered the courts again to try to stop the four-stripe shoe, claiming it was too similar to its own Adidas shoes. In some countries the courts ruled in Adidas' favor; in others, the four-stripe shoes were permitted. Figure 3-9 illustrates what the two shoe variations look like.

Due to the high visibility of shoe trademarks in advertising, competitive companies have been known to remove existing side stripes or flashes and to sew on their own identifying brand

3-7. Tiger's side stripes were originally designed as a special reinforcement to provide support to the instep and sides and prevent the upper from stretching.

mark. This practice has been particularly evident in cases involving "name" athletes. Quite often, after wearing a certain brand for many years, an athlete is reluctant to change (for reasons of fit or superstition, usually). However, when the financial stakes escalate, a compromise is often struck. The player may retain his or her favorite shoe, but with a new identity—the visual design of the company now paying his/her endorsement rights.

As a result, one company has often ended up suing another and the involved athlete. In several cases, the company that changed the original brand mark was ruled at fault. Close-up photography of actual doctored specimens have been used in the courts along with testimonial evidence to support the plaintiff's claims of misrepresentation and damage to the brand mark. Regular trade announcements similar to the Nike ad (see Figure 3-8) have been placed in trade publications to scare off imitators and those who would otherwise misuse a trademark.

THE VISUALLY ENDORSED PRODUCT IS BORN

After World War II sports quickly regained popularity and the demand for specialized shoes grew. The Olympic Games were

3-8. Adidas (left) and Nike (right) advertisements illustrating the importance of their trademarks.

held again in London in 1948 after a lapse of 12 years, the previous Games having been held in Germany in 1936, and soccer's World Cup was contested in Brazil in 1950.

In the early 1950s the playing style in soccer, the world's largest participation sport, began to change. Previously the traditional English style of "kick and rush" predominated, but now a more strategic ball control game, perfected in Europe, became more popular. Hungary was the leader of this soccer revolution. To prove its dominance, Hungary defeated England at Wembley in 1953 by the score of 6–3, the first team ever to defeat England at home. To further convince the world that the old style of play was dead, the Hungarians played the English team a few months later in Budapest. This time the final result was even more overwhelming: 7–1. These two victories made Hungary the heavy favorite to take the 1954 World Cup in Switzerland.

Germany, recovering from World War II, also entered its first West German team. A small sport shoe specialist in West Germany, Adi Dassler, was cooperating with his country's leading national players by making them lower cut, lightweight, soft toed soccer shoes that were well designed for the new style of play. Dassler added another touch to his shoes—a touch that was calculated to add more strength to the girth of the shoe. He stitched first two, and later three, leather stripes of contrasting colors around the girth of his shoes. Finally, he invented the replaceable stud so the shoes could be customized to the playing conditions.

In the 1954 World Cup the entire West German team wore Dassler's shoes. As fate would have it, a heavy rain soaked the field, rendering the Hungarian's short studs virtually useless. The Germans simply screwed in longer spikes and won the coveted championship, 3–2, in front of a massive world-wide television audience. What did the world see? A finely honed team whose members were all wearing shoes made by Adidas, a family company that had been in business since 1920.

THE MEANING OF VISUAL ENDORSEMENTS

If you look at someone else's street shoes, in most cases you can't tell who makes them or what brand they are. The shoes are simply ladies' high heels, men's brogues, sandals, clogs, etc. When you look at a running shoe, however, even from quite a distance, you can immediately identify the brand names. Therefore, everyone who wears these shoes is advertising them.

If a world or national champion wears the shoes, he/she too advertises the brand, because all who watch the champion perform will recognize the visual brand mark. In fact, the significance of a star athlete wearing a particular brand may be more convincing than anything else the company can say about itself. The typical consumer reasons, well, if brand X is good enough for a professional athlete or a world champion, then it's certainly good enough for me.

At least that's likely to be the consumer's first reaction. Upon further thought, he may reason that just because the world's fastest human could run 100 meters in 9.5 seconds in brand X does not mean that brand X will do the same for him. In fact, even if the shoes are the best for one runner, they may not be the best for another. There are too many other variables to consider. Still, the testimony of a world champion performing in major competitions remains a powerful one.

In the late 1960s advertising agencies in North America began paying close attention to the visual advertising methods of Adidas, Puma and Tiger, especially after the controversial Mexico City Olympics where it was first revealed that the best runners were being paid to wear certain shoes. Curiously, not one of the top four international athletic shoe brands, including Nike from 1972–1976, used the services of a professional advertising agency during their initial rise in popularity. Instead, they preferred to rely on word of mouth and their highly visible side stripes to penetrate the marketplace. Direct consumer advertising, generally for placement in sports publications, was created inside the companies rather than outside. The manufacturers reasoned that their market was small and specialized and that few but themselves could appeal to the market.

Ignoring the original function of the stripes and trademark application, the advertising profession in general viewed the new look as a gimmick thought up to highlight what they began calling "the visually endorsed product." Many marketers were intrigued to learn how a company could gain notoriety and market penetration without normal advertising techniques or even the services of professional advertisers.

What in fact was creating interest at the advertising and consumer levels was the age-old visual identity of a product coupled with a new approach. Now companies were exposing their products in the media through the use of highly visual sports personalities. Who else could get regular front page advertisements or hours of television exposure without directly paying for it?

The older, more traditional sport shoe companies weren't familiar with the potential of this advertising technique. Or at least it seemed to catch them by surprise. Only after one or two "trademarked" brands had surged ahead in the marketplace did the more established companies get on the bandwagon. The fastest acting companies included two newcomers—Nike (formed in 1972) and New Balance (acquired by Jim Davis in 1971) started with distinguishable trademarks and made sure their product got on the feet of wellknown athletic stars. Today there is hardly a company in the business whose products you can't recognize at first glance. Needless to say, the cost of these athletic endorsements has risen steeply through the years.

ATHLETIC FOOTWEAR ENDORSEMENTS

The pros and cons of celebrity footwear endorsements have long been debated by all segments of the sport shoe industry.

3-9. *Top left:* Noted athletes often take the opportunity to publicize their shoe sponsors. This one not so subtly. 3-10. *Top right:* Former President Jimmy Carter (foreground) taking an early morning jog along the Mississippi River. He did much to promote sports activities during his administration. 3-11. *Bottom left:* Prime Minister Margaret Thatcher (right) visits the Reebok showroom in London accompanied by Joseph Foster (center), grandson of the shoe company's founder J.W. Foster, as Steve Jones (left), who broke the world champion marathon record in Chicago in 1984, looks on. 3-12. *Bottom right:* Alberto Salazar (left), former world record holder in the New York Marathon, at the White House with President Reagan (right). Salazar competes for the Nike-sponsored track club Athletics West.

3-13. Tennis star Jimmy Connors (far right) considers fit first before switching brands in 1981.

3-14. Tennis star Ivan Lendl sports the complete accessories package.

The overall consensus of opinion, from both retailers' and manufacturers' statistics, is that endorsements by star athletes increase shoe sales. The exposure and credibility they provide seem to have a positive affect on the consumer's purchasing habits.

However, in some situations an athlete endorsement can be a liability. Some within the industry wonder if the upward spiralling costs of such endorsements don't have a negative impact on profits. Others point out that an endorsee can quickly lose form and/or popularity, and consequently his or her value as an advertisement for a particular brand.

The value of endorsements for athletic footwear can be traced back to at least 1880 when Daniel O'Leary, one of the great "pedestrians" of that era, was used in an advertisement promoting the bootmaking skills of McSwyny in New York City. Baseball stars were sought after as early as 1930, when Spalding paid Kiki Cuyler, Jr. for endorsing its product.

With or without endorsements, every athletic shoe brand wants to promote itself with a winning image. As the sport shoe market has matured in the 1980s, even becoming somewhat saturated with brands, companies have turned to price and value as another promotional approach to attract consumers. This avenue has rarely been taken by the leading brands, however. Retailers are notorious for using the value approach either to promote slow moving merchandise or to capitalize on a "hot selling brand." Since most shoe companies also sell clothing and accessories today, another sales method is the fashion or "coordinated look" approach.

MEDIA ADVERTISING

Serious sport shoe companies long apportioned somewhat less than 50 percent of their advertising budgets to direct media advertising. The other half of the budget was divided up among endorsements, donations, direct consumer promotions and public relations.

The largest portion of funds spent in direct consumer or trade (dealer) advertising went to print campaigns. Nevertheless, there exists no standard formula for successful sport shoe advertising.

Similar patterns of creative work and direction of ad placement have developed over the past decade. Most "right wing" companies, believing in the importance of their specialization, prefer to advertise in vertical publications, that is, those magazines dealing directly in their specific sport, be it tennis, running, soccer, or other.

3-15. *Top left:* Ivan Lendl pictured in front of the Adidas name and logo.   3-16. *Top right:* Jimmy Connors has been loyal to one racquet company during his dynamic career but has changed shoe brands at least four times.   3-17. *Bottom:* Chris Evert Lloyd has endorsed only one shoe during her long, distinguished tennis career.   3-18. *Bottom right:* Hana Mandlikova, Czechoslovakia's international tennis star, first wore an American brand shoe made in Taiwan, then a German brand and now wears a British brand made in Korea—that's International.

3-19. Adidas' famous "Melbourne" track spike from 1956. Signed by U.S. Olympic users.

3-20. Outstanding track model of its day—1960, Rome.

The technical format to advertising has become the most accepted creative approach. This method emphasizes the functional features of performance footwear for serious athletes. Advertising headlines such as "The Science of Sport" are familiar in these campaigns.

The oldest creative advertising features star athlete endorsees, who bring heightened awareness and credibility to the brand. Endorsee advertising must be constantly updated to take advantage of the latest winners and losers. This advertising naturally follows the theme, "If it's good enough for me, it must be good enough for you."

Inevitably, with sales as well as competition between brands, continuously increasing television advertising has begun to become a factor as an appeal to the mass market. Mostly tied-in with major sports events, such as Olympic games, World cup soccer events or Grand slam tennis titles, sport shoe companies have opted for short action-filled ads heavily stressing the image of the company with the serious star athlete approach.

THE RECIPROCAL ADVERTISING ARRANGEMENT

By the 1960s the stage was set. The traditional sport shoe companies and the concept of the visually endorsed product lined up on the one side. The other side found the world's best athletes, amateurs and professionals, lining up for innovative and improved product as the world audience for their performances increased dramatically.

It was obvious what would happen. The shoe companies gave free shoes to leading soccer and track athletes in exchange for the athletes wearing (advertising) the shoes. Both sides benefitted from the deal. Top athletes no longer had to buy their own performance shoes, while shoe companies, for the cost of nothing more than a pair of shoes, gained the world's best performers to test and advertise their products. As early as 1954 in soccer and 1956 at the Melbourne Olympics, the word began spreading among athletes: Once you reached a certain level, the shoe companies would line up to give you free products.

GETTING OFF ON THE RIGHT FOOT IN THE WRONG SHOE

This open competition of shoe companies for athletes was originally restricted to the sports the companies were concentrating their sales efforts on, namely soccer and track and field.

Later, as the once-national firms became international and as more sports markets opened up, the spectrum broadened to include all major sports.

The competition was keen but fair until some years after the end of World War II when a major public relations development took place. An Olympic athlete heavily favored to win the Gold Medal in his event had previously run all his competitions in Brand X. Because he was well known, Brand X took quite good care of this athlete, providing him with training shoes, racing shoes and accessories, such as equipment bags.

Early in the competition, the athlete wore his normal Brand X shoes. As he moved towards the finals, he suddenly showed up on the track in Brand Y. When questioned, the athlete said he had switched because he thought that Brand Y fit better and improved his performance. Coincidentally, after the Olympics, this athlete began driving to many of his races in a new sports car.

This Olympic incident was an early sign of the well publicized shoe business scandal that was to rock the amateur sports scene and in particular the Olympic International Committee. The tension soared considerably when, several years later, open warfare erupted between several top brands fighting for the best athletes.

The years between 1960–1968 included a number of other bitterly contested dramas that were to have far reaching ramifications for international, political and national sports governing bodies such as the IOC and International Amateur Athletic Federation (IAAF). By 1974 everyone knew about under-cover payments to amateur athletes by shoe companies. The amounts usually didn't exceed a couple hundred dollars, or a plane ticket, but they breached existing amateur rules all the same.

Professional athletes were easier for shoe companies to handle in the usual, straightforward business manner with payments for one season, one fight, or whatever could be agreed to. Professionals had a good reputation for sticking to the terms of the agreement, but of course they were expensive. Amateurs, on the other hand, hamstrung by the regulations of their sports, were happy for any handout they might receive. At least until they could come up with a better offer. In other words, they often didn't live up to whatever agreements shoe companies thought they might have struck. This brought up a new set of rules prompted by the athletes themselves.

THE INCENTIVE SCHEME

By the late 1960s many shoe companies had determined that it was devilishly difficult to decide what athletes were worth sign-

3-21. The first shoe to run 10.0 sec. for 100 m. Armin Hary's world record performance in 1960.

3-22. One of Ron Clarke's world record 5000 m. shoes at the Adidas Museum in Herzogenaurach, West Germany.

ing to a contract. There had always been basically three categories of athletes: the up-and-coming; those at the pinnacle; and those who were slipping off the top (but might quickly return). The only fair way to keep some standards and guidelines among the top athletes was to classify sports as "major" and "minor" with regard to mass participation and exposure.

The best athletes in major sports were then placed on an incentive program. They might earn bonuses, for example, for Olympic medals or for high placings in World Championships or other events that captured the public's attention. Teams were handled in the same way, provided all team members could be persuaded to wear the same equipment, meaning not just the same colors but the same shoes.

Accessories became more and more important to major branded companies, as t-shirts, training suits, equipment bags and shorts often provided more advertising value—showing up more clearly and more frequently in still photos and television clips—than shoes. The big drawback to accessories was their lack of subtlety. It was one thing for an amateur athlete to wear a pair of shoes with an indentifying brand mark. It was quite another when the same athlete began turning out in bold t-shirts that openly advertised the name brand to the public.

In 1963 one athlete-shoe company exchange backfired on both parties. Eastern bloc athletes, like their Western counterparts, were courted with free equipment. When that wasn't enough, they were offered money just like the Westerners. One such Eastern athlete was a world record holder in track and field. He and the participating shoe company were quite happy until one of them became greedy. The athlete approached another worldclass trackster and offered to pay him to switch brands. The sought-after athlete was not only talented but a good Communist as well. He took the shoes and the money to his sport's governing body, who took them to the country's politicians. To them the shenanigans represented capitalism at its worst, and the soliciting athlete was banned from competition, the shoe brand was banned from the particular country, and all other Eastern bloc countries took close note.

Luckily for the athlete in question, he was smuggled into the West before facing further reprisals. There he continued participating in track and field, but he soon faded from the world scene, mainly because Eastern block athletes refused to go up against him. He became more of an embarrassment to the shoe company and the country that had adopted him than he was worth. This incident brought into play another very interesting consequence of allowing athletes to advertise shoes or even to select the brand they preferred.

Eastern bloc countries acknowledged that one or two Western countries produced shoes superior to those made in the East and that it was a disadvantage for their athletes to have to wear an inferior product. However, to avoid the potential pitfalls of free choice and capitalism, they wouldn't allow their athletes to pick their favorite shoes. Instead an entire country would settle on one brand that everyone had to wear. The decision was made by the national governing body and the shoes were purchased from the chosen company, not received as gifts.

What a great coup for the lucky shoe brand! They gained a monopoly on all the athletes in, say, the Soviet Union or East Germany, which had many world record holders. And the cost of this advertising was no cost at all. The athletes wore the shoes because they had to—their country wouldn't allow them to use any other—and they couldn't accept payments. A shoe company that understood how to deal with the rigid framework of the Eastern countries stood to gain considerable advertising advantage in the international marketplace.

THE DEDICATION OF THE COMPANIES

Other similar situations have occurred over the years at major Olympic events. In one case, a star athlete was seen trying on a new shoe brand during his workout. Not wishing to lose a sure "Gold Medal," a representative of the shoes the athlete normally used asked him what shoe he planned to wear the next day. He was told the other brand. The reasons given were both logical:

First, the athlete said he preferred the other brand because the spikes were shorter at the front, making them better shoes for his event. Second, he admitted to receiving money from the second company, a clear rules violation.

The shoe representative reminded the athlete about his own company's loyalty over the years, but the talk achieved nothing. Then he offered to match the money. The athlete agreed to the offer, provided the front spikes of his old shoes could be shortened. The poor representative sat up most of the night filing down the spikes to the exact length the athlete specified.

As a result, the athlete won the Gold Medal wearing the same shoes he had always worn. The point to be made is, it isn't always the shoe company's fault when money becomes a big issue in the sport. Most athletes don't make outrageous demands and are genuinely grateful for the help and assistance of free equipment. A few, unfortunately, have played one company against another, especially at major events such as World Championships and Olympic Games.

3-23. Tiger's entry into long-distance running shoes started in the early 60s. Pictured is a shoe used at the 1964 Tokyo Olympics.

OPEN WARFARE IN 1968

When *Sports Illustrated* magazine ran a major article on the "payola" system that existed at the 1968 Mexico City Olympics, the I.O.C. decided to do something about it. By this time all segments of sport—including athletes, coaches, sports governing bodies, commercial companies and even governments—were involved.

Either by coincidence or smart planning, one of the larger sport shoe companies had made an arrangement with the Mexican government several years before the Olympics. By the terms of this agreement the company gained license to manufacture shoes in Mexico in return for exclusivity of its own brand in the country during the time period that included the Olympics. When rival shoe companies tried to import their shoes, strictly for promotional purposes (giving them to Olympic athletes), the shoes were stopped at the Mexican border.

One public relations man ended up in jail after he tried to smuggle shoes past the authorities. Only competing athletes were allowed to carry in their own personal shoes. All other companies were locked out. One company was fortunate to have enough "loyal friends" among athletes to get in all the shoes it required. The public relations fighting quickly developed into the dirtiest war ever fought between sport shoe companies. There was so much mudslinging and open payments that the I.O.C. had to step in. Athletes were even cashing their shoe company checks at Olympic Village banks. The I.O.C. asked the companies to back off and threatened reprisals if necessary.

WHITE SHOES ONLY

Shortly after the Olympics the I.O.C. and I.A.A.F. thought they had come up with an answer to the visual advertising syndrome, which had clearly gone too far in Mexico City. The governing bodies in track and field and skiing, where illegal payments were also common, attempted to step in with a ruling that stated, "In all international competitions (including the Olympics), only white shoes with no identifying brand marks would be allowed."

The ruling was scheduled to take effect in 1969, after the major shoe companies had reduced their existing stocks. However, two of the three largest manufacturers arranged a secret meeting, at which they agreed there was no sense in staying with the sport if identifiable branding were outlawed. By this time their business had expanded to the point where only two percent of production was geared to track and field. If these two companies carried through with their plan, approximately 97

3-24. This advertisement, taken by Nike in *Runner's World* magazine in 1976, shows another example of a major athletic shoe company's commitment to sport and the athlete.

percent of the world's supply of track and field shoes would immediately disappear. No other manufacturer could possibly fill the gap, especially when you consider the many small quantities of highly technical shoes that were being made for specialized track and field events.

The world's leading athletes weren't happy with the "white shoes" ruling either. It would mean no more free shoes for them. They were already receiving next to nothing when compared with athletes in other sports.

Before long, immense pressures were brought to bear on the sport's governing bodies and the whole ruling was quashed before it ever came to a vote. As a result track and field remains a vibrant sport today, with the companies competing for nearly free advertising almost as vigorously as the athletes compete for medals.

After the tremendous publicity generated by the 1968 Olympics, the sport shoe giants continued to increase their business on a world-wide basis. With centralized product development, public relations and advertising, plus solidarity of image around the world thanks to the exposure of the best athletes, the marketing formula was complete and huge sales increases followed. While one company grew the fastest and picked up the largest percentage of the world's leading track and field athletes, smaller companies started to emphasize big name professional stars. Soon Pele, Mohammed Ali, Rod Laver, Ken Rosewall, Wilt Chamberlain, Fran Tarkington, Eusebio, Reggie Jackson and Bobby Orr were among the professionals aligned with an athletic footwear company.

Famous coaches were also caught up in the game. Sir Alf Ramsey, John Wooden, Pancho Segura and Tony Trabert were just a few of the internationally recognized names who associated themselves with sport shoe makers and their brand marks. Many still do. Today the coaching influence has gone far beyond the big names. Recent newspaper stories have reported that certain coaches are paid as much as $25,000–$50,000 per year, along with free merchandise, to influence their college athletes to wear the coach's brand.

THE COMPLETE ACCESSORIES PACKAGE

By the time of the Munich Olympics in 1972 a new image package was emerging. The larger companies had expanded strongly into accessories, which included equipment bags, training shoes, t-shirts and shorts, all emblazoned with the brand name and trademark. Clothing had become a more significant factor, and it offered the same advantages as the testimonial trademarked shoes.

The use of branded apparel was approached in the same professional manner that had accompanied shoe design. Clothing was developed, first, for functional athletic use. Product innovation came from the athletes themselves. As with the booming shoe business, brand marks and logos were heavily exposed through elite athlete programs. The athletes, of course, received their equipment free. Originally developed as true

3-25. Lasse Viren became the Finnish distributor for Tiger brand shoes after his gold medal performance in Munich Olympics, 1972.

accessories to shoe marketing, these apparel items became so popular with the public that larger shoe companies seized the opportunity to enter the sportswear business in a major way. Today, many leading footwear companies derive half of their sales turnover from non-shoe articles.

In 1972 many national Olympic teams were offered a complete package: shoes, both for training and competition; training suits; rain suits; equipment bags; t-shirts; shorts; socks; and so on. Companies were willing to give away all these materials for free, and in the national colors, provided everyone on the team would wear the gear as part of its national uniform. The only thing that wasn't quite clear was whose national stripe was represented . . . the country's or the sport shoe manufacturer's.

This complete public relations donation program helped cut down somewhat on instances of "blackmail," as teams were encouraged to wear identical uniforms and shoes rather than a mixture of individual brands. However, today most athletes still are given the right to choose their own favorite shoe brand (for whatever reasons) even if the national uniform they must wear was provided by a different company.

By 1976 the sport shoe business was reaching multi-billion dollar sales figures. New companies were entering the marketplace, and some old companies were revitalized. In the U.S. especially, the picture was beginning to change. Both new and old firms had recognized the power of "visually endorsed advertising." At the same time, and perhaps more importantly, companies were beginning to design their shoes with more biomechanical features. Several companies mimicked the successful West German formula, incorporating gait laboratory analysis into their shoe research. Results were almost instantaneous, as competition for new designs got fiercer and fiercer.

MONTREAL 1976

Prior to the 1976 Games, one company negotiated with COJO (The Montreal Olympic Games Organizing Committee) to acquire rights to the Montreal Olympics symbol. However, through some legal misunderstanding, it turned out that the company hadn't obtained world-wide rights. COJO had sold rights separately to Europe, Asia, Canada and the United States. On each continent, then, a different shoe company had logo rights. The original shoe company was none too pleased to discover its lack of exclusivity and decided to interpret its original contract in the most literal sense.

According to the contract, each participating company would be allowed to set up a shoe service and selling area—the same size for each of the companies—inside the Olympic Village. No other public relations or service centers were permitted inside a radius of two miles from the Village or the Olympic Stadium. A heavy fine would be levied against any offenders. Three of the four official suppliers abided by these terms; the smaller, unofficial suppliers kept their distance.

The original negotiating company set up its promotions and service center in a hotel 100 yards from the main village. When the Olympic Organizing Committee discovered this, it sent over a delegation to insist that the company immediately desist, since they were breaking the rules of the contract. The sport shoe company, instead of arguing, surprised the Committee by admitting it had broken the contract. In addition, the company announced that it was going to pay the fine and maintain its service center in the hotel. "Cash or check?" the company asked the startled Committee.

Uniform donation programs have grown steadily. Once limited to athletes and then coaches, the programs nowadays extend to timers, judges and other officials, not to mention program hawkers, peanut vendors and beer salespeople. This form of "free" advertising is commonplace at major sports events.

In fact, sport shoe companies don't even bother to stop once they exit the stadium. Anyone who commands the public eye is a prime candidate for an enterprising company. Film, television and music stars are particularly sought after. Nor must a famous sportsman or sportswoman be one whose shoes contributed heavily to victory. If Mark Spitz, the swimmer who won seven Gold Medals at the 1972 Munich Olympics, can raise high his favorite athletic shoes, what can we expect from stars in other sports?

IN THE MOVIES

Placing branded shoes in movies, especially huge box office smashes like Sylvester Stallone's "Rocky" series, has become a business in and of itself. Although movie memories may be subliminal at best, several leading sport shoe companies have fulltime public relations personnel working on movie placements alone. Several commercial companies woo the shoe industry, and guarantee making the silver screen promotional gold for fees comparable to television advertising rates. When you consider that successful movies may be viewed by more than 50 million peope world-wide, and that manufacturers are allowed to use movie "stills" in their advertising, you can see that movies may have advertising merit to shoe companies.

3-26. When Sylvester Stallone donned a warm-up suit designed by Adidas for "Rocky IV", the company promoted its placement with posters and t-shirts.

MOSCOW 1980

Despite the boycott of the Moscow 1980 Olympic Games by much of the Western world, Adidas had contracted to equip all 34,000 officials with its shoes and sportswear. The company also agreed to start manufacturing shoes through a licensee near Moscow. If it hadn't been for the boycott, the Moscow Olympics might have been the most competitive ever for sport shoe manufacturers. In addition to the traditional toe-to-toe battle between Adidas and Puma, Pony budgeted for a large Olympic expenditure and the cancellation of television coverage in the U.S. forced Nike to rethink its planned major involvement.

Because of the boycott, Moscow became an Olympics of more clearly defined and straightforward dealings between track stars and athletic shoe companies. Incentive contracts either sanctioned or ignored by national governing bodies offered top athletes amounts in the six-figure range per year for Olympic, World and National records.

3-27. Shoe presented to Adidas Museum by Alan Wells, 100 m. gold medal winner at 1980 Olympics.

LOS ANGELES 1984

True to its Hollywood image, Los Angeles presented yet another spectacular background for major athletic shoe companies in 1984. The traditional combatants were joined for the first time by two giants from the host country—the fast-resurging Converse and the now mature Nike. According to several estimates, Converse paid nearly $9 million to be designated the "Official Olympic shoe" world-wide. Nike, on the other hand, opted for exposure via advertising muscle. As an added consumer boost aimed at ensuring that Nike's prize athletes would indeed appear larger than life, the company commissioned wall murals depicting its stars.

Nonetheless, it was the traditional rivalry between Adidas and Puma that flared again in the law courts, as Puma sued Adidas for $10 million over the loss of four U.S. women stars. Charging a violation of the contract by the athletes themselves, Puma also claimed breach of a voluntary industry agreement by 15 major athletic footwear companies with regard to respecting each other's athlete contracts.

The outcome of this lawsuit could have interesting world-wide implications. Although agreeing with Puma and issuing a temporary restraining order before the Games, the L.A. judge remained sympathetic to the age-old "the shoes are hindering my performance" explanation. He allowed the athletes to compete in the shoes of their choice as long as the shoes weren't provided free by a competing company. With a multi-thousand dollar contract in hand, the involved athletes presumably weren't too upset over having to purchase a pair of shoes at retail. The final outcome of the suit could take several years to resolve. Meanwhile, observers note that shoe companies have more lawyers on staff than ever before.

SEOUL 1988

As early as 1985 the forthcoming Korean Olympic Games were already shaping up as the "National Sport Shoe Olympics." The Korean government, having studied the domestic protection schemes used in Tokyo, Mexico City and Moscow, has let it be known that only Korean-produced brands will be considered as official suppliers to the 1988 Games.

As the world's largest supplier of sport shoes, Korea has already conceived rules to improve their marketing status by stipulating that a designated "local brand" must be one whose export volume exceeds $290 million.

No wonder the major international sport shoe powers with little or no facilities in Korea are concerned about being locked out of an important role in the 1988 Summer Olympic Games. These companies include Puma, Mizuno, Tiger, Converse, New Balance, Etonic, Brooks and others. Nike's and Adidas' production quantities in Korea have already assured them "local status." Reebok and Kangaroo also have large Korean production capacities. Adidas became a qualifying official supplier in 1986 by switching large amounts of Oriental production to new Korean sources.

Another of Nike's rivals has secured a large percentage of a company that holds exclusive world-wide marketing rights to the International Olympic Committee's five-ring symbol and to the Olympic mascot logo. This major involvement of industry, national governments and Olympic sports committees serves to illustrate the size and importance athletic footwear has reached in a 20-year period.

CUSTOM MADE SHOES

Prior to the era of mass production of performance footwear, the top quality shoes used by famous athletes were either custom made or adapted from production models. Today, only the truly elite are offered this service. Custom made shoes are now the exception, even in the most important international competitions.

However, some companies do still cater to the special requirements of leading athletes, such as a particular foot problem. In addition to athlete payments and advertising benefits,

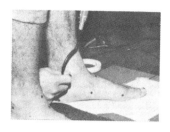

3-28. Pittsburgh Steelers quarterback Mark Malone had his feet printed, photographed, and copied at the Converse biomechanical lab in Wilmington, Mass. for a custom pair of football shoes. Rick Bunch (lab director) digitizes points on Malone's feet and later wraps plaster strips around them. The strips will form a plaster cast that will be used to make a special shoe last for Malone. John Ruiz works at a lasting machine to form a shoe for Malone who later tries on his custom made shoes and lets Converse designers know how they feel.

this genuine service arrangement is highly prized by top performers. Adidas, the largest and most respected brand, offers its athletes the most comprehensive personal service, catering to hundreds of athletes in dozens of sports world-wide. Nike and Puma also have special teams in their product development departments, as does Tiger in Japan. Smaller athletic shoe companies that realize the importance of this work as the "heart" of the industry assign product development technicians to make a few pairs at a time for star athletes on their rosters.

This is another way in which even the largest companies maintain ties to their roots as specialized custom shoe makers. On a smaller scale, several athletic shoe specialists have survived (or have recently started up) by catering to individual requirements in specific areas of athletic footwear. Among these are: S.P. Teri and Harlicks in skates; Linds in bowling shoes; Hersey in running shoes; and Limmers in hiking boots.

PUBLIC RELATIONS AT THE NATIONAL LEVEL

Around the middle 1960s the free shoe programs filtered down to the national level as the larger companies began to set up distributors around the world. Each country then established its own, small donation program. Soccer and track and field athletes were always the first to be taken care of. Then tennis, basketball and football all became targets for advertising donation programs. By the early 1970s nearly half a shoe company's advertising was spent on the donation program. This represented a tremendous boost for sports in general, and amateur sports in particular. The minor amateur sports had long been starved of adequate funding. In keeping with the pattern started by Adidas and Puma, Nike reportedly spent over 50 percent of its advertising and promotion budget to sponsor athletes and events.

Each sport had its priority, and each country followed a similar but slightly varying game plan. Here are some examples of the ways different sports are handled at the national level.

SOCCER

To influence professional teams, money was a necessity. Mostly shoe companies negotiated with entire teams. In Germany, team management encouraged or made it mandatory for players to wear the brand supporting the team. Special amateur teams were generally not given shoes unless the team was playing in televised cup finals.

Since soccer is the world's most popular sport, the stakes are high, and never higher than at the national team level. After all, these are the teams that go to the World Cup every four years. Probably the most ludicrous situation in soccer is the stranglehold one major sport shoe company holds over its national team. This company has "owned" the national team for over 25 years. No player on this team can enter the stadium unless he's wearing the chosen shoe brand.

As it happens, even a star player on the team who may have worn brand X all his life and is paid independently by brand X and plays on a team that wears brand X must switch to brand Y when he plays for the national team. That is how deep and tight some of the shoe contracts extend. While the player loses some personal freedom in this situation, it must also be pointed out that the funds paid by the shoe company are generally poured back into junior and other programs that help the sport grow.

TRACK AND FIELD

In Peter Cavanagh's *The Running Shoe Book*, he wrote, "Shoes became the currency of international track and field with Nike, Adidas and Puma the bankers."

Most of these public relations and donation programs are arranged directly with individual athletes, although in Eastern bloc countries it may be necessary to make special agreements at the national level. Since track and field remains predominantly amateur, it is open to more abuse than the professional sports. Most leading athletes are first solicited when they are competing at the junior level. The companies hope to cement loyalties and obligations early in the athlete's career.

Nevertheless, athletes will and do change companies, particularly those who ascend to the international rankings. Then he or she will be interested in more than equipment bags and several pairs of shoes. Top contracts for international track stars can exceed $100,000 per year.

Even before the advent of open payments to track athletes, it was common for international stars to make excessive demands for shoes and other equipment. Then these supplies would be given to relatives and friends or in some cases sold directly for cash. The shoe companies were always aware of such abuses but still considered their donation programs a relatively effective form of advertising.

Selecting athletes who will be included in donation programs varies from sport to sport. Companies lean toward those performers who do or will receive considerable media attention, or those who are internationally ranked. In track and field, the selection process starts at the junior level. Opinions of coaches already loyal to the brand play a major role in earmarking what tomorrow's potential stars will be wearing.

Rejecting an athlete who ranked fourth or fifth as a junior can prove a costly mistake if that individual overtakes all his rivals and goes on to become an Olympic champion or world record holder. Similarly, former greats may retire or drop in ranking for a year due to injury, causing them to be let go quietly by one company; but then the next season they may return to their earlier status, this time wearing a different brand shoe. For these reasons, good athletic shoe companies maintain promotions and public relations people who are close to the sport.

Some great athletes, amazingly, vacillate back and forth between shoe companies. This practice has sometimes reached ludicrous heights, such as when a high jumper performs with brand X on one foot and brand Y on the other. Perhaps in this case the jumpers loyalties can assume to rest with the shoe on his takeoff foot.

The arrangements between shoe companies and athletes come out into the open more when the athlete is selected to work as a public relations consultant to the company. These are salaried positions provided for international class athletes to help service other team members and solicit new or younger athletes to the brand. Since these public relations representatives are usually established team members, they're in a good position to monitor brand changes of other team members and to make contacts for loyal brand users in visiting countries.

In 1979 John Walker, the 1976 Olympic 1500 meter champion and first man to break 3:50 for the mile, became the first athlete to sign an open shoe endorsement contract. Since then many leading track stars have added their names to shoe models. In addition, many shoe companies today are prime

3-29. *Top left:* Soccer star Diego Maradona of Argentina wears three different logos—on shoes, shorts and shirt. 3-30. *Top right:* Sebastian Coe, middle distance world record holder and Olympic gold medalist in 1980 and 1984. 3-31. *Bottom left:* Members of the Oakland Raiders football team. 3-32. *Bottom right:* Dallas cowboys all-time leading rusher Tony Dorsett.

sponsors of major track teams such as Tiger International, Reebok T.C., Team Adidas. Brooks Racing Team, Puma Athletic Club, New Balance T.C. and Team Kangaroos. As purists and instigators of the track-club concept for shoe companies, Nike has always kept a low profile about its ownership of Athletics West. Track stars, despite being regarded as amateurs by much of the public, make plenty of money extolling the merits of shoes as well as other commercial items. So much so in fact, *Runner's World Magazine*, published track's top 20 incomes for 1984 ranging from $200,000 to over $750,000.

AMERICAN FOOTBALL

American football, like many other sports, was not at all familiar with the "visually endorsed product," so it went through all the phases of the shoe advertising program.

> PHASE 1: The team buys shoes directly from the company.
> PHASE 2: The team gets free shoes directly from the company.
> PHASE 3: The company pays the team to wear its shoes.

Today at the professional level, most athletic shoe companies have found it impossible to work agreements with an entire team. Some star players are paid on contract and act as "advisors." Other players' lockers look more like a specialty athletic shoe store than a changing area. Lacking an actual shoe contract, these professional athletes will select the shoe that they genuinely feel contributes the most to their performance.

Special order shoes in team colors and certain sizes still play a major role in influencing football players' choice of footwear. Throughout the 1970s, donation shoes, accessories, colors, loyalty, service and fit were the key determinants. Today these are still important but contracts and financial incentives play a bigger role.

Naturally, the better the team performs, the more visual it becomes. This can create a situation where a player who receives nothing at the beginning of a session will end up being well paid if his team progresses to the finals of, say, the Grey Cup in Canada or the Super Bowl in the U.S. So called "double coverage" was redefined in Super Bowl XIV when a Los Angeles running back wore Adidas on one foot and Pony on the other throughout the game.

RUGBY

Once regarded as among the final bastions of amateur sport in Great Britain, the Rugby Football Union has taken steps to negotiate shoe contracts as well as other collective contracts for equipment for its players. This action followed a 1982 scandal over payments to amateur rugby players. One of the biggest problems with payments to amateurs, above and beyond the regulations of the sport's governing body, was brought to light by the British Inland Revenue department. Players who had received free equipment and fees from shoe companies neglected to report these to the tax authorities. This raised the question of whether the company or the athlete was responsible for paying the tax.

In professional rugby, it was decided, players signing endorsement contracts were subject to the same employment regulations as professional athletes in other sports.

ROAD RUNNING

Prior to 1975 the sport of long distance running, whether on the track, roads or cross-country, could have been categorized and covered under the same heading as track and field, at least from the athletic shoe promotion standpoint.

By the early 1980s, however, the running boom born in the U.S. had transformed top runners from impoverished devotees to successful celebrity businesspeople. What had taken two decades to occur in sports like soccer, football and tennis was accomplished in just five years in road running. One simple reason for this was the road running shoes had obvious casual use, unlike field sport shoes for example.

It's not surprising that with so much sales volume at stake a company's fortunes can depend on what runners are wearing its logo. The once quiet business of long distance running shoes, clothing and books has become a multi-billion dollar industry. Top marathoners can win bonuses up to $100,000 for setting a new world record and double or more that amount in footwear endorsements.

In fact, payments at races and for endorsements have become so prevalent that many national governing bodies of track and field, including the Athletics Congress in the U.S., have set up trust funds that allow athletes to take payments while retaining their international eligibility. Conflicts still remain nevertheless, as many TAC delegates are fulltime representatives of shoe companies.

Many leading road runners have lucrative contracts with shoe companies in addition to commercial interests in retail stores, clothing companies and other running-related businesses. Some clubs, such as Nike's Athletics West, are open promotional vehicles for shoe companies.

The best athletes often have agents manage their financial affairs, including commercial negotiations, trust funds and appearance fees. The evolution of Bill Rodgers serves as a good example of how road racing has changed. In 1975, the year he first won the Boston Marathon, Rodgers competed in a hand-lettered t-shirt that he had found in a garbage dumpster, unidentifiable shorts and Nike shoes. Six years later Rodgers' became involved in his own signature clothing line. For a number of the best road racers, the asphalt and concrete surfaces on which they compete have turned to gold.

BASEBALL

Baseball is handled in much the same manner as American Football. Since it is among the most traditional sports, at least in the U.S., baseball held on tenaciously to the "black shoes only" rule until the mid-1960s. Then pressure from within the sport and from European public relations specialists turned the sport toward identifiable footwear.

Initially, to preserve the team uniform concept, team members were forced to wear the same product and color. But with the flamboyant and winning Oakland A's of the late 1960s, white shoes and individual brands were introduced, marking another victory for visual endorsements. The problem with dealing with

3-33. *Left:* Boston's star Jim Rice puts his best foot forward for the Red Sox and Puma in 1984.   3-34. *Right:* Bill Rodgers—marathon running's first businessman.

3-35. Tennis star John McEnroe has been used in advertising campaigns for Nike Shoes.

entire teams seems to be that all players genuinely do not like the same shoes. This is especially true, of course, if one or two superstars on the team can make a separate deal with another company.

In one case a company new to shoe donation advertising signed a deal with a professional team for all members of the team to wear their product for an entire season. The fee was $10,000. Eighteen of the 25 players subsequently refused to wear the shoes, claiming they weren't comfortable and didn't perform well. This time the company was at fault. Their product truly wasn't up to par and no amount of money in the world could guarantee the professional players would wear an inferior shoe.

The baseball diamond was also the battleground for a 1981 confrontation between Nike and Brooks that made headlines in many national newspapers. Mike Schmidt, the Philadelphia Phillies slugger, was called to testify in a lawsuit concerning the removal of one brand mark from a pair of baseball shoes and its subsequent replacement by another side stripe. The courts ruled in favor of Brooks, upholding the principle that it was illegal to misrepresent one brand with another identifying mark. However, there was little reprisal or penalty for the offenders.

TENNIS

Tennis today is a professional sport with players who are handled individually in terms of their footwear. Few of the world's hundred top ranked players don't have lucrative shoe contracts. In a sport that has the distinction of creating the youngest millionaires in sports history, tennis shoes, like the sport itself, have come a long way from the "pure white image."

Originally tennis created some minor problems for the sport shoe companies. It is a major participation sport but the rules stipulated the wearing of white shoes by everyone. Luckily, the rules of the game relaxed enough to permit contrasting side stripes. Even if they hadn't, innovative sport shoe manufacturers came up with the achilles tendon patch or back stay treatment, which is not only functional but highly identifiable.

As the top players travel around the world advertising their shoe brand, and its accessories, they are well treated by the shoe divisions of host countries. In addition to presents of appreciation, the players find it easy to meet their shoe and equipment needs, as the models differ little from country to country.

During one stay in Canada, Rod Laver called up the local supplier of his shoe brand and requested two pairs of his favorite model. This puts to rest another myth. Most top athletes don't

3-36. Adi Dassler with Mohammed Ali's boxing boots from a championship fight in 1968.

wear shoes that are specially fashioned for them and them alone. Nor do good sport shoes need a long break-in period. There are exceptions of course, such as ski boots and hiking boots, but little break-in of lightweight competitive models is necessary (although it's never a bad idea, and new shoes should always be worn for several minutes in the store to check for flaws). I have personally given athletes shoes straight from the box and seen them set national and international records just minutes later.

BOXING

Although boxing is not a major participation sport, it has enormous spectator appeal, mainly through television. An obvious attraction to shoe companies is that boxers are featured up close, increasing exposure of their footwear. Shoe makers, therefore, consider boxing a prime market. At the amateur level, little is done outside the Olympics and World Championships. Big name professional fighters have been known to ask as much as $250,000 for wearing a pair of shoes for a single bout. It can be worth the price when a boxer, and his shoes, appear in a close-up photo on the front cover of *Sports Illustrated*.

BASKETBALL

Basketball shoes hold two records in footwear advertising—the first endorsement by a name athlete and the longest-running one. In the 1920s Converse introduced the Chuck Taylor All Star model, while "Dutch" Lonborg, coach at Northwestern University was designing and promoting his model in 1932.

In professional basketball, more and more companies are vying for a limited supply of players. Thus the price of the best National Basketball Association pro's rockets upward. By the mid-1980s the average player on the roster was costing a shoe company $5,000; the best were commanding up to 20 times that amount. As the prices continue to rise, escalating retail shoe costs, consumers will at some point presumably resist purchasing the shoes of the stars.

Basketball has played another important role in the visual endorsement story. In one case a major shoe company filed legal action against a player under contract to them for wearing a competitor's brand. Shoe companies have been forced to seek justice from the very athletes they try so hard to please.

ICE HOCKEY

This is one sport that has remained less obvious in its brand identity. That is not to say that companies haven't reached for greater brand identity. The traditional brands, mostly Canadian, have incorporated more visual cosmetics in their shoes. However, these brands haven't caught on at the professional level, which has prevented them from becoming a market force.

Several players on the highly regarded Soviet team, which established itself as a dominant international force in the 1970s, began wearing a well known branded skate in the 1980s. If more world class athletes begin wearing a visually endorsed brand, it will soon gain a big retail following. Star hockey players are already used to advertising boot and blade construction improvements made during the last decade. Although not producing any equipment for the sport specially, Nike has taken to adding its blade-like logo to hockey sweaters including that of the "Great Gretzky."

CYCLING

Cycling also has not accepted heavy brand identity without some modifications. A large participation and spectator sport, particularly in Europe, cycling is of considerable interest to shoe companies. During the experimentation and testing period for the newer cycling shoe products launched during the 1960s, it was quickly determined that extra forefoot thickness wasn't desirable. It also obscured the brand mark to some degree. This caused concern among shoemakers, who came up with an interesting and somewhat ironical solution.

The simple solution was to reduce, or remove, the branding identification to another part of the shoe. This seemed to solve the problem for both riders and the sport shoe companies. The irony is that the brand mark identification was originally designed as a functional feature of the shoes. Now this function was being rejected but the cosmetics were moved to another part of the shoe—a "trademark" for its visual function alone.

GOLF

The design and function to golf shoes has remained traditional. As with ice hockey, more heavily branded products have been tried but have yet to gain a foothold in golf. Golf shoe companies use leading pro's in the traditional endorsement advertising scheme. At the very least golf can claim the most expensive production sport shoes ever made—the $6,800 model of mink-lined, ruby and gold trimmed shoes produced by Stylo Matchmaker of Northhampton, England. Recently, as if struggling with the adversion to heavily branded products, Nike has reversed its swoosh trademark on its golf shoe models as if to compromise tradition with the advantages of visual identity.

3-39. Harti Weirather—world champion downhill skier—1982.

ALPINE SKIING

Like tennis, alpine skiing is a heavily advertised participation
sport. Unlike tennis, skiing is still largely an amateur sport at the
top level. This of course leads to the same abuses as in track and
field, only in a more diverse way. A runner only competes
visually in shoes, vest and shorts. A skiier also wears helmet,
gloves, suit poles, boots and skiis. The governing bodies of
Alpine skiing and the Winter Olympic Games Association have
tried to tone down the visually endorsed products, but everyone
knows that amateur skiiers receive payments from equipment
makers.

In skiing, as in other amateur sports, the governing body has
suggested an open pool arrangement. This system, they argue,
would support national teams and developing athletes rather
than the stars alone, and supporting companies would be
promoted for their contributions. This works well in some sports
but does fly in the face of the star athlete wishing to maximize
his own value, which often exceeds that of the team, at least to
the shoe company.

REFEREES, UMPIRES AND LINESMEN

Not to be neglected for their advertising exposure, major league
referees, umpires, linesmen and other prominent officials also
receive overtures from athletic footwear companies.

Visual endorsement and logo exposure have become so valuable that many officiating bodies negotiate directly with companies on a contractual basis. In the 1960s and 1970s many of these same officiating bodies had objected strongly to the placement of identifiable logos on their shoes and clothing. The argument was that officials should remain neutral and not wear dress that conflicted with the players'.

Some associations still hold to this notion, but many more leave it to the discretion of the individual, or negotiate on behalf of the entire association. The FIFA (soccer) bylaws clearly state that officials must wear "black shoes or black shoes with white manufacturer's design." By design, many governing bodies continue to let officials associate with manufacturers.

3-40. Official FIFA uniform with "black shoes with white manufacturer's design."

GLOSSARY OF
ATHLETIC SHOE COMPANIES

In this listing of athletic shoe brands I have attempted to compile, in alphabetical order, a complete index of all specialized manufacturers and distributors of sports footwear in the world.

As there are many companies entering into and dropping out of the sport shoe business each year, this listing attempts to be as accurate and up to date as possible at the time of printing. If there are any brands or companies not listed with full details, these should be supplied to the author and publisher for updating in subsequent printings.

Many of the companies distributing sport shoes may not be prime or source manufacturers. These branded lines rely on other shoe manufacturers to design and manufacture to specification for other companies. Consequently, some of the larger shoe producing factories, such as Bata or large manufacturers in Korea and Taiwan, may produce shoes under license for many popular athletic shoe brands. Many of the private or house branded lines of sport shoes are also produced in the same factories as some of the better known international brands.

This listing is compiled from companies being represented or exhibiting to the Sporting Goods retail trade through the major sporting goods association shows around the world, such as the N.S.G.A. and S.G.M.A. in North America, I.S.P.O. and S.P.O.G.A. in Europe, T.S.G.T.F. in Japan, the Korean Sports Exhibit and Taiwan S.P.G.D.S. Exhibition in Asia and International Cycle Show in New York, Ski Industries Association Exposition in Las Vegas, U.S.A.

COMPANY	BRAND	COUNTRY OF ORIGIN	YEAR FOUNDED	ORIGINAL SPECIALTY
Aaltonen Tehtaat	Aaltonen Sarvis	Finland		
Absdorf Ltd		Hong Kong		Windsurfing
Academy Broadway		USA		Outdoor
Adam	Adam	Germany		Hiking
Adidas Sportschufabriken	Adidas	Germany	1948 (1923 as Dassler Bros.)	Soccer
Adler	Adler	Japan		Ski boots
Admiral	Admiral	England		
Adonis	Adonis	Japan		Golf
Aero Shoe Corp.	Aero	USA	1983	Running
Aerobic/Eurex	Aerobic	Taiwan		
Aigle/ Hutchinson	Aigle	France	1853	Rubber footwear
Airform	Airform	Canada	1981	Running
Alba Sports	Alba	Italy		Tennis
Alfa	Alfa	Norway		X-country running
Alfa Sport Di Zamboni Orlando	Alfasport	Italy		Sport shoes
Allfine Trading Company	Allfine	Taiwan		Sport shoes
Alpargartis	Topper	Argentina		Soccer

Alpina and Elan	Alpina	Germany		X-country ski
American Athletic Shoe		USA		
American Footwear		USA		Outdoor
AMF	Head	USA	1972	Alpine ski
Anderson and Thompson		USA		Hiking
Anotonini Sport	3A	Italy		Sport shoes
Anwelt-AFC		USA		Hiking
Arcadia	Arcadia	Japan		Golf
Arizona		Germany		
Artex	Artex	Hungary		
Ascot Sports Ltd	Ascot	England		
Asics Tiger	Tiger	Japan	1949	Basketball
Aspri	Aspri	USA	1982	Hunting
Asolo Sport SAS	Asolo	Italy		Soccer
Astrup				X-country ski
Atalasport Padova	Atalasport	Italy		Outdoor
Athletes Foot		USA/Int		Training
Aurora Ind. Co.	Aurora	Taiwan		Sport shoes
Autry Ind.	Autry	USA	1950	Training

Avenir	Avenir	Italy		Cycling
Avia (Pensa Inc.)	Avia	USA	1980	Running
Avocet	Avocet	Italy		Cycling
Ballerina Gym. GMBH	Ballerina	Germany		Gymnastic
Bally Shoe Co.	Bally	Switzerland		Dress shoes
Bancroft (Div.)	Bancroft	USA		Tennis
Bard Int.	Bard	USA	1979	Tennis
Barry, R.G.	Quoddy	USA		Outdoor
Bata Ind.	Power/Bata/ Tigre/ Athletes World/ Belmar	Czech (Canada)	1894	Footwear
Bauer Div. (GREB Footwear)	Bauer	Canada	1928	Ice skates
Bauer Hendrich		Germany		Roller skates/ ice skates
BC Products	Grippeez	USA	1985	Sailboarding
Bean, L.L.	L.L. Bean	USA	1912	Hunting
Bear	Bear	Japan		Basketball
Beker Herm	Gloria	Germany	1873	Ice skates
Benner Ski	Benner	Germany		Alpine ski
Bergans	Bergans	Norway		
Bernbaum H.	Zebra/High Sierra	USA		

Beuchat Sub Int.		France		Windsurfing
Bianchi, G.	Bianchi	Italy		Cycling
Black and Black	Jasper	Japan		Golf
Black Country	Black Country	Japan		Hiking
Bleyer, Richard	Bleyer	Germany	1954	Gymnastics
Boiani	Star	Italy		Roller skates
Bootmakers of Sturgeon Bay		USA		Outdoor
Borsumij	Freetime	Germany		
Botas	Botas			
Botterill Sports Ltd.	Botra	England		Soccer
Boylan		Ireland		Oudoor
Brancale Canguro	Brancale	Italy		Cycling
Brehm/K.G.	Brehm	Germany	1971	X-country ski
Bridgestone Sports	Bridgestone	Japan		Golf
Brixia S.R.L.	Brixia	Italy		Alpine ski
Brooks, Wm.	Rocky Boots USA		1932	Outdoor
Brooks Shoe (div. W.W.W.)	Brooks	USA	1923	Baseball
Brookfield Athletic (Hyde Ind.)	Colt/Braunbilt/ P.F. Flyers/ Brookfield	USA	1956	Ice skates

Brown H.H.	Watermocs	USA	1883	Outdoor
Browning (Div. F-N-H. sa)	Browning	Belgium		Firearms/ outdoor
Brunswick Co.	Brunswick	USA	1845	Bowling
Brute Group	Brute	USA	1974	Wrestling
Budem	Budem	Japan		Golf
Butterfly (Tamasu Tokyo)	Butterfly	Japan		Weightlifting
Caber	Caber	Italy		Alpine ski
California Footwear Inc.	Sako	USA	1983	Running
	CAF	Korea		Basketball
Calz. Gimar	Gimar	Italy		Sport
Calz. Scarpa	Scarpa	Italy		Outdoor
Calzados Deportivos	Yumas	Spain		Sport
Calzaturificio Brasilen	Brasilen	Italy		Soccer
Camaro		Austria		
Cando		Germany		Tennis
Cannondale Corp.	Cannondale	USA		Cycling
Cardin, Pierre	Pierre Cardin	France		Atheleisure
Carell Di Bruno	Carell	Italy		X-country ski
Cavalero		France		Windsurfing

C.C.M. (Sport Maska)	CCM	Canada	1899	Ice skates
Century Sports Inc.	Centurion/ Bengal/ Gladiator	USA	1972	Racquet sports
Cheetah Sports	Cheetah	Taiwan		Sport
Chen Y. Co. Ltd	Leader/Contax	Taiwan		Sport
Chicago Roller Skates Co.	Chicago/ Panther	USA	1905	Roller skates
Chippewa Shoe Co.	Chippewa	USA	1901	Outdoor
Clark's Shoe Co. Hanover Shoe	Bostonian	USA	1899	Dress/golf
Cobec	Cobra	Brazil		Sport
Cober	Cober	Germany		
Converse Rubber Co.	Converse	USA	1908	Tennis/rubber footwear
Convert	Convert	Japan		Rugby
Cooper Buxton	Cooper	Canada		Ice hockey
Corbeil J.P. Co.	Delta/Orbit	Canada		Ice skates
Corti SPA	Corti Sport	Italy	1969	Health sandal
Crispi Sport	Crispi	Italy		Sport
Dachstein International	Dachstein/ Hagan	Germany	1925	Outdoor
Dae Woo		Korea		Footwear
Daiwa	Daiwa	Japan		Golf
Dalbello	Dalbello	Italy		Alpine ski

Dalex AB	Kompassrosen Dalex	Sweden	1968	X-country
Danner Shoe	Danner	USA	1932	Outdoor
Daoust Lalonde Inc.	Daoust	Canada	1891	Ice skates
De Coram S.A.		Switzerland		Roller skates
Detto Pietro		Italy		Cycling
Dexter Shoe	Dexter	USA	1963	Golf
Di G.Gregorace	Gierrebi	Italy		Soccer
Diadema S.R.L.	Diadema	Spain		Tennis
Diadora	Diadora	Italy	1948	Hiking
Dinsport Scarpe Da Fondo	Dinsport	Italy		X-country ski
Dolomite Spa	Dolomite	Italy	1897	Alpine ski
Dominion Skate Co.	Dominion	Canada	1946	Rollar skate
Donella Sport	Donella	Italy		Gymnastics
Donnay	Donnay	Belgium		Tennis
Donner Mountain Corp.	Donner	USA		Outdoor
Doss Soccer Supply Inc.	Doss	USA		Soccer
Dovre				X-country ski
Dragon Fly Brand Co.	Dragon Fly	China		
Duarig, Audry		France		

Dubarry Sports	Jaco	Ireland		Outdoor
Duegi	Duegi	Italy		Cycle
Dunham	Dunham	USA	1885	Outdoor
Dunlop	Dunlop	England		Tennis
Dynafit (Div)	Dynafit	Austria		Alpine ski
Eagle Footwear Inc.	Eagle	USA	1985	Field sports
Eaton, Charles (Div. Tretorn)	Etonic/Fred Perry	USA	1876	Street shoes
E.B. Sports	Brutting	Germany	1962	Track & Field
Edsbyjerken		Sweden		X-country ski
E-HSIN Corp.	Turntec	USA/Taiwan	1984	Running
	Allsport	USA	1982	
Elite Skate Manuf. Co.	Roos	Canada		Ice skates
Ellesse	Ellesse	Italy	1982	Tennis
Endicott Johnson	EJ	USA	1890	Golf/bowling
Envoys (Trans World Shoe)	Kangaroos	USA	1979	Atheleisure
Estrie (div) Maple Leaf	Estrie	Canada	1976	Golf/X-country ski
Euro Linea	Euro-Linea	Italy		
Exico A.G.	Exico	Czech		
Fabiano	Fabiano	USA		Outdoor
Fabra, SRL	Fabra	Italy		

Falco (Intertiss S.A.R.L.)	Falco	France		Windsurfing
Falkenschuh	Majola	Germany		
Famax	Famax	Mexico	1951	Soccer clothing
Famolare	Famolare	Italy		Atheleisure
Feetfirst	Feetfirst	Japan		
FESL	Fesl	Germany		Ice skates
FILA	Fila	Italy		Clothing
Filler Products Inc.	Filler	USA		Motor racing
Fisher Kluppelberg		Germany		Alpine ski
Footjoy Inc. (Ascushnet)	Footjoy/ Greenjoy/ Softjoy	USA	1927 (1857 as Field & Flint and Brockton Footwear)	Golf
Footlocker (Kinney)	Lynx	USA		Retail sports
Form Sport SNC	Formsport	Italy		
Frankl	Frankl	Germany		Sport
Franklin Sports Ind.	Jaclar	USA	1945	Baseball/boxing
Futaba Golf	Futaba	Japan		Golf
Galibier	Galibier	France		X-country ski
Garmont Spa	Garmont	Italy	1965	Alpine ski
Garmish	Garmish	Germany		

Geka Sport	Geka	Germany		
General Rich	Double	Taiwan		Court
Georgia Boot (div USI)	Northlake	USA	1982	Outdoor
Gepard F.S.A.	Gepard	Germany		Atheleisure
Gierrebi	Gierrebi	Italy		Soccer
Gijima	Gijima	S. Africa		Running
Gill Sportshoes	Gill	Italy		Soccer
Glen Shoe Co., Inc.	Glen	USA		
Goedings		Holland		Outdoor
Gola Sport (WM Lamb)	Gola	England	1928	Training shoes
Gold Seal Rubber	Sporto	USA		Outdoor
Golde		Germany		Outdoor
Goodin	GJ	Japan		Golf
Gotham Shoe	Gotham	USA	1919	Dress shoes
Goudie Squash Int.	Goudie	England		Squash
Graf & Co.	Graf	Switzerland		Ice skates
Granada Lina Shoe		Belgium		
Grand King	Grand King/ Caravan/ Sporia	Japan		Outdoor
Great Power	Great Power	Japan		Outdoor

Grimmeisen Th. Sa.	Springcourt	France		Tennis
Growhill	Growhill	Japan		Ski boots
Guterman International, Inc.	A.G.	USA	1976	Tennis
Hanil Textile (Kukje)	Pro Specs Specs	Korea	1949	Shoes
Hanson	Hanson	Germany		Alpine ski
Hanwag Schumgabrik	Hanwag	Germany		Hiking
Harimaya	Harimaya	Japan		Running
Harken	Harken	USA	1985	Boating/yacht
Harlick & Co.	Harlicks	USA	1935	Roller skates/ ice skates
Hartjes Fussform Schuh KG	Hartjes	Austria		
Haugen	Haugen	Norway		X-country ski
Hawkins, G.T.	Hawkins	England	1980	Outdoor
Heil, Peter	Sun Point	Germany		Hiking
Heirling	Heirling	Switzerland	1885	Outdoor
Helle Fabriker		Germany		Outdoor
Hengst Inter.	Galop	Holland	1901	Training shoes
Herman Jos. M. (div Stride-Rite)	Survivors/Santa Rosa	USA		Outdoor
Hersey	Hersey	USA	1983	Running
	Hey! Sailor	USA	1986	Boating

Hi Peaks		USA		
Hirschuner, Klaus		Germany		
Hi-Tec Sports Ltd.	Hi-Tec	Gt. Britain	1983	Squash
Holmenkol		Germany		
Howell	Cycle Binding	USA		Cycle shoes
Hsin KWO Ind.	HK Sport	Taiwan		Training
Hudora, Dornsief-Sport	Hudora	Germany		Ice skates
Hummel	Hummel	Germany		Soccer
Hungacoop	HC	Hungary		
Hunt	Hunt	Sweden		Racquet sports
Hyde Ind. Inc.	Hyde/Saucony/ Spot-bilt	USA	1910	Football
Ice Master		Germany		Ice skates
Ideal	Ideal	N.Z.		Training shoes
Iise Wahl	IWA	Germany	1981	Gymnastic
Inter Football Ltd. (Holland)	Inter	Holland	1968	Training
Intermark		Germany		
International Bussum B.V.	Inter	Holland		
International Shoe	Eight Wheels	USA	1978	Rollar skates
ISBA S.A.	ISBA	France		Outdoor

Jalas Urho Oy	Jalas	Finland		X-country ski
Jarl AA/S		Norway		
Jarvinen		Finland		
J'Hayber S.A.		Spain		Sport shoes
Jofa (div. Volvo)	Jofa	Sweden		Ice skates
Johnson & Murphy	Johnson & Murphy	USA		Golf/dress
Jung Shoe Manuf.	Sheboygan	USA	1892	Work boots
Juvenille Shoe Corp.	Lazy-Bones	USA	1942	Golf/children
Kaepa Inc. Div. W.W.W.	Kaepa	USA	1975	Tennis
Karhu-Titan	Karhu	Finland	1916	Track & field
Karrimor Int.	Karrmor	England		Mountaineering
Kastinger	Kastinger	Austria		Alpine ski
Katimpex	Bermuda	Germany		Fishing
Kaufman	Sorels	Canada	1907	Rubber footwear
Keds Corp. (div. Stride-Rite)	Keds Pro Keds	USA	1916 (Uniroyal)	Basketball
Kelme Sport	Kelme	Spain	1975	Tennis/jogging
Kenkatehdas		Finland		
Kikut	Kikut	Norway		X-country ski
King Boot SRL	F. Llifabbi	Italy		Equestrian
Koflach Sportgerate Ges. M.B.H.	Koflach	Austria		Alpine ski

K. Swiss	K. Swiss	USA	1966	Tennis
Kubus B.V.	Windy Surf Parts	Holland		Windsurfing
Kunnan Ind.	Pro-Kennex	Taiwan		Tennis/racquet
Kuraray Co. Ltd. (div. Marubeni)		Japan		
Lackner		Austria		
La Campeginasport		Italy		Outdoor
La Crosse	La Crosse	USA	1897	Rubber
Lakesport (Lee Katz & Co.)	Lake	USA		Cycling
Lambert, Alfred	Acton	Canada		
Lamel Inc.	Vital	USA	1985	Sport shoes
La Mondial		France		
Lange Inc.	Lange	USA	1960	Alpine ski
La Robusta	La Robusta	Italy	1941	Hiking
La Sportiva	La Sportiva	Italy		Outdoor
Lazer (Lydiard)	Lazer	N.Z.		Running
Le Coq Sportif	Le Coq.	France (as Camuset)	1948 1929	Soccer (Textiles)
Legar S.A.	Legar	Spain		Sport
Lewis, William	Lewis	USA		Cycling
Lico (Link GMBH)	Lico	Germany	1932	Ice skates
Peter Limmer & Sons	Limmers	Germany/USA	1895/1919	Mountain climbing

Lind Shoe Co.	Linds	USA	1919	Bowling
Look	Look	France		Cycling
Lotto Spa	Lotto	Italy	1973	Ski/tennis
Lowa Schuhfabrik	Lowa	Germany		Outdoor
Luch's	Luch's	Germany		Equestrian
Lupa	Lupa	Germany		
Lynx	Lynx	Japan		Golf
MacGregor	MacGregor	USA		Golf
Manlova		Germany		
Mansfield		Canada		
Mapa/Viking	Mapa	Germany		
Marathon Rubber	Marathon Slicker	USA	1910	Fishing
Markwort Sp. Gds.	Markwort	USA	1931	Sport
Marresi	Marresi	Italy		Cycling
Maruman	Maruman	Japan		Golf
Mason Shoe Manf. Co.	Mason	USA	USA	Outdoor
Mec Sport	Ferrari Quiko	Italy		Soccer
Meindel	Meindel	Germany		
Mephisto S.A.	Mephisto Raglers	France	1963	Outdoor
Merrell Boot Co.	Merrell	USA	1981	Hiking
Micron Sports	Micron	Canada	1976	Ice skates

Michielin, Carlo	Michielin	Italy		Outdoor
Mitre (div. Genesco USA)	Mitre	England	1947 1817 (Benj. Crook)	Soccer
Mizuno	Mizuno	Japan	1906	Volleyball/ baseball
Mont Blanc	Mont Blanc Duoform	Japan		Soccer
Montan-Schuh GMBH	Montan	Germany		
Monteco Italia	Monteco Kronos	Italy		
Montelliana		Italy		
Montello Di Negrin Celeste	Montello	Italy		Outdoor
Mountain Gear Inc.	Hummingbird	USA		Climbing
MTS	Bepal	Japan		Golf
Multi Schuh	Multi	Germany		Sport
Munari Spa	Munari	Italy		Alpine ski/ skates
Nanlien Int. Corp. (div. Imperial Universal)	'Nic' Sport USA			
Nash Mfg. Inc.	Cruisers	USA	1950	Skates
Nautilus Footwear & Apparel Div.	Nautilus	USA		Exercise machinery
Nester Johnson MFG.	Planert	USA		Speed skates

New Balance Ath. Co.	New Balance	USA	1906	Orthotics
Nike (BRS)	Nike	USA	1972	Running
Nikolaus, Otto GmbH.	Niko	Germany	1935	Street shoes
Nippon Rubber Co.	Topwin/Asahi	Japan		Tennis
Nittaku	Nittaku	Japan		Table tennis
Noel Sport/ Ligne 7 Noel	Noel/Ligne 7	France		
Nordic		USA		
Norge	Viking			
Nokia	Nokia	Finland		Rubber
Noone, Frank Co.		USA		Golf
Nordica	Nordica	Italy		Alpine ski
Norrona	Norrona	Norway		X-country ski
Normark				X-country ski
Norski		USA		
Nort SRL		Italy		Winter boots
Nvevos Calzados		Spain		
Oberhamer Shoe Co.	Oberhamer	USA	1929	Roller skates
Okespor. (div. Junkermann GMBH)	Okespor	Germany		Windsurfing
Orma Sport	Orma	Italy		Bocce

Osaga Inc.	Osaga	USA/Japan	1973	Running
Ospra	Ospra	USA	1984	Downhill ski
Otterbeck Otter Schuhe	Otterfit	Germany		
Ours	Ours	France		Court shoes
Paioli Meccanica		Italy		Roller skates
Palladium Phoenix	Palladium	France		
Pantofola D'oro		Italy		
Paredes		Spain		
Patrick S.A.	Patrick	France	1929	Sport
Performance Bicycle	Performance	USA	1983	Cycling
Perssons Skofabrik		Sweden		
Phoenix	Phoenix	Germany		
Pichler Mowtan	Ice King	Germany		Ice skates
Polar Werke		Germany		
Poloni Calz	Skill	Italy		Outdoor
Pony Sports & Leisure Inc.	Pony	Canada	1969	Training shoes
Porvair Ltd.	Porvair	England		
Powerbilt	Powerbilt	Japan		Golf
A.J. & M. Pradet & Cie	Hunga	France		Sport
Prago Export		Yugoslavia		

Prepro Sports Equip.	Prepro	USA	1985	Sports shoes
Pronzat, Giuseppe	Gipron	Italy		
Pro-Shu Co., Inc.	Pro-Shu	USA	1946	Golf
Puma Sportschuhfabriken Rudolf Dassler K.G.	Puma	Germany	1948	Soccer
Pusch, Frank A. Becker	Pusch	Germany		Squash
Quick	Quick	Holland		Soccer
Rachle Molitor				
Raichle Boot Co., Inc.	Raichle	Switzerland	1909	Outdoor
Ram Golf	Ram	USA		Golf
Rawlings	Rawlings	USA	1888	Baseball
Reebok Int.	Reebok	England	1900 (as Fosters)	Track shoes
Rettinger Importing Co.	Retco	USA	1911	Outdoor
Richter Doris-Liane		Germany		Gymnastics
Riedell	Riedell	USA	1945	Ice skates/roller skates
A.S. Rigger		USA	1985	Boating shoes
Risport Calz.	Risport	Italy		Winter/outdoor
Rivat	Rivat	France		Cycling

Road King (Don Bergins)	Road King	N.Z.		Running
Robustus GMBH	Robustus	Germany		Equestrian
Roces	Roces	Italy		Ice skates
Rockport	Rockport	USA		Atheleisure
Roller Derby Skate Corp.	Roller Derby	USA	1936	Roller skates
Romika Lemm & Co. GMGH	Romika	Germany	1936	Equestrian
Rossignol Ski Co.	Rossignol	France		Alpine ski
Royal Esihockey		Germany		Ice skates
Rucanor	Rucanor	Holland		
Rubberworld Inc.	Grosby	Philippines/ Australia	1976	Sport shoes
Rupiger Pommerening		Germany		
Rutilius	Rutilius	Italy		Sport
Salewa		Germany		
Salomon	Salomon	Germany		
Sanga Ltd.	Sanga	Malta		
San Giorgio	Sangiorgio	Italy		
San Marco Int.	San Marco	Italy	1935	Alpine ski
Sasaki	Sasaki	Japan		Gymnastics
Schwartz, Jack	Pro Player	USA		Sport

Sebago	Docksider	USA	1948	Boating
Segarra Inc.	Segarra	Spain	1883	Golf/regular footwear
Servus Rubber	Northerner	USA		Rubber
Shalldan	Shalldan	Japan		Golf
SICO	SICO	Italy	1982	Motorcycle boots
SIDI	SIDI	Italy		Cycle shoes
Silver Fox	Silver Fox	Japan		Roller skates
Simod	Simod	Italy		
Simpson	Simpson	USA	1959	Motor racing
Sir/Gal Footwear Inc.	Fore 'n' Aft	USA		Boat shoes
SK Sport Shoes	SK	Canada	1966	Ice skates/roller skates
Skiing (div. Runa)	Skiing	Italy		
Skiing Finn		Finland		X-country ski
Skilom		Norway		
Slazenger	Slazenger	England		Tennis
Soffadias S.A.		France		
Soho				
Spalding A.G. (San Shoe Licencee)	Spalding	USA	1876	Baseball
Sporden	Sporden	Japan		Golf
Sport Brux		Germany		

SP-Teri	SP-Teri	USA	1962	Roller skates/ ice skates
SSS Corp.	SSS	Japan		Ice skates
St. Peter Sp. Gds.	St. Peter	England		
Stamm, Jos.		Germany		
Star Z.		Germany		
Stefan	Stefan	Austria		
Steinkoegler		Austria		
Stride-Rite Corp.	Sperry Topsider	USA	1935	Boating
Strider, Justin's Inc.	Strider	USA	1983	Football
Strolz	Strolz	Austria		Downhill ski
Stuburt	Profile	England		
Stumpp		Germany		
Stylo Matchmaker	Stylo/Kudos	England		Golf
Sugi Canada Volbi	Sugi	Canada		Badminton
Summit				X-country ski
Sunbeam Shoes Ltd.	Bowlmaster	Canada	1913	Bowling
Sunny Inc.		Taiwan	1974	Sport
Superga SPA (Pirelli Group)	Superga	Italy	1929	Sport/tennis
Suveren	Severen			X-country ski

Tabata USA Inc.	Tabata	Japan	1953	Aquatic sports
Tacchini Sergio	Tacchini	Italy		Clothing
Tachikara Co. Ltd.	Tachikara	Japan		
Tamazawa	Tamazawa	Japan		Baseball
T.B.S. (Eram)	T.B.S.	France		Tennis
Tebbutt & Hall	Scorpion	England		
Tecnic Sport S.A.	Tecnic	Spain		Soccer
Technica S.P.A.	Technica	Italy	1955	Hiking
Telemark				
Tempo Golf & Tennis		USA		
Tepa Sport	Tepa	Italy		Sport
Tespo		Germany		
Tiesse		Italy		
Tikkurila		Finland		
Timberland Co.	Timberland	USA	1933	Outdoor
Trabert Schuhvfabrik GMBH	Trabert	Germany		Outdoor
Trak		Germany		X-country ski
Trappeur	Trappeur	France		
Trattner KG	Tratto	Germany		Sport
Tred II	Tred II	USA	1973	Resoling

Tretorn AB	Tretorn	Sweden	1891	Tennis
Trezeta S.R.L.	Trezeta	Italy		Ski/skates
Tri-Union Trading	Lion	USA		Sport
Trivoving-Ballangrund	Ballangrund	Norway		Speed skates
Trostel	Trostel	Germany		Gymnastics
Truglide		USA		
Turntec (E-HSIN)	Turntec	USA	1984	
Tyrol		Rumania		X-country ski
Unisport (div Uniroyal)	Unisport	USA		Rubber
Universal		Poland		
Universal Skates		Canada		Roller skates
Van Ackeren Sport GMBH	Klevas	Germany		Soccer
Van Doran Rubber	Vans/Off the Wall/Serio	USA	1966	Tennis
Vasque (div. Red Wing Shoe Co.)	Vasque/Red Wing	USA	1905	Outdoor
Venson	BIG	Japan		Golf
Viko Dour	Viko	Yugoslavia		
Ving	Ving			X-country ski
Vittoria	Vittoria	Italy		Cycling
Viva SRL	Viva	Italy		

Volkl		Germany		
Walker Shoe Co.	Golden Retriever	USA	1947	Outdoor
Walsh	Walsh	U.K.	1981	Running
Weather Rite Inc. (div. Fuaua Ind.)		USA		Outdoor
WECO Whehmeyer		Germany		
Weinbrenner (div. Bata)	Wood 'n' Stream	USA	1892	Outdoor
Weinmann	Weinmann	Germany		Alpine ski
Wilson Sp. Goods	Wilson	USA		Tennis
Wolf, Bob	Bob Wolf	USA	1964	Sport
Wolfrum & Gerbeth	Woge	Germany		Sport
Wolverine W.W.	Wolverine/ Wilderness/ Hush Puppies/ Kaepa/ Brooks	USA	1906	Tanning
World Diamond	World Diamond	Japan		Crochet
Yamaha	Yamaha	Japan		Racquet sports
Yamato Takkyu	TSP	Japan		Table tennis
Yasaki	Yasaki	Japan		Tennis
Yassasport Chemotrade	Yassa	Germany		Soccer

Yasudo	Yasudo	Japan	Soccer
Yonex	Yonex	Japan	Racquet sports
Yume International Inc.	Dream	Japan	Windsurfing
Zamberlan S.R.L.	Zamberlan	Italy	Outdoor
Zermatt	Zermatt	Italy	X-country ski
Zeta Nord	Zeta Nord	Italy	
Zett	Zett	Japan	Baseball

PART 2

• SHOEMAKING •

"Ne Sutor Ultra Crepidam"

"Let the Cobbler Stick to his Last"

CONSTRUCTION OF
ATHLETIC FOOTWEAR

Because athletic shoes do depend on function for credibility, shoe construction must yield optium performance. For example, while the tubular construction of running shoes produces a lightweight, flexible upper, this certainly wouldn't be the best way to produce roller skate boots. Most of the major methods of shoe construction are also used in the manufacturing of functional sport shoes. After all, although the marketing and product development methods are somewhat different, the specialized sport shoe business is still shoemaking and from this standpoint does not vary dramatically from the traditional shoe industry.

Many of the early leather sport shoe makers such as Hyde, Etonic and even Adidas started as work boot makers. Until the decade of the 1960s, leather sport shoe manufacturing was more closely allied to heavy grade work boots than fine dress shoes. Over the past 30 years refinements to older companies and the entrance of some fine traditional Italian shoemakers, such as Diadora and Lotto, have reversed manufacturing trends. Also the once dominent rubber shoe giants such as Uniroyal, Dunlop and B.F. Goodrich have either reduced their original shoemaking operations or sold them to more specialized shoe companies.

The following pages explain the common shoemaking components and construction methods.

FIRST: THE LAST

In the process of manufacturing any athletic shoe, all upper work is done around the "last"—a three-dimensional form based upon

5-1. Author, Mel Cheskin, in Korea with the world's largest sport shoe made with identical materials used in regular sized models.

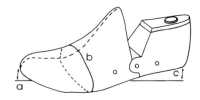

5-2. The Last: (a) toe pitch; (b) girth; (c) heel height.

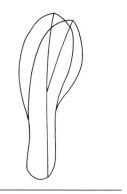

5-3. A curved last and straight last.

the shape and movements of the foot. The last, therefore, determines the shape, size and dimensions of the shoe. To help accommodate variations in foot shape, which occur with different movements of the foot and leg during sports activities, the last is designed with several special features. The two major ones are the Toe Spring and Heel Pitch, which affect the rocker or pivoting motion of the foot, particularly important in court shoes (see Figure 5-2).

The shape of the toe area is determined by the last, as is the instep, girth, bottom curvature and feather edge. The biggest last variations occur in the girth (or widest part of the forefoot) and in the heel width. These allow for snug or loose fitting. The amount of extension at the toe will permit or retard forward movement of the foot.

STRAIGHT AND CURVED LASTS

Most feet have a slight inward curve. Therefore, a corresponding inward curve in the last will improve fit and comfort. Athletes with a high or flexible long arch may prefer curve lasted shoes. Sport-shoe companies work with lasts curved approximately seven degrees. The greater the curve the more likely it will be suited for the under pronator. Straight-lasted shoes, appropriate for about 30 percent of athletes, tend to provide better support to the medial side of the foot. Therefore sensibly the best for athletes with flat feet.

ANATOMICAL LASTS

These are technical lasts with builtup bottoms or plantar sections that make the last conform better to the sole of the foot. Heel cups, raised insteps and metatarsal bridges can be incorporated into these lasts. This is an alternative to building the same features into a flat sole bottom shoe by using a contoured sockliner.

COMBINATION LASTS

This refers to any last that varies from a proportionally standard last to accommodate a combination of fitting or dynamic movement characteristics required in certain sports lasts. For example, a long jump track last may incorporate a narrow heel width, a standard waist area, a wide girth and a narrow toe area to best suit the long jumper's requirements. A standard last would not have differing width specifications at girth, instep or back part.

LAST VOCABULARY

BACK CONE: Portion of the cone surface between the "V" cut and the back end of the last.

BACK CONE HEIGHT: The vertical distance between the heel featherline plane and the back cone top plane.

BACKPART (REAR FOOT): Portion of the last extending rearward from the break of the joint to the back of the last.

BACKPART WIDTH: The width of the heel end measured parallel to the heel featherline plane at a specified distance from the heel point.

BASE PLANE: The plane to which the last in its proper attitude is referenced for the purpose of defining certain terms.

BREASTLINE: An arbitrary line defining the forward boundary of the heel seat.

CROWN: The lateral curvature of the bottom of the last.

FERRULE: Metal sleeve through the heel end of the last to permit attaching heel.

FOREPART (FORE FOOT): Portion of the last extending forward of the break of the joint to the toe.

FOREPART CENTERLINE: The best line of symmetry of the forepart bottom pattern.

FRONT CONE: Portion of the cone surface between the vamp point and the "V" cut.

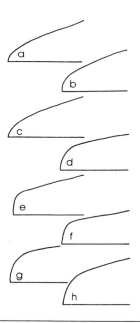

5-4. Last Shapes: (a) narrow/round; (b) oxford; (c) oval; (d) oval/round; (e) natural shape; (f) high/wide; (g) high; (h) high/round.

FRONT CONE PROFILE: A side view profile of the front cone.

FULL IRON BOTTOM: A last with a full sheet metal bottom surface from heel to toe.

GRADE INCREMENT: The change per size and/or width of any last dimension.

GRADE RATE: The ratio of the change in girth per size to the change in length per size.

HALF IRON BOTTOM: A last with a sheet metal bottom surface extending from heel to ball (joint).

HEEL CURVE: A side view profile of the back end of the last from the top of the last to the heel seat or featherline.

HEEL CURVE ANGLE: Angle between the heel featherline plane and heel point 2½ inches (63mm) up from the heel point intersecting the heel curve.

HEEL ELEVATION (PITCH): The vertical distance between the base plane and the heel point is the heel elevation.

HEEL FEATHERLINE: A line that defines the heel seat shape.

HEEL PLATE: A sheet metal bottom surface covering the heel area.

HEEL POINT: The rearmost point of the heel featherline.

HEEL SEAT: The bottom surface of the heel end of the last from the breast line back.

HEEL SEAT WIDTH: The greatest width of the heel seat measured from featherline to featherline perpendicular to the heel centerline.

HINGE: A metal piece connecting the front and rear section of the last. The break to foreshorten the last occurs at the hinge.

HINGE CUT: The "break" cut which provides for the two parts of the last to be "broken."

INFLARE: Asymmetrical inward swing of last shape.

INSTEP GIRTH: The dimension around a last passing through the instep point.

JOINT GIRTH: The greatest dimension around the last passing through the break joint.

LAST BOTTOM CENTERLINE: A line defined by the toe and heel point.

LAST BOTTOM FEATHERLINE: A line that defines the bottom shape of the last (last bottom pattern).

LAST BOTTOM WIDTH: The width across the ball area of the last bottom at its widest point.

LAST JOINT BREAK: Point located at the intersection of the shank and the forepart, tangent to heel point and perpendicular to last centerline.

LONG HEEL GIRTH: The dimension around a last passing through the instep and heel featherline point.

LONG HEEL PLATE: A sheet metal bottom surface extending

from the heel to midway of the shank area.

RIDGE: A well defined intersection of the wall and the conical section of the forepart.

SHANK: The bottom area of the last between the breastline and the joint break.

SHANK PLUG: A metal piece inserted in the shank in order to clinch metal shank fasting staple.

STICK LENGTH: Overall length of a last measured with a last size stick.

TACK HOLE PLUG: A plastic insert in the bottom of the last for receiving insole tacks.

THIMBLE: A metal sleeve inserted in the top heel end of last providing an opening for a mounting spindle or last pin.

THROAT OPENING: The distance in a straight line from the vamp point to the back seam tuck.

TOE PROFILE: A side view profile of the toe end of the last.

TOE RECEDE: The slope of the top surface of the last extending from the toe point to the point of full toe thickness.

TOE SPRING: The vertical distance between the base plane and the toe point of a last having the desired heel elevation.

TREAD POINT: The point of the bottom forepart in contact with the base plane.

VAMP LENGTH OR DEPTH: The distance measured along the toe profile from the vamp tack to the toe point.

VAMP TACK: An arbitrary point on top of a last forepart marked by a tack, measured from the toe.

V CUT: The portion of the cone which is removed to permit "breaking" of the hinge.

WAIST GIRTH: The smallest dimension around a last between the joint girth and the instep girth.

WALL: Straight sides around the periphery of the forepart of certain style lasts.

WEDGE ANGLE: The angle between the heel featherline plane and the base plane, with the last positioned on the base plane.

THE PRODUCTION OF LASTS

No new last can be formed before certain criteria are gathered. In the case of a custom made last, this comes from individual measurements. A standard last is fashioned to conform to the particular segment of the market for which it is intended.

To produce an individual last, the following measurements are necessary:

1. A draft outline plan of the weight-bearing foot;
2. An impression that shows the weight distribution;

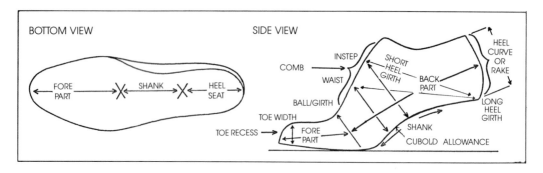

5-5. Last Division and Measurements.

3. A profile to show the height of the big toe and instep contour;
4. Overall length (stick length);
5. Width taken from draft;
6. These girth measurements from draft—
  A. Joint (around metatarsal-phalanged joint)
  B. Waist (smallest girth behind joint)
  C. Instep (smallest girth passing over prominence)
  D. Long heel (seat to instep)
  E. Short heel (seat to lowest crease in front ankle)
  F. Ankle (around and above ankle boots)

By determining a statistical average of as many individuals as possible in a market segment (for example, women runners), last makers are able to form an "average last" for that market segment.

LAST MANUFACTURE

Original lasts are still carved from blocks of wood, usually maple. Wood's flexibility enables the lastmaker to refine each characteristic and measurement.

The process begins when the lastmaker cuts the wood to the rough shape using a band saw. Then he shapes, files and sands the last block to exactly the required three dimensional shape, which does not have a single straight line measurement on it.

After an original model has been turned—the lastest Incoma machines can turn two pairs, both lefts and rights, at once—exact plastic or metal replicas are reproduced and graded either up or down for mass production. Hinges, hardware and markings are applied to the production lasts to suit the shoemaking construction method required. It is the last shape itself that primarily affects the fit of the shoe. Added sockliner inserts and upper pattern modifications are secondary fitting modifications that should be incorporated into the last fitting specifications.

5-6. Olympic sprinter McDonald Bailey's wooden shoe last, circa 1955. Note the high toe spring.

LASTS AND FEET

The essential differences between the human foot and the shoemaking last can be summarized as follows:

SURFACES—Last surfaces are smooth to enhance the appearance of the shoe and to enable the upper to be molded more easily to shape. The surfaces of the feet are irregular and vary with individuals.

OUTLINE—The outline of a last is regular and continuous with a sharp feather edge around the seat and forepart to assist lasting and give a clear defined edge to the finished shoe. The foot has no feather edge.

SUBSTANCE—The last is hard and firm, while the foot is softer and more flexible.

TOES—The foot has separate toes; the toe end of a last is solid.

HEEL CURVE—greater on the last to help the upper grip the foot.

HEEL PITCH—not present on the foot.

COMB AREA—thinner on the last to help the shoe grip the foot around the quarters.

JOINT GIRTH—sometimes greater on the last to allow the foot to flex in the shoe. This depends on the upper material and style.

LENGTH—The last is longer than the foot to prevent pressure from the shoe on the big toe.

TOE PROFILE—Depth gradually decreases to a feather edge on most lasts, but not on the foot.

TOE DEPTH—The last is normally deeper at the front then the foot to avoid pressure on toes.

TOE SPRING—not present on the foot.

GIRTH AND SIZE INTERVALS—regular on lasts, irregular on feet.

DIMENSIONS—identical on a pair of lasts; rarely identical on a pair of feet.

STYLING—The foot is incapable of being modified to give a square or pointed toe shape, for example; so any last styling of this nature must be carried out outside the limits of the foot to be fitted.

FUNCTION—The last is used for shoemaking; the foot is used for weight bearing and propulsion.

Lasts used to be made of wood but are now generally made of plastic. Metal lasts are used when direct or injection molded soles are applied to the upper, because of the heat and pressure involved. The last not only determines the shape of the shoe but also the area of mass that will be replaced inside the shoe by the foot. The volume inside the shoe can be greatly affected by heel wedges, molded footbed insoles or orthotics. These inserts can be accommodated in the original shape and mass of the last, but if such inserts are added to the shoe without being considered in the last, they will change the inside mass and fit of the shoe.

Many lasts are hinged or split to ease removal from the shoe after it is lasted. In the case of slip lasting, the hinge enables the upper to be stretched comfortably over the last.

MATERIALS USED IN SPORTS FOOTWEAR

It's possible to oversimplify the basic material groups used in sports footwear construction into leathers, nylons, rubbers and vinyls. However, a more detailed inspection reveals the true impact of Polymer Science in developing new materials that help athletes perform better.

A brief chronology of Polymer Science, the era of synthetic organic chemistry, dates back to the mid-1700s.

> 1751—François Fresnau and Charles Marie de la Condamine discovered rubber (``casutchouc'').
>
> 1770—The name ``rubber'' is credited to Joseph Priestly, an English chemist.
>
> 1791—Englishman Samuel Peal introduces the first commercial use of rubber.
>
> 1820—Handcock invents the prototype of the rubber processing mill, which has also found extensive use with elastomeric plastics.
>
> 1826—Regnault first prepares vinyl chloride, although it's not used commercially as PVC until 1934.
>
> 1839—Charles Goodyear discovers the vulcanizing process for natural rubber.
>
> 1860—Grenvill Williams isolates the main constituent from natural rubber and names it ``isoprene.''
>
> 1869—The basic cellulose nitrate patent is issued in the U.S. The plastics industry dates from this year when John Wesley Hyatt makes his first billiard ball.
>
> 1879—French chemist A & G Bouchardat makes a rubbery gum from isoprene monomer through the process of heat cracking rubber.
>
> 1884—Chardonnet produces the first artificial silk.
>
> 1892—W. Tilden makes a rubbery gum from synthetic isoprene.
>
> 1909—Dr. Backeland develops his ``heat and pressure'' patent—known as ``Bakelite''—for phenolic resins.
>
> 1915—DuPont creates commercial polyester in the U.S.
>
> 1921—Commercial rayon is introduced. A Soviet chemist improves the method of making butadiene rubber.

1923—U.S. and German chemists develop emulsion polyer-
ization.

1926—Eckert & Ziegler marketed their first injection molding
machine.

1935—Dupont introduces neoprene. Germany develops
Buna S—a styrene butadiene—and Buna N—a nitrile butadiene, oil-resistant rubber.

1951—The first polyester fibers are produced.

1959—All the basic polymers important to footwear manufacture are in use commercially.

ORGANIC POLYMERS

First came the natural organic material like wood, flax, cotton,
silk, oils, fur, rubber and leather. These are made up of cross-
linked or chain molecules. Natural compounds such as resins,
starch, cellulose, lignin and proteins are obtained from organic
polymers. The replacement or man-made polymers were developed later.

SYNTHETICS, PLASTICS AND MAN-MADE MATERIALS

One of the problems in explaining synthetics is the matter of
nomenclature. In the shoe industry at least, the terms "synthetics," "plastics," and "man-made materials" are all interchangeable. This group of inorganic substances can be technically
defined as:

"Any one of a group of materials consisting wholly, or in
part, of combinations of carbon with oxygen, hydrogen, nitrogen
and other organic and inorganic elements. While solid in the
finished state, they are made liquid at some stage in their
manufacture and are capable of being formed into various
shapes usually through the application of heat and pressure."

Synthetic materials can be divided into two groups—
thermoplastic and thermosetting. Thermoplastic materials become soft when heated sufficiently and then harden when
cooled. No matter how often the process is repeated, thermoplastics become pliable, then stiff. This group includes such
materials as ABS, acetal, acrylics, ethylene-vinyl-acetate (EVA),
nylon, polyethylene, polycarbonate, polypropylene, polystyrene, vinyl and some urethanes.

Thermosetting materials, in contrast, are set into permanent
shape when heated and molded; reheating will not soften them.
This group of plastics includes melamine, epoxy, phenolic, polyester and silicones.

PROCESS FLOW SHEET
WET OPERATIONS
1. TRIMMING AND SORTING
2. SOAKING
3. FLESHING
4. UNHAIRING
5. BATING
6. PICKLING
7. TANNING
8. WRINGING
9. SPLITTING AND SHAVING
10. RETANNING, COLORING, FATLIQUORING
11. SETTING OUT

DRY OPERATIONS
12. DRYING
13. CONDITIONING
14. STAKING
15. BUFFING
16. FINISHING
17. PLATING
18. MEASURING
19. GRADING

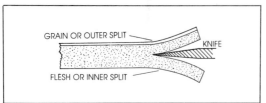

5-7. *Top left:* Author, Mel Cheskin, inspecting material testing equipment in Korea's largest shoe factory.   5-8. *Right:* Typical Tannery Process Flow Sheet (Courtesy of New England Tanners' Club.) 5-9. *Bottom left:* Split Leather Diagram.

UPPER MATERIALS

LEATHER UPPERS

Leather can come from the skin of any animal, bird, fish or reptile. However, only a few leathers are used in manufacturing athletic footwear.

Although leather consists of three layers, only two are used in shoemaking, namely the grain or outermost (hair) side and the inner corium central layer (after the epidermis has been removed). Leather is the most traditional material for shoe uppers. It has the ability to stretch and retain the stretched shape of the last. Leather will also absorb and transmit perspiration (that is, it "breathes"), and it has good resistance and resilience in flexing. It is also a fairly durable and abrasion-resistant material.

In the production of athletic footwear, the most used leathers are:
- Calfskin leather (box or willow)
- Kip leather (cowhide)
- Pig leather
- Antelope leather
- Goat leather

LEATHER THICKNESS GAUGE									
MMS.	OZS.	IRONS	THOUS.	INCHES					
				128	64	32	16	8	4
.2	.5	.4	7.8	1					
.4	1.	.8	15.7		1				
.6	1.5	1.1	23.6	3					
.8	2.	1.5	31.4			1			
1.0	2.5	1.9	39.3	5					
1.2	3.	2.2	47.2		3				
1.4	3.5	2.6	55.1	7					
1.6	4.	3.	62.9				1		
1.8	4.5	3.4	70.8	9					
2.0	5.	3.7	78.7		5				
2.2	5.5	4.1	86.6	11					
2,4	6.	4.5	94.4			3			
2.6	6.5	4.9	102.3	13					
2.8	7.	5.2	110.2		7				
3.0	7.5	5.6	118.1	15					
3.2	8.	6.	125.9				1		
3.4	8.5	6.4	133.8	17					
3.6	9.	6.7	141.7		9				
3.8	9.5	7.1	149.6	19					
4.0	10.	7.5	157.4			5			
4.2	10.5	7.9	165.3	21					
4.4	11.	8.2	173.2		11				
4.6	11.5	8.6	181.1	23					
4.8	12.	9.	188.9			3			
5.0	12.5	9.4	196.8	25					
5.2	13.	9.7	204.7		13				
5.4	13.5	10.1	212.6	27					
5.6	14.	10.5	220.5			7			
5.8	14.5	10.9	228.3	29					
6.0	15.	11.2	236.2		15				
6.2	15.5	11.6	244.	31					
6.4	16.	12.	252.						1
6.6	16.5	12.4	259.8	33					
6.8	17.	12.7	267.7		17				
7.0	17.5	13.1	275.6	35					
7.2	18.	13.5	283.5			9			
7.4	18.5	13.9	291.3	37					
7.6	19.	14.2	299.2		19				
7.8	19.5	14.6	307.1	39					
8.0	20.	15.	315.0				5		
8.2	20.5	15.4	322.8	41					
8.4	21.	15.7	330.7		21				
8.6	21.5	16.1	338.6	43					
8.8	22.	16.5	346.5			11			
9.0	22.5	16.9	354.3	45					

5-10. Leather thickness gauge.

- Deerskin leather
- Buckskin leather (Nubuck)
- Kangaroo leather
- Split varieties of the above (finished split)
- Suede varieties of the above

Of all these leathers, Kangaroo has the highest tensile strength and the lightest weight. Different thickness and grades of leather are available; the thinnest would be Kangaroo at 0.5mm in track shoes, and the thickest 3.5–4.0mm in mountaineering boots (see Figure 5-10).

Tensile Strength: Tensile strength may be defined as the longitudinal stress a material can withstand before tearing apart. Leathers can withstand a pull of 2,000-4,000 pounds per square inch.

Tear Strength: The structure of leather, with its fibers formed in a random arrangement that's interwoven through three dimensions, provides good tear strength. This occurs because the fibers aren't oriented in any fixed direction.

Elongation: When mulled or steamed to preform stretch over a last, leather can stretch as much as 20–30 percent.

Flexibility: The matrix of leather fibers allows it to flex freely without damage under extreme temperature and humidity, as well as exaggerated foot movements.

Puncture Resistance: Leather's irregular fiber pattern resists penetration by sharp objects often encountered in sports activities.

Moisture Absorption and Transmission: Leather can be treated to resist or repel water, but it will still retain its ability to transmit perspiration vapor when heat builds up within the shoe.

Tanning: Tanning is a treatment or preparation that aids the leather in retaining strength, flexibility and appearance. It also enables leather to accept coloring and different finishes. There are two types of tanning processes: 1.) vegetable tanning; and 2.) mineral, or oil tanning (such as chromium salts, hence chrome leather).

Finish and Dyeing: In order to improve appearance; cover blemishes; produce special effects; protect and improve water resistance; and retain the protein in the leather to avoid further bacterial breakdown of the tissue, leathers are treated in the following manner:

- Dyeing—
  drum dye (garment leathers) Nappa
  staining and brushing
  spray dyeing

- Finished and Grain Surfaces—
  aniline (clear wax finish)
  protein (casein, or milk)
  resin (gloss)
  patent or wet look (PVC or PU coated)

glazing (high gloss)
rub off (antiqued finish)
pearlized (lustre)
metallized (metal like lustre)
bronzed (metal coating)
gold and silver (metal coating)
natural grain/full grain (untreated or highlighted)
corrected grain (buffed and printed surface added)
embossing and printing (imprinted)
boarded grain (fine roll creases)
suede (buff or reverse nap)
water repellant (silicone or fluores-carbon treated)

RUBBER UPPERS (Synthetic or natural rubbers are

polymeric materials possessing characteristic elastic properties.)
Rubber uppers are used in golf, fishing and hunting shoes, due
to the various weather conditions and elements encountered in
these sports. This type of footwear usually has a fabric interfacing or lining on the inside. Most rubber footwear is made from
the vulcanizing process, and rubber uppers are waterproof.

FLOW MOLDED UPPERS (Coated or laminated

thermoplastic vinyl)
These uppers are PVC coated leathers or fabrics that have been
formed into a single piece of upper material without stitching
(except for at the back seam). This process uses silicone rubber
dies that are produced from original completed or decorated
uppers as a thin film and bonded to the backing material. Fine
details such as stitching lines and overlays are accurately reproduced, simulating a stitched upper. This technique is used
primarily on golf shoes.

SLUSH AND DIP MOLDED UPPERS (Thermoplastic

vinyl material)
These uppers are PVC molded, using the dip molding process or
slush process to produce a solid skin of PVC that has some
application in skates and waterproof footwear.

PVC OR PLASTIC INJECTION MOLDING (Mono-Bloc

Casting; Thermosetting plastic material)
This process has led to great innovation in athletic footwear
since the mid-1960s. Used almost exclusively in ski boots now
and for skates and other sports requiring rigid, protective boots,
this type of boot is made in a casting or injection molding
process with PVC and Acrylic monomer hardeners. Padded

leather and material liners are added to complete the inner boot. The sole and upper are of course produced "all in one" in this process.

SOFT NYLON (Synthetic fibers made from synthetic polyamide resins with related but not identical chemical compositions)

This material consists of a woven fabric (Taffeta) doubled or interfaced with a thin foam and tricot (skin fit) lining. It has become very popular since 1970 due to its strength, light weight, softness and flexibility. The range of denier used in most sport shoes is from 70 denier at the finest to 420 denier at the coarsest. The closeness of the weave is also a factor in the strength, durability and breathability of the material.

MESH NYLON (Nylon fabric, same as soft nylon)

This knitted material is available in varying degrees of strength and hardness (durability). Mesh has the added advantage of breathability (if not heavily interfaced with foam and tricot lining). Mesh has essentially the same features as soft nylon but, used in coarser grades, it gives added strength and body to the shoe. The usual denier of mesh nylon thread is about 400; it can be used in single, double or even triple mesh knits. All nylon materials may be treated with a spray finish in order to maintain varying degrees of stiffness.

PVC COATED FABRICS (Thermoplastic material: Vinyon is the generic term for vinyl chloride textile fibers.)

These materials, used primarily on less expensive grades of sport shoes, consist of a woven, knitted or non-woven base coated with a layer of plasticized PVC.

POROMERICS AND POLYURETHANE COATED FABRICS (Microporous and permeable coriaceous sheet material consisting of a urethane polymer material reinforced with polyester)

These materials are later developments to the PVC coated materials and vary considerably in their structure and make-up. Most have a textile woven base that is coated on either one or both sides with a PU foam or film. These materials, due to the cellular structure of PU, have some breathability and permeability to moisture vapor.

CANVAS AND OTHER FABRICS

The fabrics normally associated with athletic shoes are plain, one-on-one weave cotton or synthetic mixtures known as can-

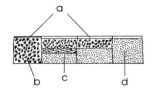

5-11. Diagrammatic cross-section of various structures of poromerics: (a) PU surface film; (b) microporous PU; (c) woven fabric interlayer; (d) impregnated non-woven fabric.

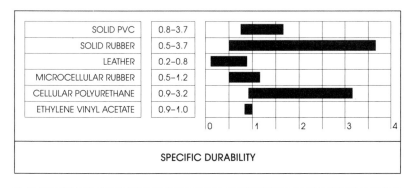

		SPECIFIC DURABILITY			
SOLID PVC	0.8–3.7				
SOLID RUBBER	0.5–3.7				
LEATHER	0.2–0.8				
MICROCELLULAR RUBBER	0.5–1.2				
CELLULAR POLYURETHANE	0.9–3.2				
ETHYLENE VINYL ACETATE	0.9–1.0				

5-12 Specific durability ranges for soling materials.

vas, or a twill weave cotton or synthetic mixture known as twill. Other fabrics are used as lining materials. A new cotton mesh provides excellent breathability, due to its very open weave.

SUEDINE OR PANDA SUEDE (Coated vinyl or rubber
substrate, also known as Bradford suede, Rae suede and Yamanashi)
This imitation suede, actually a flocking of fibers stuck to a PVC coated fabric or rubber backing, is used on less expensive shoes and for trim.

MATERIALS USED IN SOLING
Rubber soling has traditionally been the most widely used soling material because of its versatility, durability and all-around performance. Rubber can be used in unit, sheet form or direct vulcanizing process. It is used primarily in a highly compressed molded form or with a blowing agent in microcellular form (MCR).

Two definitions will help guide us through a further discussion of soling:
* Rubber—Natural and synthetic rubbers are polymeric materials possessing characteristic elastic properties.
* Elastomers—Any substances, including mixtures containing natural rubber, that have rubber-like qualities.

The two most commonly used rubber compounds in athletic footwear soling are Carbon rubber SBR and Styrene-Butadiene rubber SBR. Black carbon rubber is the hardest wearing rubber and is often used in running shoe soles. Styrene-Butadiene rubber is the other hard rubber type most used in tennis, basketball and other flat-soled shoes.

SBR can vary greatly in quality and composition. Basically it is a mixture of a natural or synthetic rubber base with additives such as accelerators, vulcanizing agents, coloring, filler and softeners. SBR can be any color and quality, depending largely on the composition and purity of ingredients. Usually a gum color or semi-opaque sole indicates a higher quality rubber containing purer materials, but this can be deceiving. No visual test can determine the quality of rubber soling. Only a laboratory analysis or wear test will indicate true durability and traction.

The rubber and elastomer forms used in footwear include:

Raw rubber—Plantation Crepe, Natural Rubber NR
Styrene—Butadiene Copolymers SBR
Acrylonitrile—Butadiene Copolymers (Nitrite Rubber)
Polychloroprene Elastomers (Neoprene)
Isobutylene—Isoprene Copolymer (Butyl Rubber) IIR
Ethylene-Propylene—Diene Monomers EAM
Polybutadiene BR
Chlorosulphonated polyethylene
Organic polysulphide copolymer
Polyurethane PU
Silicone Rubber (Gum Rubber)
Carbon & Hydrocarbonated Rubber SBR

MICRO-CELLULAR RUBBER (MCR)

MCR is a compounded mixture of natural rubber and additives that has a cellular structure and is used mainly for midsoles and wedges, although it can also be used as an outsole material on certain shoes (such as curling shoes). MCR is a rubber elastomer compound that contains a powdered blowing agent that decomposes during the vulcanization process to form a cellular structure (density, 0.5; approximate hardness, 50 shore A).

ETHYL VINYL ACETATE (EVA)

EVA is a chemical blend of ethylene and vinyl acetate known 'as a Co-Polymer and blowing agent that, when vulcanized, forms a cellular structure (density, approx. 0.2; hardness, 30–35 shore A). Used in cellular or polymeric form for lightweight midsoles and heel wedges, EVA is probably the most popular material used in good quality running shoes, due to its lightness, flexibility, density, elongation and impact resistance. EVA may be used in prefabricated (sheet) or compression molded forms.

POLYURETHANE (PU)

Polyurethane is a liquid polyester or polyeither two-part component that can be mixed·with a liquid catalyst or resin hardener to cause a chemical reaction, forming a blown cellular structure (density, 0.55; hardness, approx. 30–60 shore A for softer compounds and 80–90 shore A for harder compounds). PU can be injected directly or cemented as a unit sole. Incredibly versatile, PU can be used as a midsole and heel wedge component, while it is also light weight and durable enough for outsole material.

Dual density PU is a combination of a lightweight midsole and wedge with harder outsole material. PU finds use both in the cellular (blown) state and as a hardened elastomer form in multi-studded soles, golf shoes and others.

PVC
PVC is a mediumweight polyvinyl chloride resin plastized with a suitable plastizer and stabilizer at low temperature (density, 1.2; approx. hardness, 60–65 shore A). Elvaloy (or a similar substitute is a resin based modifier that adds rubber-like performance to PVC. Other PVC mixtures include thermoplastic rubber (T.P.R.) and thermoplastic elastomer (T.P.E.)

NYLON (Polyester Elastomer Resin, sometimes called
nylon sole)
This is a polyester resin with a higher melting point that can be used to form a harder outsole when injected (density, 1.1; approx. hardness, 95 shore A). Nylon is used for spike plates and base where attachments such as screw-in studs will be used.

Common hardness grades include Nylon 6, 11 and 12. Nylon 6 is the hardest; Nylon 12, the softest. The hardness grade refers to the number of carbon atoms in the nylon molecule.

LEATHER (Organic polymers)
Splits leather (bends) and coarse full hides are used on some athletic shoes, such as bowling shoes.

THE DESIGNER (OR MODELLISTA)
The successful shoe designer must be part creative artist, part skilled technician. The four primary functions of the designer are:
1. Sketch an idea or concept;
2. Transfer idea onto the last;
3. Develop the standard and cutting pattern off the last;
4. Produce the prototype sample shoe.

The most famous design and shoe making schools are Cordwainers in England (so named from the days when goat skins were imported from Spain's Cordova district) Deutsche Schuhfachschule, Pirmasens, Germany and Ars Sutoria in Italy.

5-13. *Top left:* Adi Dassler as he appeared during his active sportsman days. *Top right:* Adi Dassler shown with the first screw-in-stud soccer shoe which he produced. *Bottom left:* Bill Bowerman, co-founder of Nike,ꞏ shown in his running days (second from left). *Bottom right:* Bill Bowerman at work on his revolutionary waffle shoe.

None of these schools specializes in sport shoe design.

Although a good sport shoe designer does not have to be an active sportsman, it is essential for the designer to appreciate the needs of the athletes for whom the shoe is being designed. The most famous sport shoe technician was probably Adolf Dassler, better known as Adi Dassler, who had over 800 worldwide patents and patent applications to his credit before his death in Germany in 1978 at age 77.

Because the movements of the body are so critical during sports activities, podiatrists, sports physiologists and biomechanical experts have contributed significantly to the design and function of athletic footwear.

GRADING OF PATTERNS

A designer usually works on one size only in the initial designing stage. The normal working size is 9 for men's shoes and 6 for women's shoes. The standards and sections for the other required sizes for any given series must be obtained by grading.

which refers to the proportional enlargement and reduction of patterns for various sizes. The system of grading, originally calculated mathematically, based on a geometric principle of properties of similar triangles, is today calculated by machine or computer.

PROPORTIONED COMPONENTS
The outsoles, midsoles and insoles are originally optimally designed for the sample size (size 8 or 9 in men's and 6 in women's). As the grading of sizes is completed for both smaller and larger sizes, the dimensions, density and hardness is proportioned to each size for maximum comfort and performance.

If proportioned components are not used, while economical, this results in too much bulk in the smaller sizes and too little support and shock absorbency in larger sizes.

THE UPPER
The material used in the upper (outer and lining) comes in about 16–20 pieces that are first die-cut from various materials and then sewn together. The largest pieces of the upper, namely the quarters and vamp, can be cut in different ways.
1. one piece upper pattern;
2. two sided pattern with front seam joined;
3. three quarter cut vamp pattern;
4. vamp and two quarters.

Inside quarters are often cut higher than outside quarters for better medial support. This is called an asymmetrical pattern. It is generally best to have as few joins or seams as possible in the upper, as these can cause irritation to the foot. Identification of the quarters (medial and lateral) is obtained by a system of nicks

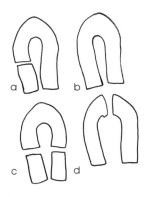

5-14. The Upper—(a) one-piece upper pattern; (b) two-sided pattern with front seam joined; (c) three-quarter-cut vamp pattern; (d) vamp and two-quarters.

5-15. *Left:* Author, Mel Cheskin, checking automatic toe and side lasting machine in Pusan, Korea.
5-16. *Right:* Author, Mel Cheskin, inspecting upper stitching on stitching line in Pusan, Korea.

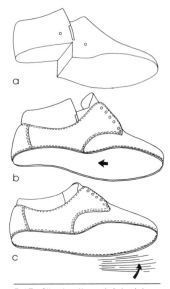

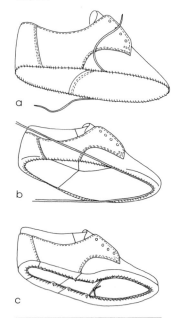

5-17. Slip Lasting: (a) last broken to receive upper; (b) slip lasting the upper onto the last; (c) closing of last tightens the upper.

5-18. String Lasting: (a) the upper with the string sewn at the edge; (b) the upper is being lasted as the strings are pulled; (c) the string is tied and hooked on pins.

on the inside or outside quarter pattern. Many of the popular trademark stripes or flashes are used to conceal the seams or joins. Sewing the pieces together accurately is achieved with pre-marked chalk stampings that guide correct placement of the pieces.

The shoe industry has long been a labor intensive, multi-work station operation, particuarly with regard to the sewing operations. Most sewing is still done on manual machines assisted by relatively simple electro-mechanical production devices. Computerized sewing systems have been introduced, however. They will no doubt play a key role in increasing efficiency, reducing costs and "de-skilling" the entire operation.

Most sport shoe uppers consist of soft nylons, mesh nylon, leather, suede canvas and man-made poromeric materials such as Kangoran. Vinyl and synthetic materials may find their way into lower grade footwear.

Once sewn together, the upper is stretched over the last to form the top-line, which is the opening for the foot; the feather edge, which is the lower extremity where the upper meets the sole or insole. In most methods, a margin called lasting allowance is added to the feather edge underneath the last.

The principal exceptions to stitched uppers are monobloc injection, as seen in ski boots and flow molded uppers as in some golf shoes. Sport shoes that aren't monobloc injected are flow molded. Flow molded uppers are stitched at the back seam and can be lasted in the conventional manner. Vulcanized rubber uppers are used to provide waterproofing for fishing and some golf shoes.

METHODS OF LASTING

There are some 14 or so methods of lasting that can be employed in shoemaking. Generally it is better to pre-form or pre-heat the sewn upper before applying it to the final lasting process. Certain lasting methods (such as hot melt cement, machine pulled) will consistently fit a tighter upper around the last than, say, hand-pulled string lasting.

THE TURNSHOE

The turnshoe or slipper construction is the earliest form of upper. It is the forerunner of the moccasin and tubular designs, and consists of the sole and upper being sewn together, then reversed to place the seams on the inside of the shoe. Most early track shoes were made this way. These types of shoes were called "pumps."

1. Slip Or California Lasting (also called force lasting)—With this lasting method, the last is inserted into a completely sewn upper, thus forcing it to take the shape of the last. A sock lining (called a slip-sock) usually takes the place of an insole. Features include: light weight, excellent flexibility, no torsional rigidity, no lasting insole.

2. String Lasting—A pull-string is sewn around the edge of the upper (under the last), then drawn tight so that the upper conforms to the shape of the last. Features: light weight, good flexibility, no torsional rigidity, no lasting insole.

3. Flat Lasting (cement, tack, staple)—Here the upper is pulled over the last and fastened to the insole with hot, quick-drying cement, tacks or staples, first at the toe, then at the heel, then along both sides under the last. Features: good torsional rigidity, platform stability, form fitting.

4. Moccasin Construction (forced lasting)—The mocassin style is used primarily with suede or leather uppers. In this method, the upper is placed under the last and extends up and around to form quarters and vamp. The upper is usually completed by stitching in a plug. Features: excellent flexibility, wrap-around effect.

5. Tubular Construction (forced lasting)—This is similar to moccasin construction. However, although the leather (or other material) is completely pulled under the sole, it is joined with one or more seams under the shoe. This method is heavily used in athletic footwear, particularly in running and track shoes. Features: excellent flexibility, wrap-around effect.

6. Rib Lasting—Rib lasting is used for welted footwear. The upper is pulled over the last and attached with nylon, wire staples or cement to a rib on the underside of the insole. Features: strength, durability.

7. Flanged Lasting—The upper is shaped over the last with the edge of the upper turned outside. This flange is stitched to the upper surface or directly to the sole. Features: strength, durability.

8. Combination Lasting—It's possible for more than one lasting method to be used on the same shoe. For example, a shoe can be tack-lasted at the heel and cement-lasted at the toe and sides. Moccasin construction shoes are often slip-lasted in the forepart and cement-lasted in the heel. Rigid insoles or part insoles are commonly added to more flexible constructions to improve torsional rigidity. Combination lasting offers unique customized features suited to high performance footwear.

5-19. Stitchdown or Flanged Lasting: (a) upper stitched down or flanged outwardly; (b) lasting insole.

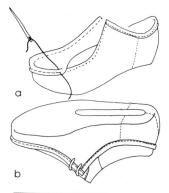

5-20. Moccasin: (a) sewing or lacing of the plug onto the vamp; (b) shoe lasted.

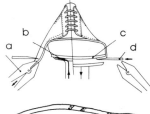

5-21. Flat Thermo Lasting: (a) pulling over action; (b) thermo cement application; (c) lasting insole; (d) wiping action.

DESIGNS AND CUTS OF UPPERS

Footwear fashion evolves from seven basic styles—Oxford, boot, pump, clog, mule, sandal and moccasin. Style is a basic profile or concept, whereas fashion is a current or popular version of a style. Styles are permanent; fashion is not.

The oldest style is the moccasin dating back some 14,000 years to the American Indians. The most recent style is the Oxford, from Oxford, England. This lowcut lace style was first introduced in 1640. Athletic shoes, due to their functional design, generally restrict styling types to just two of the seven basics.

Within these two styles, Oxford and moccasin, the designs can be virtually infinite. However, the main variations can be simplified as:

1. the U-throat (a full lacing pattern down to the toes, in the shape of a U);
2. the vamp or blucher pattern (cuts across the instep of the foot and does not extend to the toes);
3. the balmoral, or circular vamp or brogue (such as is found in golf shoes); and
4. the lace-to-toe pattern (an extension of lacing as in the U-throat but pulling both quarters together across the foot, where maximum support is required. The medial quarter may also be cut higher as in an asymmetric pattern as opposed to a symmetric pattern where both sides are the same).

Because a snug fit around the ankle is critical in lowcut (Oxford) athletic shoes, the top-line opening is not more than 10-11 cm or approximately 35 percent of the average size 8 shoe. Regular lowcut shoes tend to have a larger foot entrance of about 11-13 cm.

Regular or speed lacing can be incorporated into any of the above patterns. The moccasin or tubular cut can be termed a styling pattern as well as a construction method, since the upper must be cut in a certain style to accommodate the construction method.

MOLDS

This part of the shoemaking process creates the intricate sole patterns on shoe bottoms. Mold making, though not strictly a shoemaking function, is an extremely important part of the end product. The mold will affect grip and traction of the outsole, as well as flexibility, weight, durability and even shock absorption.

Molds are required for unit soles, outsoles and for direct injection attachment as in PU injection. There are several differ-

5-22. U-Throat

5-23. Flap Over Vamp

5-24. Blucher

5-25. Lace To Toe

5-26. Extended Eyeletstay

5-27. Strap Over Toe

5-28. Wing Tip

5-29. One Piece Toe

5-30. Apron

5-31. Extended Apron

5-32. Stitched Joined Toe

5-33. Derby

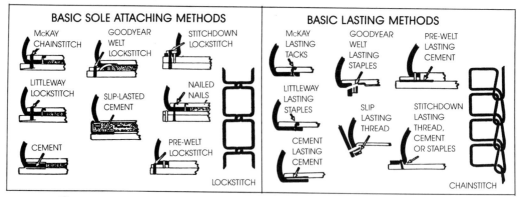

BASIC SOLE ATTACHING METHODS

McKAY CHAINSTITCH

GOODYEAR WELT LOCKSTITCH

STITCHDOWN LOCKSTITCH

LITTLEWAY LOCKSTITCH

SLIP-LASTED CEMENT

NAILED NAILS

CEMENT

PRE-WELT LOCKSTITCH

LOCKSTITCH

BASIC LASTING METHODS

McKAY LASTING TACKS

GOODYEAR WELT LASTING STAPLES

PRE-WELT LASTING CEMENT

LITTLEWAY LASTING STAPLES

SLIP LASTING THREAD

STITCHDOWN LASTING THREAD, CEMENT OR STAPLES

CEMENT LASTING CEMENT

CHAINSTITCH

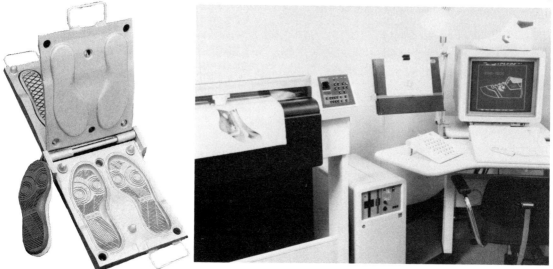

5-34. *Top:* Basic Lasting (showing various fastenings used for retaining the lasted-over margins) and Sole Attaching Methods (Courtesy of USM Corporation). 5-35. *Bottom left:* Typical rubber outsole molds. 5-36. *Bottom right:* CAD/CAM—Computer Design Equipment.

ent types of molds, basically depending on the dimensional areas involved. For example, sheet rubber molds are normally two dimensional, whereas unit sole molds are three dimensional. Molds used for direct injection attaching can have a bottom plate and split side rings in order to accept and release the lasted shoe for the bottoming operation.

When a sport shoe sole pattern is designed by shoe technicians, biomechanists and athletes, the sole design and features must first be translated by hand on drafting tables to the machine shop. Then most of the mold work is performed on the aluminum or steel blocks by hand operated tool and die cutting machinery.

In the early 1980s computer technology (CAD/CAM, for computer aided design/computer added manufacture) had cut in half the waiting time for mold design and production. Those shoe companies investing in the technology claim it will keep them ahead of others in developing styles and designs for future production. It should also increase availability of production molds on popular models.

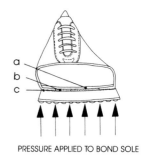

PRESSURE APPLIED TO BOND SOLE

5-37. Cement Construction: (a) lasting insole; (b) filler; (c) cement.

THE BOTTOMING PROCESS

The other main operation in shoemaking is called "bottoming," which follows lasting. In bottoming, the sole and other bottoming components are attached to the upper. While the upper determines the fit and support a shoe will provide, the sole keeps the athlete in touch with the ground and determines traction and shock absorbency. Soles come in various thicknesses and materials, as well as layers. Having discussed soling materials previously (on page 135) let's look at the various construction methods.

Cement Construction (probably the most commonly used in sport shoe construction)—The sole or bottom unit is glued or cemented directly to the lasted upper. The upper is usually roughed or treated chemically to insure a better bond with the lasting margin. This method can be reinforced with stitching or rivetted for added strength. Cement construction soles are placed by hand after the soles and uppers have been heat activated. They are then placed on a heel and toe press or a bag press; the pressure applied insures a good bond between sole and upper. Any riveting or stitching is completed after the sole has been stuck (see Figure 5-37).

Vulcanized Construction—There are two types of vulcanized rubber soles, both of which are heated to adhere to the upper.

1. Built up—The sole is cut from a slab or sheet of rubber. Other layers of rubber are used as cushioning or fillers between the upper and the outsole. A strip of rubber foxing is glued around the sole and upper. The shoes are then placed on lasts in a vulcanizing oven (autoclave) and cured for approximately 90 minutes. The upper, sole and foxing are bonded together in the heating process. Some of the shoes made this way include tennis, basketball and boating shoes.
2. Direct Vulcanizing Process—The lasted upper is placed

5-38. Vulcanized Rubber Built Up Shoe.

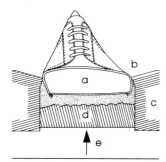

5-39. Direct Vulcanization of a Rubber Sole Onto a Shoe—the complete mold is heated in order to vulcanize the rubber and flat conventional lasting or slip lasting is used. (a) steel last; (b) sealing edge; (c) side mound; (d) piston; (e) pressure of 1000 to 1500 lbs.

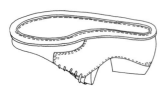

5-40. Goodyear Welt Construction.

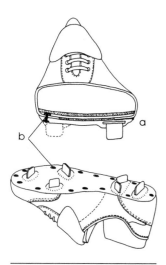

5-41. Cement and Rivet Construction: (a) rivet; (b) cement.

on a metal last and prepared for a mold cavity. An unvulcanized blank of rubber is added to the mold cavity, which has a base plate and side molds. The mold and metal last are heated to soften the rubber, which then takes the shape of the mold. The rubber is vulcanized in the mold, thus bonding the sole permanently to the upper.

Outside Stitchdowns, Lockstitch (Inside fastened; Littleway, McKay)—In stitchdown construction, the lasted edge of the upper is flanged outward and lockstitched to an insole (sometimes called a runner). The outsole is then cemented over the insole to form the bottom. The lockstitch method involves the stitching of the lasted upper through the margin and insole to the outsole in one machine process. This method is used in bowling shoes and some field shoes.

Goodyear Welt and Double Upper Stitchdown (Norwegian welt)—This is the traditional sturdy shoe construction whereby the sole is stitched to a welt diagonally through the lasted margin of the upper and insole, and vertically to the outsole in such a manner that the sewing cannot be seen from inside the shoe. This construction is used for hunting, hiking and mountaineering boots and for other categories.

When a double upper is used either welted or flat lasted (flanged), this method combines the stitchdown process with Goodyear welted or cemented constructions.

Cement and Rivet/Screw—This process is used with nylon (or unit rubber) unit soles. The semirigid nylon or rubber unit sole is drilled or predrilled with rivet holes. Then the sole is cemented and pressed to the upper. The complete shoe is next rivetted through the lasting margin, either all around (approximately 10 rivets) or at heel and toe for strength.

This method is used for football, soccer (screw-in studs), baseball and cross-country shoes. In some hiking boots the outsole is cemented and screwed to the midsole section.

Direct Injection Or Extrusion Molded Process—This method is generally used for PVC (something of the Elvaloy type which, when added to PVC, improves the gripping and wearing properties), PVC extenders or Thermal Plastic Rubbers (TPR). The main difference between injection and extrusion molding is that rubber cannot reach a molten stage to be successfully injected, as can PVC. Therefore rubber must first be extruded into the mold much like toothpaste from a tube.

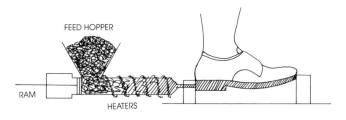

5-42. Direct Injection Process—single color thermoplastic injection (PVC - TPR)

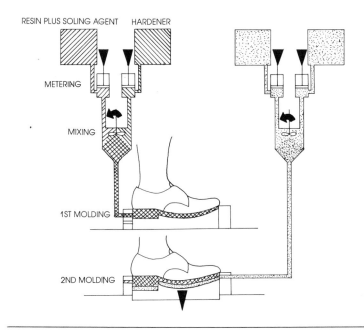

5-43. Direct Injection Process—double color polyurethane sole.

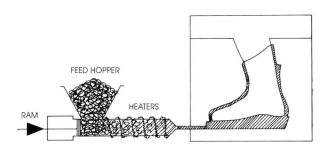

5-44. Monobloc Ski Boot Injection—(PVC—thermoplastic polyurethane injection) or (casting of two parts polyurethane).

Metal molds that have bottom pistons and side rings form a complete sole mold. The lasted upper on a metal last is placed in the mold and the rings closed to seal the mold. When cooled, this leaves the sole bonded to the upper. A heel filler can be used for weight saving.

This process is employed to make cross-country, soccer and field shoes and other categories.

Single, Dual and Triple Polyurethane Injection (Re-action Molding)—This is basically the same molding process as described above. However, with polyurethane the two chemicals that make up the compound are mixed together in the mold to react. This reaction releases a gas that forms bubbles in the compound, producing a cellular or blown structure within the mold.

The two compounds are mixed as liquids immediately prior to entering the mold through two injection heads. The cellular sole is formed immediately; it requires no cooling-off period. A bond is naturally formed with the upper. A silicone spray is applied to the molds as a release agent, causing a slight film to form on the outside of the sole. In the dual injection case, the process is repeated in separate parts of the mold before being bonded by the joining midsole layer to the upper. The three color process is a further advancement of the technique. By varying the chemical composition of the polymer mixture, a different hardness or density can be obtained.

Dual density (or two shot) injection occurs when one density is injected into a mold through one injection head, while a second density is introduced through a second head. When the first completed slab is joined to the second injection shot, the two densities of PU are cemented and bonded to the upper. This process is used for court and outdoor shoes.

Polyurethane may be pre-mixed and poured into a mold in liquid form to harden later. This soling method is called "Poured PU." It is normally used for unit soles that will later be cemented to the upper. It can, however, be poured to make a direct attachment to the upper.

Direct Injected Plastic Boots (Mono-Bloc Casting)—Over the last 30 years plastics technology has become increasingly important to the shoe trade. Since the mid-1960s for example, rigid plastic alpine ski boots have gradually dominated the downhill ski market. The same process is now making headway in the manufacture of skates.

The direct injection process is the same in principle as the other mold processes except mold blocks form the complete

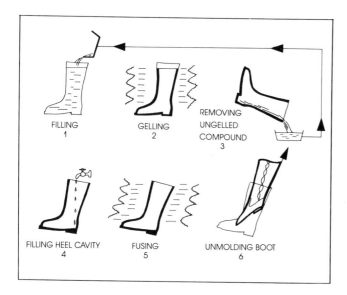

5-45. *Left:* Slush Molding Process.   5-46. *Right:* Leather upper fully stitched rubber shell sole.

shoe and not just the sole. The block mold splits in the middle and the metal last is incorporated into the mold. When the mold closes, the cavity left between the metal last and the inside of the block mold forms the shape of the complete unit.

As with the other injection methods, injection of the compounds occurs through an injection head. The boots produced this way are often made in two pieces and hinged to provide some forward lean flexibility. Different thickness and flexibility in the upper and sole can be achieved simply by the shape of the mold cavity. The boot is completed when liners and attachments are added.

Slush Molding Process—This method of shoemaking has
been used primarily for winter or protective footwear but has some application for skates, fishing, hunting and riding boots. PVC is poured into a cavity mold (similar to the shape of the boot) and "rinsed" or "slushed" around the inside until a shell or skin is formed inside the mold.

When heated the compound hardens and is then pulled out of the mold as a complete unit. Liners and outside attachments are added to complete the boot.

A dip molding process (a film is formed on the outside of the mold) produces a similar boot. However, as no' detailed finish can be obtained on the boot's outside, the result is a plain look such as is found on lower priced riding boots.

THE OUTER SOLE

The outsole is the portion of the shoe that makes contact with the ground. In other words, the wearing part of the sole. The outsole, when referred to as such, is usually attached to a midsole and wedge to form a prefabricated complete sole. The outer sole may be of flat-wedge type, one-piece inside heel type or two-part sole and heel.

Most flat sole shoes have outer soles of synthetic solid or blown rubber compounds that provide general flexibility and durability. Gum rubbers are hard-wearing and grip well on most surfaces. PU is less versatile but also suitable for outsole material. Nylon, leather and PVC have specific outsole application for certain sports.

OUTSOLE DESIGNS AND PROFILES

The outsole profile design of a sport shoe may include several different features that will aid performance and decrease injury likelihood. A few of these include: cushioning, traction, pivoting, flexpaths, wear plugs and weight saving. The selection of the most suitable materials is, of course, central. The lateral heel plugs found in running shoes; the radial edges on tennis shoes; and the pivot points on court shoes are all fully discussed under their separate sports categories in Section IV of this book.

It's probably safe to state that there exists a single optimal performance outsole for each sport, for every specific weather condition, on each type of surface and to suit each weight/movement ratio. Some common profile design examples include:

- Reinforced wear areas in running shoes;
- Cantilevered shock absorption designs in running shoes;
- Traction outsoles for running shoes;
- Flex path outsole designs on running shoes;
- Pivot points on court shoes;
- Herring-bone, multi-traction outsoles on court shoes;
- Bi-level traction outsoles on court shoes;
- Suction cup designs on court shoes;
- Multi-claw or stud designs on field shoes;
- Radial edges on court shoes;
- Asymmetric stud patterns on field shoes;
- Traction and wear lugs on hiking and climbing boots.

MIDSOLES, WEDGES AND HEELS

These are used as separate soling components in conjunction with an outsole. The midsole and wedge (or heel) are sandwiched between the upper and the outsole, attaching to both.

These components primarily give the shoe heel lift, rocker and toe spring. They are also crucial for cushioning and shock absorbency.

UNIT SOLES
Unit soles usually contain the outsole, midsole, and wedge or heel all in one. These types of soles are most suitable for use when the sole doesn't come into contact with the ground as, for example, with roller skate boots. Unit soles may be made of any of the previously mentioned harder soling compounds such as rubber or PVC and are also used for field sports where little heel lift is required. They tend to be heavy and offer less flexibility than prefabricated or combination soles. Unit soles are normally cemented, riveted and/or stitched to the upper and offer good torsional rigidity.

SHELL DISH OR CUP SOLES
These are unit soles with foxing sides, forming a cavity in which the lasted upper is cemented. Stitching can be added around the foxing to give added strength. Rubber or PU types are most common with inside cells for cushioning and lightness.

COMBINATION OR PREFABRICATED SOLES
To obtain optimal performance, combinations of materials are now commonly used for sport shoes. Rubber unit or shell soles often contain EVA or PU midsole and wedge inlays. The improved cushioning, varying densities and weight-saving advantages first introduced into running shoes can also be found in court, aerobic and even some field sport areas. Insets in direct attached soling, such as high density PU, also give certain features to a sole. These inserts can be cemented or encapsulated in the mold.

OTHER COMPONENT PARTS

HEEL COUNTERS
The heel counter is a hard or semihard moldable or premolded strengthening device in the heel area of the upper. These counters serve to stabilize the heel and reduce heel drift. Premolded fiber, polyethelene or plastic counters are all accepted. In recent years, heat-activated counters have improved dramatically and gained in usage. Many categories of sport shoes have elongated counters on the medial side for additional pronation control, contoured or notched counters reduce Achilles tendon pressure.

5-47. *Left:* Premolded Fiber or Plastic Counter. 5-48. *Center:* Thermoplastic Counter. 5-49. *Right:* Toe Box.

BOX TOES

Box toes are stiffeners inserted between the lining and upper. In running shoes, these are usually small or nonexistent. Box toes lend protection to the toes when correctly inserted, which is crucial in contact sports. Where a high or adequate toe box is recommended, the inserted stiffener helps to prevent the collapse of the upper material in the toe area.

5-50. Side Foxing: (a) cement; (b) foxing to reinforce lateral movement and sides of shoe wear.

FOXING

Foxing is support material, usually suede or rubber stripping, that gives medial and lateral support to the outside of the shoe. In running shoes the most important foxing is at the toe, where it's called the toe cap. In court shoes the foxing runs completely around the sole for lateral support.

5-51. Heel Stabilizer.

VARIABLE WIDTH LACING

This principle is simple and logical. A variable, or wavy, eyestay pattern with two sets of eyelets allows conventional lacing to be adjusted for wider or narrower feet. The wider or lower spaced eyelets allow the lacing to exert more control on the quarters of the shoe and are thus more suited to a narrow foot. Conversely, the narrower or higher spaced eyelets allow for more width variation, benefitting the athlete with a wider foot.

ADDITIONAL HEEL STABILIZING LACING

This system of lacing around the heel and top quarter offers adjustment to the heel width and top line. Heel stabilizing lacing is used on running shoes as well as on field shoes, where the feature was first introduced as an adjustment to the top line.

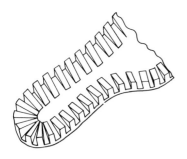

5-52. Cantilevered sole with shock absorption and stabilization effect.

CANTILEVERED OR ANGLED RADIAL OUTSOLE

This is a specially designed shock-dissipating outsole that is used for running shoes and other court and aerobic models. A variation is the longitudinal channel design (sometimes called biokinetic outsole) that brings a greater proportion of the sole into the shock absorption and motion control process.

DOUBLE VAMP LACING SYSTEM

This design splits the vamp into two separate sections with separate laces, which permits variable lacing adjustments in both the upper and lower portions of the eyestay.

5-53. Two-lace/split-vamp lacing system.

LASTING INSOLE AND SHANK

As explained earlier, in the first stage of shoemaking the upper is lasted and attached to the insole. Insoles will vary in thickness according to the weight and strength requirement. Insoles are usually composition board. The heel region of the shoe needs to be more rigid. The back part of the insole (or the reinforcing material added to the back part) is called the shank. Additional shanks are not common in wedge soled shoes, but are considered important for torsional rigidity in shoes with heels to support the metatarsal arch.

In conventional (cement) and other forms of lasting methods, such as tack lasting, the upper is attached to a cellulose fiber board called an insole board. This insole (not to be confused with the insock or sock liner) adds torsional rigidity to the shoes. Insole boards can be added after lasting to other constructions to improve platform and torsional rigidity. Insoles are manufactured in various thicknesses and variations that incorporate features such as built-in shank support, flex cuts and premolded shapes.

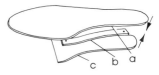

5-54. Reinforced Lasting Insole: (a) lasting insole; (b) steel shank; (c) hard fiber shank.

TONGUES

Tongues are designed primarily to protect the dorsal closure area of the foot from lace pressure and to prevent dirt and moisture from entering the shoe through the eyelets and throat of the shoe. Tongues are usually lightweight, well padded and in some instances, such as in field sports, protective. Ventilation is another feature that can be incorporated into tongue design.

Some sport shoes have special tongue features designed into them, including the flap-over or Kilty tongue, which keeps laces dry and prevents lace entanglement with cleats or spikes; or the bellows tongue, which is sewn to the eyestay to prevent wetness from seeping through. Lacing loops or tongue slits are popular to help prevent the tongue from slipping to the side. Tongues are usually made from leather, high frequency molded PVC or padded nylon.

5-55. Shawl Tongue.

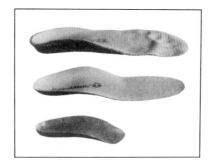 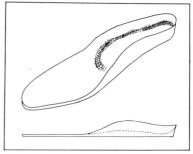

5-56. *Left:* Sock Linings, Arch Supports and Inserts. 5-57. *Right:* Molded Footbed Insole with Arch Support.

LININGS

Upper linings are often used in conventionally stitched athletic shoe uppers for comfort, sweat absorption and added strength. Linings may be made from soft leather, fabric or a woven or knitted nylon material'called nylon tricot or skinfit. Nylon tricot is usually foam backed, which adds minimal weight to the shoe.

Arch bandages, which act as longitudinal reinforcers, and full linings give added support to the upper and prevent stretching, particularly if the upper material has a tendency to stretch when wet.

SOCK LININGS, ARCH SUPPORTS AND INSERTS

In today's athletic shoes, sock linings do much more than just cover the insole and improve comfort and appearance. They can be sophisticated molded lightweight soft support systems that are designed to reduce heel shock and overpronation. Also, they can absorb perspiration and mold to the plantar foot surface, acting as an anatomical shaping for the foot contour. Some sock liners will even aid air circulation inside the shoe.

Regular insocks should be comfortable and perspiration absorbent. Arch supports, built-in heel cups and other types of padding, usually made of sponge rubber or EVA, can serve other functions, including support, special canting requirements and resistance to foot drift and overpronation of the medial arch.

To accommodate these inserts inside the shoe, a last allowance must be made or the quarter height adjusted. Sometimes there is already sufficient room in the last so as not to effect the original fit of the shoe.

Shoe manufacturers are careful to avoid use of the term "orthotic." These are corrective devices prescribed by or used in conjunction with qualified podiatrists. Orthotics may be of various hardnesses. Shoemakers prefer terms of more general application such as contour molded, footbed insoles and soft support system. To avoid confusion on this point, especially if concerned about the effect a particular insert may have on their performance, athletes should always consult a practicing podiatrist.

The lastest in shoe technology, pioneered by the ski industry (Sidas® and Superfeet® systems) is custom molded "foothotics." These are semirigid insole devices that take the exact bottom shape of the athlete's foot, thus helping to increase comfort, absorb shock and improve performance. Such custom insole devices can be used for any sport provided the inside of the shoe has enough room to accommodate the insert.

NEW COMPONENTS AND INNOVATIONS

AIR SOLES
By introducing ridges or tubes of air into the insole, midsole or heel wedge, manufacturers can increase sole cushioning. Tests have proven that these air-inflated soles exhibit superior shock absorption and rebound energy potential, but perform poorly in stability and offer a limited platform during the midstance and toe-off positions of running and jumping. As air cushioning has been embraced by the U.S.'s largest athletic shoe company, research on the instability problem has led to improvements that promise to get ever better.

Water or oil soles have also been tried but without great success due to the weight disadvantage and instability.

PERFORATED AND COMBINATION MIDSOLE AND HEEL WEDGE
To lighten the sole and make it more flexible, holes can be perforated through the midsoles or heel wedge. The same result can be achieved by using different prefabricated materials in the midsole and wedge construction. These modifications are then covered with a harder wearing outsole material.

AIR VENTILATED SYSTEMS
Several athletic shoe companies, realizing the importance of good ventilation in their products, have introduced innovative ways to pump fresh air inside the shoes. Adidas and Allsport market shoes with a compression system that pushes air inside the shoe through the sole. Romika and others use upper ventilation methods to achieve the same result.

5-58. Customizing chair and some of the equipment required to modify orthotic insole devices. Note the heating oven for thermoplastic setting materials.

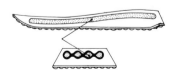

5-59. Air Cushioned Sole (air chambers within sole).

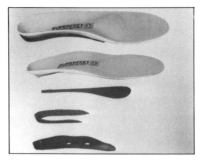

5-60. *Top left:* Turntec's optional removable running sole introduced in 1985.
5-61. *Top right:* The first pronation control device shoe—"The Brooks Vantage."
5-62. *Bottom left:* Customizing materials used to modify a soft support system sockliner.   5-63. *Bottom right:* Lotto's safety running lights introduced in 1983.

5-64. *Left:* Puma's Computerized Micro-Pacer Shoe.   5-65. *Right:* The computer running shoe complete with software package, program, program disk, connector cable and main menu display screen.

FLEXIBLE INSOLES

These are special flex portions inserted directly into the insole to give a better flexpath. The same effect can be achieved by slitting the insole board for greater flexibility.

REPLACEABLE PLUG SYSTEMS

Three replaceable plug systems have been introduced into sports footwear in recent years:

1. Adidas designed a rearpart shock absorption plug system that allows three different hardnesses of replaceable plug to be inserted into the heel wedge.
2. Pro Keds used a replaceable wear plug system on the outsole with the idea of prolonging sole life by replacing the areas that wear most quickly.
3. Brooks marketed a pronation control system, which is inserted on the medial side of the heel in column form to allow varying degrees of pronation to be controlled by inserting harder plugs.

REMOVEABLE/REPLACEABLE OUTSOLES

Removeable outsoles were long thought about but always rejected as too impractical or "gimmicky" until Jerry Turner introduced removeable outsoles on his Turntec line in 1985. The outsoles are attached to the midsole by a hook-and-loop (Velcro-like) closure system. Where little lateral stress is placed on the shoe, as in running, the concept has tested well. However, an all-purpose application of this principle for use in many different sports has not yet been perfected.

REARFOOT STABILIZING SYSTEMS

First introduced on running shoes in the early 1980s, this feature has now been transferred to other categories such as tennis shoes. The external component (a solid outside counter attachment) is made of PU or PVC. The idea is to give extra strength to the rearfoot area while helping keep the foot correctly aligned inside the shoe.

PRONATION CONTROL DEVICES

These were first introduced by Brooks in 1978, using Dr. Steve Subotnick's varus wedge concept. There have since been many modifications or new applications aimed at controlling overpronation in runners. Most fall into two categories:

1. A harder density or structure built into the midsole and/or heel wedge to compensate for the rolling-inward action of the foot.

2. An added component to the inside or outside of the shoe that prohibits it from collapsing on the medial side.

Results from the latest studies indicate a need to focus attention on a total foot control device rather than simply the rearfoot.

SPORTS LIGHTS

A flashing safety light component for running shoes was introduced by Lotto from Italy in 1983. This heel innovation has also been made available as an optional attachment that can be cemented to any brand of shoe as a night-running safety feature. Although these innovations were inspired by a genuine need for safer road running at night, it is interesting to note that natives of South America and the West Indies tie several large, brightly blinking cucuyo fireflies to their boots to light their way along nighttime paths.

COMPUTERIZED MICRO-PACER SHOES

The most advanced technology introduced in the mid-1980s has been in running shoes with built-in electronic devices that communicate with a computer. By marrying the running shoe with the computer, runners can now benefit from technology that automatically measures distance, time and caloric energy expended during the run. The microsensor or pacer is stored in one shoe (with compensating balance in the other) to collect data at footstrike during the run. Following the run, shoe information can be inputted into a computer terminal and calibrated, stored or combined with previous personalized data to supply current information and update goal files on an ongoing basis. The software package allows the program to be used by one or many runners on the same system.

NEW MATERIALS

Chemical suppliers to the footwear trade are constantly innovating and inventing new component pieces, linings, footbeds and so on. Some of the more recent materials that have caught on include: Sorbothane, Cambrelle, Thinsulate and Poron.

Shoemaking, like most other crafts, changes with improved materials and technology. Generally speaking, shoemaking is becoming less labor intensive and more dependent on scientific contributions. As in the automobile industry where cars that are designed and raced for performance are often forerunners of innovations that will effect the whole industry, world-class athletes will be the first to wear new shoe materials or components that later will spread to the masses.

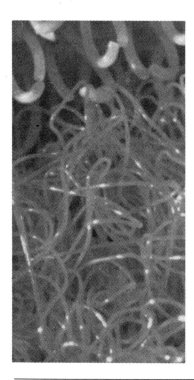

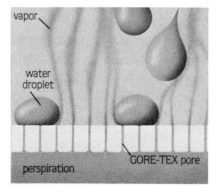

vapor

water droplet

GORE-TEX pore

perspiration

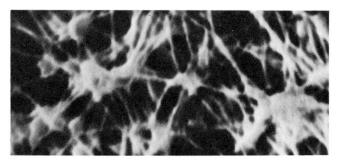

5-66. *Top left:* Velcro fabric membrane magnified. 5-67. *Top right:* A close-up of the Gore-Tex membrane properties. 5-68. *Bottom right:* Gore-Tex fabric membrane magnified.

FAMOUS COMPONENT PARTS BY BRAND NAME

Brand Name	Company	Use
Bondtex®	Georgia Bonded Fibers	Insole Material
Cambrelle®	Faytex Corp.	Lining Material
Champ®	McNeil Eng.	Golf Spikes
Clarino®	Kuraray Co. Ltd.	Synthetic Upper
Cordura®	Du Pont	Nylon Materials
Dunova®	Bayer	Interlinings
Frelonic®	Freudenberg	Insock Materials
Gore-Tex®	W.L. Gore & Assocs.	Waterproof Uppers
Indy 500®	Goodyear Corp.	Outsole Material
Infinity®	Quabaug Rubber Co.	Outsole Material
MK®	Mitchell & King	Ice Skate Blades
Nash®	Kuraray Co. Ltd.	Synthetic Uppers
Nomex®	Du Pont Corp.	High Temperature Aramid Fiber

Odor-Eaters®	Faytex Corp.	Sock Liners
Perfecta®	St. Lawrence Manf.	Ice Skate Blades
Phillips®	Phillips	Golf/Field, Spikes/ Cleats
Poron®	Rogers Corp.	Sockliner Materials
SLM®	St. Lawrence	Ice Skate Blades
Skywalk®	Skywalk S.P.A.	Outsole Materials
Snyder Skate®	Snyder Skate Co.	Roller Skate
Sorbothane®	Spectrum Sports	Sockliner
Spenco®	Spenco Med. Corp.	Sports Medicine
Sure-Grip®	Sure-Grip Int.	Roller Wheels
Surlyn®	Du Pont Corp.	Soling/components
Texon®	Texon Corp.	Insole Material
Tuuk/ICM®	Canpro Sport Inc.	Ice Skate Blades
Thinsulate®	3 M Comp.	Insulation
Uhl®	Uhlsport Gmbh.	Sole Components/ Spikes Studs
Vanguard/Vanthane®	Vanguard Manf. Co.	Roller Wheels
Vibram®	Vibram/Quabaug Co.	Soling Materials
Velcro®	Velcro USA Inc.	Closure Systems
Visa/Fast Break®	Manning/Milican	Upper Materials
Wilson®	John Wilson Ltd.	Ice Skate Blades
Wingfoot XL®	Goodyear Rubber Co.	Sockliner

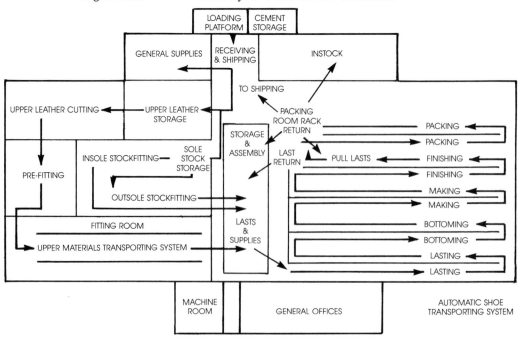

5-69. Work Flow Diagram For a Single Floor Shoe Factory (Courtesy of USM Corporation).

MANUFACTURING PROCEDURES— INSIDE THE SHOE FACTORY

In addition to describing shoe construction, it's important to explain the shoe manufacturing process for a full understanding of how an athletic shoe is assembled. The shoe industry, largely labor dependent, has became more automated and more reliant on chemical innovations in the past 50 years and will certainly continue to move in this direction.

Most shoe factories are alike in their organization and the procedures they follow to manufacture shoes. Some are much larger than others, particularly a few in South Korea that have the capacity to turn out 200,000–300,000 pairs per day. Factories using injection molding are more mechanized. The largest polyurethane injection machine has 72 stations, or the capacity to sole up to 240 pairs per hour.

It is possible to categorize a factory's major work areas and group them according to the functions each fulfills.

THE RECEIVING AREA

The raw materials are received, inspected and stored in this area until they are ready to be forwarded into manufacturing. The materials include sheeting for soles, rolls of leather, suede, nylons and PVC materials, and shoe findings (hardware such as eyelets, etc.).

PRIMARY RUBBER AND CHEMICAL MIXING

Many large shoe manufacturing companies have their own primary chemical mixing operations. These areas, which contain large Banbury mixers, rollers and presses, are usually run in conjunction with chemical engineers as well as factory shoe personnel.

FORMULA AND TESTING LABORATORIES

These areas are usually small departments headed by chemical engineers. In the factory lab, new soling materials are formulated; shoes and materials are destruction tested and approved for manufacturing; and returned shoes are analyzed for chemical and structural breakdowns.

CUT AND SEW OPERATIONS—THE FITTING ROOM

With the exception of specialized shoe constructions such as slush molding, monobloc casting and PVC flow molding, all shoe uppers are die cut and sewn in the fitting room. Materials and

5-70. *Left:* Assembly line for ski-boot liners at Koflach factory in Austria. 5-71. *Right:* Author, Mel Cheskin, inspecting directly attached PVC/PU multi-studded soccer sole at a factory in Canada.

leathers are die cut or hand cut singularly in a process called "clicking." Leathers, suedes and other materials are manipulated to produce as little waste as possible. The assortment of gang die cut parts are marked into position and individually sewn to complete the upper. Eyelets, speed lacing, buckles and other attachments are completed at this stage of the operation. The completed uppers are then hung by size to await the bottoming or soling operation.

LASTING

The lasting process, which may include the attaching of the insole board, is the method of pulling the finished upper over the last to create the upper shape. The basic lasting operation includes the insertion of the heel counter, box toes and shanks, which are incorporated into the lasting insole, if used. In the bottoming operation, lasting methods such as string and slip lasting may be completed before injection on the metal last, mounted on the injection machine. Plastic or wooden lasts are generally used in other lasting methods.

BOTTOMING AND SOLING OPERATIONS

Injection soling, with either string or slip lasting, is completed in one operation. Other types of soling (either prefabricated with wedges, midsoles and outsoles, or unit type injected, or vulcanized soles) are completed and trimmed before being attached to the upper. The bottoming operation is basically the completion of any separate soling unit for the sole laying operation.

SOLE LAYING

Sole laying is the attaching of the sole to the upper either by cement, rivet or built-up vulcanized rubber soling. The sole, already sized and trimmed, is matched to the upper and pressed, riveted or glued to the lasted upper for permanent bonding.

FINISHING AND PACKING
After the upper and sole have been permanently attached, the shoe is passed through a finishing stage where marks are cleaned off, sock linings and laces inserted, and inspection is completed.

GLOSSARY OF SHOE TERMS
ACRYLIC RESIN: Synthetic resin prepared from acrylic acid.

ADHESIVE (Cement): Substance capable of holding materials together by surface attachment.

AGLET: Metal or plastic tip of lace.

ANILINE: Leather tanning finish.

APPLIQUÉ: Logo or other ornament in the form of a piece of leather or material sewn to the shoe.

APRON CUT: Design of the toe cap.

ARCH BANDAGE: Reinforcing strips of fabric stitched inside the shoe on the medial and lateral quarters.

ARCH CUSHION: (Cookie) support pad for the medial arch of the foot.

ASYMMETRICAL: In shoemaking this applies to lasts and patterns that have uneven shapes, the right side different from the left.

A.T.P. (Heel Horn): Extended padding at the back heel collar to protect the Achilles tendon. (Achilles tendon protector)

AUTOCLAVE: Vessel or oven in which chemical reaction or cooking takes place under pressure such as in the vulcanizing construction method.

BACK SEAM: Stitching line at the back of the heel joining quarters.

BACKER: Lining material.

BAGGED EDGE: Clean inside seam hiding stitching.

BAL: (Balmoral) design where quarters meet and the vamp is stitched over the quarters at the front of the throat.

BANBURY: Apparatus for mixing compounds.

BELLOWS TONGUE: Outside attached tongue to prevent snow entry.

BIAS CUT: Cut away upswept heel.

BINDING: Reinforcement for the edge of material used in upper.

BLOWING AGENT: Chemicals added to plastics or rubber that generate cellular structure.

BLUCHER: Design where front quarters or tabs are stitched over the vamp for a short distance at the throat.

BOTTOM: The sole up to the breast of the heel. On a wedge sole the term covers the complete sole.

BOTTOMING: The operation of attaching the completed sole to the upper.

BOX TOE: Hardener used to maintain shape of front toe area.

BREAK: Flex point or path.

BREATHABILITY: The ability of the upper to transpire, thereby ventilating the foot.

BUCKSKIN: Leather or deerskin with suede finish.

BUILT-UP: Construction used in vulcanized rubber process.

BUMPER: Rubber toe strip attached over front toe area.

BUTADIENE: A gas obtained from petroleum, used to make plastics.

CALENDER SOLE: Sheet sole pressed between rollers.

CALFSKIN: Leather of young cattle.

CARBON BLACK: Pigment added to outside rubber for better durability.

CELLULOID: A termoplastic material.

CELLULOSE: Natural polymeric.

CEMENT: (see Adhesive)

CEMENT PROCESS: Construction stuck-on bottoming method.

CHAINSTITCH: Sewing method used for stitching uppers to soles.

CHROME TANNING: Leather, mineral tanning process.

CIRCULAR VAMP: Design vamp extended from toe to heel breast.

CLEATS: Metal studs extended out from the sole.

COLLAGEN: Fibrous protein layer of hide.

COLLAR: Top line of the shoe quarters. Many are padded.

COMBINATION LAST: Last with wider forepart and narrow heel fitting.

COMPACTION: Permanent flattening and deformation of sole material (bottoming out).

COMPRESSION MOLD: Shaping materials by heat and pressure.

CONTOUR INSOLES: Foam insoles capable of retaining pressure pattern of the foot.

CONVEYOR: Mechanical belt for continuous transport.

COOKIE: Arch pad in shoe.

COPOLYMER: A natural or synthetic compound.

CORRECTED GRAIN: Leather-type finish added and embossed to correct blemishes, etc.

COUNTER (POCKET): (See Heel Counter)

COWHIDE: Leather from cattle.

CREPE RUBBER: Natural rubber soling material.

CUTTING: First step in die cutting of uppers.

DENIER: Weight of synthetic fibers. (Measure of fineness)

DENSITY: Weight per unit volume of a substance.

DERBY: Design quarters overlapping vamp and tongue.

DESIGN: Pattern or cut of upper.

DIE CUTTING: Cutting of upper or sole materials with metal dies.

DIENE: Chemical compound of molecules having two double bonds (mainly in gas).

D.I.P. CONSTRUCTION: Direct injection process.

DOUBLER: Interfacing between upper material and lining.

D-RINGS: Lacing rings (for speed lacing).

DUO PROCESS: Method of upper assembly construction by cementing instead of stitching edge.

DUROMETER SCALE: A method of determining material hardness on a scale of 0–100, with lower readings indicating softness.

D.V.P.: Direct vulcanizing process.

ELASTOMER: Term used for synthetic rubber.

ELVALOY: Resin modifier added to PVC.

EMBOSSING: Depressing a specific pattern in leather or fabrics.

E.V.A.: Ethylene-vinyl acetate.

EXPANDED VINYL: Soft, nonbreathable PVC (stretchy base) material as opposed to nonexpanded vinyl: harder, nonbreathable (rigid base) material.

EXTENDED EYESTAY: A design wherein the eyestay is extended to form the toe cap.

EXTRUSION: Construction method of injecting T.P.R., nylon, etc.

EYELETS: Holes for lacing (blind) with metal reinforcements or eyelet hooks.

EYESTAY: Reinforcement around lacing holes.

FEATHER EDGE: Last bottom profile.

FILLER: Cheap additive to plastic.

FINDINGS: Small component parts of shoemaking.

FINISHING: End of manufacturing process.

FITTING ROOM: Department where upper parts are prepared.

FLANGING: The edge where the upper is turned outside for attachment to outsole or midsole.

FLARED HEEL: Wider flanged heel for landing.

FLEX PATH (Break): Girth area at the main metatarsal of foot which must flex as foot pushes off from ground.

FLOW MOLDING: The construction method of molding PVC coated materials as an exact replica of original uppers.

FOREPART: Area of foot from the ball to the toe.

FOXING: Rubber striping bonded to the upper and sole around the shoe.

FRICTION TAPE: A tape sewn to the bottom of an upper to

strengthen adhesion under the foxing.

FULL GRAIN: Outermost layer of the leather still present in finished product.

GHILLEY LACING: Form of speed lacing with loops.

GIRTH: Widest part of the last.

GOODYEAR WELT: Construction method of stitching uppers to sole.

GRADING: Method used by designers to size original patterns.

HEEL BREAST: Front part of heel.

HEEL COUNTER: Stiffened heel cup inserted between lining and upper material.

HEEL COUNTER POCKET: Rearpart upper material pocket containing heel stiffening material.

HEEL PITCH: Amount of rise at back of last when last is held level.

HIGH CUT: Over the ankle shoe design.

I.M.P. (Injection): Injection molding process form of shoe construction (see also "lasting insole").

IMPREGNATION: Process of thoroughly soaking material with oil or resin.

INSERTS: Metal threaded retainers for spikes or studs.

INSOLE: Padded sock inserted into shoe next to foot (not to be confused with lasting insole).

INSTEP: Medial inside arch area of the shoe.

IONOMER RESINS: A family of thermoplastic resins.

ISOPRENE: Fundamental rubber molecule.

KANGAROO: Leather from Australian Kangaroos.

KID: Leather from goat skin.

KILTY: Shawl tongue covering eyestay lace area.

KIP: Leather from young cattle.

LACE-TO-TOE: A design where the eyestay is extended down to the toe box area.

LAP SEAM: A simple sewing method where one material is laid over another and sewn through.

LAST: Three dimensional facsimile of the foot.

LASTING: The process of pulling the upper over the last.

LASTING INSOLE: An insole used to attach an upper to an insole before bottoming; the bottom surface of the upper.

LATERAL: The outside area of the foot.

LATEX: A milky liquid exuded from rubber trees.

LINING: The inside backing material for uppers.

LITTLEWAY: A method of stitching the sole to the upper.

LOCKSTITCH: A method of sewing the upper to the bottom.

LOW CUT: Below the ankle shoe design.

McKAY: A shoe construction method that uses tacks and a stitched sole.

M.C.R.: Microcellular rubber.

MEDIAL: Inside area of the foot.

MESH: Woven or knitted nylon material for uppers.

METATARSALS: The long bones of the foot between the toes and ankle.

MIDSOLE: The sole between the insole and outsole.

MOCCASIN: A method of construction whereby the upper is placed under the last and extended up and around to form the quarter and vamp.

MOLD: A cavity used to shape plastic or rubber by pressure and heat.

MONO BLOCK (CASTING): An injection molding process that casts upper and sole together (as in ski boots).

MULLING: The steaming or dampening of leather for stretching purposes prior to lasting.

NAP: The surface pile or layer of textile fabric.

NEOPRENE: An elastomer, polychloroprene.

NUBUCK: An imitation full grain leather buckskin made from cattle hide.

NYLON: The generic name for all synthetic fiber forming polyamides.

OIL TANNING: A method of treating leather that's particularly good for water repellency; tanning with oils and greases.

OPEN TOE: Shoe design with no front center seam.

ORTHOTIC: Corrective device inserted into shoe to aid functionality.

OUTSOLE: The outside sole area in contact with the ground.

OVERLAY: Trimming material attached to the upper.

OXFORD: A shoe design with a laced, low cut shoe.

PATTERN: The cut out pieces making up the design of the upper.

PERMEABILITY: The passage of gas, liquid or solid through a barrier.

PIPING: Rounded braid sewn between seams to cover raw edges in upper materials.

PISTON: The bottom plate of a mold.

PIVOT POINT: The rotation area on sole under ball of foot.

PLASTIC: Synthetic or man-made polymeric substance, excluding rubber.

PLIMSOLL: The English name for a vulcanized, canvas shoe.

POLYETHYLENE: A thermoplastic material or ethylene.

POLYMER:A molecular compound, natural or synthetic.

POLYMERIZATION: A chemical reaction linking molecules.

POLYPROPYLENE: A tough lightweight plastic.

POLYSTYRENE: A transparent thermoplastic.

POLYURETHANE RESINS: A family of resins from which PU is produced.

POLYVINYL ACETATE: A thermoplastic material.

POROMERIC: A breathable upper material usually consisting of textile based material coated with polyurethane.

PREFABRICATED: A sole unit built from more than one layer.

PU: Polyurethane (cellular plastic).

PVC: Polyvinyl chloride (plastic material).

QUARTER: The major pattern piece making up the sides of the upper.

RAYON: A general term for cellulose fibers.

RELEASE AGENT: A lubricant used to coat a mold cavity.

RESILIENCY: The ability to regain quickly the original shape (return energy rebound).

RESIN: Solid organic products of natural or synthetic origin.

ROUGHING: The process of grinding the underside of the lasted upper.

RUBBER: An elastomer or natural rubber compound.

SADDLE: A piece of leather extending from the shank over the vamp.

SEAM: Sewing that joins together pieces of the upper.

SEMI CUT: A design cut just on or over the ankle. (Also called three-quarter cut.)

SHANK: The reinforcement under the arch between the heel and the sole.

SHELL (DISH) SOLE: A unit sole with foxing sides molded to the bottom. (Also called a cup sole).

SHORE HARDNESS: The durometer hardness on a scale of from 0–100.

SILICONE: A slippery polymeric material used in treating shoes for water repellency.

SKINFIT: Nylon tricot lining.

SKIVE: The thinning down of edges of leather or poromeric material.

SLIP LASTING: The lasting method whereby a closed upper is formed before being stretched over the last.

SLIP SOLE: A half-sole from toe to shank.

SLUSH MOLDING: A PVC construction molding process.

SNEAKER: The American name for vulcanized, canvas rubber shoe.

SOCK LINING: The material (regularly called an insole) inserted between the foot and lasting insole next to the foot.

SOLE: Bottom or ground contact area of footwear.

SPECIFIC GRAVITY: The density of any material.

SPEED LACING: A lacing method that uses D-rings.

SPIKES: Metal appendages protruding from the shoe sole.

SPLIT: The flesh or the underside of the leather hide after the grain side had been removed.

STABILIZER: An ingredient used in formulating elastomers and synthetics.

STITCHDOWN: A method of sewing the uppers to the bottom.

STUDS: Large knobs protruding from the sole.

SUCTION CUPS: Indentations on the outsole that provide traction on smooth surfaces.

SUEDE: The buffed reverse or flesh side of leather.

SYMMETRICAL: In shoemaking, this applies to lasts or patterns that have even sides, the right side the same as the left side.

TANNING (TANNAGE): A method of preserving skins prior to finish and coloring.

TENSILE STRENGTH: The pulling force expressed in measuring leathers or fabrics.

THERMOPLASTICS: Plastics capable of being softened by heat and hardened when cooled.

THROAT: The topline of the vamp in front of the instep.

TOE CAP: An additional protective device on the frontal toe area.

TOE SPRING: The vertical distance between the ground and the toe point giving the shoe frontal pitch.

TONGUE: The flap that extends up the front of the shoe to protect the foot from the laces.

TONGUE GUIDE: The tag or slit in the tongue through which the laces are slotted to hold the tongue in place (lace keeper).

TOP LINE: The open area of the shoe around the ankle.

TORSION: The stress caused by twisting a material.

T.P.R.: Thermo plastic rubber.

TREAD: The soling configuration of the outsole.

TRICOT: Lining, skinfit.

TURNSHOE: An early shoemaking technique; the reverse of the simple stitched shoe.

UNIT SOLE: The bottom unit with sole and heel portions molded together as a single piece.

UNIVERSAL LAST: A standard last used by sport shoemakers for all width fittings.

UPPER: The material making up the "top" part of the shoe.

URETHANE: A resin combination with polymers.

U-THROAT: A lacing eyestay pattern at the front of the shoe.

VAMP: The top or front part of the upper over the toe and lacing area.

VEGETABLE TANNING: Tanning that uses plant or vegetable materials.

VINYL: A PVC material that's available in expanding and nonexpanding types.

VULCANIZE: A method of shoemaking in which the rubber sole and/or foxing is cured by heat after attaching to the upper.

WAIST: The narrow part of the shoe between the heel and toe.
WATER REPELLANT: Shoes treated so that they will shed water.
WATERPROOF: Shoes treated so that water cannot penetrate.
WEDGE: A tapered one-piece material that replaces the heel.
WELT: A narrow strip around the outside of the sole, stitched between the upper and the sole.
WIDTH: A coded method for shoe girth sizing.
WING TIP: The design of the toe cap.

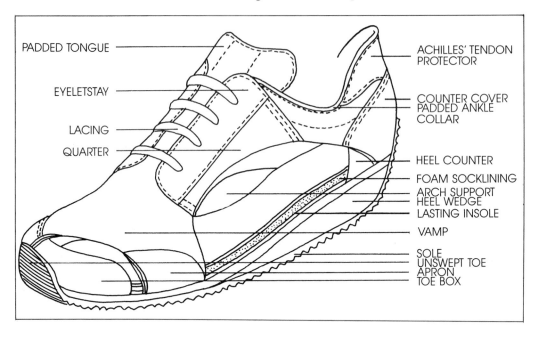

5-72. Anatomy of a Shoe.

"An *object at rest will remain at rest until acted*
upon by an outside force."
Law of Inertia, Sir Isaac Newton

C H A P T E R 6

BIOMECHANICAL FOOTWEAR DESIGN

Biomechanics is the study of the human body in motion. By applying principles from mechanics and engineering, biomechanists can study the forces that act on the body and the effects these forces produce. One application of this science is in the design and testing of sports equipment. In the area of sport shoes, this biomechanical or functional testing represents a relatively new innovation.

The design and/or evaluation of any piece of sports equipment must be based upon a sound understanding of the activity and the demands placed upon the equipment by the individual performing the activity. The equipment influences the dynamics of the human body. This is why so much is written and discussed about the performance of athletic shoes relative to the impact forces experienced by the runner, basketball player or other athlete. With regard to running in particular, it has been suggested that more research has been devoted to the design of running shoes in the last decade than has gone into all other areas of the footwear industry collectively.

Through gait laboratory research and the use of high speed photography, biomechanists and podiatrists have learned that a three-hour marathon or three-set tennis match place specific severe strains on a foot and the shoe encompassing it. This discovery, passed along to shoe technicians, has helped produce significant improvements in shoe cushioning, weight, flexibility, and support to name only the most obvious features.

HISTORY OF BIOMECHANICS IN ATHLETIC FOOTWEAR

Prior to the 1930s almost no research or product development was directed toward the design of athletic shoes even though lab testing and mechanical analysis (early forms of biomechanical research) dated back to a century earlier. Most performance footwear was either handmade or adopted from traditional styles. Little attention was given to function except for some concern for protection and traction. The "solid toe" soccer shoe, the canvas and rubber soled "sneaker" or Plimsoll for running and tennis and the traditional brogue shoe with spikes added for golf were all products of the early sport shoe industry passed from generation to generation with little or no change.

Later changes in athletic shoe design were primarily the result of trial and error. Visual analysis of leg and foot motions, usually too fast to be seen clearly, were translated into shoe designs that experienced athletes then evaluated by subjective "feel."

For example, players' requests for a lowcut basketball shoe were finally met when a Converse sales agent, Grady Lewis, simply cut down the original hightop and had his wife sew binding on the new top line. After several attempts he had an under-the-ankle version that would stay on the foot. Thus the lowcut basketball shoe was born in Chicago in the early 1930s.

Twenty years later a traditional shoemaking business in Germany started to specialize in making a better grade of soccer boot. The shoemakers, Adolf and Rudolph Dassler, had been operating the Dassler family shoe business since 1920. By discussing the inadequacies of previous shoes with leading players, they were able to design new shoes with an eye toward improved function. Their experiments resulted in a new soccer shoe more in tune with the changed style of soccer play (more ball control and running). The toe styling was changed to a softer version for better "feel" of the ball. Reinforcing strips were added for strength. The timing for this early biomechanical work on soccer shoes coincided with the German World Cup Soccer victory in 1954, drawing international attention to the new style.

First through ideas, then trial and error, then experimentation, similar improvements were introduced in other sports, primarily track and training shoes. Although laboratory testing remained minimal, the design of sport shoes moved away from craft and ever closer to science. The use of high speed photography (100–150 frames per second) in the 1970s was probably the first truly scientific attempt by shoemakers to design more functional shoes.

WHY IS A BIOMECHANICALLY DESIGNED SHOE DIFFERENT?

The answer to this question begins with the traditional shoe trade. Early forms of foot coverings or shoes were very functional. The goal was protection from the elements and from injury. Once these were achieved, comfort became the next objective.

Protection and comfort are both functional features of any shoe. However, style and fashion are not. Here is the key departure from performance footwear. When shoes become fashion articles, styling and form play the most important roles; function is often sacrificed. The primary concern of the true sport-shoe technician is design, components and materials that meet performance criteria. Styling and logo treatments are then blended to create the "look" of the shoe. Usually, if the shoe functions well and becomes popular with athletes it becomes a "fashion." Dedicated athletic footwear designers never lose sight of the shoe's original purpose. That is why athletic footwear manufacturers are far ahead of regular street footwear makers in their understanding of leg-foot-shoe biomechanics.

BIOMECHANICAL DESIGN AND EVALUATION

Doctors and scientists have been studying leg anatomy and function for many centuries. The application of their knowledge has only recently been applied to the testing of athletic footwear, however. European specialty companies have closely guarded their accumulated experience. Only with the advent of new sport shoe companies into the field in the last 20 years have the established firms been forced to change direction. The result has been a higher level of importance for biomechanical design and testing.

Originally, the research resulting in shoe modification all came from actual wear-testing by the athletes. This had obvious drawbacks. Because personal variables such as fit and style of performance vary from athlete to athlete, a more uniform set of criteria was needed for standardized testing. The companies knew they needed more information than they could get by asking several athletes, "How does it feel?"

The answer was biomechanics. By studying the motions of an athlete engaged in a sports movement, biomechanical engineers can apply mathematical and engineering principles to derive functional criteria for the problems encountered by the

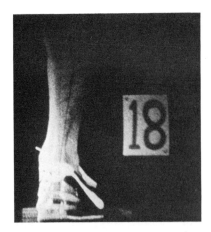

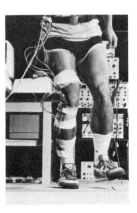

6-1. *Top left:* Frame from slow motion picture showing rearfoot landing angle. 6.2. *Top right:* Dr. Peter R. Cavanagh, author of *The Running Shoe Book* and leading biomechanist. 6-3. *Bottom left:* Vibration shock testing equipment at Tiger testing laboratories in Osaka, Japan. 6-4. *Bottom right:* Athlete strapped with transducers on force plate during shock absorbency testing.

human body in motion. They can use machines that simulate the normal or the extreme movements of the lower extremities as they affect footwear components. By using high speed motion pictures in conjunction with a force measuring platform, scientists have identified the ways the foot contacts the ground and the magnitude of the impact forces generated. Consequently, we now know that the foot and shoe must absorb forces equal to two to three times the body's weight with each step. The capacity of shoes to lessen these forces can save the athlete from their punishing effects, which often lead to injury. In an attempt to control these impact forces, shoemakers have introduced new soling and midsole materials along with new shoe designs. Materials tests have indicated that a considerable amount of cushioning can be lost after the equivalent of only 200 miles.

Used shoes will eventually perform differently from new shoes in other areas, also. A shoe may become more flexible with wear; less stable with material breakdown; or provide less traction with sole wear. Only mechanical testing can evaluate these changes accurately. A new generation of shoes—the so called "computer shoes"—may someday monitor these changes for the athlete, providing him with data about loss of shock absorbency and other crucial qualities.

In general, good sport shoes must have a balanced combination of characteristics with no one feature dominating. Characteristics such as lightness, flexibility, and injury protection are recognized and sought after by all. However, the shoemaker must be careful that one quality isn't sacrificed when another is maximized.

For example, the incorporation of softer midsole materials to attenuate the high impact forces will often result in an undesirable degree of side-to-side instability which may simply result in a different type of injury.

WEAR TESTING VS. LABORATORY TESTING

Some athletic shoe companies still regard lab testing of shoes suspiciously. In his book, *The Running Shoe Book*, Dr. Peter Cavanagh quotes famous New Zealand coach, Arthur Lydiard, to the effect that "the Pennsylvania State University biomechanics team members are not experts at rating shoes."

The arguments in favor of wear-testing are strong and logical. After all, it is the athlete who must wear the shoe and perform in it. He or she should have the last word with regard to shoe function. Nonetheless, certain criteria can only be tested in a lab. These would include such factors as reduction of shock absorbency after prolonged use and water permeability.

Prior to 1970 only a few shoe manufacturers had sufficient expertise and facilities to test shoes. A decade later lab testing had assumed a major role in running shoe evaluations. This resulted from the tremendous running and jogging boom in the U.S. and gave birth to many new shoe companies and other running related firms. One of them, the popular running magazine, *Runner's World*, started to discuss functional shoe design with manufacturers and to offer readers advice about choosing shoes that would prevent injuries.

Before long several companies were developing new products according to these guidelines and with the help of athletes, coaches and podiatrists. *Runner's World* then devised a method of rating shoes on a comparative basis. In addition to a panel of top runners, podiatrists and magazine staff members, *Runner's World* sought a biomechanics lab for shoe testing. Several shoe companies offered use of their labs but the magazine thought this would introduce a conflict of interest, and continued looking for an independent lab. The Pennsylvania State University Biomechanics Laboratory was selected and the first comprehensive lab testing program was initiated. The data from the lab tests were first published in October, 1977.

For a manufacturer to advertise that its shoe was superior, or for a leading athlete to visually endorse a shoe, was one thing. But when a popular magazine actually ranked shoes on the basis of comparative tests, the results had a huge influence. Highly rated shoes experienced incredible sales gains. Not everyone was happy, though, since some shoes would inevitably fall to the bottom of the rankings. There were also allegations about the propriety of the *Runner's World* rankings. One company was so enraged that it advertised an indignant rebuttal to the rankings in the next magazine issue.

Whatever the opinions of manufacturers, the public became familiar with testing procedures and demanded more of the same. The stature of biomechanical testing grew significantly. It now had two purposes:
   1. to influence design features; and
   2. to evaluate the design features on a comparative basis.

SHOE-SURFACE RELATIONSHIP
During the past 25 years playing surfaces have changed considerably. In addition to previously used indoor surfaces of wood and outdoor surfaces of cinder or actual turf, man has added combinations of resins, rubbers, various asphalt types and artificial turf. It is a complex relationship; however the simple fact is shoes and playing surfaces make a diference to performance and affect injury. In the past decade much biomechanical study has been devoted to this subject. A collection of such studies on this subject by leading biomechanists has been published under the title *Sport Shoes and Playing Surfaces* (E.C. Frederick, Phd., Published by Human Kinetics Publishers, Inc.)

Movements, common in sports activities, such as sliding, non-sliding (traction) or rotation or pivot are dependent upon adequate shoe-surface frictional or traction characteristics. The evolution of soling materials used to bottom athletic footwear

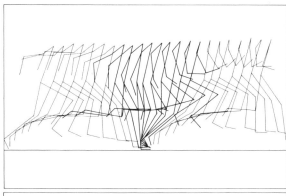

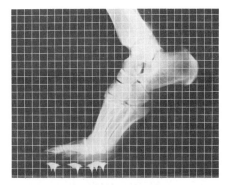

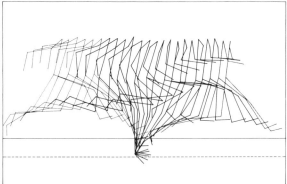

6-5. *Left:* Computer sequences showing running positions are obtained by digitizing the points marking a runner's major limb joints in a motion picture of running and then connecting those points on a digital plotter. The same runner is shown on a hard, or stiff, surface (top) and on a soft, or springy, one (bottom). 6-6. *Top right:* X-ray photography showing track-spike placement under forefoot. 6-7. *Bottom right:* Co-author, Dr. Barry Bates, "running" his own testing on a force platform at the University of Oregon.

has generally kept pace with the increased demands required by athletes to perform better and stay injury free. The primary soling materials used in sports shoes are natural and synthetic rubbers, polyurethane, nylon and PVC. If the traction or coefficient of friction is not sufficient by using these materials in multiple tread or stud patterns then spikes or cleats are used. Due to the variance of movements in sports action, the friction force desirable in one sport or on one surface may not be the ultimate in aiding performance on another surface. For example, it was quickly determined by American football players after the introduction of artificial turf in the 1960s, that the traditional screw-in seven stud cleat system was not adequate. Players first turned to the 13–15 multi-studed soccer shoe before manufacturers eventually produced the currently accepted 130 appendage astroturf sole.

What is desirable is the optimal performing sole for the given movements of a sport on a certain surface with maximum consideration given for injury protection and individual variables, such as body weight. Given the number of variables, this is not typically achievable in a single pair of shoes.

There appears to be a correlation between the frequency of pain and selected injuries to the hardness and type of playing surface. For example, granular (sand) surfaces are the least likely to cause impact injuries increasing through synthetic granular (cinder), synthetic surfaces (rubber), wood court, felt/carpet to concrete/asphalt. The methods used for testing surfaces can also be used for testing shoes, however, there are so many variables in a shoe that this is often not very practical. A sole is neither homogeneous nor isotropic.

Ongoing study, experimentation and testing of sport shoes must be combined with the abstracts of creativity required in crafting the end product design. Major athletic shoe manufacturers have devoted large proportions of their product development budgets into both areas to rapidly evaluate the effects of specific sole performance. Thus through laboratory testing and ongoing objective opinions of ever improving athletes the closer we can get to producing the ultimate performing sole for a given surface.

LABORATORY SHOE TESTING

Lab shoe testing is not new to the shoe trade. The Shoe and Allied Trade Research Association (SATRA), founded in 1919 in Northamptonshire, England, in the heart of the early British shoe industry, has long helped shoe companies test and improve their products. The testing of such features as cold-flexing for winter boots and adhesives for new materials are regular SATRA services for its members, some of whom are in the athletic footwear business. A few of the tests SATRA performs include measurements of: materials, seam strain, adhesion, durability, cold-flex and shock absorption.

Using similar machinery and adapting new machines for specific tests (for example, simulating the toe drag on a tennis shoe—sliding test apparatus Stuttgart—or the flex point for cross-country boots), some European athletic shoemakers began to lab test sport shoes in the mid-1950s. Over the following 15 years European companies made tremendous progress in developing sport shoe tests based upon biomechanical information. In the process they achieved a number of important innovations. In the early 1970s other athletic shoemakers began to take note when they recognized that one or two progressive

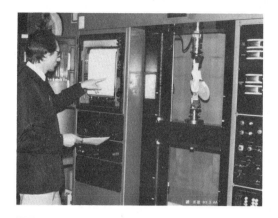

6-8. *Left:* Author, Mel Cheskin, checking adhesion pull tests in Pusan, Korea.   6-9. *Right:* Author, Mel Cheskin, checking flex tests in Pusan, Korea.

companies were starting to command sizeable portions of the sports shoe market thanks to their sophisticated testing procedures.

TESTS CONDUCTED ON RUNNING SHOES

The most publicized laboratory tests on sport shoes in the past decade were those conducted by the Pennsylvania State University Biomechanics Lab in conjunction with the annual *Runner's World* magazine shoe survey. The tests were included as part of the survey for the first time in 1977, using a series of machine tests designed to simulate the stresses placed on various, important shoe components. The components were selected from runner surveys, clinical experience and biomechanical research; and were changed and modified over the years as more information became available. Although all the tests were mechanical in nature, they were based upon biomechanical criteria.

The first test battery in 1977 included five objective evaluations: heel shock absorption, forefoot shock absorption, upper durability, sole durability, and flexibility. By 1982 the number of tests had been expanded to 10. The new areas of evaluation were: midsole longevity, rearfoot control (three tests), shoe weight, and permeability. The test for upper durability was dropped. A detailed description of the testing procedures and results was published in the October, 1981 issue of *Runner's World*.

The objective of lab testing is to allow a simple, quantifiable comparison among shoes based on relevant performance crite-

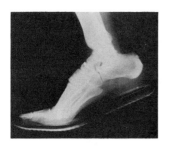

6-10. X-ray photography inside shoe to determine foot movement.

ria. These types of tests are accurate, replicable, and allow many shoes to be evaluated and compared with relative ease and efficiency. There is little question but that these evaluations have led to vast improvements in running shoes.

However, since runners are complex functioning biological mechanisms, it's not surprising that use of simple mechanical testing procedures has sparked great controversy. Critics ask: Do the tests really evaluate functions that occur while the athlete is running? This approach has led other labs to test shoes from a different perspective, that is, to evaluate shoe function while the runner is performing with shoes on his feet. The University of Oregon Biomechanics Laboratory and the University of Calgary Biomechanics Laboratory, to name two, have followed this path.

Typically, runners are evaluated in a gait laboratory using high speed cinematography and a force platform to assess the interactive effects between the shoe and the runner. The primary components evaluated are: rearfoot and forefoot shock absorption, and rearfoot control. These functions are the most variable and the most dependent upon the dynamic situation. Although laborious and too expensive for use in evaluating large numbers of shoes, this testing is truly biomechanical and provides valuable insight regarding dynamic function. Its primary purpose is to validate the mechanical or machine tests and/or to suggest the need for additional ones.

BIOMECHANICAL TESTS AND TESTING PROCEDURES

Traditionally the shoe industry has concerned itself with the testing of materials, adhesion, attachment, seams and fatigue due to structural breakdown of the shoe with use. Most countries with large shoe making industries have their own central institute for conducting tests for member firms. The United States, Germany and Italy, for example, have well-known testing facilities. The largest association remains SATRA in Northamptonshire, England.

Biomechanical testing, on the other hand, is relatively new and primarily concerned with dynamic performance of the shoe in action and the resulting stresses imposed on the human body. The sections that follow identify a number of critical concerns for which tests have been devised.

FOREFOOT AND REARFOOT IMPACT TESTING

Protection of the foot from excessive impact forces is one of the two primary functions of a shoe. Forces in excess of five times body weight can result from activities such as long jumping, and runners regularly generate forces two to three times their body weight when they train and compete. Gait laboratory tests have shown that when a 180 pound basketball player leaps from an 18 inch high platform, he strikes the ground with a force of 700 pounds. A 250 pound player generates a force of one ton when he drops from a height of three feet.

The two primary areas of force concentration are in the heel region and the forefoot portion of the foot. The ability to make shoes that protect the athlete's foot from these large forces has significantly reduced foot and leg injuries.

Several testing methods have been employed to measure impact forces. These include vertical and pendular impact testing, as well as tensiometer tests using sophisticated instruments such as the Instron computer controlled servohydraulic system. The best known method is probably the vertical impact tester formerly used by Dr. Peter Cavanagh of Pennsylvania State University when he performed the shoe testing for *Runner's World* magazine.

In this method a weighted shaft with attached accelerometer is dropped from a fixed height to impact the desired portion of

 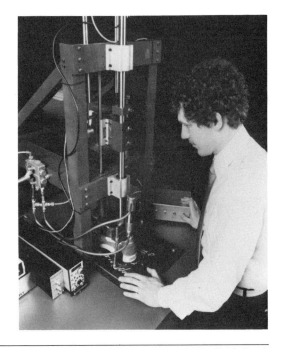

6-11. *Left:* Biomechanical testing on a force plate for jumping and landing pressures. 6-12. *Right:* Shock absorption testing equipment at Converse biomechanical gait laboratories near Boston, U.S.A.

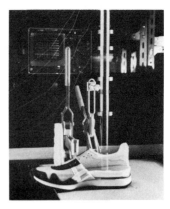

6-13. *Left:* Close-up shot of shock absorption testing at Converse biomechanical laboratories near Boston, U.S.A.   6-14. *Right:* Shock absorption testing machinery at Tiger laboratories in Osaka, Japan.

the shoe. The weighted shaft and drop height are adjusted to approximate the characteristics of runner impact between the shoe and running surface. The accelerometer measures the shoe's cushioning response (in multiples of acceleration caused by gravity) in addition to the time of peak force/acceleration. The value of acceleration is an index of the shock that will be transmitted to the body at various points during ground contact.

If the missile strikes a hard surface, the acceleration will increase rapidly to a large peak value. If, however, the contact surface is softer, the peak value will be lower, indicating greater cushioning. Due to material characteristics, it is important to put the shoe through 25–50 test cycles before measurements are taken.

Both the heel and forefoot impact are influenced by an individual's weight, with heavier people requiring more protection. Another important factor is the cushioning material's response to impact over time. Some materials retain their cushioning capability far longer than others.

While it's crucial to minimize the shock forces, it's equally as important to establish firm rearfoot control, and these two characteristics are often inversely related. In other words, soft material that provides good cushioning results is a very unstable base. As a result the shoemaker must find a compromise between these two characteristics or design an integrated system that eliminates the adverse relationship.

Other impact tests use other methods that differ in the way they apply the load and record the data. The important point is that the applied load should be as similar to the real event as possible to obtain meaningful results. A limitation of all the currently used impact tests is that they can only approximate the real event, because in athletics the load is simply not applied in a fixed vertical direction.

Some progress is being made, however. To more closely simulate the human foot's flexibility and weight transfer, the Cushioning Shock Absorbing Tester devised by Bjorksten Research Laboratories in conjunction with the U.S. Army Lab in Natick, Massachusetts, uses a prosthetic foot-leg pylon assembly that is attached to a moveable carriage. When the electromagnet is turned off, the carriage falls until the shoe strikes the impact surface. An accelerometer attached to the leg pylon assembly measures the peak acceleration of the prosthesis.

Another way to measure shock absorbency in shoes is to measure the forces transmitted through the lower anatomy. This can be accomplished with devices called transducers that are attached directly to the legs and feet. Again, there are certain variables (in this case, skin and soft tissue) that may make the test data less than totally reliable. Nonetheless, both the uses of force plates and of transducers do provide some degree of comparative information between two shoes if tested on the same runner.

REARFOOT CONTROL AND TORSIONAL RIGIDITY

Stability in an athletic shoe is a generally desirable characteristic, particularly in running shoes where lack of stability is a major cause of injuries. A number of components working together are necessary to achieve good control.

First and probably most important, the medial portion of the midsole in the heel and midfoot regions must form an adequate base. At the same time it must resist compression and collapse as the foot rolls (pronates) to the inside. This feature, combined with torsional rigidity in the mid-portion of the shoe and a good heel counter, comprises the most important part of the stabilization system.

A number of lab tests have been used to test for rearfoot stability and torsional rigidity. The section that follows describes four of them. Dr. Cavanagh used the first three in his *Runner's World* studies. The best test, although the most impractical, is the fourth—filming runners from the rear and actually measuring the degree of pronation. This method is the most objective and also the most costly. For the present, it can only be used on occasion to validate other lab tests.

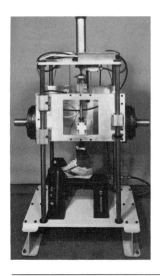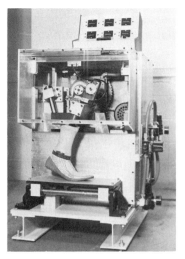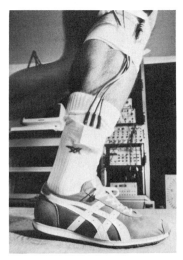

6-15. *Left:* This cushioning/shock absorbing tester uses a leg pylon and prosthetic foot which has been modified to more closely duplicate the very rigid bone structure located in the heel of a human foot. 6-16. *Center:* Prosthetic foot is driven through life-like motions by a system of mechanical and pneumatic actuators. 6-17. *Right:* Athlete strapped with transducers, running across a force plate.

Heel Counter Stiffness:
The shoe is mounted on a test apparatus with compressed air clamps. An instrumentation probe is then pressed against the medial portion of the counter toward a standardized location. The counter stiffness is the force required to cause a fixed amount of penetration. A big problem with this test is that the foot never applies force on the shoe from the outside; hence the test doesn't evaluate a real situation.

Heel Penetration:
The assumption underlying this test is that the more the heel sinks down into the shoe upon impact, the less rearfoot control the shoe will provide. This data can be collected at the same time that rearfoot impact tests are being conducted. Penetration of the missile is recorded upon impact, and a low score presumed better.

Although it is generally true that a firmer base is more stable, this test does not allow for dynamic function. The heel does not load the shoe from a fixed vertical position, of course. Also the test is likely to produce invalid results for a shoe designed to produce rigidity only on the medial side.

Rearfoot Stability:
This test measures the shoe's ability to withstand collapse along the inside border. The shoe is fitted on a form and placed under a weight bearing load intended to

approximate the runner's downward force. A hinged plate beneath the inside border is rotated with a fixed amount of energy to compress the midsole material, simulating the forces of pronation. The maximum angle of deflection of the hinged plate is then recorded. The greater the angle, the less the rearfoot control. A major problem with this test is that the compressive action is in the wrong direction, since it is the upper that rotates on the bottom.

Torsional Rigidity: Pronation is a complex full-foot movement. To overcome it, a shoe must provide rigidity or stiffness through its narrowest part (the arch area). This is especially true in court sports where the foot often lands at an angle and some torsional rigidity is desirable. The lab test consists of clamping the rearpart of the shoe securely to the test platform with the forepart (front 40 percent) clamped to a platform that is allowed to rotate around either the inside or outside border of the shoe. The front platform is then lifted alternately on the medial and lateral sides to tilt the front of the shoe to an angle of 25 degrees to the horizontal. The more pressure required to tilt or twist the shoe, the greater its torsional rigidity.

FLEXIBILITY
Both the regular shoe industry and athletic shoe companies have used flexibility testing for many years. The flex path in the forepart of the shoe is an important feature. Since a shoe flexes 3,000–4,000 times during a five-mile run, energy savings and comfort are greatly increased if the shoe flexibility is good. Also, most clinicians agree that a flexible shoe is less likely to cause certain injuries.

The major factors affecting shoe flexibility are: materials used in the sole/midsole construction, outer sole pattern, the amount of toe spring in the last, the lasting method and upper design. For testing flexibility, the shoe is mounted on a hinged platform or on two separate platforms with both the rear and front portions clamped to the testing jig under a fixed amount of pressure. For some tests the upper material may be cut away if the sole alone is to be tested.

Special clamps can be constructed to allow for more realistic testing of the entire shoe. The shoe is carefully aligned with the flex point positioned at 60 percent of the distance from the heel to the toe. Different options exist as to the orientation of the flex path relative to the long axis of the front portion of the shoe. Some tests use a right angle while others have tried to establish an angle more compatible with the alignment of the metatarsal heads. In either case, once positioning is completed, the shoe is repeatedly flexed with some sort of cam and push-rod mechanism to a fixed angle (usually between 10 and 45 degrees) for a number of cycles.

Since shoe flexibility generally improves with use, it is important to pre-flex the shoe for a controlled number of cycles before actually making the test measurements. *Runner's World* suggested 2,400 cycles through a 40 degree angle. The evaluation records either the energy necessary to flex the shoe or simply the torque required. In either case, a lesser value is more desirable.

TRACTION

Resistance to slippage, particularly in court sports, has long been a selling feature for companies claiming exclusive tread patterns or outsole designs. Again, the only way to accurately evaluate outsole materials and designs is to formulate laboratory tests. To measure traction, the tests must determine the coefficient of friction (and, consequently, the slip resistance characteristics) for shoes or materials under varying surface conditions. A widely accepted industry standard for testing traction uses a device called a James Machine.

Two types of slippage are possible in most activities. The foot can slip forward or sideways upon initial contact with the surface, or it can slip backward during the pushoff phase. Slips usually occur when a foreign substance such as water, sand or even dust comes between the shoe and the surface. Although the most dangerous slip is probably in the forward direction, most tests have been done to simulate pushoff slip.

The James Machine is designed for materials testing, but the holding mechanism can be modified so that whole-shoe testing can be accomplished. Either way, the coefficient of friction is determined by gradually changing the angle of an applied standard force. Initially, the force is directed straight downward so that no slip can occur. As the test begins, the angle of force application is gradually changed so that it begins pushing in the direction that the slip will occur in a manner similar to a leg pushing off from a surface. Eventually, the shoe slips and the two components (vertical and horizontal) are determined for that moment, and the coefficient recorded. The greater the value, the better the traction. The test can be performed on any shoe soling material and on varying types of surfaces, wet or dry.

Sliding Test Apparatus Stuttgart: A measurement of sliding behavior is performed using the sliding test apparatus Stuttgart. Here the resistance against movements of shoes caused by friction is measured. This apparatus mainly consists of a prosthetic foot on a spindle. The foot is mounted on a revolving verticle spindle. The foot as it moves downward touches a surface with the sole of the foot. The torque caused by the sliding resistance is measured by transducers mounted inside the foot. The sliding behavior is described by the parameter "sliding friction coefficient".

Friction problems are complex depending on the combination and abrasion of sole material and surface used. Any variant such as dust, water or aging may effect the friction coefficient.

SOLE WEAR

Outsole wear is an important feature of any shoe. Many athletes use outsole wear to judge when it's time to-buy their next new pair of shoes. In addition, excessive wear is related to loss of performance and potential injury.

SATRA and other labs have conducted standard abrasion tests for years. Most of these have been done on soling materials with little or no concern for function and wear patterns. For most runners the primary area of wear is the outside edge of the heel due to scuffing of this region at foot contact. The second most worn region is the center forefoot section due to a combination of pushing off and forefoot rotation. Functional laboratory tests expose these stress points of the shoe to an abrasive surface. Shoes used in racquet sports are particularly subjected to toe-drag wear.

Several machine testing methods can simulate "action" conditions. Most involve placing a last or prosthetic foot inside the shoe to maintain a standard force between the shoe and the wear surface. The wear surface may be a moving abrasive belt or an inert concrete or pavement surface. Most wear tests exaggerate the conditions (force, contact time, surface abrasion) to create an accelerated test. The final test score is usually given in amount of time to reach some criterion such as wearing through the outer sole.

PERMEABILITY/BREATHABILITY/TEMPERATURE

The fact that the shoe covers the foot results in an inside environment different from the surrounding air. The temperature and humidity will always be greater inside the shoe. The more the upper materials can transmit moisture, the greater the reduction of perspiration around the foot and the cooling effect from evaporation.

Shoe breathability is determined with a standard industry test. The upper material is used to seal a container filled with a

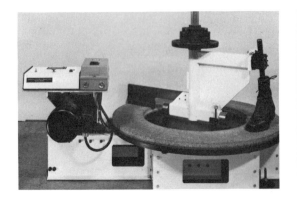 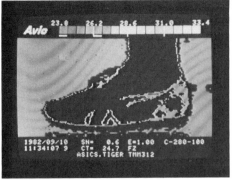

6-18. *Left:* A mechanical abrasion tester determines sole wear and durability.   6-19. *Right:* Thermography photography showing heat build-up inside shoe during marathon running.

known amount of calcium chloride. After weighing, the container is placed in a climate-controlled chamber for a designated period of time. Afterward the container is weighed again to determine the amount of moisture absorbed by the calcium chloride. The more moisture absorbed, the more breathable the material, resulting in greater comfort.

Man-made materials are usually not as permeable as leather. The most common man-made materials in running shoe uppers are nylon taffetas and nylon meshes. Other sport shoes some-times use artificial leathers or plastics. The use of combinations of materials is common, as is layering. All these factors affect overall breathability of the shoe. Simple perforation or the newer laser piercing can be used to improve the breathability of any material.

As far as tests for keeping water out of the shoe, or water-proofing it, the United States Army developed a machine that moves the shoe on a mechical foot through normal walking motions. The whole process can be carried out in a tank of water while time moisture sensors monitor seepage into the shoe. Cold intrusion is similarly studied by embedding an array of thermocouples in a prosthetic foot. Different types of insulating materials, seam designs and construction techniques can be evaluated by monitoring the temperature at various locations within the footwear as the outside temperature is reduced.

WEIGHT

Determining the weight of a shoe is a simple matter and doesn't require biomechanical testing. Shoes can be weighed accurately, and various competitive models of the same size compared.

For most athletes the weight of the shoe is an important consideration. Wearing heavy shoes results in greater energy demands, thus hindering performance. Of course, carried to its extreme, this concept would dictate the complete elimination of shoes. However, because of the sacrifice of other obvious features such as traction and cushioning, few athletes choose this path.

Either directly or indirectly, weight is related to other shoe characteristics. The general trend is, and should be, to reduce shoe weight as much as possible without sacrificing performance, protection and comfort characteristics.

UNDERSTANDING LABORATORY TESTS

Due to the influence of lab tests on the consumer and the media, mechanical testing of footwear has come under considerable criticism. Possible reasons for this include the fact that the approach is a relatively new one and the testing procedures are not well understood. In addition, there has been considerable controversy over which tests are important and whether or not the tests really evaluate their claimed functions. Shoe manufacturers and retailers are greatly affected when any accepted sports authority or organization begins to rate or rank shoes, especially when the rankings are supported by scientific data.

While it is true that the so called "personal variables" (fit, weight of the athlete, running style and footstrike pattern) affect the performance of any athletic shoe, shoemakers who do not use biomechanical tests are left with only their trial and error methods. There is little doubt that lab testing and the subsequent ranking of shoes has made everyone within the industry aware of certain key characteristics that should be incorporated into athletic shoes. In addition, testing has helped improve functional quality of the shoes.

Some characteristics thought to be important have been found detrimental when taken too far. An example of this would be the overly wide heel flare, which resulted in many runners getting injured. Another problem is overemphasis on a particular characteristic such as weight.

Shoe weight must be evaluated relative to other features. Even though the foot and shoe weigh little, the weight factor is an important one to consider. Since the foot and shoe are at the farthest distance from the hip axis, any added weight requires a much greater muscle force to move it. Also, the foot moves through a longer distance than any other part of the leg.

Nonetheless, if the reduction in shoe weight comes at the expense of other important features (for example, cushioning or control), the athlete will want to think twice before selecting the lightest shoe.

Another major concern is that if all shoes are subjected to the same tests, they will end up being designed only for those tests. If this happened, the result would be many brands of shoes with very little to distinguish among them, giving the consumer a narrower choice. No doubt the best approach is to combine laboratory testing with wear testing procedures using knowledgeable performers. This dual approach should result in the most meaningful improvements in future sport shoes.

DESIGNING ATHLETIC FOOTWEAR

The design of any sport shoe must begin with a sound knowledge of the activity to be performed along with an understanding of the demands placed upon the shoe by the athlete. In other words, shoe function must be defined. Through biomechanical analysis, shoemakers can deduce exactly at what points the shoe will benefit from maximum traction, shock absorbency, stress reinforcement, etc. Once the functional components are identified, the most appropriate construction method can be chosen to accommodate the required features.

Next a last must be developed or identified that will result in the best possible fit for the group of people who will participate in the activity. Fit is closely related to comfort and no matter how many functional features a shoe might possess, if it doesn't fit, people simply won't buy it. Finally, after all functional considerations have been met, the shoe designer decides upon the cosmetic features. This is not to relegate appearance to a minor role. Again, as with fit, if the shoe is basically unappealing to the eye, most consumers won't buy it. The shoe should be both functionally and cosmetically attractive.

As an example, consider the golf shoe, which has remained largely unchanged for over 100 years. From the time when early golfers walked onto St. Andrews links in Scotland in their brogue shoes, little change has taken place in the design of golf footwear. True, metal cleats have been added for grip while man-made materials have largely replaced leather soles, but the shoe has remained relatively unchanged.

In redesigning golf shoes some functional features can be identified without an intensive research effort. Common sense indicates that light, waterproof or water repellent materials are desirable since much walking occurs through wet grass. Replacing metal cleats with nylon can reduce weight and eliminate possible rusting problems. Contour insoles might increase comfort.

Features related to foot function, however, are not so easy to identify. Expensive laboratory testing would be necessary to pick out functional demands requiring a shoe re-design. To date, few companies have taken this scientific approach with golf shoes.

Only after all these features have been studied and analyzed can a prototype be worked up and handed over to golfers to evaluate. With their recommendation the athletic shoe designer can then determine which features are desirable and likely to meet wide acceptance, and which have little or no effect on performance.

Sometimes functional features dictate style, such as with the flared heel incorporated into many running shoes in the late 1970s. When this feature was added to improve rearfoot control and stability, many traditionalists were shocked at how "ugly" the shoe looked. They forgot that the shoe was not designed for looks but for function. Despite the radical look, some runners tried the new design and found it an improvement over past shoes. Eventually the concept became widely accepted, and today most running shoes have some sort of flared heel.

BIOMECHANICS OF RUNNING

Biomechanical studies of running were intitiated to gain a better understanding of the prevention and treatment of running related injuries. Obviously, the shoe is only one of many factors implicated in running injuries, but some studies have indicated the shoe as the cause/cure of 10 to 20 percent of these injuries. As a result, sports medicine specialists became involved in shoe design and helped create features like the "varus wedge," the contoured support systems and various heel stabilizing designs.

Before long researchers began studying the entire foot-shoe-running surface system to better understand the complex interactions between the various components. The use of high speed cinematography and force platforms allowed for a degree of sophistication not achieved in the past. Forces could be measured and the effects of various designs documented. This information translated into more effective and efficient footwear. The following is a list of selected running shoe features and corresponding design functions that have resulted from this research:

FEATURE	FUNCTION
Kinetic Outsoles	Shock absorption and traction
Dual-Density Midsoles	Shock absorption and control
Flared Heel	Control and stability
Heel Counters	Control and stability
Contoured Support Systems	Control, stability and shock absorption
Arch Support	Pronation control
Toe Pitch	Smoother push-off
Tubular (Moccasin) Construction	Flexibility
Soft Nylon	Lightness and comfort
Mesh Nylon	Lightness, comfort and breathability
Width Fittings	Fit, comfort and support
Different Last Design (Women's)	Fit, comfort and support
Orthotics and Corrective Wedge or Inserts	Support, control and stability
Solid Carbon or Blown Rubber Outsoles	Durability, traction and lightness
Padded Tongue, ATP Collar	Comfort
Perforated Porometric Uppers	Lightness and breathability
Soft Seamless Linings	Comfort
Traction Soles	Durability and grip
Reinforcements	Support and durability

Inspite of our increased understanding of the biomechanics of running, each runner is still a unique individual with certain subtle characteristics that are difficult to quantify. People are and will continue to be anatomically and functionally different, and therefore their footwear requirements are different. Consequently, there is no such thing as the perfect running shoe.

Perhaps someday someone will design a totally adjustable running shoe that can be fine tuned for each individual, but until that time we will have to settle for good approximations. This is already being achieved, at least in part, by shoemakers who design certain models for specific user groups, such as those with a certain foot type and shape, a particular running style or a particular training mileage and speed.

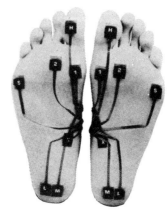

6-20. *Left:* Co-author, Dr. Barry Bates, running across force plate at University of Oregon. 6-21. *Right:* Electrodynogram testing begins with a series of sensors being placed on the foot of the subject, each sensor placed precisely at prime biomechanical function points.

BIOMECHANICS AND OTHER SPORTS

The principles and some of the features described for running shoes can naturally be applied to all sport shoes, since running is a part of so many sports. However, it must be remembered that each sport and each event is different, calling for footwear with special characteristics. Among the most technical sports shoes in an already specialized area of footwear are Alpine and cross-country ski boots and cycle racing shoes. As we move through the 1980s, performances in all major sports continue to improve. Part of this improvement results from better equipment. Biomechanists and other shoe technicians continue their efforts to improve the function and quality of all athletic footwear, hoping to help athletes better their performances while avoiding injuries.

A DIRECTORY OF SHOE RELATED DEFINITIONS

ABRASION TESTER: A machine used to determine the quantity of material lost by friction (wear) under specified conditions.

ACCELEROMETER: A device that measures acceleration or the rate of change of velocity as it relates to impact force.

ANATOMICAL: Pertaining to the structure of the body.

ANATOMY: The study of the structure of the body and the relationships between its parts.

AXIS: A reference line for making measurements. Ground reaction forces are usually evaluated relative to a set of three orthogonal axes: vertical, longitudinal (direction of motion), and transverse (right angle to direction of motion).

BIOMECHANICS: The study of the internal and external forces acting on the human body and the effects produced by these forces.

CAM: A projection on a wheel or shaft that changes a regular circular motion into an irregular rotary motion or a back and forth motion.

CINEMATOGRAPHY: The study of movement using high speed film (usually 100–500 frames per second).

COEFFICIENT OF FRICTION: A number between 0 and 1 indicating the slip-resistance of a material like a shoe sole on a particular surface. The greater the value, the less likely any slipping.

COEFFICIENT OF VARIATION: The ratio, expressed as a percentage, of the variability (standard deviation) of a test parameter to the average value (mean) of the parameter.

COMPRESSION DEFLECTION: The amount of deformation observed in a material after it has been subjected to a compressive or impact load.

COMPRESSION SET: The amount of permanent deformation observed in an unloaded material following a single or multiple load application.

CONFIGURATION: The relative position of parts, or the manner of their arrangement.

CONTACT FACE: The surface brought into contact with another surface or object.

CYCLIC: Moving or occurring in cycles.

DECREMENT: A gradual decrease or lessening in quality or quantity.

DIFFERENTIAL LOADING: The application of forces of varying magnitudes.

DIGITIZING TABLET: A device that allows film data to be converted to numerical data, usually for computer analysis.

DRIVE SHAFT: A shaft that transmits power from an engine to various working parts of a machine.

ELECTRODYNOGRAM: An instrumentation system consisting of individual sensors to measure pressure at selected locations on the bottom of the foot.

ELECTROMYOGRAPHY: The measurement of the electrical activity associated with muscular contractions.

EXERCISE PHYSIOLOGY: The study of the effects of exercise on the biochemical function of the body and its parts.

FLEXIBILITY: The rigidity of the shoe bottom composite usually evaluated in the forefoot region of the shoe.

FLEXION CYCLE: The act of bending a shoe or object through a fixed angle a single time.

FLEXION ENERGY: The energy required to bend a shoe or object through a flexion cycle.

FORCE: A pushing or pulling effect that produces motion or deformation of an object or material.

FORCE PLATFORM: An instrument used to measure forces on its surface. The device is typically imbedded in a surface across which a person can walk or run.

FORCE TIME CURVE: The output of a force measuring device indicating the forces applied to the foot as a function of time.

FRICTION TESTER: A piece of equipment used to determine the slip-resistance (coefficient of friction) between two materials such as a shoe and a running surface.

FUNCTIONAL ANATOMY: The study of the effects of body structure on performance.

GAIT LABORATORY: A testing lab equipped with specialized equipment for the study of walking and running.

GAS ANALYSIS: The evaluation of expired respiratory gases used to determine such things as oxygen consumption, which relate to energy output.

GONIOMETER: An instrument used to measure angles. It can be employed to evaluate motions of the joints, particularly the knee and ankle joints.

HINGED: Two pieces or parts jointed in such a way that both are free to rotate about a common axis.

HISTORESIS CURVE: A graphic representation of the relationship between the stresses or forces required to deform an elastic material and the observed forces when the load is removed. The area inside the closed loop represents the energy dissipated within the material.

IMPACT TESTER: A piece of equipment used to evaluate the shock absorbing characteristics of shoes or materials.

INSTRON TESTER: A sophisticated computerized hydraulic testing machine capable of performing numerous shoe and material tests of loading and deformation.

INTERFACE: The surface forming the common boundary between two bodies or spaces.

JAMES MACHINE: A machine used to test traction.

JIG: Any of a number of various mechanical contrivances or devices used to maintain the correct position of a shoe or material during a test.

JOULE: The unit of work or energy in the MKS system.

KINEMATICS: The science of pure or abstract motion.

KINETIC ENERGY: Energy associated with motion.

LOAD DEFLECTION: The amount of deformation observed in a

material after being subjected to a load.

LONGITUDINAL FORCE: The force generated in the direction of motion by a walker or runner during foot contact and related to the slip characteristics of a shoe. Also referred to as the anteroposterior force.

MEMORY: The speed and extent to which a material recovers to its original shape after load compression.

MILLISECOND: A unit of time equalling .001 seconds.

MOTION ANALYSIS: The analysis of total or partial body movements for the purpose of better understanding how the body functions. The analysis is usually done in conjunction with high speed filming and computers.

MOUNT (dismount): To prepare or place in position for use or testing (to remove).

NEUTRAL POSITION: The most efficient functional position for the foot producing the least amount of stress on the joints, ligaments and tendons.

NEWTON: The unit of force in the MKS system.

ORTHOGONAL FORCE COMPONENTS: The three components of the group reaction force measured relative to a set of mutually perpendicular axes in the vertical, longitudinal (direction of motion), and transverse (right angle to direction of motion) directions.

POTENTIAL ENERGY: Energy associated with position.

PRONATION: A complex multi-joint action of the foot that is usually estimated from the inward rotation of the heel relative to the leg producing the inward rolling motion that takes place in the foot and ankle joint following footstrike during running.

PROPRIOCEPTOR: A sense organ that receives stimuli from within the body.

PROSTHETIC FOOT: An imitation foot closely resembling the shape, texture, flexibility and weight of a human foot. Used in testing procedures.

PUSH ROD: A rod that functions in conjunction with a cam to open or close valves.

REARFOOT STABILITY: The ability of the shoe to control foot pronation during the initial 40 to 50 percent of the support phase.

RETEST RELIABILITY: The ability to reproduce the same test results on two separate occasions.

RUNNING MACHINE: A piece of equipment, used to test shoe characteristics, that simulates the actions of running on a shoe.

SHEARING FORCE: A force that causes or tends to cause two parts of a body to slide relatively to each other.

SPROCKET: A projection on the rim of a wheel or cylinder that engages the links of a chain.

STANDARD DEVIATION: A standard measure of dispersion of a frequency distribution about the average value. A distribution is typically made up of three standard deviations on either side of the average value.

STRAIN GAUGE: A device for measuring forces by monitoring the change in resistance to a small wire that has been deformed by the force.

SUPINATION: The outward rotation that takes place in the foot and ankle joint during the latter portion of the support period during running. The opposite of pronation.

TENSILE STRENGTH: The resistance of a material to being pulled apart.

TERMINAL WEAR CONDITION: A condition in which the outsole of a shoe is worn completely through to the midsole or underlying material.

TORQUE: A force that causes or tends to cause rotation of an object about an axis. The torque (also called moment) is the result of the magnitude of the force, its direction, and distance from the axis of rotation.

TORSIONAL RIGIDITY: The amount of stiffness in the shank and waist of a shoe.

TRACTION: The amount of friction or resistance to slip between a shoe outsole and the contact surface.

TRANSDUCER: A device that converts an applied load or force into an electrical signal.

TRANSVERSE FORCE: The force generated at a right angle to the direction of motion by a walker or runner during foot contact and most closely related to rearfoot stability. Also referred to as the mediolateral force.

TREADMILL: A rotary machine-driven belt that allows subjects to run in a confined space.

VERTICAL FORCE: The force perpendicular to a level surface. The dominant force generated by a walker or runner during foot contact and most closely related to the shock absorption characteristics of a shoe.

WEAR TESTER: A piece of equipment used to evaluate the resistance of the outsole of a shoe to abrasion.

WEIGHTED SHAFT: A shaft with a weighted end that is used to impact shoes or material.

"You cannot put the same shoe on every foot"
Publius Syrus

C H A P T E R 7

FITTING REMARKS
FOR ATHLETES

A thletes are more concerned with fitness than with the fit of their shoes. Very little material is available on the actual fitting of shoes from either the traditional shoe trade or the "new" athletic shoe industry. Even the runners bible, *Runner's World* magazine, in their annual rating of shoes, quickly sidesteps the controversial issue of fitting by stating, "fit is no longer a factor in the survey. Since everybody's foot is different and there are too many variables involved in production, the only one truly able to judge . . . is the individual runner." This is true, but only a shoe that fits well gives the foot enough support, shock absorbency and comfort to take full advantage of all the biomechanical features that are so sought after in today's athletic footwear. And above all, these criteria must be achieved in the lightest possible shoe.

This chapter will examine the benefits of shoes that fit well. These benefits are basically:

1. Proper stability and support for the foot
2. Protection from foot injuries
3. Adequate shock absorption and comfort
4. Prolonged wear and retention of shoe shape

To properly discuss shoe fitting, we should first consider some basic foot anatomy and common foot ailments. We should also consider the characteristics of the form on which a shoe is made, the "last," and relate these to the foot. Materials and the actual construction of the shoe have their effects on fitting, as do foot measuring and measuring devices.

Your foot is an ever changing, flexible system that responds to heat, stress, rest, humidity and weather conditions. Your shoe

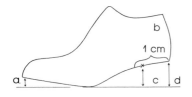

7-1. Last Specifications: (a) toe spring; (b) heelbreast; (c) heel height; (d) heel pitch. For example, size 4D—ball measurement = 20.5mm; heel height = 40mm; heelbreast = 45mm; toespring, ladies' shoe medium heel = 6mm, men's shoe = 8mm. (Heel height to be measured 1 cm behind the heelbreast.)

on the other hand, is a relatively inflexible covering. Much work has been done by the athletic shoe industry to introduce materials that mold to the foot and compensate for how the foot changes. Having a detailed knowledge of foot anatomy and the technical characteristics of shoes is certainly helpful when you are looking to find a shoe that fits correctly, but there is a lot to remember and it is easy to get confused. Fitters should recognize the difference between a flexible foot and a rigid foot. The former will require motion control, while the latter will need more shock absorption. You do not buy shoes every day, so let's concentrate on a few essentials that you can remember the next time you choose a sport shoe.

Remember, the fit of all shoes depends largely on the shape of the form, or last, upon which the upper is fashioned or "pulled" around. A last is a three dimensional facsimile of a foot. Last-making is an art that determines the look and style of a shoe. In athletic footwear, the design of lasts match the characteristics of the shoe to the functions athletes need the shoe to perform (see Fig. 7-1).

There are classically recognized differences in foot types. These are defined by arch and racial types (see Chapter 8). There is an argument that holds that a shoe last upon which you can build a shoe that will fit well on an Oriental foot cannot be used to build a shoe that will fit well on a European foot. Most manufacturers have tried to take this argument into consideration in the design of their lasts. They have either modified their original last shape or tried to design additional fitting improvements into the pattern of the upper. If the market is large enough, a new last may even be developed—Tiger shoes made in Japan for the large United States market, for example.

In the specific instance of running shoes, the last is usually made wider in the front, or girth, for comfort and flex, and slightly narrower in the heel for a more snug fit. Combination lasts that are used in some sport shoes provide narrower fitting qualities—a thinner instep, waist and heel, while the length and girth are standard.

Curved lasts are better suited for athletes who have a pronounced, inflared foot shape or athletes who must do a great deal of running, which places more pressure on the lateral side of the foot. People with high or flexible arches may be best suited by a curve-lasted shoe.

Straight lasts tend to provide more support to the medial side of the foot, and are better suited for athletes with low arches or for runners who do not have a severe pronation movement. As a general rule, slower athletic movements require more medial support, which is provided best by a straight-lasted shoe, while faster movements, which place more stress on the outside of the foot, are best served by a curve-lasted shoe.

IF IT FITS, IT FITS THE FIRST TIME

Today's designs and materials have largely eliminated the need to "break in" shoes used in training or competition. Shoes should feel comfortable the first time you put them on, an instant, happy marriage.

SOCKS AND FIT

When you are selecting a new pair of shoes, be sure to wear the socks or hose you normally wear when training. The thickness of hose, or its absense, makes a great difference in how shoes fit and feel. If you wear orthotics, make sure you try them in the shoes you are considering. Smoothing out all the wrinkles in your socks before putting on your shoes will help prevent blisters. Socks are also the most critical component in minimizing the absorbency of perspiration inside the shoe. Fine chamois skin inserts (once known as pushers) can still help stop blistering in shoes which have uppers made of hard leather or synthetic materials.

LACES

Make sure the laces are loose when you put on your shoes. This prevents unnecessary stress on the eyelets, counter and back tab. Begin at the bottom and pull the laces one set of eyelets at a time when you tighten them. This makes the shoes fit more comfortably and takes unnecessary stress off the top eyelets. Remember that the greater the number of lace eyelets, the easier it is to adjust the eyelet throat.

Conventional lacing, using the crisscross to the top-of-the-shoe method generally works most effectively for the majority of athletes. But just as one shoe model cannot meet every athlete's needs, neither can one lacing system. Specific lacing methods can help you alleviate certain injuries or biomechanical problems.

Many sport shoes today incorporate variable-width or dual lacing systems. **Variable-width,** first introduced by Nike, simply and effectively gives the shoe an alternative set of eyelet holes deeper into the quarter. This allows the user to lace on a wider or narrower eyelet spacing—giving you more or less lace across the throat. More lace on the wider spaced eyelets offers the narrow foot more control to pull the eyestay tighter. Less lace on the

7-2. Variable width lacing—left for wide fitting, right for narrow fitting.

7-3. Independent lacing system using two laces.

7-4. Kaepa's feature patented two-lace/split-vamp lacing system that allows for custom-fit adjustment.

7-5. *Left:* Crisscross alternative #1. 7-6. *Right:* Crisscross alternative #2.

7-7. *Left:* Square box lacing. 7-8. *Right:* Single lace cross.

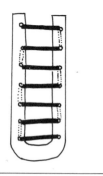

7-9. Show lacing.

narrow spaced eyelets gives the broader foot greater potential to open the eyelet stay wider. For maximum effect use only alternate eyelet holes.

Dual lacing systems such as three punched holes and three speed rings mainly serve the purpose of giving even pull to the eyestay and speed of closing and opening.

Independent lacing systems, first popularized by Kaepa, use two laces on each shoe. One lace for the front quarter, the other for the back quarter. One lace may be tied tightly, the other loosely thus relieving strain or pressure on the forefoot, plantar fascia or dorsal area of the foot.

Crisscross alternative # 1 is to lace conventional crisscross until the next-to-last eyelet. By looping the end of each lace and using the loop as an eyelet you can obtain a better pull on the laces for a more secure fit. This method is useful to help prevent heel slippage, usually the result of wide heel fitting.

Crisscross alternative # 2 offers relief from specific dorsal soreness or boney prominences on the first metatarsal ray. Lace conventionally to just under the trouble spot. Then lace to the next eyelet vertically up so the lace does not cross over the eyestay at all (usually missing one eyelet hole is enough). Continue using conventional lacing after problem area has been bypassed.

Square box lacing also helps to distribute lace pressure more evenly on the dorsal area of the foot and alleviate traditional crisscross lace strain on the foot. In this method the laces pass under the eyelet stay and do not *cross* over the top of the foot at all. This may help athletes with high arched or rigid feet alleviate full lace pressure.

Single lace cross (or dress shoe) method may offer help to the athlete experiencing problems with blackened, sore or tender toenail difficulties. One lace runs from the inside front eyelet to the opposite last eyelet. The other end of the lace goes side to side through every remaining eyelet. This helps to lift the toe box up off the toe area thus relieving any pressure on the toenails.

Combination lacing simply uses any of the above methods on a different foot thus personalizing the lacing method best suited to the athlete's individual foot requirements.

Show lacing is not practical for wearing purposes. However, for retailers and manufacturers wishing to present their footwear attractively a single lace method alternately bringing one lace vertically up and across showing no undercross is regarded as the professional way to lace a shoe. A correctly shaped shoe tree, not stuffed paper, shows the shoe to its best advantage. Professional shoe photographers prefer to photograph the lateral side of the shoe.

YOU HAVE TWO FEET

Be sure you try on both shoes when you select a new pair. After you have laced both of them, walk around to be sure that both of them are comfortable. Very few people have two feet with the same width (girth) and length measurements. According to The Prescription Footwear Association, "Men's and women's feet are equally mismated. In about three-fourths of men and women where one foot is longer than the other, the difference amounts to one-half the shoe size. In the remaining fourth the difference amounts to a full shoe size or more. In three out of five people the width across the ball of the foot (or girth) will be different in one foot than in the other. The width of the heel also differs between the two feet in three out of five persons. In almost all people the weight-bearing spread, "both length and girth, varies from one foot to the other." Sixteen percent of the time, the left foot is longer than the right; 10 percent of the time, the right foot is longer.

Your feet swell during activity, so choose a shoe size that is right for your largest foot. There are some competitive sports, such as track where the shoes may be worn for only a short time, or downhill skiing where there is little or no foot movement, in which shoes that best fit the smaller foot may be selected. In these cases, the athlete is prepared to settle for some discomfort in the larger foot.

FLEXIBLE AT THE TOP

Check the flexibility of the shoes you are considering to make sure they flex (break) across the girth and metatarsal bones. If they don't break, you may experience discomfort when you run.

7-10. Some runners prefer shoes with the toe cap cut out—so this model comes that way.

Some uppers are designed to allow more adjustable lacing than others. Lace-to-tip, double quarter designs, top-line lace stabilizers and variable eyestay patterns all help adjust the fitting of the shoe on the foot. The perfectly adjustable shoe has yet to be designed, but new elasticized materials for uppers and shoes with specially designed asymmetric, lace-to-toe adjustable lacing will soon be available. Recently, open-toed running shoe models have been made in New Zealand and Germany.

TIGHT SHOES, LOOSE SHOES: BLISTERS

You may get blisters from your shoes whether they are too tight or too loose. Your foot can drift and slip inside the shoe if it is too loose and cause the same discomfort as a shoe that is too tight.

7-11. Side lacing system on a training shoe.

7-12. Checking prototype ski boot closure at Koflach factory in Austria.

HOW SPORT SHOES ARE CLOSED

1. **Laces.** The "X" lacing pattern is universally accepted. It supplies even pressure, security and strength. There is one set of eyelets on each side of the eyestay, which may be cut various ways. The staggered or "variable" eyelet system allows greater control over how the upper fits. There are many combinations of eyelets you can use when you lace your shoes to create a custom fit. Speed or "Ghilly" lacing is a system of rings or loops that make it possible to tighten laces quickly.

2. **Velcro and Hook-and-Eye.** This method of closing a shoe is used mainly on casual or atheleisure shoes but it has been used successfully on competition shoes. World records in track were set in shoes with Velcro closures in the U.S.A. in 1968. Velcro straps are easy to adjust and can be quickly tightened and released.

3. **Buckles.** Buckles are used on ski boots. We'll talk about them under Alpine Ski Fitting.

4. **Hook Eyelets.** Hook eyelets are used on hiking boots and ice skates. We'll discuss them when we come to those sports.

HALF SIZES

Most athletic shoes come in half sizes, so make sure you take advantage of it. About 80 percent of those who use athletic shoes take the same size in their sport shoe as they do in their regular shoe. Remember, in fitting a shoe, make sure the weight of the body is completely on the lasting insole, not bulging or overlapping onto the upper.

In many sports books, coaches and authors recommend that a sport shoe be a half size smaller than their normal shoe for a snug fit. This is a dangerous recommendation. The complexities of fitting and the stresses a shoe is subjected to in performance make it wise to have a test fitting. Don't ever assume your shoe size; models and sizes vary from manufacturer to manufacturer.

OLD SHOES

If your old shoes have caused you problems, it may help to bring them with you when you go to purchase a new pair. Explain the problems you have had with the old shoe to a qualified salesperson and what you have done to overcome them. The salesperson may be able to recommend a shoe that corrects the problem or better matches the characteristics of your foot.

FOOT MEASURING DEVICES

Devices designed to measure feet are the best way to measure for shoe size. Many of them, such as the Ritz, the Brannock, and the Scholl devices, are available to retailers, but it is fitting to note that many do not currently use them. Before you put your foot into one, pull out the toes of your socks—tight fitting hose may squeeze your toes and give an incorrect reading.

Good foot measuring devices will consider:

1. overall length from the tip of the most prominent toes (as in Morton's foot) to the heel—the normal full size measurement equals one-third inch or 1 cm (see Fig. 7-14);
2. ball joint position in relation to the heel (short or long toes) and the arch length;
3. girth measurement or the width of the foot—this measurement is generally given by a letter (A to E, with A, AA and AAA being the narrow fittings and E, EE and EEE being the widest) (see Fig. 7-15).

A shoe fitter should be able to use these three measurements to recommend a size that will afford a good overall fit.

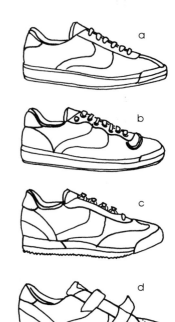

LAST WIDTH STANDARDS (GENERALLY ACCEPTED)

AMERICAN MEN'S			INCHES/CM	INCHES/CM
8A			8½ (21.6)	8¹¹/₁₆ (22.1)
8B	9A		8¾ (22.2)	8¹⁵/₁₆ (22.7)
8C	9B	10A	9 (22.9)	9⅛ (23.2)
8D	9C	10B	9⅛ (23.2)	9⅜ (23.8)
8E	9D	10C	9¼ (23.5)	9⁷/₁₆ (24.0)
8EE	9E	10D	9½ (24.1)	9¹¹/₁₆ (24.6)
8EEE	9EE	10E	9¾ (24.8)	10 (25.4)

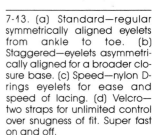

7-13. (a) Standard—regular symmetrically aligned eyelets from ankle to toe. (b) Staggered—eyelets asymmetrically aligned for a broader closure base. (c) Speed—nylon D-rings eyelets for ease and speed of lacing. (d) Velcro—two straps for unlimited control over snugness of fit. Super fast on and off.

WIDTHS AVAILABLE

AAAAA	A	E
AAAA	B	EE
AAA	C	EEE
AA	D	EEEE

The most common regular shoe fittings are C for men and B for women, but they vary from one manufacturer to another. The average athletic shoe fitting increases to D for men and C for women. This reflects additional allowances for foot expansion and movement during sport, and last allowance for contoured padded sockliners and footbeds (orthotics). Approximately one-quarter inch (6.5 mm) is used as a standard joint width fitting between the whole sizes at the widest part of the foot. For

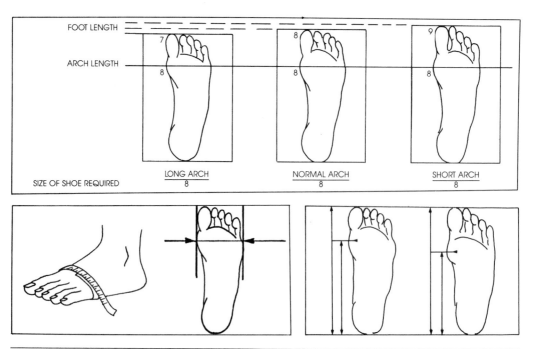

FOOT LENGTH

ARCH LENGTH

SIZE OF SHOE REQUIRED

$$\frac{\text{LONG ARCH}}{8}$$ $$\frac{\text{NORMAL ARCH}}{8}$$ $$\frac{\text{SHORT ARCH}}{8}$$

7-14. *Top:* Length Measurement. 7-15. *Bottom left:* Width Measurement. 7-16. *Bottom right:* Ball Joint Fitting.

example, a width of 8D is approximately nine and one-quarter inches (23.5 cm) at the girth, where a width of 8E is nine and seven sixteenths (24.0 cm) and 8EE is nine and nine sixteenths (24.3 cm).

Width fittings are rare in athletic footwear. This is because previously the low quantities of these shoes that were sold make it uneconomical to produce many specific lasts. Athletic shoes are generally built on "universal" fitting lasts that incorporate wide adjustments into the patterns of the lacing system.

THE FITTING AREAS

Let's look in detail at the various areas where the shoe fits the foot once you have it on:

Toe (Metatarsal) Area. The fit in this part of the shoe should correspond to the toe-to-heel length. You should have enough toe room in the front of the shoe so that your toes don't bunch or cramp. The shoe should be long enough so that the toes can't be jarred by the upper. Usually it is sufficient to leave one-half inch (13 cm) open from the end of the longest toe (considering Morton's foot). The box toe is another important factor in fitting this area. The box should be high enough to accommodate all the toes so that the uppers do not come in contact with the nails. (Note: the more pointed the shape of the last, the longer the shoe; for better protection against toe bruising.)

Ball Joint Fitting. The area from the ball to the heel including the arch is the crucial flex point one reads so much about. This is the widest part of the foot. Be sure there is enough material in the upper so that your foot can flex and spread. The girth should have a comfortable to snug fit. If in doubt, check for bulges or pressure points. Avoid excessive wrinkles in the upper. Your foot should not drift or "slop around" in the shoe, particularly across the girth.

You can check for slack material simply by pressing the upper down onto the lasting insole with your thumb. All toes should lie on the insole. They should not press the upper over the feather edge.

The arch should fit snugly. Feet with high insteps or arches are usually helped by an arch support. People who have more pronated feet or feet with lower arches often have trouble adapting to an arch support. You can remove the arch supports of most shoes if you like. Some arch supports are too soft to have any real function other than to fill up the shoe.

Most athletes feel that support systems, or contour-molded insoles, give their feet better support. However, if you have difficulty in fitting or have problems adjusting your shoe, you should consult your podiatrist. If you try to insert a molded insole into a shoe that does not have enough mass to accommodate one, you may get a tight fit or even push your foot out at the quarter or heel.

EYESTAY SPACING

Checking the spacing of the eyestays or eyelets is a good test of the fit across the girth. The eyestays of a laced shoe should be parallel from top to bottom. If they are pulled too tightly or bulge, your shoe is being over adjusted to make it fit. (see Fig. 7-17)

The width of eyestays varies with the type of design; e.g., U-throat, lace-to-toe, blucher cuts. Most athletic shoes with conventional lacing have an average width between eyestays of three-quarters inch to one inch (2–2.5 cm). The eyestays are cut wider on hockey and figure skates to allow for more width adjustment because these shoes must fit snugly to give the

TOO WIDE OPENING
UNCOMFORTABLE

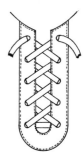

NORMAL OPENING
COMFORTABLE

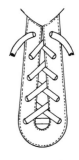

TOO NARROW OPENING
IMPROPER TIGHTENING

7-17. Lacing Test for Proper Fit.

needed degree of support. The Kaepa double vamp and lacing system offers an adjustable upper and lower vamp lacing or two lacing systems.

FLEX POINT

You flex your foot 6,000 to 7,000 times each day. Runners who cover eight miles in an hour can add twice as many steps to that total. That is why running shoes should have flexible foreparts. You can check the flexibility of a shoe by holding it between your hands and pushing gently at the toe. The easier it bends, the more flexible it is. The flex point should be across the metatarsal joints, not in the middle of the shoe.

You can improve the flexibility of shoes you own by making small cuts across the sole along the flex path or by pressing the toe up to the top line of the shoe and holding it there for a minute or two. This helps breakdown the adhesion of the sole and insole.

FITTING THE HEEL AND REAR OF THE FOOT

Heel fitting is potentially the one area of your shoes that can cause the most problems. Keep the following points in mind when you try on shoes:

1. The shoes should have smooth seams in the lining of the heel. Better yet is no seams at all.
2. Many A.T.P. (Achilles Tendon Protection) heels come up fairly high on the achilles tendon. If the shoe you are considering has such a heel, make sure the padding is soft and flexible enough not to irritate you when you run.
3. The heel counter, which lies between the lining and the outside material of the shoe, should be firm enough to support your heel and to prevent heel slippage and drift when you run. It should fit snugly. Many athletic shoes have elongated medial counters for additional arch support.
4. The shock absorption of the heel area is vital in running and court shoes, particularly if you perform on hard surfaces such as concrete. Be sure the sole area in the back of the shoe offers adequate platform. When you run, you come down on your foot with three to five times the force of your normal body weight. The more weight that is shifted to the rear of the foot on impact, the slower you run. The faster you run, as in racing, the more weight is shifted to the middle and forepart of the foot.

THE EFFECTS OF MATERIALS AND CONSTRUCTION

The inside shape of the shoe does not get bigger or smaller after the last is removed, but some materials and construction methods can cause changes to occur in the upper. These changes can occur either during the making of the shoe or while they are being worn. The stretch in the leather (the amount of "lasting margin") and the lining also affect how the shoe feels and acts. Uppers made of synthetic materials generally have a small amount of permanent stretch. Leather uppers, on the other hand, have a larger degree of dimensional recovery. Most of these factors are considered in the manufacture of a shoe, but you should still keep them in mind when you buy softer leathers.

WHEN TO TRY ON SHOES

Your feet tend to swell as the day progresses, so the best time to try on a pair of shoes is during the afternoon or in the evening. You will get a truer fit.

Those are the basics of fitting a sport shoe, but not the whole story. Unlike street shoes, sport shoes have specific functions to perform that vary from sport to sport. A tight-fitting shoe may be right for one sport but disasterous in another. Let's look at these functions sport by sport.

SPECIFIC CATEGORY FITTINGS

SKATES

It is crucial that skates fit well. Ice skates carry all your body weight on two blades approximately three millimeters wide. What is more, between strokes all weight is transferred to one foot. Skating boots must fit snugly in the ankle to give it adequate support and keep it erect, while maintaining sufficient blood flow. Poor fitting boots or boots in which the ankle area contains soft material can cause excessive ankle movement. Few people who skate actually have weak ankles; it's the fit of their boots that convince many people that they do. The ankle area should flex slightly, but if your boots are laced properly there should be little or no buckling around the ankle when you bend from the knee. A skate needs a firm heel counter for a snug fit at the rear of the foot. You want little or no movement in the heel area. Try a half size smaller shoe than you normally use for other athletic shoes. Try on a skate while you are wearing the socks you will wear when skating. Medium to thick socks are preferred in skating so that you can lace more tightly around the ankle without restricting your blood circulation. Your feet will stay warmer if blood can flow freely through the area. Many skaters prefer not to wear socks at all, reasoning that this is the best way for them to get that all important warmth and "feel." Leather linings are a good idea for these skaters. When you lace your boot, be sure not to lace too tightly at the toe. Lacing hooks make this a little easier on the hands.

The lasts of skate boots generally are medium to narrow fitting and have a semi-pointed toe. This allows a snugger fit thereby giving your foot more control over the edges of the boot. The shape of the last should give you sufficient lateral support without lacing tightly. Leave a little play when you lace up. You want tight lacing only at the ankle and at the top of the boot. A good way to lace highcut boots such as ice or roller skates is to lace the boot halfway up at one tension and the rest of the way at another. Just twist and knot the lace in the middle.

Many excellent skates have elongated medial counters or arch supports in the waist of the shoe. A well fitting, high quality boot upper will gradually mold to the foot but still stay rigid enough to keep its shape and give good support. Remember to make sure the laces are loose all the way down the boot when you put it on; otherwise you may incorrectly think the boot is too small when actually your foot is being restricted by the laces. Sometimes the blade needs to be repositioned on the boot for a skater to obtain a perfect skating position on the ice. When it needs to be done, this repositioning is usually toward the medial side. Repositioning the blade can only be done satisfactorily if the blade is screwed not riveted onto the boot. Because skates must be stiff, new boots need to be broken in slowly. It takes three or four sessions to break in a new boot. During this period, do not lace the boot to the top hook. It is better to gradually lace higher as the boot molds to your foot and ankle.

Many advanced ice and roller skaters prefer to have their boots customized to meet their individual needs. Extra support, padding and heel height can be built into a customized boot to provide needed support and counter the pressures that are applied against a boot.

HOCKEY SKATES

Besides fitting well, ice hockey boots must also protect the foot from the puck, sticks and blades. They have a wide fit protective toe boxes, tendon guards and tongues. Except for the toe area, they are fitted the same as figure skates. The need for a good medial counter or arch support for the medial arch cannot be over stressed. The elongated medial counter should be pre-molded. It should "cup" the arch and hold it firmly in the proper skating position. A hockey skate should allow sufficient forward and backward flex for the ankle to bend. The boot should be laced as tightly as comfort will allow in the front but permit enough anterior and posterior movement of the ankle. Hockey boots are cut slightly higher at the tendon guard than figure skates. The blades are also lower and narrower (3/32 mm compared to 3 mm) than those of figure skates.

PU Molded Boots. A customized molding machine (the Micron Medafit System), similar to the shell expanding systems used for plastic downhill ski boots, has been introduced. It can heat specific spots of a PU skate shell so that it can be reshaped to relieve pressure on bone spurs, bruises and the like.

CROSS-COUNTRY SKI BOOTS
A cross-country ski boot should be fitted similarly to a leather training shoe. The toes should have adequate clearance from the inner edge of the tip because of the flex and forward pressure movement in the shoe. Be sure to wear a thick sock or normal skiing socks when you are fit for a ski boot. The boots should fit snugly in the heel, waist and girth and have room at the toe. Because you spend a long time in the boots on touring trips it is important for the boot to be comfortable. Large fitting will tend to reduce control of the skis. Small fittings reduce warmth, cut off blood circulation and cause blisters. It is important for the boot to flex across the girth or ball of the foot. Be sure to avoid boots that are too tight or have stiff ridges over the toe area when you raise your heel and flex your toes.

COURT SHOES
The stop-start and lateral movements in court sports create a set of considerations you will need to keep in mind when you go to purchase court shoes. They are:
1. Your shoe should have sufficient room in the toe box area. If your toe touches the shoe when you stamp your foot forward then your shoe may be too small.
2. A court shoe should fit snugly in the heel, waist and girth. You get the most lateral support when your foot is "bound" snugly. A snug fitting, firm heel counter is

important to keep the heel firmly in place, but make sure there is no pinching in the lateral toe area (the little toe).

3. Many court athletes wear elasticized anklets, or two pairs of socks. If you are one of them, then be sure to buy new shoes wearing the same thickness of hose you wear when you play.

4. Look for the best gripping sole for the surface on which you normally play. The best sole on clay is not necessarily the best on indoor court surfaces. There are special indoor court tennis shoes, for example, that are best on those surfaces.

5. People who play court sports tend to spend long periods of time on the court, therefore make sure that your court shoes breathe.

6. Adequate padding and insoles are very important in a court shoe. Contour-molded footbeds or anatomical footbeds help redistribute the stress of quick stops and changes of direction over the entire foot.

SOCCER SHOES

In soccer, the foot makes direct contact with the ball—that's the whole idea of the game. In order to "feel" the ball, a tight fitting shoe is required. Soccer shoes should be made of soft flexible leather and have good ankle padding. A soccer player is in contact with the ball for only about two percent of the game; the rest of the time he is running or walking. Lightness is therefore important in a soccer shoe. The soccer shoe is also the one exception where it is desirable to have the shoe upper slightly overlap the insole, thus giving the foot better contact with the ball.

On hard ground, the multi-studded sole is most comfortable because it has more surface area and distributes the body weight more evenly. On softer fields, the screw-in stud type of shoe affords better traction.

CONTACT FIELD SPORTS

For sports where protection is needed, look for well padded high or semi-cut boots with good firm toe boxes and heel counters. Good quality leather of adequate thickness offers better protection than more flamboyant but less functional nylons and suedes.

TRACK SHOES

Optimal performance is more important to the track athlete than the comfort and durability of his shoes. Comfort and durability are sacrificed for lightness, tightness of fit and traction. The faster an athlete runs, the more pressure he applies to the forepart of his shoes. Good waist and girth fitting of track shoes is essential to performance. Semi-pointed lasts reduce space in the forepart of the shoe to cut down on movement inside this part of the shoe. Track shoes have been described as shoe gloves—that's how snugly they need to fit.

HIKING AND MOUNTAINEERING BOOTS

These boots need to be roomy because feet tend to swell during confinement as heat builds up inside the boot. When you are fitted for a hiking boot, try the one foot test: standing on one foot applies extra weight to it, which causes it to spread more than usual. If the boot feels comfortable while you stand on one foot then it is not too small. A wide girth and narrow heel and instep are best in a hiking boot. Check the length of a boot by sliding your foot forward and sliding a finger between your heel and the boot. Unlace the boot before you put it on and try this test. Spend a little time in the boots when you are trying them on to see if there are any pressure points or if there is discomfort. These boots should be broken in before you take to the hills in them.

DOWNHILL SKI BOOTS

Because modern high-shafted plastic ski boots are so rigid and inflexible in the lateral ankle region they are probably the hardest form of athletic footwear to fit. Again, the requirements of the sport make an exact fit of the padding or the inner boot crucial to comfort and control. The pressure inside the liner of the boot is great because of the rigidity of the outer shell. This pressure will cause pain if it is not distributed evenly over the foot. The closest thing to a natural movement a skier experiences in a downhill boot is a forward and backward movement of the foot inside the boot. There is enough flexibility or suppleness in the older style leather ski boots, as there is in other leather athletic boots, for the configuration of the ankle and foot to impose their impression on the boot. The plastic outer shell of modern boots is not so forgiving. The tongue, or in some models, the outer shell of the boot must be hinged so that you can be comfortable in the forward flex position without raising your heel. This forward lean or cant may vary from 12 to 27 degrees from the upright position of the shaft.

The lateral fitting of a ski boot is also very important because of the amount of side slipping or edging that occurs in the sport. The lateral fitting may vary up to six degrees. In their normal forward stance position, most skiers tend to apply lateral pressure on the lower or downhill ski. For this reason the boot shaft should be canted to the lateral or outside. Some boots have devices that regulate flex and canting built in to the inner liner or outer shell of their boots. These devices should allow you to obtain the most comfortable angle for your leg and foot stance and still keep the needed ankle stability afforded by rigid plastic boots. Such boots generally limit lateral ankle flex. Lateral movement is predominantly from the knees in rigid plastic boots.

When you try on a downhill ski boot, kick your heel to the back of the boot before you fasten it. The heel pocket should hold your heel firmly. Then fasten the boot and stand up. There should be no slippage inside the boot. You want a toe fitting that is as close to the front of the boot without pressing against it as possible. Bend into your normal ski stance and adjust the boot for the desired forward lean flex. Check to see if the boot is correctly canted for your leg structure (see Fig. 7-19). Also check the boot for any canting systems or the like that allow you to make lateral shift adjustments. A beginner can loosen one or two buckles for more lateral flexibility. After the boot is completely adjusted, bend into your forward stance and your left and right side-edging stances. Check for pressure and pain. The boot fits if it does not irritate any of the main pressure areas and feels relatively pressure free in skiing positions. Wear one pair of woolen socks when you are being fit for a boot. The main pressure areas are:

1. top of the shaft (tibia pressure)
2. ankle bone area
3. anterior dorsal ankle flex area
4. bunion joint (great toe joint)
5. base of the fifth metatarsal.

There are several devices available that can help relieve some of the discomfort and pressure that may develop as you use your ski boots:

1. **Shaft or Shin Soreness.** For shaft or shin soreness try premolded narrow sponge tongues, ankle cuffs with elastic stirrups, nylon covered sponge foam or the plastic wing pads you can wear between your socks and boots.
2. **Ankle Soreness.** The ankle bone—particularly on the medial side—should fit into the cups or indentations in the inner shaft padding. If you have problems with ankle comfort, loosen the boot and raise the heel so that you can feel the indentations. If your ankle fits into the cups better after you raise the heel, then insert a rigid heel wedge to keep the heel in the elevated position. You can

 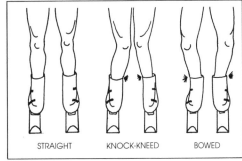

STRAIGHT KNOCK-KNEED BOWED

7-18. Special equipment required for stretching or adjusting monobloc injected ski boots for better fit. 7-19. Typical Leg Structures.

also try inserting "spoilers" at the back of the shaft. These devices are semirigid rubber or plastic wedges that increase forward lean and add support to the back of the achilles tendon area. Heel wedges that should be cemented into your boots are also available. Or try sponge foam "doughnut" rings that function in much the same way as ankle cuffs. The rings are available in several thicknesses.

3. **Soreness in the Dorsal Flex Area.** The dorsal flex area is at the top of the foot near the ankle. Downhill ski boots do not flex in this area as do most other types of footwear. This is where the straps and buckles of many boots can cause pressure when you are in your forward lean. Soft foam padding or moleskin, or a long, pre-molded, sponge boot tongue can help relieve the pressure.

4. **Soreness in Other Area.** You can insert thin, hard rubber padding between the inner and outer boot to help relieve discomfort at other pressure points. Moleskin may also help in other areas where soreness commonly develops; use it to cover seams, buckles, rivets and the like which irritate blisters, bunions and corns.

Many good ski shops have shell expander systems that reshape both the liner and the plastic outer shell of poorly fitting rigid boots when they are inserted into the boot liner and opened. Some boot stretchers have pressure "bumps" that leave indentations at pressure points. The Superfit® shell expander uses specially designed hydraulic tools and attachments to remold both the width and the length of a boot shell without scarring or defacing the plastic finish.

CYCLING SHOES

A racing cycle shoe is fit much the same way as a spiked track shoe. The shape of the lasts are very similar, and neither shoe is made for normal surfaces. Cycling shoes, however, do have different cleat attachments to affix the sole into rattrap pedals. The positioning and angle of the cleat at the correct pressure point under the forefoot is critical for maximum efficiency and comfort. There are specific cleat shapes for cyclo-cross, racing and road and track events; if you are not an experienced cyclist you should get advise from expert riders or coaches about the right cleat for each event. Individual adjustments can be made by experimenting during practice rides.

Toe clips with straps can be attached to the soles of most cycle shoes to prevent your feet from sliding off the pedals. Make sure you get the right size toe clips. They come in three sizes: SMALL, to fit American shoe sizes six through eight; MEDIUM, to fit American shoe sizes eight and a half to 10; and LARGE, for sizes 10½ to 12.

The toe of your shoe should not touch the medial edge of the clip. If the shoe is particularly uncomfortable, or if you have a foot with a wide girth, a larger shoe size may be in order. Aluminum spacers and longer toe clip bolts may be needed for you to get the correct pedal position if you have a large shoe.

SIZES AND FITTINGS

Shoe sizes were created in England during the reign of Edward II (1324). The original sizing was based on the measure of barleycorns (the longest man's foot being 13 barleycorns in a row). It was hardly a scientific approach. Today, sizing methods vary from country to country. There are four basic international scales in use:

1. English sizing
2. American standard
3. Continental or European sizing (Paris points—a metric system based on a terrestial measurement that was adopted by Napoleon in 1790)
4. Centimeter (metric) system.

(Note: the International Standards Organization (ISO) has proposed an international shoe size marking system called mondopoint, but it has not been adopted in most parts of the world.)

WOMEN'S SHOE FITTING

In today's specialized market the sizing of women's athletic shoes is equivalent to women's usual street shoe sizes. In the

INTERNATIONAL SIZE-SCALE COMPARISON CHART

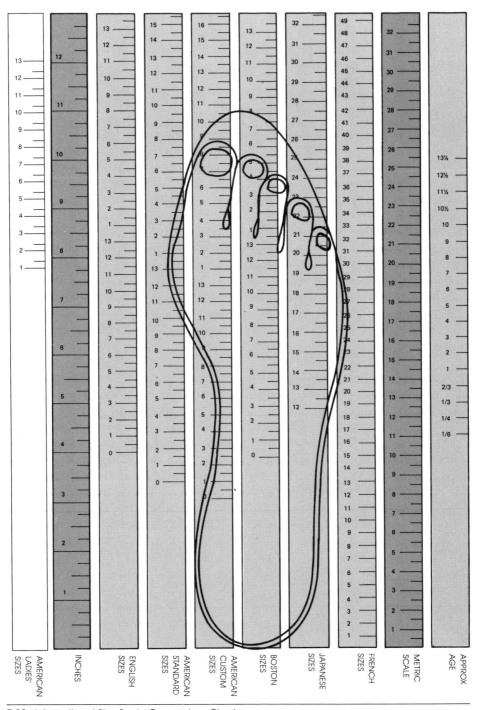

7-20. International Size-Scale Comparison Chart

event that a specific woman's size is not marked, the woman's size is one and a half to two sizes down from a man's size—that is, a woman's seven is equivalent to a man's five.

The women's fashion shoe industry is at least 10 to 15 percent larger than the industry for men's shoes. However, it has only been since the 1970s that a large number of sport shoes specifically for women have been manufactured. Prior to then there were only a few sports, golf for instance, in which there were shoes designed for women. Most sport shoe makers tended to produce a universal fitting last that naturally decreased proportionately in width as it became progressively smaller. Now that more women are participating in athletics, especially in running, court sports and winter sports, there are more and more athletic shoes available for them.

Women's sport shoes do not function any differently from men's models, but women's feet tend to be narrower than men's, averaging an A or B width fitting. Women's feet tend to have a shorter and narrower support structure than men's. Women also complete the heel-to-toe gait in a shorter time than men, which causes a greater impact at heel strike. The lasts used in women's sport shoes, therefore, are narrower in the girth. Some manufacturers offer last fittings that are narrower particularly in the rearfoot area. Lace-to-toe upper patterns are not recommended for women who need a narrow shoe. More pointed U-throat and extended U-throat patterns are popular for both fitting and appearance. The designs of uppers tend to be more streamlined with narrower toe shapes. Keep in mind the important transition from a high fashion heel to the much lower heel lift of an athletic shoe. This transition can cause stress problems on the achilles tendon and the ankle and knee joints. Women may want to compensate for this extreme variance in heel height by making sure the heel lifts and cushioning in their athletic shoes are adequate. During pregnancy, a woman's foot must bear extra weight, which may cause the inner longitudinal arch to flatten and the forefoot to turn out. Ligaments and muscles may stretch.

The only other difference between men's and women's sport shoes is that women's shoes come in different color combinations to fit the more sensitive female eye.

CHILDREN'S SHOE FITTING

Generally, the human foot stops growing around the eighteenth year. Shoe fitting during the formative years is critical. Sport shoes are purchased less frequently than regular shoes, and are often expected to last longer or to get one through "one more season." A young person should allow extra toe room when he

7-21. Correctly proportioned children's sport shoes have been stressed in the 1980s.

or she gets a new pair of athletic shoes to accommodate growth. The fit of the heel should still be snug and the ball of the foot should rest comfortably on the sole at the widest point of girth. Passing a shoe along from older to younger child is not recommended—you may pass along a problem as well as a shoe. The shoe size of a young person should be checked regularly with a measuring device. Here is a guideline:

Age 2 to 6—check every 1 to 2 months
Age 6 to 10—check every 2 to 3 months
Age 10 to 12—check every 3 to 4 months
Age 12 to 15—check every 4 to 5 months
Age 15 to 20—check every 6 months
Age 20 on up—check every time shoes are purchased.

Athletic shoe companies have started to put emphasis on the design of children's shoes. Lasts have been developed to accommodate the anatomy of a child's foot, which tends to be somewhat "square" and have softer bones.

Another specific factor being taken into consideration is the systematic adjustment of mid-sole and heel height according to shoe size. This compensates for a child's body weight increasing faster than the plantar surface area of his or her foot between the ages of two and 15. Adjustments in the mid-sole and the heel heights can assure the underdeveloped foot the needed amount of cushioning, stability and protection in each shoe size.

The fetal skeleton of the foot consists of cartilage. Cartilage is slowly transformed into bone starting as early as the ninth week of fetal development. This process, called ossification, continues until the child is about eighteen. The long bones of the foot and leg can be distorted if too much weight is applied before the process has gone far enough. Pressure from ill fitting shoes or too tight socks can force the bones to be incorrectly aligned at the joints, especially under the stress of athletic activity. This reasoning supports the argument to restrict children under 12 or 13 from engaging in heavy sports training.

A child's foot grows proportionately more in length than in width or girth. The rate of growth on the average boy's foot slows down from age 14 and ceases around the age of 17. The rate for an average girl slows down around the age of 11 and ceases around the age of 15. An infant's foot may grow two sizes (three-quarters inch) in length in a year, and a child's foot may grow one size (one-third inch). The joint girth of the average young foot increases approximately 3/16 inch for every one third-inch (one size) increase in length. The average foot continues to increase in girth and bulk for a few years after it ceases to grow in length. The metatarsals and phalanges gradually become more parallel while the big toe grows longer and becomes less straight until it is at an angle of approximately 70 degrees to the inside tangent line.

HOW TO CORRECT AN IMPROPER FIT

If one of your feet is larger than the other, for comfort fit your shoes according to the larger foot. You can use Spenco medical tape in the shoe on the smaller foot. This tape is a rubber-backed adhesive foam; with it you can narrow the heel cup so that the length of the shoe is slightly reduced and the heel can be better grasped. The use of foot bed insoles or cushion wedges will also help fill in a large shoe and reduce the length slightly without creating a significant imbalance in the shoe.

If you experience discomfort because of pressure on a bunion, corn or the like and find that the pressure is not alleviated by the leather or suede of the upper, you can adjust your shoes with a stretching machine. These shoe stretchers, with external "bump" attachments, can be inserted into a shoe and opened up after the shoe is tightly laced. The shoe is then steamed or sprayed to soften the leather.

Remember to include size measurement of your foot (toe-to-heel, girth outline) and any peculiarities of shape. These guidelines should help you get a proper fit. If you have difficulty getting a proper fit, talk to a podiatrist or orthopedic surgeon.

IF THE SHOE FITS WEAR IT!

Remember many shoe sellers are more concerned with the sale and price of a shoe than with a proper fit. Many sales people are not trained in measurement techniques or even basic shoe construction. When in doubt make sure there is no pressure points on your foot and that you, the athlete, are completely happy with your fitting. There are enough varieties of athletic shoes around to suit almost everyone. Few companies offer width fittings, so you should try on several different brands before you chose a shoe. Do not buy because of brand name alone. Many top brand name shoes are not made in the original factories or even in the countries of their origin.

FIT FEET

The information in this chapter was intended to help athletes and sales people fit athletic shoes more expertly and choose a sport shoe best suited for the athlete's feet. Shoes that fit properly will last longer. They give better protection and support. They can also make sport healthier and more enjoyable.

P A R T 3

• MEDICAL CONCERNS •

The foot, "a masterpiece of engineering."
                                    Leonardo da Vinci

8

FOOT STRUCTURE AND FOOTWORK

I t is essential for the athletic shoe specialist to have some knowledge and understanding of the foot's structure and basic movements. Throughout this book there are constant references to running, lateral and medial movement, balance and center of gravity.

All lower extremity movements are affected by the footwear worn. You could say that shoes are to an athlete as tires are to an automobile. Shoes worn for athletic performance must aid the foot, assisting the natural movement of the lower body. In many cases well designed athletic shoes can even compensate for the failure of the foot. Proper footwear can certainly help prevent injury.

It is not the purpose of this chapter to overstate the role of the podiatrist or the exercise physiologist in sports footwear. Many excellent books have been written on foot function by learned and experienced doctors. Podiatrists are specialists who are trained to treat problems of the function and movements of the foot and lower extremity. Many leg and foot problems can be traced to inefficient or incorrect use of sports footwear. Before you can understand sports footwear, however, you must first understand the structure of the foot and how it functions. It is hoped that this chapter will relate these basic movements to the functions performed by sport shoes, to show how a shoe can help you go higher, faster and longer.

The foot is our foundation and contact with the ground. Any shoe that is worn, therefore, immediately changes this contact in some way.

Conversely, there are different foot types, and shoes act differently from one to another. Let's look first at the foot in its natural state, without shoes. The human foot has evolved from performing an arboreal (tree climbing) function to a terrestial one. The foot is an extremely intricate structure and probably the most overlooked vital mechanism in the body. It has 26 bones and its complexity of tendons, ligaments, nerves, blood vessels, muscles and tissues work efficiently even under the excessive strains and conditions to which it is subjected in most sports activities.

BONES

The skeletal framework of the foot gives strength and supports the weight of the body. Muscles attach to the bones for movement, softer tissue such as tendons and ligaments are also attached to the bones by means of periosterum, which is a group of cells that cover the outside surface of the bones.

The 26 bones of the foot can be divided into three major groupings: tarsus (the back group), metatarsus (the middle group) and phalanges (the distal group).

The tarsus group consists of the following seven short bones: The calcaneous (oscalsis), known commonly as the heel bone, carries a large proportion of the body's weight. The talus (astragalus), which links the foot to the leg, helps distribute the weight of the body to the forepart of the foot and the heel. The remaining bones are the scaphoid (navicular), the cuboid on the lateral side of the foot, and three cueiform bones, the inner, middle and outer.

The metatarsus group consists of five long bones joined to the cueiform (first three) or cuboid (fourth and fifth).

The phalanges consist of the fourteen long bones that form the toes.

CARTILAGE

Cartilage is the specialized material that covers the ends of the bones. Cartilage provides a surface over which other bones move. It also provides shock absorption. Joint fluid called synovial fluid provides the lubrication to the cartilage.

JOINTS

Joints exist in the skeletal system where two or more bones meet. The main joints in the lower extremity are the hip, the knee, the ankle and the toes.

Joints where little or no movement occurs are held firmly together by strong elastic tissues called ligaments. Joints where movement is necessary are called synovial joints. These joints may be either ball and socket type joints such as the hip, hinge type joints such as the knee, or gliding type joints such as the subtalar.

LIGAMENTS

Ligaments are like elastic bands. They strap around the bones to keep them in place and prevent dislocation. Articular and capsular ligaments contain joints that prevent bone displacement by allowing little movement. Facior ligaments or spring ligaments hold in tendons and have more elasticity. They are found where joint movement is necessary.

MUSCLES

Muscles are the prime organs in the body as far as motion is concerned. They pass from bone to bone, usually traversing one or more joints. A tendon is the fibrous cord in which the fibers of a muscle end and by which the muscle is attached to a bone. There are four groups of muscles in the leg that act on the foot.

1. **Front or Anterior Group.** This group includes the four muscles in front of and between the tibia and fibula. The tendons of these muscles pass in front of the ankle joint. These muscles raise the foot, turn the sole in and out and extend the toes up.

2. **Outside or Lateral Group.** This group includes the two muscles that join the fibula. The tendons of the muscles pass behind the ankle joint. They bend the foot down and turn it out.

3. **Surface Back Group (the calf).** One of the muscles of this group is joined to the thigh bone (femur) and the other is joined to the tibia and fibula. They pass, via the achilles tendon, over the back of the ankle and bend the foot down.

4. **Deep Back or Posterior Group.** This group consists of the four muscles under the calf. The tendons of these muscles pass behind the ankle to flex the toes down and turn the foot in.

   As for the actual muscles on the foot, the muscles above the skeleton extends the toes and the others under the skeleton control the other movements of the toes.

NERVES

Nerves stimulate muscle contraction through voluntary, involuntary or reflex action. When a muscle contracts, the fibers which compose it shorten. This produces tension through the muscle-tendon unit. The final result is a movement from bone to bone. Each group of muscles has a compensating or opposing group of muscles called antagonist muscles. This arrangement prevents excessive or jerky movement.

THE BLOOD CIRCULATORY SYSTEM

This system nourishes all body tissues, removes waste and provides repair materials. Blood vessels carry blood to perform these functions.

SKIN

Skin is the protective layer of the body, our contact with the environment. In terms of movement, its function is to stretch with movement of other organs. The skin has nerve endings, blood vessels, sweat glands and hair folicles. As the skin and nails of the foot are what make actual contact with your shoes (usually through socks), we will discuss the skin more in "Injuries Related to Athletic Footwear."

ARTERIES AND BLOOD

Blood is carried from the heart and lungs to muscles through arteries. Veins return used blood back to the heart and lungs for replenishment. The feet contain much more blood than is needed for their nourishment. This allows them to play a large part in temperature control. The feet are subjected to extreme heat in sports like basketball, which causes them to perspire. They can also be subjected to extreme cold in winter sports and are susceptible to frost bite.

SWEAT GLANDS

There are more sweat glands per square inch of skin on the foot than on the skin of most of the rest of the body. According to a Dr. Scholl's publication, "There are 250,000 sweat glands in a pair of feet, pouring out half a pint of moisture, salts and acid into shoes each day." Perspiration plays a major role in controlling body temperature, so when the body becomes heated from muscular activity even a larger quantity of moisture is produced.

Before we look at the movements that interact with the foot let's consider the physiology of the lower extremities. In addition to the 26 bones in the foot, there are four bones between the ankle and hip. Together, these 30 bones compose the foundation of the lower extremity of the body. The complete lower anatomy of the body accounts for approximately one-third of the body's weight.

The hip bones (pelvis) join the lower extremity to the rest of the body. The thigh area lies between the hip and knee, and the leg is between the knee and ankle. The foot includes the ankle joint and below. The rearfoot is composed of the heel bone (calcaneus) and the ankle bone (talus). The joint between the talus and the calcaneus is called the subtalar joint. The remaining bones are the lesser tarsus, the metatarsus and the phalanges.

Let's look at four views of the foot, from the top (dorsal), bottom (plantar), outside (lateral) and inside (medial). These four views will give us a thorough picture of the foot and its complex bone structure (See Figs. 8-1, 8-2, 8-3 and 8-4).

Any position of the body is a result of movement. We have already referred to the components of the physiology of movement (bones, tendons, cartilage, nerves, blood vessels, ligaments, blood and skin).

Let's look now at the joints of the lower extremity and the actual mechanisms involved in motion.

THE HIP

The hip is the only joint in the lower extremity that can move in all directions. The pelvis transmits the energy created by the lower anatomy to the rest of the body. The proximal (closer to the center of the body) end of the femur acts as a ball in a ball-and-socket mechanism. This allows the quadriceps and femur in the thigh to rotate medially (toward the inside), laterally (toward the outside), anteriorly (forward) and posteriorly (backward). The hip allows the knee, ankle and lower joints to retain straight ahead positions during forward movements such as running.

THE KNEE

The distal end (the end away from the center of the body) of the longest bone in the body, the femur, connects to the top of the knee. The proximal ends of the tibia and fibula (often referred to as the shank) connect to the other end of the knee. The knee is a hinge-type mechanism that allows mostly the motions of flexion and extension. Some lateral and medial rotation is possible, but not to any great degree. The knee is the largest joint in the body. It is probably subjected to more sport injuries than any other joint in the lower extremity.

THE ANKLE

The distal ends of the tibia and fibula join at the ankle. Like the knee, the ankle is also a hinge-type mechanism. It allows dorsiflexion (upward movement) and plantarflexion (downward move-

DORSAL VIEW

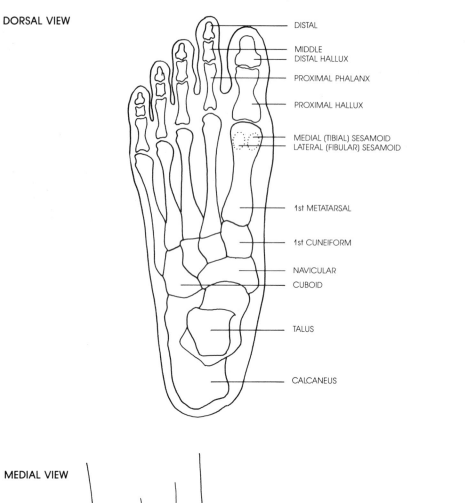

DISTAL

MIDDLE
DISTAL HALLUX

PROXIMAL PHALANX

PROXIMAL HALLUX

MEDIAL (TIBIAL) SESAMOID
LATERAL (FIBULAR) SESAMOID

1st METATARSAL

1st CUNEIFORM

NAVICULAR

CUBOID

TALUS

CALCANEUS

MEDIAL VIEW

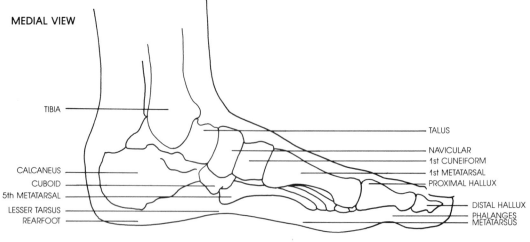

TIBIA

TALUS

NAVICULAR
1st CUNEIFORM
1st METATARSAL
PROXIMAL HALLUX

CALCANEUS
CUBOID
5th METATARSAL
LESSER TARSUS
REARFOOT

DISTAL HALLUX
PHALANGES
METATARSUS

8-1. *Top:* Dorsal view of the foot.   8-2. *Bottom:* Medial view of the foot.

PLANTAR VIEW

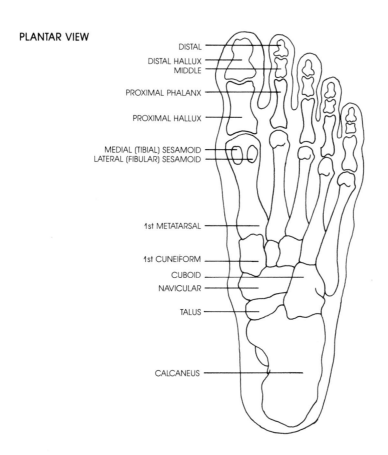

DISTAL
DISTAL HALLUX
MIDDLE
PROXIMAL PHALANX
PROXIMAL HALLUX

MEDIAL (TIBIAL) SESAMOID
LATERAL (FIBULAR) SESAMOID

1st METATARSAL

1st CUNEIFORM
CUBOID
NAVICULAR
TALUS

CALCANEUS

LATERAL VIEW

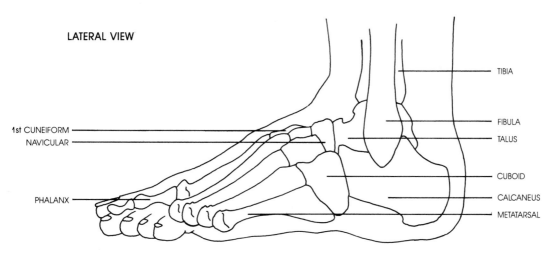

TIBIA

FIBULA
TALUS

CUBOID

CALCANEUS
METATARSAL

1st CUNEIFORM
NAVICULAR

PHALANX

8-3. *Top:* Plantar view of the foot. 8-4. *Bottom:* Lateral view of the foot.

ment) of the foot. The ankle is most important in maintaining the body's center of gravity during forward or backward motion.

THE SUBTALAR AND MIDTARSAL JOINTS
These two joints are below the ankle. In addition to aiding in the dorsiflexion and plantarflexion of the foot they play a major role in the movements of supination and pronation (defined below). These two motions are needed for the foot to function properly and efficiently. They help absorb the retrograde shock at heel strike and help the foot change from a rigid lever for propulsion to a mobile adapter during the contact phase of gait. Pronation is a complex series of movements that involves these two joints as well as the entire lower extremity. Pronation can be described for the sake of simplicity as the lowering of the medial (inside) arch. It is composed of three movements, eversion, abduction and dorsification, which are basically up and out movements. Supination is the opposite of pronation. It involves inversion, adduction and plantarflexion, which are down and in movements.

METATARSAL-PHALANGED JOINTS
These joints include the ball of the foot. They allow dorsiflexion and plantarflexion of the toes in a simple hingelike manner. These joints and the individual phalangeal joints enable the grasping movements of the toes.

PHALANGEAL-PHALANGEAL JOINTS
Phalanges are the little bones at the distal end of the metatarsals. The great toe, the "hallux," has two phalenges, the lesser toes each have three. Like the metatarsal-phalangeal joints they are hingelike and permit toe grasping.

FOOT TYPES
Like a finger print, every foot is different. Shoe makers must categorize feet into groups in order to design lasts and shoes for sports performance. They share this need to categorize feet with podiatrists. The two common methods of categorizing feet are by race and by arch type. Both methods are considered in the design of shoes for the people of some nationalities, but let's look at them separately.

RACIAL DIFFERENCES
Most sports equipment can be used by almost anyone almost anywhere in the world. A tennis racket designed in one country

fits the needs of a tennis player in another. There are two deviations from this generalization. One is clothing and the other is footwear. Although most athletic shoe companies do not vary the characteristics of their lasts to accommodate racial differences, they agree that definite physiological differences from race to race exist. Heredity and the trends of fashion affect the foot types of each generation.

1. **The Negroid Foot.** The classic negroid foot is broad in the forepart and narrow in the heel. The toes are flared out to straight, probably reflecting generations of walking barefoot on soft grounds. Black women tend to have slightly narrower and straighter feet. In an American study it was determined that blacks had a greater thickness of fat tissue under the calcaneus at 2.3 cm than a corresponding caucasian group at 1.78 cm.

2. **The Oriental Foot.** The classic Oriental foot is short and broad in the forepart and heel. The toes are straight with a large space between the big and the second toe, which possibly accounts for the popularity of the Oriental thong-type shoe. The feet of Oriental women are similar in shape to those of men only smaller. Although heel lift has been largely standardized by the major makers of shoes, Oriental people tend to prefer a smaller lift than other people.

3. **The Caucasian Foot.** This foot type is an equal mixture of high, normal and low arches. It has been affected by fashion trends and climatic conditions. In warmer climates such as Australia, the southern United States and part of South America, the male foot tends to be broad with straight toes. Fashions such as the vogue for pointed shoes, the negative-heel earth shoe and the anatomically shaped wooden clog have all played major roles in shaping feet while they grow. Caucasian women tend to have narrow feet, a tendency greatly influenced over the years by the fashion for pointed shoes.

ARCH TYPES

Although the percentage vary from one race to another, all arch types are found in all races.

1. **High Arch** (Cavus Foot Type). This type of foot has one or more high arches in the foot. Thus the front forefoot and heel areas generally carry the predominant degree of pressure or weight. The high-arched foot requires exceptional shock absorption or anatomical plantar surface fitting, since exercise exerts a tremendous force on the

ball and heel of the foot.

2. **Normal Arch.** The normal arch distributes weight evenly over the forefoot, the lateral border and the heel area. The long inside arch is raised.

3. **Flat Arch.** Collapsed or low arches distribute weight over the total foot area. This puts extra pressure on the outside border areas of the foot.

STRUCTURAL DIFFERENCES BETWEEN MEN AND WOMEN

Women are biomechanically and structurally different from men. Certain physical characteristics of women cause effects in foot function that are different from the effects seen in men. The wider pelvis of a woman creates a greater angle in the pelvis to hip joint than a man has. The femur connects the hip to the knee at approximately a 15 degree lateral angle. This larger angle of the longest bone in the body increases the possibility of lateral knee injury. It also makes the structure of the female leg less biomechanically efficient. Less muscle mass is supported and the ligaments, tendons and cartilage may be more delicate. This flexibility may result in less power but allows for more fluid movement. The shorter and narrower foot structure of a woman helps to complete the heel to toe gait movement quicker. This causes greater impact in the heel area at foot strike.

ATHLETIC MOVEMENTS

Let's now look at all the basic athletic movements that are performed on or by athletes' feet. Those sports in which shoes are not worn (gymnastics, swimming, karate, et. al.) will not be considered.

Balance and the Body's Center of Gravity. When the foot hits the ground, the weight of the body is distributed across the foot from the talus to the calcaneous at the heel, to the heads of the metatarsals in the forepart, along to the outer longitudinal arch. The pressure of bearing the weight causes the inner longitudinal and the anterior metatarsal muscles to become lower and longer. The foot increases in length from the heel to the metatarsal-phalangeal joint, and the width of the joint becomes wider. The heel area also gets wider. The girth of the joint increases slightly and the toes lengthen, the great toe helping to provide balance. This increase in length may be as much as one half to one full size. Dimensional changes such as

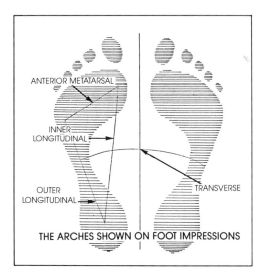

ANTERIOR METATARSAL

INNER
LONGITUDINAL

OUTER
LONGITUDINAL

TRANSVERSE

THE ARCHES SHOWN ON FOOT IMPRESSIONS

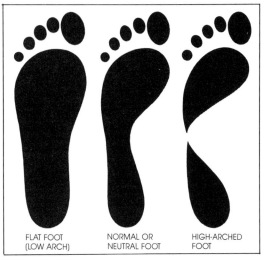

FLAT FOOT
(LOW ARCH)

NORMAL OR
NEUTRAL FOOT

HIGH-ARCHED
FOOT

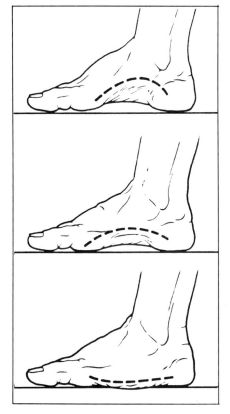

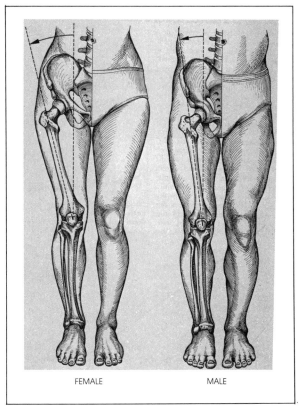

FEMALE

MALE

8-5. *Top left:* Arches shown on foot impressions.   8-6. *Top right:* Types of Arches—(a) flat foot (low arch); (b) normal or neutral foot; (c) high-arched foot.   8-7. *Bottom left:* Relationship of arch angle to flexibility. A high arch angle indicates a tight heel cord and tight-jointedness. A low to flat arch generally means loose joints, more typical in the female foot type.   8-8. *Bottom right:* Structural differences between men and women.

these occur in increasing degree as the whole weight of the body becomes concentrated on specific parts of each foot. This is common in most active sports performance.

Balance is needed by an athlete during all movement, no matter if the movement is forward, backward, upward or to a side on one leg or two. Usually, the next coordinated motion is not possible if an athlete loses balance and does not become possible until balance is restored. The arms, torso and the lower extremities all play a role in maintaining balance. Practicing certain movements also improves balance and allows the body to adjust more quickly and more efficiently. The lower extremities, with their complex structures of joints and muscles, play the major role in repositioning an athlete's center of gravity, which is essential to maintaining balance.

Normal stance or normal gait means that all involved structures are working synchronously and harmoniously with each other, and that there are no abnormal imbalances or influences from inside or outside the body. Under normal conditions, the function of the foot is to cushion the body, to aid in balance and to provide leverage for traction and movement. When an imbalance occurs, as it frequently does in sports motions, the legs and feet must compensate and give the body a base of support so that balance can be regained. The body's center of gravity in relation to the ground is adjusted by movements of the joints and muscles, creating greater stability.

Running.
Besides being a discipline in itself, running is a core action in many sports. There are several types of running. Basically, they are slow running or jogging, middle pace running or striding, and fast running or sprinting.

In long distance running, as in walkng, a foot usually completes a full cycle from heel landing through midstance to toe off. Ground contact occurs on the lateral side of the shoe while the nonweight-bearing foot goes through a swing phase in a cycle of support and recovery. In walking, one foot is always in contact with the ground. Both feet are air borne if only for a moment in even the slowest running.

Middle distance running differs from long distance running mainly in the way the foot strikes the ground. Most middle distance (800m to 5000m) runners land on the midfoot and rock back for a split second onto the heel; or they land simultaneously on the midfoot and the heel. This changes the body's center of gravity, making it come closer to a straight line as forward speed increases.

A sprinter has a completely over balanced center of gravity

at take off. The stride increases in length when full stride is achieved. The muscles of the legs and feet drive the legs forward to maintain the balance of the upper torso. Leg speed naturally increases when optimal stride length is achieved. Over or under striding, along with slower leg speed, reduce the speed of the forward motion of the body. When athletes sprint "off center," as they do in many sports in order to change directions quickly or to maintain their balance, they use a wider foot plant for a lower center of gravity and greater stability.

The two basic motions that occur in the foot during running are pronation and supination. The foot strikes the ground in a supinated state (arch elevated) when heel contact occurs. From the point of heel contact through midstance and just prior to toe off, the foot goes through a series of pronation-supination movements, with pronation being the more prevalent. During this pronation dominated stage the foot becomes in essence a loose bag of bones, which allows the foot to adapt to the terrain and absorb retrograde shock from impact on the ground. Just before toe off, or propulsion, the foot resupinates. This changes the loose bag of bones to a rigid lever that provides the proper mechanism for an efficient toe off.

Lateral Movements. Lateral movements are the side-to-side motions of the body. During a lateral movement, the center of gravity either repositions the body or it sets the body so that it can perform arm or upper body movements. During lateral movements the joints of the lower extremity are required to move in either a lateral or a medial fashion so that the muscles can work to retrieve the body's balance. Injuries such as ankle sprains can result when too much stress is applied to these lower extremity joints.

Jumping. Your can jump off of one leg or off both together. During a jump the center of gravity is kept low and the basic upward thrust comes from the gluteus, thigh and calf muscles. These muscles force the hip, knee and ankle to extend. At take off, as upward thrust occurs the foot changes from a pronated to supined position.

Landing. Just as you can leap off either foot or both, you can land on either or both. A correct platform position is necessary when you land or injury can result. The incidences of injury are even greater in landing than in propulsion because of the G. forces when landing add weight to the body. Malalignment of joints, particularly the ankle, is common.

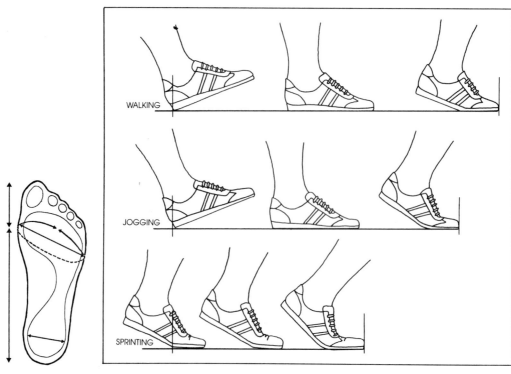

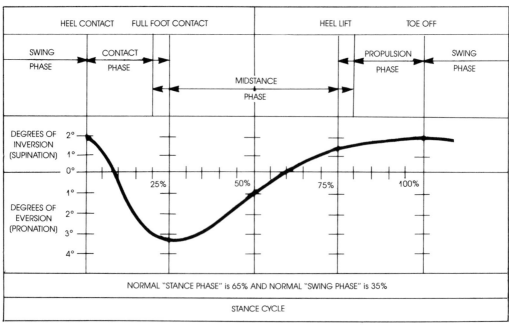

8-9. *Top left:* Increases in dimension due to weight-bearing. 8-10. *Top right:* Ground contact of foot in various modes of displacement. 8-11. *Bottom:* Stance cycle graph.

In a natural landing the forefoot area makes contact with the ground first. It hits ground in a supined position but quickly becomes pronated. Eversion, abduction and dorsiflexion occur simultaneously with this action. The foot must either absorb whatever of the tremendous shock is not dispersed throughout the lower anatomy or transmit these forces back up the body.

Kicking. Kicking is the one sports motion where the foot is deliberately brought into contact with an object, usually a ball, with ballistic force. A kicking action can be achieved in three ways: in a soccer or rotated swing style, in a straight-on toe style, or in a punt or drop-kick style.

In soccer-style kicking the nonkicking foot is planted even with or slightly behind the ball. The kicking leg is raised back then swung in an arc, pivoting at the hip. The knee is extended and the foot is placed in a stiffened position so that the dorsal (top) or the medial (inside) or the lateral (outside) of the foot can make contact with the ball. The foot is in a direct line with the ball. The body's center of gravity moves from a backward position to a forward position during the follow-through of the kick. This puts the weight of the kicker into use during contact with the ball, varying it according to the type of kick that is intended.

The straight-on kick, used mainly in place kicking in American football, uses the same type of action as a soccer kick except that the toes of the kicking foot are the only point of contact with the ball. A special block-toe shoe is recommended to avoid injury. The kicking leg is swung in a straight line to the ball through contact. The transfer of body weight and the follow through are similar to what happens in soccer-style kicking.

Punting or drop kicking requires the kicker to make contact with the ball while it is in the air, or to kick the ball directly out of the hands, or to kick it on the half volley immediately after it has bounced off the ground. Here a much more exaggerated leg swing is made. The foot and the leg extend high into the air after contact and into the follow through. The ball can be kicked great distances this way. In a punt, when contact is made with the ball, the dorsal area of the foot assumes a platarflexed position. When the ball is kicked on a half volley, it is struck more with the toes and the foot assumes a dorsiflexed position.

Cross-Country Skiing. Although the edges of the skiis are used occasionally when ascending or descending slopes, the main motion in cross-country skiing involves a forward movement. The foot, linked by shoe-binding-ski, comes in contact with the ground, as it does in walking; in fact, cross-country skiing is much more like walking or jogging than it is like downhill skiing. Like so many specialized sports, cross-country skiing involves specialized movements and requires special footwear. Cross-country skis and footwear are kept light because during use they must be raised and lowered. The foot is connected to the ski only at the toe area.

During motion the heel is raised and the ski is slid forward in a smooth, gliding motion. The anterior and posterior muscles of the leg work much the same as they do in jogging or striding; however, the foot functions differently. The weight-bearing foot remains pronated with the heel kept down to act as a platform. This keeps the body in balance as the foot swings through. The ski slides smoothly and the foot goes from a supined to a pronated state. The full weight of the body is then supported by the foot and ski and the leg goes into an upward motion and replicates the cycle. As in walking one foot remains in contact with the ground while the other moves through the swing cycle. Ankle support is not needed in cross-country skiing, but some skiers prefer highcut boots to keep out the snow. Special fore-foot and heel plate attachments help stabilize the boot when the edges are used for episodes of downhill skiing during a cross-country trip. Poles are used for propulsion and balance.

Downhill (Alpine) Skiing.

There is nothing else remotely like downhill skiing, with the possible exception of water skiing, in terms of the biomechanics and kinesiology involved. The edges of the skis must act as extensions of the leg and foot. The feet are literally anchored to the skis for maximum control. This is accomplished with a rigid ski boot that minimizes lateral ankle and foot joint movements. The edges of a ski are controlled mainly by the upper leg muscles, the knee and the hip. The boot is hinged to allow forward ankle flexing and forward lean; this allows a shift in the center of gravity in either an anterior or a posterior movement. The ankle and foot became simply extensions of the upper leg, which transfers messages from the upper joints and muscles to the platform and edges of the ski. The feet and ankles are locked in a dorsiflexed position with a pronated heel. In order to allow some lateral movement of the subtalar and midtarsal joints within the rigid boot, some boots are equipped with adjustable varus wedges or with canting devices. As the feet and the lower joints have very little mobility in the rigid boots, it is essential that specially padded or molded inner liners conform to the shape of the ankle and foot for comfort.

A skier in good skiing position is flexible at the hip and knee and has his or her body weight balanced forward over a low center of gravity. Because of the speed achieved in downhill skiing, the balance needed and the types of terrain traversed, injuries to the lower anatomy, particularly to the bones and joints below the knee, are common. As the foot is "locked" to the ski, quick-release pressure bindings allow the foot to escape if need be to avoid injury.

Ice Skating. In ice skating all body weight is transferred to, and must be balanced on, thin metal blades. This may seem to be a pretty dramatic definition of skating, but anyone who has tried to skate will verify that it is one of the most difficult things to teach the body to do. As in downhill skiing the edge and angle of the blade determine how body weight is distributed and thus how balance can be achieved.

Ice skating, be it figure, hockey or speed skating, requires a great variety of movements. All leg muscles and joints of the entire lower extremity are used. Excessive transverse or frontral movements below the ankle are detrimental to good skating; thus a tight fitting, highcut boot is needed to stabilize the ankle and subtalar joints. "Pushing off" requires some movement of the foot, which stays in mainly a pronated position. Some flexibility in the subtalar, midtarsal and metatarsal joints is also necessary. Between strokes, a skater's weight rests on one foot, so the ankle must adopt an erect position to support it. Because stresses are placed on the medial arch in skating, a pronated condition must be corrected by firm arch support for a correct skating position to be achieved.

Roller Skating. Balance and stability are somewhat easier to maintain in roller skating than they are in ice skating. Instead of a thin blade, the foot lies atop four wheels. Most of the motions performed in roller skating are similar to those in ice skating. One difference is how a roller skater stops, with a toe stop at the front of the track.

"Pedaling" Technique in Cycling (sometimes called "Ankling"). This is another movement that is unique to its sport with effects on athletic footwear. This technique, along with a stiff sole plate permits more efficient pedaling because it uses muscles more effectively. The foot is clamped onto the pedal with the forefoot positioned at the correct angle and longitudinal position. The foot is flat or at right angles to the shin when the pedal is in the 12 o'clock position. The foot and ankle remain locked in that position until the complete downstroke is accomplished and the pedal is in the six o'clock position. As the foot moves past six o'clock, the heel is pulled up. The foot assumes a slightly plantar-flexed position as it passes nine o'clock and returns to 12 o'clock. Ankling may be changed by pointing the toe into a more plantar-flexed position on the downward stroke and into a more exaggerated dorsal-flexed position on the up stroke.

GLOSSARY OF FOOT MOTIONS AND PLANES OF REFERENCE

ABDUCTION—To move away from the midline of the body

ADDUCT—To move toward the midline of the body

ADDUCTION—Moving a part toward the midline of the body

ANTERIOR—In front; forward

DISTAL—Farthest away from a reference point, such as the center of the body

DORSAL—Top of foot, the upper surface of the foot

DORSIFLEXION—Moving the toes up toward the distal end of the foot towards the leg

EVERSION—Turning out the plantar aspect of the foot from the midline of the body

EVERT—To turn out the plantar aspect of the foot so that it faces away from the midline of the body

FRONTAL PLANE—The vertical plane that passes through the body dividing into a front and a back half

HORIZONTAL PLANE—(see transverse plane)

INVERSION—Turning the plantar aspect of the foot in toward the midline of the body

INVERT—To turn in the plantar aspect of the foot so that it faces the body's midline

LATERAL—The side away from the midline of the body

MEDIAL—The side closest to the midline of the body

PLANTAR—The bottom or sole of the foot

PLANTARFLEXION—The downward movement of the toes or distal end of the foot away from the leg

POSTERIOR—Behind, back

PRONATION—A triplane motion of the foot or part of the foot which consists of simultaneous movements: abduction, dorsiflexion and eversion; basically, a movement away from the midline of the body, up and out; lowering the medial foot arch; the opposite of supination

PROXIMAL—Closest to a reference point such as the center of the body

SAGITTAL PLANE—The vertical plane that passes through the body from back to front dividing it into a left and right half

SUPINATION—A triplane motion of the foot or part of the foot which consists of simultaneous movements: adduction, plantarflexion and inversion; basically, a movement toward the midline of the body, down and in; elevation of the medial foot arch; the opposite of pronation

TRANSVERSE PLANE—The horizontal plane that passes through the body from side to side and back to front dividing it into an upper and lower half

The runner's weakest link traditionally has been his or her feet"   Dr. Steve Subotnick

CHAPTER 9

INJURIES RELATED TO
ATHLETIC FOOTWEAR

The competitive sportsman is generally more concerned with winning than with the maintenance of health. But any injury usually represents a marked setback. Any contribution to the avoidance of injury or ailment represents a success for medical practitioners.

Podiatry is the branch of medicine which specializes in treating diseases and injuries of the foot and leg. The podiatrist (DPM—Doctor of Podiatric Medicine) is the specialist who treats these problems. He is totally cognizant of the direct interrelationship between the foot and lower extremity (the hip, thigh, knee and leg). He knows that the foot is a dynamically functioning structure which is constantly changing and adapting to the terrain and for sport. The foot must function smoothly and efficiently so that correct function of the lower extremity is ensured. The foot must be able to make a smooth transition from a mobile adapter at heel contact to a rigid lever at toe off. If this motion occurs unimpeded the rest of the lower extremity will effortlessly follow. If this smooth motion is restricted to any degree, however, either by inherent structural problems or external forces such as the wrong shoes, then pathology develops in the lower extremities. In the athlete this pathology occurs most often in the form of an injury. The study of this interrelatedness of human motion is known as biomechanics.

A thorough knowledge of biomechanics as it relates to the lower extremity is vital to both the sports podiatrist and the shoe manufacturer. For the podiatrist, this knowledge enables him to understand the mechanism of the injury and therefore able to properly treat it. For the shoe manufacturer, this knowledge makes possible the design and construction of a specialized sport shoe, suited to the wide range of motions the lower extremity goes through during a particular activity. The close relationship of biomechanics and the design of athletic footwear is critical to maximizing the efficiency of the athlete and minimizing the possibility of injury.

For an athlete any injury, regardless of its severity, is the most feared thing that can happen to him. An injury can cause an athlete to lose valuable time from a training schedule, or even force an early retirement from the particular sport altogether. Sports injuries can be easily categorized in two ways: 1) acquired, 2) inherited. The acquired injury is a direct result of involvement in the sport; a twisted ankle, for instance, or a broken bone. The inherited injury is not truly an injury. It means that the athlete has an inherited biomechanical abnormality which may predispose a possible injury while participating in the sport.

A recent survey by a leading American running magazine indicated that the entire lower extremity is subject to injury to varying degrees. Chapter 8 has succinctly described the major foot motions: pronation and supination. If either of these motions becomes excessive a potentially dangerous situation results. An imbalance develops between the agonist and antagonist muscles. The body attempts to compensate for this imbalance by increased stimulation of muscles, tendons, and nerves. The result is that the athlete is now functioning with weakened and fatigued tissues. Consequently the chance of injury has increased. It must be asked whether athletic shoes have any effect on the wearer with respect to foot and lower extremity sports injuries.

Sporting shoes today are designed for a variety of purposes, depending on the activity. The most common of these are:

1. support
2. protection
3. accommodation of foot injuries
4. balancing of foot abnormalities
5. shock absorption
6. increased traction.

If the shoe is poorly constructed, then the athlete will already be predisposed to possible lower extremity injury. This predisposition is heightened if the athlete has any biomechanical abnormalities. The selection of the correct shoe will often aid the performance of the athlete. It may make the difference between winning and losing. More importantly, a properly designed and constructed shoe will help to protect the athlete from both external and internal forces which may lead to injury.

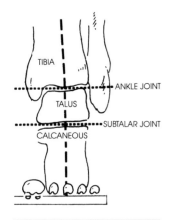

9-1. Criteria for the ideal "normal" foot and leg.

TIBIA

ANKLE JOINT

TALUS

SUBTALAR JOINT

CALCANEOUS

THE NORMAL FOOT

Before the abnormal foot and its relationship to injuries is discussed, the criteria for a normal foot must be known and understood. According to the basic principles of podiatric bio-mechanics of Dr. Merton Root, normal is "that set of circumstances whereby the lower extremity and particularly the foot will function in such a manner that it will create no adverse physical or emotional response to the individual as long as it is used in an average manner, in an average environment as dictated by the needs of society at that moment."

A "normal" foot is the ideal rather than the average. The following is the criteria for the normal (ideal) foot:

1. The calcaneus is parallel with the leg and perpendicular to the supporting surface.
2. The plane of the forefoot (metatarsal heads) is perpendicular to the calcaneus and parallel to the supporting surface. All five metatarsal heads lie on that surface.
3. The ankle joint must be able to dorsiflex at least eight to 10 degrees.
4. There are no external forces from the leg to the foot in any of the three body planes causing it to dorsiflex or plantarflex, adduct or abduct, invert or evert.

THE ABNORMAL FOOT

A discussion of the bony abnormalities found in the abnormal foot must include the following:

1. Metatarsus adductus, a transverse plane abnormality in which the metatarsal bones are pointed inward relative to the rear foot producing a "C" shaped foot.
2. Forefoot varus of forefoot valgus, a frontal plane deformity of the forefoot in which it is either inverted or everted on the rearfoot respectively.
3. Subtalar varus (the most common osseus abnormality of the foot) or subtalar valgus (relatively rare), in which the frontal plane of the subtalar joint is either inverted or everted on the leg respectively.
4. Equinus (more commonly called talipes equinus), a boney abnormality of the ankle in the sagittal plane which causes an inability of the ankle joint to allow the foot to dorsiflex on the leg at least 10 degrees. This deformity affects the midstance phase of the gait and midtarsal joint of the foot.

Two other abnormalities which exist above the foot yet influence foot function are tibial varum and tibial valgum (bowleg or knock knees), and limb length discrepancies. The leg length

9-2. *Top:* Supinated foot—rigid with high arch (side view), heel swings inward (rear view); *Center:* Rectus foot—stable with moderate arch (side view), heel and lower leg aligned (rear view); *Bottom:* Pronated foot—low arch (side view), heel swings outward. (Courtesy of *TENNIS* magazine; Illustrations by Diane Teske Harris.)

differences may be functional (caused by excessive pronation of more than 12–15 degrees), structural or a combination of both. The one common denominator which ties most of the above-mentioned inherited abnormalities together is the resultant compensatory pronation which occurs in most of these problems. As a result of this abnormal pronatory motion, injuries do occur in the various areas of the foot (toes, forefoot, arch, rearfoot and ankle), leg and knee.

One of the best methods of treatment which the podiatrist employs is the use of foot orthoses. By definition, these are orthotic devices or appliances that support the foot in a neutral and functional position. In essence, it rebalances the abnormal foot. In most cases with judicious use of these orthotics most of the symptomatology produced by these inherited abnormalities has been greatly reduced and very often eliminated. The orthotics are used as a treatment in conjunction with the proper exercise strengthening/flexibility regimen and also with the proper selection of athletic shoes.

The acquired injuries are for all intents and purposes self-inflicted. That is, they are a direct result of participation in a particular sport. This type of injury can be equated with an industrial accident. A specific object or movement results in a definitive injury to a specific part of the body. In the case of the athlete, it's often the lower extremity.

When an athlete pushes the body beyond its physical limits, a stress reaction in the form of an injury occurs at the weakest segment in the body. This situation is termed the "overuse syndrome". It is standard practice to interchange the terms overuse and underconditioning. Overuse syndrome is a direct causative factor of the acquired injuries.

For simplicity, we will divide the acquired injuries into areas: 1) the thigh-hip area, 2) the knee, 3) the leg, 4) the ankle and 5) the foot. The farther up the leg and away from the foot the structures are the less effect the athletic footwear will have on them. Therefore this discussion of the interrelationship of the shoes and athletic injuries will be confined to the area from the knee to the foot.

The next few sections will list the various anatomical parts which are subject to trauma, possible etiological factors and various treatment methods and shoe modifications used to alleviate and often correct the problem.

INJURY STATISTICS	
KNEE	25%
ACHILLES TENDON	18%
SKIN	15%
ANKLE	11%
HEEL	10%
ARCH	8%
HIP	7%
CALF	7%
HAMSTRING	6%
FOREFOOT	6%

9-3. Injury Statistics.

TOES

Although they are among the smallest of the various anatomical structures of the foot and leg and also one of the most neglected, they are prone to many injuries, some of which may be incapacitating. Nail problems, such as ingrown nails (onychocryptosis) and black toe nails (subungual hematoma) are most prevalent. These problems usually result from repeated trauma of the toe against the toe box or tight-fitting shoes across the toe area. In either case the matrix (nail root) or nail plate has been damaged, thereby resulting in some nail deformity. A sufficiently high and wide toe box, a shoe that is properly lasted for the foot, and preferably a square toe (rather than a pointed toe) would reduce the incidence of injury.

Corns (heloma dura) are areas of hard skin (hyperkeratosis) formed on the tops of the toes at the joints or knuckles. They result from the toe joint rubbing the inside top of the toe box. If the toe is bent, as in a hammer toe, then the knuckle becomes more prominent and a corn usually results. A high toe box (and a proper shoe fit) usually eliminates this problem. Surgical correction, a simple office procedure, will easily correct the hammer toe. The application of store-bought corn pads or lamb's wool will protect the area. Fractures and soft tissues inflammation of the toes may result from someone stepping on the foot or from a hard object striking the foot. Standard medical therapy is employed to aid healing. If the sport requires one, ensure that the shoe has a rigid and therefore protective toe box.

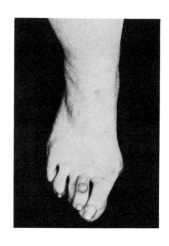

9-4. This picture clearly demonstrates the presence of a bunion (hallux abductus valgus); hammertoe on the second toe with concomitant corn; and a hammertoe fourth digit.

FOREFOOT

(For the purpose of this discussion, forefoot will refer to the metatarsal area or the ball of the foot.)

Blisters. Blisters are a direct result of friction. Blisters may be produced by a shearing force between skin layers or by the skin rubbing against the sock lining of the shoe. Refer to the section on "Basic Foot Care" for the treatment of blisters. Applying a piece of moleskin or zinc impregnated adhesive tape to the blister affords relief. A shoe which has a cushioned sock liner such as Spenco® is also helpful.

Calluses. Calluses are areas of hard skin found on the plantar aspect of the foot. Like corns, calluses are friction-related. They usually occur directly under a metatarsal head. Abnormal pronation is one of the major factors in producing calluses. A shoe which incorporates a cushioned sock liner will decrease the callosity thickness. Some shoe manufacturers incorporate Spenco® insole or anatomically contoured foot beds or other forms of compressible shock-absorbing friction-reducing material. An orthotic device, prescribed by a podiatrist, worn inside the shoe will eliminate the excessive pronation and therefore greatly reduce the callus and its build-up. A pre-molded contoured sock liner or foot bed is the shoe manufacturer's version of a soft orthotic. A proper lacing pattern on the shoe will create a more stable foot and thereby reduce, and possibly eliminate, any shearing between the foot and the shoe.

Metatarsalgia.
Metatarsalgia is a generalized term meaning forefoot pain. This is usually indicative of biomechanical imbalances, over-pronation in particular. Metatarsalgia may also refer to a pain in the metatarsal phalangal joint area. Some of the possible causes are: 1) a thin foot pad, 2) excessive pressure on the heads of the metatarsal, resulting from mechanical imbalances, 3) capsulitis (inflammation of the capsule around the joint) resulting from overuse of the joint or excessive pressure on the area and 4) interdigital neuromas. A proper lining and a flexible forefoot in the sole of the shoe will offer great relief from metatarsalgia.

If the correct shoe girth, or last, is worn, the chances of cramps in the forefoot are eliminated and so is the pain. If pronation is the problem, then an orthotic is the treatment of choice. Many running shoes have an external pronation control device built into the shoe. In many cases, it will be enough to control normal pronation.

Sesamoiditis.
Two small little bones (sesamoid bones) are located under each big toe joint. They act as a fulcrum for the muscles that pass over them. Because of their location, they are excessively prone to injury. Landing hard on the area will produce pain and inflammation. Many times an imbalanced foot will result in excessive weight distribution on this area. Again pain will result. If poor biomechanics is the cause than orthotics may be prescribed by the podiatrist. If, however, poor shock absorption in this area is producing the sesmoiditis, then a shoe which has excellent shock absorbing properties must be worn to protect the area and prevent future problems.

Interdigital Neuroma.
Interdigital neuroma is not a true injury. It is a thickened nerve which is located between two metatarsal heads, normally the third and fourth. Excessive pronation or pressure from the shoe are prime causes of its formation.

As the foot pronates, the adjacent metatarsal heads compress the nerve which courses between them. This process continues intermittently. The end result is a thickened nerve which produces a characteristic pain. A simple office surgical procedure may be the treatment of choice. The athlete will be able to return to his or her sport within three weeks after this office procedure.

Stone Bruises. A stone bruise results when the foot lands heavily on a hard object. The athlete should be certain that the footwear has adequate forefoot protection and cushioning in the sole and sock liner to prevent this from occurring.

Tendonitis. Tendonitis (inflammation of a tendon) may affect any of the tendons that pass over either the plantar or dorsal aspect of the metatarsal joints. This injury is usually sustained either from an overextension (such as hyperextension or hyperflexion) or from an overuse syndrome (such as compensation from abnormal pronation). Tendonitis may also occur if the toe box is not protective enough or the forefoot of the athletic shoe is not flexible enough. A podiatrist or orthopedist should always be consulted as to the diagnosis and treatment of the aforementioned problems.

The cutaneous nerves which provide sensation to the skin lie just below its outer surface. Their location makes them vulnerable to compression and/or entrapment. Nerve compression is a direct result of wearing irritating or tight fitting shoes. Ski boots and ice skates are the two major types of athletic footwear which produce this problem. Surgery, or some other inflammatory process (such as an injury), usually produces a fibrous band around the nerve. Injections or surgical intervention is the treatment of choice for this problem.

Bunions are not considered a frank injury. Consequently they will be discussed in the section on "Basic Foot Care."

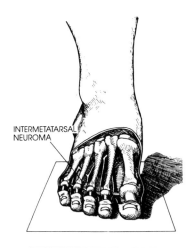

INTERMETATARSAL NEUROMA

9-5. Intermetatarsal Neuroma most often found in the third interspace. The neuroma is in fact a fibrous envelope around the nerve.

ARCH

The foot has two arches, a longitudinal and a transverse. This section will discuss the injuries associated with the longitudinal arch, which is the concave portion on the medial aspect of the foot. The shape and integrity of the arch is maintained by a strong plantar ligamentous band—the plantar fascia. It arises from the plantar aspect of the calcaneus and inserts into the area of the metatarsal heads. This ligament is extremely prone to injury—either strain or partial/complete rupture. If the plantar fascia becomes inflamed (plantar fasciitis) then the athlete cannot perform to his/her capacity. Weight bearing becomes in some cases excruciatingly painful. If the athlete is cursed with an abnormally pronated foot or excessively flat foot (pes planus), then he or she becomes susceptible to a plantar fascial strain. An athletic shoe which is constructed with a proper shank support will afford some protection.

Some footwear, especially running shoes, incorporates a compressible arch pad or "cookie". The various shoe companies either state or infer that this "cookie" will help control pronation. How can a thin compressible piece of material control the foot when up to three to four times body weight passes through it during the gait cycle? Sometimes these arch pads cause blisters or pressure pain because of their improper placement within the shoe in relation to the foot. Like other injuries which are a direct result of abnormal pronation, plantar fasciitis due to mechanical imbalance is best treated with an orthotic device, either rigid or semi-rigid. If the fascial strain is a direct result of an injury, then relief may be obtained by taping the foot, or employing the various over-the-counter arch supports. These supports, like the prescription orthotics, are slipped into the athletic shoe. A sports wedge or a varus heel pad in both shoes may also be of some benefit. Flexible flat feet may be prone to fascial injuries. Consequently, the athletic shoes should have a good supportive shank and arch.

HEEL

The heel is one of the most often traumatized parts of the lower extremity in sports-related injuries. In any running sport, such as field or court sports, at least three times the normal gravitational force passes through the heel and its associated structures. These tissues are subject to tremendous force. If the athlete lands on the heel from a relatively high point, the calcaneus is subject to possible stress fractures. The shoe should therefore have a sturdy, shock-absorbing heel area. This will also reduce the incidence of bone bruises to the calcaneus.

Plantar Fascia. The plantar fascia originates its attachment to the plantar aspect of the calcaneus, and that area is consequently extremely prone to injury. If the plantar fasciitis is confined to the tendonous junction a local bursitis (an inflammation of a fluid-filled sac), periostitis (inflammation of the bone covering) or tendonitis may occur. These problems may be the eventual consequence of abnormal pronatory stresses, or they may result directly from an athletic injury. An orthotic will usually prevent the problem in the first case. A varus heel pad or sports wedge placed in the shoe may also offer some symptomatic relief. To prevent injury a good shanked shoe with a shock absorbing heel is required.

If the plantar fasciitis persists, a bone spur will eventually develop. This spur is basically a shelf of bone which has been produced by long-term intermittent pressure at the bony-tendonous junction. The spur grows out from the existing bone. If a spur develops various treatments may be used to eliminate the problem. These range from heel cups (made of plastic or rubber), or foam pads with a cut-out hole, to orthotics (rigid and semi-rigid) and ultimately to surgical removal. It has been found that a reasonably sturdy yet flexible forefoot in the shoe greatly reduces the stresses which pass through the plantar fascia—calcaneus complex.

Children. Children are not immune to injuries. The heel is a prime area of trauma from athletics. The calcaneus has at least two growth centers (apophysitis). When trauma occurs the heel becomes tender and the child experiences pain when weight is placed directly on the heel. Rest is the best treatment with possibly the ingestion of a few ASA to relieve some of the pain and to reduce swelling. Athletic shoes cannot prevent calcaneal apophysitis from occurring. However, with the addition of a firm yet shock-absorbing heel area in the shoe, the injury incidence may be greatly lessened. The insertion of heel cups of foam rubber or either expanded PU or EVA into the heel area of the shoe normally provides some shock absorbing properties and therefore lessens the reactive forces which pass through the calcaneal area.

Bursitis. Often a localized bursitis will develop either between the calcaneus and Achilles tendon (retrocalcaneal bursitis) or between the skin and the Achilles tendon (subcutaneous bursitis). Usually the injury is caused by an irritation of the post aspect of the calcaneus—Achilles tendon unit with the shoe's heel counter. This may be the result of 1) an ill-fitting shoe, 2) a poorly padded heel counter or 3) excessive heel motion. A properly fitted shoe together with a well-padded heel counter, sometimes called Achilles-tendon padding (ATP), will most often eliminate the prime cause of the bursitis. Some athletic shoes have incorporated higher than normal ATP on the assumption that the higher heel horn offers greater protection. This assumption is highly questionable. An excellent feature that has been introduced recently is the Achilles tendon notch. This is simply a design feature cut-out to better accommodate the Achilles tendon, especially when the foot is plantar flexed.

The Achilles tendon. The Achilles tendon is the strongest tendon in the body. The posterior aspect of the calcaneus is the attachment point for this tendon. If the athletic shoe has poor forefoot flexibility or an excessive bias-cut heel, this will increase the strain. Eventually a local tendonitis may occur, bounded by an area approximately 5 cm. above the tendonous attachment to the calcaneous. Achilles tendonitis is almost always a tri-plane injury. A low heel elevation in the shoe may also be a contributing factor to this tendonitis. As in other types of overuse injuries which are a result of excessive pronation, orthotics are most beneficial.

Hagland's Deformity. This is an acquired deformity. The back part of the heel bone forms small irregular bumps usually between the Achilles tendon and the heel bone. This problem is still referred to as "pump bumps" since it most often plagued women who wore dress shoes with hard unyielding counters. When shoes, either running or dress, rub against these bumps, they become painful and swollen. This constant rubbing and pain occasionally stimulate extra bone growth in the area. Most athletes who are afflicted with this problem are tall with high arched feet. They also tend to have a tighter Achilles tendon than normal. To prevent irritation, a shoe with a well padded Achilles tendon pad (ATP) should be worn. Heel lifts can be worn to elevate the foot in the shoe and reduce irritation. Stretching of the Achilles should also be down. If biomechanics are the prime corrective factor, then a pair of orthotics from a podiatrist will most likely eliminate the pain and irritation by controlling the side-to-side motion of the lower ankle and upper foot areas.

ANKLE

This section will discuss ankle sprains and a condition called the tarsal tunnel syndrome. An ankle sprain may either be an "inversion sprain" (which accounts for more than 75 percent of all ankle injuries) or an "eversion sprain". The former occurs when the foot turns in, or inverts, relative to the leg. Sports involving walking, running or jumping frequently cause this injury. The latter is incurred when the foot turns out, or everts. Jumping sports may precipitate this injury. If an athlete is prone to any form of ankle sprain, he should ensure that his athletic shoes have a solid heel counter. A moderately flared heel will greatly benefit the runner. Athletic shoes worn for court or field sports may offer some increase in stability if they are highcut rather than lowcut. Hockey skates and alpine ski boots offer ankle support but they also must be flexible enough to ...normal foot and leg motions to occur during those sports. Boxing shoes are cut high strictly for fashion. There is no functional importance to their height. Tapings, various shoe wedges and orthoses are all employed to varying degrees in the treatment and prevention of ankle sprains. Adidas developed a therapeutic boot expressly to speed-up the rehabilitation period for athletes suffering ankle strains. The boot has adjustable ankle strapping to accommodate inflamed tissue as well as braces that help transfer foot pressure directly to the tibia and fibula thus bypassing the ankle joint to a great degree.

The classical tarsal tunnel syndrome is not a frank injury. When it occurs in conjunction with sports activity an overuse syndrome is usually a concomitant feature. The athlete with elongated feet is more apt to be afflicted than the athlete who does not have pronated feet. The tarsal tunnel syndrome is an impingement and compression of the major nerve (posterior tibial nerve) as it courses under the medial malleolus. Either trauma or abnormal pronation causing excessive pressure of the overlying structures will usually initiate this problem. Tapings, sport or heel wedges, or orthotics are all used to treat or prevent this condition. An athletic shoe with a solid heel counter will aid, to some extent, the control of pronation and thereby indirectly help prevent the development of the tarsal tunnel syndrome. Likewise shoes with elongated medial counters or external pronation control features may help prevent this condition.

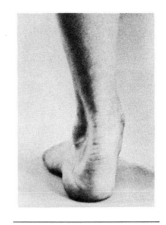

9-6. A severely pronated foot as viewed from the rear.

LEG

There is a direct relationship between the proximity of the various parts of the lower extremity to the foot and the incidence of injury as it is related to athletic footwear. Consequently the leg, knee, thigh and hip are less affected (in decreasing order) than the foot and ankle. The next few sections therefore briefly mention the types of athletic injuries which may occur to these anatomical parts and indicate, when applicable, how shoes may play a role.

Two major injuries affect the leg's soft tissue: trauma and bone fracture. The soft tissue injury and its associated pain is commonly referred to as shin splints. This is a non-specific term which normally indicates pain in the lower leg precipitated by activity. It can occur in any sport and is usually associated with a change of footwear, an inflexible forefoot in the athletic shoe, an increase in jumping or a change to harder playing surfaces. Many of the court and field sports are associated with shin splints.

Inflammation of the tendons (tendonitis), muscles (myositis), and/or bone covering (periostitis) may be the cause of the leg pain. Most of the shin splints are, however, a direct result of an overuse syndrome of these structures, secondary to abnormal pronation. Hence the previously mentioned modalities such as heel pads, varus wedges and orthotics are usually employed. If tibial varum condition is a pre-existing factor, the athletic shoe should be fitted with a heel-to-toe midsole varus wedge in order to neutralize the bowing of the legs. A podiatrist or orthopedist should first be consulted before any shoe alterations of this nature are undertaken.

If the shin splint pain is persistent for at least a three to four week period, then the possibility of a stress fracture should be considered. X-rays will indicate the presence of such a fracture. All athletic shoes should have adequate shock absorption qualities in both the forefoot and heel area to lessen and dampen the ground reactive forces. A flexible forefoot will also decrease the strain in the leg muscles, in particular the anterior muscle group. Posterior shin splints may be related to excessive arch scoop in the shoe.

Compartment Syndrome. There are seven muscle compartments in the leg, each tightly wrapped by a tissue covering called fascia. If an injury to one of these compartments/muscles occurs, inflammation results. Fluid then begins to accumulate, leading to increased pressure within the compartment. If allowed to continue, both nerve and blood supply becomes severely compromised, various symptoms from numbness, coldness, pins and needles and exquisite pain are produced. This is a medical emergency. Surgical release of the fascia, thereby relieving the pressure is the only treatment.

KNEE

The knee joint is the largest joint in the body. It functions only in the sagittal plane, allowing flexion and extension. Any other motion is abnormal and usually results in injury. The component parts which comprise the knee joint are the adjacent ends of the femur and tibia, the patella (knee cap), the thigh muscle (quadriceps), specialized cartilage on the upper end of the tibia (meniscis), and the muscles and ligaments that provide external support. Chondromalacia (softening of the cartilage), runner's knee, tennis knee, jumper's knee, and biker's knee are the various terms which have been used to describe pain in and around the knee joint. If the shoe tread offers either too little or too much traction (leverage) then the knee may become traumatized. Some of the running shoes were initially designed with an excessively flared heel. This eventually produced knee problems because of the increased stability provided by the wide heel. Dr. George Sheehan, a noted sports cardiologist, has mentioned on many occasions that one of the best ways to treat "runner's knee problem" is by treating the foot. The principle behind this statement is that abnormal foot pronation eventually leads to overuse knee injuries. Rebalancing the foot and eliminating the abnormal pronation is the treatment of choice. Prescription orthotics have been used most efficaciously in treating overuse knee problems. A shoe which has a solid heel counter will offer some control over pronation but should not in itself be the sole means of treating abnormal heel motion and therefore indirectly treating knee problems.

Converse's innovation of linking the outsole directly to the upper heel counter by rubber extensions on both medial and lateral sides has been claimed to be successful in helping overuse knee problems.

THIGH AND HIP JOINT

Cramping and strains of the various muscles may occur as a result of participation in sports. The hamstrings (posterior thigh muscles), quadriceps (anterior thigh muscles) and gluteals (hip muscles) are the three major muscle groups in this area. Fractures and dislocation may also occur. Prompt medical attention should be sought for treatment of these injuries. For all intents and purposes the construction of the athletic shoes usually is not a precipitating factor in these injuries. However, peroneal muscle spasms and lateral column pain may be caused by any over-pronation contour used to excess on shoes.

The remainder of this chapter will concern itself with the various sports categories and the shoes that are used in each. The various sports-related injuries and their relationship to athletic footwear will be mentioned. It will also discuss the numerous foot aids, appliances and the assorted features which are incorporated into the shoes. A complete list of the various sports will be found in the individual chapters discussing the specific sports categories.

TRACK AND FIELD SPORTS

Jumping—Most of the injuries associated with these sports occur as a result of landing on the foot from a height. Fractures, bone bruises, soft tissue strains and twisted ankles are the normal types of injuries. Adequate heel padding and heel-cups are desirable features in jumping shoes. Refer to the sections on the foot and ankle for shoe selection.

Throwing—Most of these sports are a mixed-motion action involving both lateral and forward motions. Blister, arch strains and ankle sprains are some of the most common injuries. Refer to the forefoot, arch and ankle section for shoe selection.

Running—Most of these sports involve a single plane motion of the foot and leg; all function within the sagittal plane. The various foot, leg and knee injuries previously listed in this chapter may befall an athlete participating in these sports. The athletic shoe should be properly constructed, with adequate heel counter, good forefoot flexibility and platform, sufficient sole traction and adequate toe box, to reduce the risk of injury. Running on softer track surfaces does not require a great amount of underfoot padding, however, off-track running on hard surfaces certainly does.

FIELD SPORTS

Contact—The most important aspect in these sports is adequate shoe traction. Different athletic footwear has specific cleats for the different playing surfaces. The cleats increase the foot's traction, providing a more stable foot to leg relationship. As a result, knee injuries become more prevalent. Heel control and protection are provided by a shoe which has a rigid heel counter. Rigid toe boxes give protection to the toes and forefeet. Ankle protection is likewise increased by the use of well padded high or semi-cut uppers.

Non-Contact—Like the contact sports, these sports involve ballistic motion (throwing, kicking), forward motion (running) and lateral motion (change of direction). Blisters, fractures, sprains and general foot and leg fatigue are common to all field sports. "Turf toe", a strain on the first ray caused by the toe jamming in the shoe, has been a common injury since the introduction of artificial surfaces in playing fields. The shoe features discussed earlier, under the "Foot and Leg" sections, should be incorporated into the footwear.

COURT SPORTS

Team and Racquet—All sports thus classified involve lateral motions and sudden stops and starts. These movements primarily cause blisters and ankle injuries. Shoes should have adequate shock absorbing and friction reducing qualities. A rigid heel counter is mandatory. The sudden changes of direction predispose the foot to nail problems and fatigue. "Tennis toe" like "turf toe" is caused by a jamming of the toe, usually the great toe, against the end of the shoe. The toe box must provide sufficient room for the toes, and the shoes must provide proper support in both the forefoot and arch areas.

WINTER SPORTS

Skating—Both figure skating and hockey require a boot that affords the maximum ankle support yet is supple enough to allow adequate foot and ankle flexibility. Hockey skates must also provide protection to both the foot and ankle. Ankle injuries are the main concern in the design of the shoe.

Skiing—Alpine (or downhill) skiing boots are designed so that the boot, ski, binding, foot and leg function as a unit. The boot must therefore be form fitting, offer superb support and still provide comfort. Blisters and cramping are common injuries from ill-fitting boots. Boot top fractures of both the tibia and fibula are common. Better engineered boots have resulted in a decrease in the incidence of ankle injuries. Rear entry boots offer more relaxed walking motion when off skiis.

Cross-country Skiing—This sport is much akin to running or jogging with respect to the biomechanics and associated injuries. The shoe is designed to accommodate the ski, keep the foot warm and dry yet still be flexible enough to allow the required foot motions to occur. Refer to the "Running" section for a discussion of the typical injuries.

Ski Jumping—In this sport, most if not all of the foot and ankle injuries are traumatic in nature. The ski boot should be protective enough around the heel and ankle to reduce the risk of injury, yet must be adaptable enough (as with the other ski boots) to permit the normal foot movements. Due to impact forces generated upon landing, a fully anatomical and well padded foot bed is a desirable feature.

OUTDOOR SPORTS

These sports are either walking/hiking related or running related. Refer to the "Running" section for the sports related injuries and recommended shoe features. Most of these shoes should have thicker than normal soles to protect the foot against various terrains. *One additional note*: Although not directly related to injury, due to the vast amounts of time, conditions and weather involved in outdoor activities such as hunting, a high degree of protection and waterproofing can save more than discomfort from the elements.

SPECIALTY SPORTS

1. **Gymnastics**—no shoe related injuries. This sport is generally performed barefoot or with a simple ballet-type slipper.
2. **Weightlifting**—no shoe related injuries. The shoe functions primarily to provide traction and support to the foot.
3. **Boxing**—no shoe related injuries. The shoe provides traction and some support.
4. **Wrestling**—no shoe related injuries. Traction and support are again the prime shoe functions.
5. **Fencing**—this is a forward motion sport with short quick steps. Due to the amount of toe and medial side drag in this sport, a correctly reinforced upper helps to prevent blisters and soreness. Refer to the section on "Racquet Sports" for associated injuries and shoe design considerations.
6. **Shooting**—no shoe related injuries.
7. **Bowling, Lawn Bowls, Boccie, Croquet**—no shoe related injuries.
8. **Golf**—blisters and walking-related injuries afflict golfers.
9. **Equestrian, Bicycling, Motorcycling, Motor Racing**—These sports are performed in a sitting position. The shoe acts strictly as a protective device. In cycling a specialized stiff-shanked sole is mandatory in preventing injuries and soreness to the plantar surface of the foot. No shoe related injuries.
10. **Roller Skating**—quite similar to figure skating. Shoes have attached wheels instead of blades. Otherwise requires the same basic features.

11. **Sculling, Rowing, Yachting**—these sports require a shoe with excellent traction. Well ventilated uppers prevent the possibilities of constantly wet, cold feet. A safety tip: Easily removed footwear using a casual style or Velcro closures can save more than a foot injury. In water related sports the probability of going overboard is always present. No shoe related injuries.

The following list describes shoe features, various aids and appliances and the anatomical sections which they affect.

FEATURES	ANATOMICAL SECTIONS
Toe Box	toes and nails
Uppers (for comfort)	toes, nails and forefoot
Forefoot Padding	forefoot and leg
Flexpath	forefoot and leg
Shank	arch, heel and forefoot
Sole Tread	ankle and heel
Heel Wedge	heel and Achilles tendon
Flared Heel	ankle and knee
Bias Heel	heel and Achilles tendon
Heel Padding	heel and leg
Varus Wedge (pronation)	leg, knee and Achilles tendon
Ankle Padding (comfort)	ankle
Arch Cookies and Support	arch and heel
Heel Cups (alignment)	heel
Moleskin	forefoot and heel
Insoles (Orthotics, Foot beds, Spenco® Wedges)	arch, heel, leg, and knee

It should be noted that many of the injuries listed in this chapter may require extensive physiotherapy, oral medications, injections or even surgery to be properly treated. A podiatrist, orthopedist or sports physician should be consulted if one suspects a potential serious injury.

Finally, to paraphrase an athletic shoe manufacturer: "People stop playing sports because it hurts or they get hurt. Keeping people from getting hurt makes good sense both business and medically speaking."

"A *man may find his happiness and the poets'*
praise . . . in triumph by the prowess of his
running." Pindar, The Pythian Odes, 498 B.C.

10

WALKING AND RUNNING MOTIONS RELATED TO SPORT SHOES

Makers of sports shoes have designed and adapted shoes to accommodate the particular walking and running motions that occur in many sports. The lateral movements of each sport—jumping, weight transfer and kicking—also affect footwear design. Still, under the major headings of walking and running we will be able to discuss the basic motions affecting the design of shoes for many sports.

WALKING

As the saying goes, you have to learn to walk before you can run. In many sports you have to walk before you can play. In fact the cycle of the walking gait lies at the core of many sports. Thus an analysis of the walking cycle is essential to understanding much athletic movement. The complete walking cycle goes from heel contact on one foot to the next instance of heel contact on the same foot. In walking the foot is a platform for propulsion. Weight transfer occurs off a base that is primarily neutral in terms of the body's center of gravity.

THE SUPPORT PHASE (PRONATION)

The first motion of the supporting phase is the heel strike of the forward or extended leg. The foot acts as a mobile adapter during this phase of walking, accommodating two forces exerted against it, a horizontal, forward force against the ground and a vertical, downward force against the ground. The horizontal, forward force slows the body's forward motion. The vertical, downward force controls the downward fall of the body's center of gravity. The body's center of gravity moves forward, directly over the supporting foot. The foot rocks forward and goes through the midstance position onto the ball of the foot where the propulsion phase can begin.

THE PROPULSION PHASE (SUPINATION)

The propulsion phase, or toe off, starts at midstance in a neutral position. The body's center of gravity moves ahead of the supporting foot. The foot changes from a flexible adapter to a rigid platform or lever. Vertical force is reduced to zero as horizontal force is exerted backwards. The horizontal or propelling force reaches maximum at the ball of the foot. The body's center of gravity comes to a forward position, the horizontal force becomes greater than the vertical force and the body is propelled forward.

THE SWING PHASE

The swing phase of the walking gait begins immediately after the push off the ball and toes of the foot. All joints of the lower extremity are involved. The hip rotates and lifts the thigh. The knee flexes and raises the leg and foot enough to clear the ground. The foot passes the center of gravity under the body. The knee begins to extend and the hip continues to rotate and extend. This slows the leg. In walking, the heel makes contact with the ground before any other part of the foot because the ankle is slightly flexed dorsally.

The heel tilts inward (is inverted) during the swing phase. Motion originates at the hip and the center of gravity moves forward with the momentum of the leg. When the heel of the same foot again hits the ground the cycle is considered complete and the weight-bearing or support phase starts again. One foot is always in contact with the ground in walking.

The contact phase takes up 25 percent of the gait cycle, the midstance phase takes up 50 percent and the propulsion phase the final 25 percent.

A foot is in contact with the ground 60 percent of the time during the walking gait; the other 40 percent of the time it is in the swing phase. The cycles of the two feet overlap about 25 percent of the time, the percentage decreasing as the speed of the gait increases. There must be some degree overlap to keep one foot in contact with the ground at all times, otherwise the gait is not considered to be walking.

RUNNING

Every runner has an individual style which is peculiar to that individual as is one's fingerprints or footprints. In addition, running plays a central role in many sports. Hence most athletic footwear must accommodate the running movement while also taking care of other sports specific needs.

The one-foot-in-contact-with-the-ground rule distinguishes walking from running. In running the gait cycle follows the same phases of support: midstance, propulsion and swing. However, the body's center of gravity is moving forward more quickly, and in an attempt to catch up, the legs move faster to keep the body from falling forward.

Running is essentially a series of collisions with the ground. As the runner's foot strikes the surface, his or her muscles contract and ultimately reverse the downward velocity of the body.

Different emphases occur in the gait cycle at different running speeds. In slow running or jogging the gait phases are similar to those in walking. The heel lands first, the foot goes into the midstance and the propulsion phases and finally into the swing phase. In faster running, the landing or the support phase may occur simultaneously with the midstance phase.

In fact analysis has shown that most runners do not land only on the heel; some part of the lateral or outside edge of the foot also strikes the ground. Many runners land flatfooted, the whole foot meeting the ground at the same time. Some runners even land on the ball of the foot and rock backwards. In terms of foot strike, running is not a continuous forward motion but a series of forward and backward pressures on the foot. This type of information is obtained from pressure patterns and force platforms in the study of the basic biomechanics of running (see Fig. 10-2).

Rearfoot control can be defined in running shoes as the relative ability of a shoe to limit the amount and or rate of subtalar joint pronation immediately following foot strike. A normal amount of pronation is helpful in decreasing peak pressures experienced by the foot and leg, but excessive pronation can be harmful if it produces increased internal or medial leg rotation causing stress in various bones and soft tissue.

In sprinting, the propulsion phase becomes more important in lifting the body's weight from the vertical force to the horizontal force during propulsion or toe off. In all running motions, as well as in jumping and hopping, both feet are off the ground at some point. As running speed increases, the flexion of the knee increases and the swing phase speeds up and increases the speed of the forward leg. Stride length also increases as the

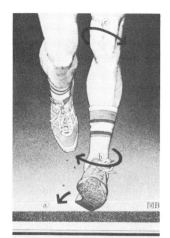

10-1. Running: (a) Upon landing, the foot moves from a supinated position through midstance to a pronated state. (b) The subtalar joint is shown in the motion of adduction. (c) The knee joint is shown in the motion of abduction.

10-2. Close-up of force platform at University of Oregon.

swing phase quickens until stride length and leg speed reach an optimal balance. Beyond this point either leg speed or stride length go out of balance and speed is lost. Hip flexibility helps to increase stride length at full stride. Runners tend to lean forward because their centers of gravity are forward.

WALKING SHOES

The activities for which there are particular walking shoes are hiking, race walking and exercise walking. Exercise walking falls somewhere between hiking and race walking, but deserves individual discussion nonetheless.

10-3. Lightweight hiking shoe. Leather and Cordura upper, steel shank, EVA midsole, Vibram outsole, Gore-Tex waterproof lining.

Hiking Boots. Hiking boots are used on rugged terrain. They are normally made of split or full-grain leather or suede (rough in or rough out), have leather linings and are highcut above the ankle for support. Lighter weight shoes made of nylon with leather supports and trim are also popular. The predominant cut or design is an overlapping ski-boot closure with D-rings or eyelet hooks.

The upper of a hiking boot should be water-resistant. There should be very few seams for both comfort and waterproofing. Those seams that do exist should be sealed or waterproofed. The construction method can be Goodyear welt, lock stitch (Norwegian welt), cement (with fake welt) or direct injection molding. The soles are heavily lugged for traction and durability and are made of rubber PU or PVC compounds; the soles of some of the less expensive shoes are made of thermal rubber mixtures. Heavily cut soles may be screwed through the midsole for extra strength.

There should be some flex in the forepart of the shoe at the main metatarsal joint. Other features of a good hiking boot include a good heel counter, a padded top line and ankle area, a smooth or seam-free lining, an ample toe box and ample girth. A wedge or a heel with a shank is also a necessary feature. Hiking boots are medium to lightweight shoes, weighing between 500 and 800 grams.

One last note—do not confuse hiking boots with climbing boots. Climbing boots have inflexible soles and thicker grade leather uppers.

Race Walking Shoes. Soles may be up to 13mm (½ inch) thick. Heels must not exceed the sole thickness by more than 13mm (½ inch). (Track and road racing, 20 km and 50 km). These specialized shoes are closely allied to track training shoes and to track running shoes. Lightness is important, and they normally weight 250 grams or less. A fine suede or nubock leather, perforated for ventilation, or a nylon upper is used. The shoe is U-throat cut and has conventional lacing. A reinforcing, nylon-tape lining or outside girth support is a desired feature. The shoe is made with a jumbo or full girth track shoe last with a form-fitting, symmetrical-cut quarter.

The construction is the same as that of a track shoe (tubular moccasin), but to obtain the necessary rigidity at toe off and to maintain good flex in the forefoot, a cement-lasted thin half insole is added to the forepart of the shoe. A minimally sized firm midsole is the choice of most race walkers. Outsoles are made from a flat rubber carbon or gristle gum rubber with possibly a reinforced wear pattern. The heel area of the shoe is extremely important as much stress is placed on the heel on landing. Heels made of firm to hard EVA or PU foam are preferred by most race walkers. A rigid heel counter is essential, and a well supported heel with outside or inside counter for reinforcement is desirable. Normally a squared or straight heel is preferred to a bias cut at the back of the shoe (see fig. 10-3).

Exercise Walking Shoes. Comfortable street shoes such as moccasins or casual footwear have traditionally been used for exercise walking, but influence from the training shoe market has been strongly felt of late. Logically, a good training running shoe will have many features desirable for walkers—lightness, a flexible forepart, a comfortable, soft upper and a shock-absorbent sole. Analysis of walkers' needs, however, has led to two new, specialized designs.

For the country walker, who traverses rugged terrain or rougher roads, there is a lowcut version of the hiking boot. The shoe differs from the traditional hiking boot in its lowcut-oxford ankle height, and in its lacing system, a U-throat or lace-to-tip design with conventional lacing. A reinforced counter design or additional outside heel stabilizer helps to control the angle of the shoe at heel strike on uneven surfaces.

10-4. Leather exercise walking shoe with blown polyester/PU sole and heel unit.

There is also a new walking shoe designed for the suburban walker. Basically it differs from the training shoe in its use of leather as the material of the upper, weight is not the major consideration and leather gives better protection and support. A well designed, adequate toe box and internal soft support system are important comfort features. The sole is also different, with a wedge or half-wedge incorporated into its design (see fig. 10-4). The tread is a smoother, lower-profiled, more conservative herringbone than the waffle tread of a training shoe.

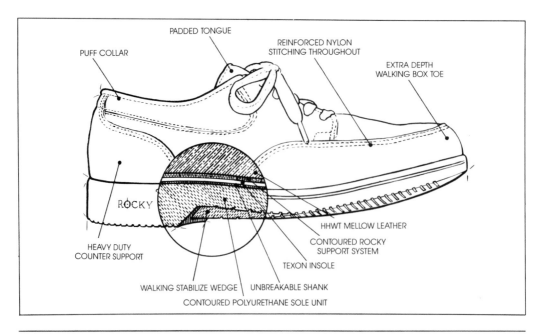

PADDED TONGUE

PUFF COLLAR

REINFORCED NYLON
STITCHING THROUGHOUT

EXTRA DEPTH
WALKING BOX TOE

ROCKY

HHWT MELLOW LEATHER

CONTOURED ROCKY
SUPPORT SYSTEM

HEAVY DUTY
COUNTER SUPPORT

TEXON INSOLE

WALKING STABILIZE WEDGE   UNBREAKABLE SHANK

CONTOURED POLYURETHANE SOLE UNIT

10-5. Drawing showing features of a "Rocky" exercise walking shoe.

10-6. Walking shoe—Leather and Cordura upper, asymmetrical counter, Gore-Tex lining, Vibram infinity outsole.

10-7. Track spike with adjustable attachments.

Many outersoles have a rocker profile to encourage the natural roll of the foot in the walking motion. This feature also helps reduce excessive flex in the forepart of the upper.

A walking shoe should have a firmer rearpart landing area than many running shoes have. The bias-out, or up-swept heel of many running shoes does not offer the landing platform needed by walkers. Most walkers also benefit from the use of a more resilient compound in the rearpart of the shoe. A heel height of 10–15 mm (⅜–⅝ inches) is recommended for exercise walking to aid the correct walking motion and reduce over-stretching.

RUNNING SHOES

Special running shoes exist for use on tracks, on roads, or cross-country (orienteering).

Spikes. Track shoes are the ultimate tool in human efforts to run faster. The lightness of the shoe saves energy in the swing phase of the gait. It makes possible maximum leg stride within the quickest gait. Fine grade leather with high tensile strength, such as kangaroo leather, is preferred. Leather of this grade also gives good support and transpiration to the foot. Nylons are also used extensively in the uppers of track shoes. Linings of nylon tape are used on the better models of the shoes for additional strength and support.

A U-throat lacing design is the lightest and strongest, but velcro closures have been used quite successfully. Velcro allows better adjustment across the total girth and waist of the shoe.

Tubular moccasin is the most common construction, offering lightness, wrap-around support and flexibility in the forepart. The lightness and support are wanted features, but a flexible forepart is not advantageous to the track runner because of the importance of propulsion or toe off in track running. The answer is a nylon spike receptacle plate that is attached as the outside sole in the forepart.

This plate not only holds the spikes but also serves as a rigid platform off which a runner propels him or herself off the ground with maximum vertical force.

Most track runners, even those who run the longer distances, land on the forepart, or the midstance and forepart of their feet rather than on their heels. Little body weight is placed on the heel in sprinting. All landing and propulsion are carried by the mid and forepart of the foot. That is why track shoes used in the faster, shorter races have only enough padding at the heel and plantar fascia to prevent bruising.

A slight wedge in the shoes worn in longer races gives more torsional rigidity and support in the shank area. Torsional rigidity is sometimes sacrificed in track shoes for lightness; however, many runners, especially fast bend runners (e.g. 200m racers) find they need some support. Track shoe lasts are form-fitting to hug the foot at the heel, waist and girth. The last is semipointed in the toe area to hold the toes from splaying under the pressure of landing and take off.

Flats. It is estimated that there are about 30 million runners in the United States alone. Therefore it is not surprising that since the 1970s more biomechanical and shoe-design study has been done in this area than in all other areas of athletic footwear combined. The starting points were a general purpose training shoe and a specific, flat marathon shoe (a track shoe upper with a thin, flat sole). By now just about every performance and injury-reducing consideration has been made, and designs are as close to optimal as is scientifically possible. Improvements in today's much tested shoe will probably come from the introduction of new materials and in the reduction of weight. The designs of running shoes have finally caught up to the development of concrete.

The features most required in a running shoe used for long distance training on hard road surfaces are:
- shock absorption in the heel
- shock absorption in the forefoot

10-8. Training flat with rear part stabilizing system.

10-9. Training flat with outside heel stabilizer.

10-10. Road running training shoe with reflective material in heel.

- flexibility in the forepart
- rigidity and stability in the heel counter area
- torsional rigidity in the waist or shank
- lightness; under 300gm for training
- traction for different surfaces
- abrasion (wear resistance of the sole)
- a good fit for support comfort
- excessive motion control and alignment

Today's good training shoes meet all these criteria.

Long distance running shoes have become increasingly specialized. The need to satisfy the individual requirements of runners has reached the stage where companies publish charts segmenting the market. They have models for forefoot-landing and lighter runners, for heavier runners and heel strikers, and for motion control and over pronating runners. Running shoes have evolved to the point that most major running shoe manufacturers produce models for specific foot types, gait patterns and running styles. This degree of individualization may soon carry over to other major segments of the athletic shoe market such as tennis or basketball.

Although the list of features needed in a running shoe is vast, most manufacturers, having gone through the critical, open analyses and brand comparisons of the 1970s, are using the same criteria in the development and production of their running shoes. Uppers are usually made of soft or breathable mesh nylon because of the lightness of the material. Even the uppers of highcut jogging boots are now being made out of nylon. Eyestays are usually made of suede and are reinforced. Suede is also used in the toe and in the outside heel pocket for better support and adherence to the sole. A rigid heel counter is essential because most runners land heel first like walkers. The fit of the shoes depends largely on the last and design (see "Chapter 7" for more details on fit).

The soles of training shoes have seen the greatest changes both in materials and shape. Again for lightness, PU, EVA and MCR are used. All these materials have good to excellent shock absorbency, and are built into prefabricated heel wedge and midsole combinations or into polyurethane unit versions. The shape of the sole is wedged from heel to toe, with approximately a double thickness from the heel to the flex point at the metatarsal joints in the forefoot. Heel height is increased because a thick heel is needed for maximum shock absorbency. To offset and stabilize the increased height, a flared heel is preferred. A square-edged heel, which reduces Achilles strain, seems to be preferred over bias or extended-cut heels.

Traction and abrasion are best obtained with a gum or

carbon rubber outsole cemented to the heel wedge and midsole. Tread design should offer good traction on roads and softer surfaces and have a wear pattern following the normal, major wear areas of the shoe (see fig. 10-11). To obtain the best traction on loose or open-terrain surfaces, such as those encountered in cross-country running, a deeper sole tread is desired. On smoother, harder surfaces such as on pavement a lower-profile sole tread offers better stability and adequate traction.

Microcellular outsoles have become popular on training and racing flats because of their extra shock absorbency; however, there is little evidence that expanded rubber or EVA outsoles improve the performance outsoles in any way other than shock absorbency. These materials have no extra value in terms of lightness, flexibility or traction. Combination outsoles that combine expanded compounds and synthetic, carbon-based rubbers in the wear areas are also available from some specializing manufacturers.

Microcellular soles should have surface areas larger than those of SB rubber for best wear. SB rubber soles can be produced with a thin base and with traction-stud designs, and they should last longer than microcellular outsoles if correctly reinforced. It should also be noted that correctly placed traction studs push up into the soft midsole or wedge material. Therefore they not only aid traction on softer surfaces but tend to act as mini, independent shock absorbers on harder surfaces.

The tubular, moccasin design, California sock or three-part insole of a flat lends flexibility to the forepart of the shoe. Flex-path outsoles and wide flex-eyestay designs also aid flexibility. The combination of a thick midsole with a wedge should give adequate torsional rigidity. Some designs, particularly PU, injected or unit soles in which an insole is not used (as in slip lasting) can be improved with an added insole board/sock lining combination.

Marathon and Road Racing Shoes.
Racing flats are used for longer distance races on roads and some cross-country surfaces. Some longer track events are sometimes also run in this type of shoe. These models have evolved from track shoes to obtain maximum efficiency in terms of weight, flexibility, support and traction. Most racing flats are built on modified track shoe lasts. They have narrow fitting heels, adequate girth for foot expansion and semipointed toe shapes for good rigidity at toe off. Weight saving is important in these models in order to conserve energy uptake by using less rotational kinetic energy. Racing shoes are approximately 25 percent lighter than regular training flats. Occasionally more radical designs such as Nike's

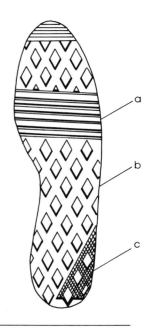

10-11. Typical Tread Pattern: (a) flexion bars; (b) heel reinforcement for stabilization and wear; (c) traction stud design.

10-12. Alberto Salazar—marathon champion and world record holder from 1981 to 1984.

10-13. Nike's Sock Racer, above, and Ligne 7's CF Racing Flat.

sock racer and Nöel Ligne 7 toe spring racer are introduced after experimentation with leading runners.

Uppers are usually made from soft taffeta nylon or nylon mesh. Lightweight pigskin or kangaroo leather are used for support in the heel counter pocket, the eyestay, the tip and foxing on the quarters. Strong, lightweight poromeric materials are sometimes used instead of leather. The uppers are often lined with thin nylon tape or tricot for additional support in the girth and for longitudinal support. The upper of a racing flat is basically similar to that of a spiked track shoe.

The soles are normally much narrower than the soles of training shoes. They are shaped to the contours of the plantar surface of the foot. These soles have a narrow, scooped waist area, a more pointed toe, a thinner, continuous midsole with less heel lift and possibly more toe spring. These modifications, again, save weight and allow the runner to feel the surface on which he or she is running. Although these features mean less rear and forefoot shock absorbency and inferior sole wear than one can get in a training shoe (statistics indicate 500 to 1,000 miles of maximum wear), many racers prefer the positive feel and weight advantage in competition. The lower, thinner midsole and heel wedge also reduces the possibility of compression set or sole lean.

Tubular and slip-lasted moccasin uppers give excellent flexibility and good flex path for more energy at toe off. Heel counters are rigid or semirigid to avoid foot drift and to keep the foot in proper alignment in the shoe on landing impact. Good torsional rigidity is also desired to compensate for any twisting of the foot on uneven surfaces.

Cross-country and orienteering shoes. These rough terrain running sports require certain features in a shoe that are not found in track or training shoes. This is the one area of running shoes that has probably been most neglected by manufacturers. The shape of the upper is basically that of a track shoe last. Nylon or polyurethane-coated materials are the predominant material for the uppers to allow water transpiration during running. Nylon, as we have already discussed, is also soft and light. Although it is by no means universally held, the accepted sole for cross-country running is a unit molded rubber sole with small rubber studs, similar to a soccer sole but with more studs and finer profile.

10-14. Rob Sweetgall cares for his feet during his 50 state solo trek across the U.S.A.

"Inside quite a few shoes there are bare feet
struggling to get out."
John Burroughs (1837–1921)

C H A P T E R **11**

BASIC FOOT AND SHOE CARE

The foot is the most used, abused and neglected part of the body. It has been estimated that a pair of feet take the average person far enough to circle the world two or three times. That's a lot of use. Most athletes quickly realize the need to maintain healthy feet, regardless of the cost. They usually administer self-aid to their individual pedal problems. When the problems become unmanageable and painful, a podiatrist is usually sought out.

One of the prime edicts of proper, basic foot care is to wash both feet daily. This may seem obvious but many people only rarely consider it. The hands and face are deligently cleaned, why should the feet be slighted? After all they are kept within a confined space, subjected to stresses and perspire with little chance to breathe. It is important to give your feet free air time. They deserve a little attention every day.

BAREFOOT VS. SHOES

Some sports have not required or traditionally ban footwear in competition. The obvious examples are swimming events and the marital arts such as Judo. However, in all other sports the protection offered by shoes against the elements is basic. The protection evident against the shearing forces caused by the friction of skidding and twisting as the foot pushes off a surface has been well documented by biomechanist. As practical evidence anyone who has attempted to perform any sport barefoot where shoes are normally worn can testify to the blisters and bruises to which feet are subjected.

11-1. Abebe Bikila winning 1964 Olympic Marathon—this time in shoes. He won the 1960 race barefooted.

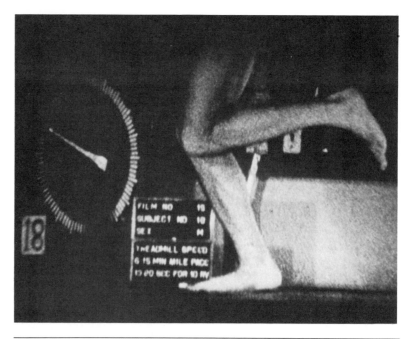

11-2. Barefoot running test on force platform in Nike's gait laboratory.

Still there are certain sports where individuals have successfully competed barefoot. Long distance running is probably the most common. Among the most famous barefooters are Abebe Bikila who won the 1960 and 1964 Olympic Marathons; Bruce Tulloch, British & European 5,000 m and 10,000 m record holder in the 1960s and 70s and most recently middle distance world record holder Zola Budd.

In addition to the traction advantages offered by shoes the other benefits are arch support, heel lift (which reduces strain on the achilles tendon and calf muscles), underfoot cushioning and shock absorbency. Protection from the elements in winter and outdoor sports as well as ballistic protection in contact sports is obvious.

However, where participating athletes successfully perform in bare feet they claim certain advantages which in discussing shoes we should at least consider. In running, for example, it has been proven by researchers that wearing shoes encourages the feet to pronate more than running barefoot. This is basically caused by wearing the midsole unevenly, thus causing the rigid anchored heel counter to tilt and sink, causing the foot to roll inward. A more elementary advantage in running is the energy saved by reducing the mass required to be moved by the legs, in other words reduced weight.

No standard shoe last however well researched and designed can fit any athlete perfectly. However slight the misfit this may effect the natural motion of the foot. Probably the greatest concern should be the swing or inflare of the last which causes instability as the outfanning foot supinates to the outside of the shoe.

Place kickers in American football often kick the ball barefoot with the dorsal area of the foot (soccer style) claiming they have a better feel for the ball. They do, however, rely on a studded shoe on the opposite or plant-foot for traction.

In summary although it is probably comfortable to occasionally run barefoot on sand or grass it is wiser to follow the other 99.9 percent of athletes and wear shoes on a regular basis.

HOT FOOT AND FOOT ODOR

Hot foot and foot odor can be helped by using good quality absorbent, antibacterial insoles and wearing shoes that breathe well. Various insoles available today have many airholes and an activated form of charcoal that reduces odor. The temperature inside a running shoe on pavement can reach 125 degrees F on a hot day. It is advisable to wear hose that is made of good quality, absorbent, natural fibers, preferably a 60/40 blend of cotton and wool. Fitted socks (toe and heel) are preferable to the tubular style.

Many athletes wear two pairs of socks. If two pairs of socks are worn, the inner pair should be a cotton/wool blend, the outer may be either a cotton/wool blend or nylon. In running sports, the outer pair usually serves as a layer of friction protection; that's why the outer layer should be the thinner of the two layers. Winter sports, on the other hand, normally require a thin inner layer and thick outer layer. For maximum breathability and evaporation of perspiration look for hose with a minimal amount of nylon content. Be sure you wear the same amount of hose when you try on sports shoes as you wear when you participate in the sport.

Before you put your shoes on, smooth out all wrinkles in your socks. This will help prevent blisters. Change socks as often as possible, especially during athletic events. Do not reuse socks a second time without washing them. Perspiration salts make socks stiff and misshapen when dry. Wrinkles become more eminent and fungus infestations more likely.

Two conditions, diametrically opposed to each other, may affect the skin of the foot. Excessive perspiration results in "wet feet" or hyperhidrosis. An inability to produce and/or deliver sweat to the surface of the skin, or anhidrosis, is the other malady.

The probable causes of hyperhidrosis vary from metabolic disorders, to an increase in anxiety to a hot, humid environment, to the use of poor quality socks. Initially upon being bothered by abnormal perspiration, an athlete should change socks at least twice a day. Daily alcohol rubs together with the use of a commercial foot powder usually help to keep the condition under control. Medical help may be needed if the condition persists or cannot be controlled through self-administered foot care.

The causes of very dry skin may include a blockage of the sweat ducts to various allergies or disease states. Hydration of the skin through the use of assorted moisturizing creams is usually the treatment of choice. Sometimes a medicated cream prescribed by a doctor is required.

Bromhidrosis or foul-smelling sweat frequently occurs on the foot. Sweat itself is odorless; however, it promotes bacterial growth, and the resultant odor is a product of the bacterial decomposition of surface protein debris. The best treatment for this problem is the daily use of an antibacterial soap together with the regimen employed to combact hydrosis.

The ultimate challenge in eliminating foot odor in recently worn shoes has been met by the P.D.Z. Corporation. By placing shoe-size pouches of a mineral called clinoptilolite, with its remarkable absorbent qualities, in shoes overnight, they reversibly absorb/desorb moisture and amonia caused by perspiration, leaving the inside of the shoe dryer and fresher.

CORNS AND CALLUSES

Corns and calluses were discussed in "Chapter 9." Suffice it to say here that one should never use razor blades, paring or pen knives, scissors or anything of the like to cut away the thick skin. Bathroom surgery can result in local infections that can become incapacitating.

The regular use of a pumice stone will help reduce callus build up. A podiatrist should be sought to treate severe conditions. Lamb's wool, cotton, moleskin and nonmedicated pads may be used for temporary relief. If you use pads make sure that they are placed around and behind the lesion rather than directly on top of it. This will disperse the pressure away from the sensitive spot. Examine your shoes to make sure they are the proper size and width. Also check for irregularities within the shoe that may be causing excessive pressure points.

NAIL CARE

Cut all toe nails straight across making sure that the sides of the nails are the same length as the centers. If toe nails are properly cut, problems at the corners of the nails will be markedly reduced. Get podiatric care and treatment if you suspect an ingrown nail.

There are two other problems that can befall the toe nails of athletes, black nails (subungual hematoma) and fungus of the nails (onychomycosis).

The problem of black toe nails was thoroughly discussed in "Chapter 9." If bleeding and pain occur under the nail, see a podiatrist. The podiatrist will drill a hole in the nail plate. The treatment is painless. Blood escapes through this hole and the pain will be eliminated.

Fungal infection of the toe nails (onychomycosis) in athletes is normally the result of an invasion of a fungus similar to a yeast infection into a nail. The fungus very easily infects any traumatized tissue such as toes and nails on the feet of runners. The best self-treatment that can be recommended is preventative: simply control the length and thickness of your toe nails. Podiatric treatment is better. Treatment may include an oral antifungal and/or a topical antifungal medication or complete removal of the nail and matrix (the nail growth plate).

ATHLETES FEET

"Athletes feet" (tinea pedis) is truly a misnomer. It is not confined to athletes. The term is a collective one that implies an infection of some part of the foot. The infection is most often localized to the interspaces of the toes, usually between the fourth and fifth. Tinea pedis is caused by the same type of fungal organism that infects toe nails. The most common organisms are *trichophyton rubrum, trichophyton mentagrophytes, epidermorphyton floccosum and candida albicans.* Symptoms vary according to infecting organism. One form may produce an oozing, macerated area with pus secondary to bacterial involvement. This type of fungal infection is primarily confined to the interspaces and is first noticed in the fourth interspace. Skin fissuring, pruritius (itching) and discomfort are synonomous with this form of infection. The other major form of fungal infection produces a chronic, often painless scaling. It usually involves the soles of the feet and extends up the sides. At first glance it may appear as though moccasin slippers are on the feet.

While fungal infections are the most common pedal skin afflictions, they account for only about one-third of all skin diseases that affect the feet. Many times tinea pedis is misdiagnosed as a nonfungal disorder. A podiatrist or dermatologist can easily confirm a correct diagnosis and then initiate the correct treatment for the specific invading organism. The treatment regimen may include soaking the foot daily, applying a topical medication or taking an oral antifungal medicine. Socks should be changed twice daily. No synthetic hose should be worn, only cotton. Shoes should be dusted daily with an antifungal powder and given at least 24 hours to dry between wearings.

BLISTERS

Blisters are a result of abnormal friction as was explained in "Chapter 9." They may be the most common of all foot problems. Improper footwear and mechanical abnormalities of the feet are the two major causes of blisters. By definition a blister is the separation of the upper most layers of the skin, creating a void into which clear or bloody fluid flows. A "hot spot" or discrete area of burning is the first indication of potential problems. Activity should be stopped when a hot spot is sensed and the area should be inspected and treated appropriately. Moleskin, vaseline or extra socks may help to reduce the friction. A full blown blister should be first cleansed with either soap and water or alcohol. Gentle pressure will force the fluid to be dispersed to one side. Puncture the area a few times with a sterile needle and the fluid can then be gently expressed out. The removal of fluid normally eliminates any pain. The top layer of skin should be left intact since it still functions. It will eventually peel away. Antibiotic cream and a bandaid, with possibly the addition of moleskin or an aperture pad are then placed over the area of the blister.

Blisters can be avoided by wearing proper socks and shoes that fit properly. Cotton or cotton/wool blend are the best hose to wear since they absorb perspiration and thereby reduce friction. "Wick Dry®" is another type of sock that can be worn. It enhances evaporation of perspiration and maintains a drier and warmer foot. The material of this sock is an olefin/nylon composition; even though it contains nylon, it is an excellent choice for any winter, court or running sport. Some commercial shoe inserts such as SPENCO® also can help reduce friction.

WARTS

Warts (verrucae) are caused by a virus and are commonly misdiagnosed as corns or calluses. They are contagious and usually infect adolescents. They may be single or multiple ("mosaic warts").

Warts differ from calluses in two major ways. Warts have a clearly defined border and a central dark brown or black spot. This spot is a small blood vessel and nerve. Warts are more painful than calluses, causing a lateral, pinching pressure than direct pressure. Calluses do not give the pinching sensation and are usually not painful.

"Common warts" (verruca vulgaris) occur on the top of the foot and look like a cauliflower. "Plantar warts" (verruca plantaris) occur on the plantar aspect of the foot and grow into the skin because of the pressure of weight bearing. Many different treatments for warts are available. Usually the application of various acids or surgical removal are the best therapeutic methods. Podiatrists can quickly determine if a lesion is a wart or a callus then take the necessary steps to treat and erradicate it.

BUNIONS

Bunion is the Greek word for turnip. The bunion is a bump or enlargement on the medial aspect of the foot at the joint of the great toe. This area can become inflamed. There are three main reasons for bunion formation: pronated feet, hereditary influence and the long term use of ill fitting shoes. Pronation is the most prevalent of these reasons. It produces a muscular imbalance around the joint of the big toe. Adolescents and the middle-age group are most affected. If left untreated, bunions will eventually produce arthritic changes in the involved joint, create discomfort and make the foot look ugly. Athletes who participate in kicking sports subject themselves to the possibility of bunion formation and traumatic arthritis.

The importance of getting early treatment for a bunion cannot be emphasized enough. This is especially true for the young, still-growing athlete. Professional help should be obtained if a bump or any deviation is noticed on the great toe joint. Redness over the area may be a result of ill fitting shoes, and appropriate measures should be taken to remedy this situation.

A "tailor's bunion" or bunionette is a protrusion or bump at the base of the fifth toe where it meets the ball of the foot. It is a prominence of the head of the fifth metatarsal without the deviation of the fifth toe. The name originated from the tailors who sat "Indian" style all day. Self treatment includes the wearing of a shoe wide enough to accommodate the bump. The nature of the shoe material will determine if that part of the shoe can be stretched to create a pocket for the prominent head. Placing half-moon pads around the lesion usually offers temporary relief. Surgery is the treatment of choice for a permanent solution.

SKIN INFECTIONS

Skin infections can be caused by penetration of a fungus, bacteria or virus. A break in the skin layer provides an excellent portal for the entry of an invading organism. Any systemic infections, such as gum infections, can also increase the susceptibility of the skin to an invading organism. If you have an infection then keep it clean. Wash it with antibacterial soap, hydrogen peroxide (37 percent) or alcohol and apply a sterile dressing. If red lines (lymphangitis), pus or drainage are present at the site of the infection, then seek medical care promptly.

The severity of a laceration can be deceiving. A small cut can bleed profusely while a deep one may bleed very little. Clean the area around a cut as soon as possible and apply direct pressure for at least two minutes. Immersing the cut in cold, running water can help clean it. Inspect the wound to determine the depth of the cut; also look at the edges of the wound. Seek medical attention if either seems abnormal. Medical help should also be sought if bleeding continues after the direct pressure is stopped.

This section on basic foot care has not been all inclusive. It should, however, have given you some basic rules of pedal care to follow. Get medical help if you are ever in doubt about a problem with your feet, or don't know what treatment to administer.

SHOE CARE

It is debatable whether a model or brand of athletic shoe can improve an athlete's performance. There are however certain criteria that athletic shoes should meet. These criteria affect all sport shoes of the same classification. They are discussed fully in the following chapters. Considering them will give you an excellent chance of selecting as good a shoe as possible for your needs. Even if it does not actually help to improve your performance, selecting the right shoe will ensure that your foot is properly supported and balanced.

Considering the right criteria when choosing a sports shoe at the very least will keep you from getting a shoe that could affect your performance adversely. Shoes play an important role in getting the maximum efficiency from your body's movements. They supply the protection, support and traction that permit the transmittal of kinetic energy through the body's center of gravity, through the lower extremities to the feet on to the ground. Shoes are the link between the feet and the various surfaces on which sports are conducted. Sport shoes are designed to enable the feet and lower anatomy to function at maximum efficiency by accommodating the biomechanical principles that govern the performance of the body. Moving on bad shoes is like driving a car with flat tires.

Maximum foot efficiency in any sport depends most importantly on correctly fitting the right shoe for the sport. Having the "best" athletic shoes also gives an athlete confidence. Sport shoes should protect the feet from abrasion and minimize the incidence of injury. They should adequately support the feet, ankles and legs and be flexible and shock absorbent enough to allow excellent performance.

The lightness of the shoes is important for best performance—obviously, it takes more energy to lift a heavier weight than a light one. However, weight can be overstressed, particularly in training or when peak effort is not required. Lightness, though important, is not more important than fit, protection, support, comfort and durability; it should not be the overriding factor chosen at the expense of others in the selection of a shoe.

Comfort and cushioning are also important considerations, especially when an athlete is subject to long periods of training or performance, or when unusual stresses occur as they do in skiing.

The durability of a shoe is more important from an economic standpoint than it is from a performance one. A sport shoe that performed well in all aspects but did not wear well would not be a popular sales item simply because it would need to be replaced often. Many professional or amateur athletes who receive free shoes do not in fact bother to consider the durability of a shoe. Many world-class tennis players, as well as players who just play a lot, need new shoes every two or three weeks because of abrasion and toe drag.

Torsional rigidity is the final consideration in selecting an athletic shoe. It is a desirable feature to have in many athletic shoes but it is often overlooked at time of purchase because it only becomes noticeable through performance or after the shoe has been broken in. An easy test for torsional rigidity is to hold the shoe by the sole at the toe and heel and twist the heel from side to side. The harder it is to twist the shoe, the more rigid the shoe is in the waist or midpart.

SHOE SELECTION

Sports shoes have become so specialized a market that there is now almost a shoe for every sport and a model of shoe for every type of performer. Still there are many shoes that are called "multipurpose" such as the multistudded shoes sold for use in field sports. The specific purpose for which the shoes are intended should be kept in mind when these shoes are considered. Remember that designs and constructions vary greatly from shoe to shoe even within the same sport.

It is commonly known that esthetics have long ruled over function and common sense in the design of regular footwear. The basic contours of the foot have been overlooked. In sport shoes, the functions of the feet have not played a secondary role to fashion. This is one reason training flats have become so popular as street shoes: they feel good. Even with all the specialization and the variety of brands, there is no one ideal shoe for all sports under all conditions.

Here is a list of features to consider when you select your athletic footwear:

WEIGHT—important but not critical in training; comfort, cushioning and support should not be sacrificed for lightness in most instances.

FIT—critical; fit depends on the shape and design of the last (see chapter on "Fitting").

FLEX PATH—important on all shoes where the foot is required to bend at the metatarsal joints.

FLEX TORQUE—important where lateral movement or plantar surface stability is needed; a shank is used in heeled shoes to support the foot between the heel of the shoe and the forepart of the sole; a wedge sole provides continuous support through the midpart of the shoe without the need for a shank.

HEEL COUNTER—prevents heel drift and cups the heel for fit and protection; a rigid form is best, possibly one that is elongated on the medial side. Additional outside heel stabilizers may help.

UPPER MATERIAL—should be suitable for the particular sport; it can be protective and supportive or flexible and breathable.

UPPER LINING—should be suited to the requirements of the sport; most desirable characteristics include breathability, comfort, a padded ankle collar and a padded tongue; it should be free of seams; can have or be accompanied by inside tape supports, arch supports, heel cups, canted soles and insocks.

SOLING—important for shock absorbency, durability, traction and support; the main methods of building the soles of sport shoes are cement, built-up vulcanized, direct injection, Goodyear® welt, lockstitch and rivet.

LAST SHAPE (curved or straight), Toe Spring and Heel Lift—toe spring provides running ease, heel lift transfers the weight of the body onto the forefoot across the width of the forepart of the shoe.

ANKLE SUPPORT—highcut designs should be selected when they are necessary.

PRACTICAL DESIGN—design features include U-throat, lace-to-toe, derby, blucher, and adjustable width; the heel and fore-part of the sole should have suitable width for stability; the toe box should fit comfortably and protect against jamming the toes.

TRACTION OUTSOLE—should be made of the correct material and have the right profile (wear pattern) for the requirements of the sport, e.g., court shoes should have pivot points under the ball of the foot and running shoes should have reinforced heels for running on pavement.

SHOCK ABSORBENCY—in order to find the optimal amount of cushioning one must consider energy loss and transfer body weight, playing surface and support. Underfoot cushioning materials often take a "compression set" (compaction) after several hours of use, effecting the above criteria.

WEAR PATTERNS IN SPORT SHOES

There is no standard wear pattern for all sport shoes. However there are certain wear patterns that exist within four general classifications of sports shoes: running and walking, court sports, field sports and winter sports.

RUNNING AND WALKING SHOES

In slower running and in walking the "normal" wear pattern of the sole runs from the rear, outside heel, rolls toward the lateral girth and middle of the shoe to the medial girth or ball of the foot (see fig. 11-3). Any variation from this pattern may indicate an imbalance of the foot or the lower limbs.

Faster running places more stress and wear on the waist or arch area, the girth and the metatarsal push-off area. Many running shoes are reinforced or carry a heavier tread pattern in the major wear areas, which increases the sole wear of the shoe.

Larger profile tread patterns are generally better suited to rough or undulating ground where maximum traction is needed. Smoother, reinforced-wear, bar sole patterns are better suited to pavement and road conditions.

COURT SHOES

Court shoes, especially tennis shoes used on hard court surfaces, have a notoriously short life span. The wear patterns of court shoes normally show most wear in the heel, the ball of the

11-3. Typical sole wear pattern.

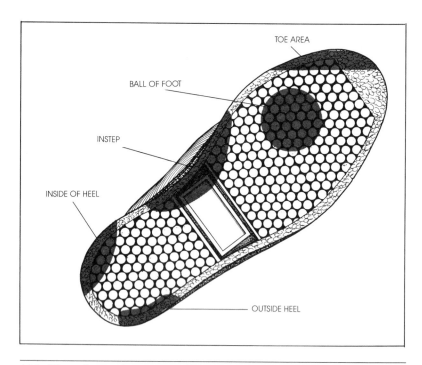

TOE AREA

BALL OF FOOT

INSTEP

INSIDE OF HEEL

OUTSIDE HEEL

11-4. Where do your shoes wear out? Toe area—A sure sign of a toe dragger. Get a shoe with a reinforced toe or change your serve. Ball of foot, instep, inside of heel— Any or all of these areas indicate an abnormally pronated foot or flat foot. Orthotics are a plus for this condition. Outside heel—A high-arched foot causes this area to wear out quickly.

foot and the toe area. Weight needs to be distributed equally on both legs and feet. The slightly forward position of the center of gravity places weight on the balls and toes of the foot. Because of the quick turning and lateral movements that occur in court sports, a wide sole with a flat or low profile will distribute wear better. Such a sole puts more surface area in contact with the court.

A pivot spot at the ball of the foot aides turning and puts more of the surface area of the sole of the shoe into contact with the court. The problem area in the wear of court shoes is located at the toe and front foxing. In racquet sports, players use their back leg for support and tend to drag the foot in their follow through after hitting the ball. Many players drag the toes of the back or trailing foot when they serve. Some court shoes even have reinforced medial vamps because players tend to stretch out the trailing foot in a sole-upwards position that drags the toe and vamp of the upper (see fig. 11-4). Shoe makers have experimented with molded-in inserts at the toe in efforts to reduce wear in this area. Prolific toe draggers will find leather, rubber and solid PU reinforcements for the toe area available, but there is nothing that has yet been devised that can eliminate the excessive wear that occurs in the toe area.

FIELD SPORTS

Most sports where the foot kicks a ball are played on a field. For protection, the uppers of shoes used in these sports are still predominantly made of leather. Sole wear on cleats and studs depends largely on the hardness of the playing surface. Front cleats or studs tend to be bias cut, or the shoe offers enough toe spring to clear the front studs when a player kicks. Play on hard ground surfaces requires the use of a stiff stud that is well buttressed at the base to keep the stud from breaking or wearing away quickly.

The studs and cleats of many shoes are replaceable. Rubber, replaceable studs for use on hard ground surfaces have been much overlooked because of the popularity of studs made with hard substances such as nylon and polyurethane for shoes used on soft ground surfaces. The popular rubber, PVC or PU molded sole of a shoe used for field sports has between 10 and 15 studs. Maximum cleat length is one-half inch. The cleated shoe distributes weight evenly on the plantar surface of the foot; it is the most comfortable shoe for use on hard surfaces.

Astroturf shoes are the latest descendants in the lineage of studded field shoes. They have smaller, more numerous studs and appendages for lateral and forward traction. Artificial turf is extremely abrasive, and the soles of shoes used on it do not last more than a few hours of playing time.

WINTER SPORTS

The sole of most types of winter sport shoes are not subjected to much wear. Ski boots, skates and snow shoes are attached to other surfaces and therefore do not directly touch the snow or ice. The leather uppers of winter shoes are normally subjected to much more wear and tear because of water absorption at the sole line and seams. Perspiration probably builds up worse in leather winter footwear than in any other kind because thick leather must be used to provide the rigidity needed and the thicker the leather the worse it breathes.

After use, boots should be opened up and allowed to dry thoroughly at room temperature. Good maintenance is essential (see ''Leather Care''). The blades of ice skates should be coated with oil or petroleum jelly to prevent corrosion. Skate runner guards protect blades when you walk on them off the ice but they should never be put on wet blades; for proper drying you should also, make sure you take the guards off when you take off the skates. Boot covers are available as well as blade guards. Be aware that the change in temperature between an ice rink and other surroundings can cause condensation to build up on the blades.

Downhill ski boots and skates are available in direct-injected plastic materials that are maintenance free. Leather skates and cross-country ski boots need to be well maintained to give maximum wear, comfort and support. Cross-country ski boots with injected soles are bonded better to the upper and are more waterproof. Generally, the fewer seams there are in a boot, the better the waterproofing.

OUTDOOR SPORTS

The shoes made for outdoor sports are generally very rugged and contain many protective features. Soles used in most outdoor sports are made from compounds especially formulated to withstand heavy wear and tear. Sole wear is not a factor as much as upper wear. Excessive heat and water, as well as the application of the wrong type of waterproofing treatments can drastically reduce the life span of a boot, especially one made of leather. Uppers not made of leather, such as molded boots, usually have few seams or joints and require little waterproofing attention. Oil-based products should be used on boots made with oil-tanned leather. In addition to keeping a seamed, leather boot waterproof, regular treatment of the leather will help to maintain its oil content; this will help keep the leather soft and water repellent. Chrome and vegetable tanned leathers with wax impregnation or treatment should be treated with wax-based or synthetic-based products. Chrome or silicone tanned leather should be treated with liquid silicone. Keep suede leather dirt free by brushing it and using a silicone spray.

To prevent water from penetrating through exposed seams and welts, a special welt seal application is recommended; this will also help to protect these areas against abrasion. Waterproofing products with a hydrophobic coating will allow the leather to breathe and vapor to escape.

GETTING YOUR MONEY'S WORTH

After going through the process of selecting and fitting the right shoe for the athletic activity of your choice, you will want to take a few simple steps to protect your investment. Generally, athletes, no matter their level of performance, want the best equipment they can afford. They make the logical assumption that the best athletes in the sport know and use the best equipment, and this hypothesis, whether true or false, is how standards of excellence are set for sporting equipment. If the world's number one skier uses skis that cost $600, bindings that cost $300 and boots that go for $450, it is reasoned, then his edge may lie in his ability to get everything out of the equipment that it has to offer, and what it has to offer is more than what other equipment can offer. There will always be customers who will follow his lead in the pursuit of their own personal bests. They will try to buy the best. Important in these efforts is understanding the materials, construction, and function of their equipment, and maintaining it after purchase so it works as it is supposed to. This line of reasoning applies to athletic shoes. Be it for prestige, confidence or improved performance, there will always be a demand for expensive, quality athletic footwear.

TAKING CARE OF YOUR SHOES

Athletic shoes are subjected to two types of wear, abrasion (wear and tear) and "aging". Aging is more a result of chemical processes than it is a matter of accumulated stress. A SATRA report stated that the primary causes of chemical breakdown and the consequent loss of comfort and esthetic appeal are friction, humidity, bacterial erosion, perspiration and heat. The aging of shoes can be appreciably delayed if the shoes are made with materials that have built-in resistence to corrosive bacterial erosion (there are sanitizing and antibacterial materials available that have this quality). Here are some suggestions that will help you to make your shoes last a long time:

- An athlete who practices or performs every day ideally should have more than one pair of shoes and switch pairs every day. The shoes should be opened fully between wearings and allowed to dry at room temperature for at least a day. This gives the shoes enough time to dry thoroughly between wearings, and should maintain their comfort and prolong how long they keep their shape.
- Shoes that are subjected to water or ice should also be allowed to dry at room temperature. Excessive heat or attempts to dry shoes quickly will adversely affect leather and suede materials, causing the shoes to crack, become stiff and loose flexibility.
- Shoes will retain their shape better if shoe trees or stretchers are inserted when they are drying or in storage. Stretchers made with absorbent coverings or materials will help shoes safely dry more quickly.
- Suede leather should be treated with a dry brush or

sponge. Suede sprays will help to revitalize reverse suede materials. Washing suede or bringing it into contact with water will cause it to crack or become stiff. Suede is a natural, reverse leather material and will tend to "bleed" into hose if it is not lined or backed.

- Leather can be smooth, chrome tanned or oil tanned. Chrome tanning is a process of removing all natural oil and replacing it with chromium salts. Oil tanning replaces the natural oil with vegetable oils. Chrome tanned leather can be treated and cleaned with a damp cloth, followed by an application of shoe cream, saddle soap (or shoe polish where applicable) or mink oil with a dry cloth. This will help to keep the leather soft and flexible.
- Unfinished or natural (vegetable) tanned leathers can be treated with mink oil, neatsfoot oil or dubbin.
- Waterproofing is improved by using dubbin or oil, silicone/ wax, sprays or creams. Leather boots and shoes subjected to water (such as cross-country shoes) have particular need for treatment with these substances.
- Nubock leather is a specially tanned, silicone-treated, soft leather. It is more absorbent than some other leathers and should dry without cracking or stiffening. Dry only at room temperature.
- Nylon materials, whether soft or mesh, are best cleaned with a damp cloth or soft brush. These man-made materials should not be treated with any creams, polishes or silicone solutions because it will block the pores of the fabric and reduce its breathability.
- Poromeric or rubber substrate materials (such as Kangoran) should be treated the same way as nylon.
- Canvas (twill, weave or mesh) is relatively easy to care for. It can be washed, but careful hand washing is better than putting them in a washing machine. The canvas doesn't mind the washer but some of the other materials in the shoe—terrycloth, latex rubber—may be affected by a continuous water soaking. Wash with a mild soap or soap flakes and a soft brush. Submerge the shoes only as long as you need to and dry them at room temperature.

If you do wish to put your canvas upper shoe in the washing machine, then make sure that the shoe's construction is vulcanized instead of cemented, which may be affected by the washer. Also make sure that there is no leather or suede in the upper—leather and suede definitely do not get along with washing machines. Take the laces out of the shoes and wash them separately in bleach, soap and water. Use the cold washing cycle of the washing machine. If you hang your shoes outside to dry, hang them from an eyelet; if you use an automatic dryer, set it at air dry instead of a heat setting.

Here's a tip that will help prevent dirt from getting into the fabric of the canvas: when the shoe is new or newly cleaned, spray the canvas with starch.

Vinyl is a plastic material that normally has a textile backing to prevent stretching. Vinyls should be wiped with a damp cloth. The use of oil or chemical-base agents on vinyls is not recommended as they can break down the PVC compound.

CARING FOR THE SOLES OF YOUR SHOES

There are many different materials that are used in the construction of the soles of athletic shoes. PVC, rubber compounds, polyurethane, nylon plastic-based compositions and leather all are used in the soles of sport shoes. In use many of these materials are subjected to water, mud and abrasive surfaces such as asphalt, concrete and artificial turf. Most soles are best cleaned with a stiff, dry brush; some can be put under a water tap and dried immediately with a dry cloth. The bottoms of roller skating boots, the wheels and wheel assemblies, should be wiped off after use to remove dirt and prevent the build up of grease and debris. Oils and chemicals should not be brought into contact with soling materials because they can cause the chemical breakdown of some compounds and lead to the deterioration of the soles.

Traditional, leather shoe constructions, such as Goodyear welt and nailed soling, were labor intensive, and the jobs of repairing and resoling shoes was commonly undertaken by local shoe repair services. The older style shoe cobbler, however, was not well equipped to attempt repairs on lighter weight, cement-soled and injected-sole athletic shoes. In the last decade resoling and repairing services specializing in running and court footwear have appeared in many parts of the western world. Prefabricated or built soles can be replaced basically by reheating the complete sole to soften the cement, and replacing the midsole, wedge or outersole with new material in the same cement method.

Tennis shoes can be "ground down" to the bare upper so that new soling with foxing can be attached to it. This gives the shoe a completely refinished sole. If this work is done well, the life of a shoe can be extended considerably. This resoling costs about one-third to half the cost of a new pair of shoes and should not have an adverse affect on the performance of the shoes. It can save money for long distance runners and tennis players, two groups of athletes notorious for burning out shoes. If soles are replaced, new sock linings or orthotic footbeds or supports should be replaced at the same time. And it never hurts to string a new pair of laces through a pair of shoes.

There are some minor shoe repairs, such as building up potential wear spots or worn down sole areas, that can be done at home. This type of work, along with the replacement of old insoles, will prolong the life of many sports shoes, especially for those who are rough on shoes like you incorrigible toe draggers out there. The work is done with one of the several sole-patching, plastic compounds on the market. These compounds are usually sold in tubes or glue guns. They go on the sole in a viscous state that is easy to spread then they harden as they dry. Outsole patching on running shoes can also be tackled in the kitchen but getting a professional resoling service to do the work is a better idea because they have the tools and the know-how.

Although it is not usually a serious problem, resoled shoes are rarely identical to the original shoe in balance, sole thickness or heel height. If you are concerned about existing foot or leg disorders, you maybe should think twice about competing in newly resoled shoes.

BREAKING IN SHOES

There are conflicting recommendations on whether athletic shoes need to be "broken in." Obviously, softer forms of foot-wear, such as soft nylon running flats, are initially easier on the feet than heavier sports shoes that must give more support, such as hiking boots, skates and ski boots. The recommendation of many manufacturers is to get the best fit you can, wear the shoes or boots for a few minutes in the store on carpeting and see if there is any discomfort or pinching. If you feel comfortable and have no second thoughts then the shoes should be ready for you to train in. To be safe, shoes that are to be worn in competition should be practiced or trained in first.

Hot foot and foot odor can be helped by using good quality, absorbent, antibacterial insoles and wearing shoes that have air holes for good breathability. Temperatures inside a shoe worn running on pavement on a hot day reach 125 degrees F—and the temperature inside a shoe worn on a hot day on artificial turf have been measured at a distressing 135 to 160 degrees F. Temperatures like these can cause feet to swell and perspire unnaturally.

You should also wear socks made of good quality, absorbent natural fibers. Hose that is fitted at the toe and heel is preferable to tube socks. Socks offering protection and comfort are being specifically designed for use in several sports. By using design features and experimenting with different thicknesses of material, sock manufacturers are also striving to come up with products that will help circulatory problems in athletic use. Socks should fit snugly. Those athletes who follow recommendations to wear two pairs of socks should wear an outer sock that is thicker than the inner sock. Of course when trying on a shoe, you should wear the same hose you will wear when you perform in the shoe. Shoes should be purchased late in the day to ensure a proper fit. The feet are swollen the most at this time and also simulate the foot size during the athletic activity.

One final note: When possible use a shoe horn to slip your foot into your shoes. It will help to save the heel counters from breaking down.

P A R T 4

• THE SPORTS •

"Citius, Altius, Fortius"—

"Faster, Higher, Stronger"
—The official International Olympic motto and the lifelong goal of Adi Dassler.

12

TRACK AND FIELD SHOES

From early childhood, humans display an affinity for physical activities, the most basic of which involve running and jumping. As children grow older, they take these activities beyond the normal boundaries of play and into the arena of highly competitive sports.

The ability to run faster or farther than another, or to jump longer or higher, becomes the sole object of the effort. In organized competitions of this kind, the athlete's attention is quickly drawn to his equipment, which he or she correctly perceives as a pathway to improved performance.

Track and field footwear is the most important part of the athlete's equipment. In terms of footwear, it may also represent the highest form of the art of shoe making. Of all types of athletic footwear available in the marketplace, track and field footwear is certainly the most diversified within one sport.

In categorizing athletic shoes, one normally discusses the various types such as field sports (with studs or cleats), court sports (indoor and outdoor court shoes), winter sports (including skiing, curling and skating), outdoor sports (from hiking to snowmobiling) and specialized footwear (the huge category that encompasses all other types).

Track and field footwear falls into this last category. However, because of the number of completely different events making up the sport of track and field, it's appropriate to devote an entire chapter to this sport and its shoes.

Track and field, or "athletics" as it is known around the world, consists of 20 events for men and 13 events for women, not including the various relays. These events can be further divided into the following disciplines:

1. Running (sprints, middle distances, long distances)
2. Hurdles (110 meter, 400 meter, 3000 meter steeplechase)
3. Throws (Shotput, discus, hammer, javelin)
4. Jumps (Triple jump, long jump, high jump, pole vault)
5. Decathlon and Heptathlon (Combinations of the above)
6. Walks (20 kilometers and 50 kilometers)

Obviously, the diversified shoes required by this sport demand much attention. Also, since track and field is a world sport that may attract more participants than any other sport (everyone has tried running at some time, and the world-wide jogging/running/fitness boom remains very strong), the sport is an extremely important one for major shoe manufacturers. In describing track and field footwear, one must investigate the demands placed on the shoe by the six major categories of the sport.

RUNNING SPIKES: SPRINTING SHOES

Anyone who has attempted to run on a soft or loose surface knows that optimal traction cannot be achieved with a flat soled shoe. The earliest attempted spikes date back to the Greek Olympic era in the eighth century B.C., which marked the birth of the "Olympic" concept by the Greeks. Metal nails were embedded into lightweight footwear to make the world's first track spikes.

Factory manufactured track spikes were introduced in England in the mid-1900s. With little improvement or sophistication, leather soled six-spike shoes (in the forepart) continued as a specialty traditional sport shoe in the hands of custom shoemakers in each industrialized country. By this time, it had been established that a "track spike" should have the following characteristics:

1. Lightweight
2. Optimal support
3. Maximum traction potential

It was considered that comfort and durability couldn't be achieved without sacrificing these three most important qualities.

Until the dawning of the biomechanical sport shoe era in the mid-1930s, the track spikes described above were the only ones known to the world. Then, just as cinder tracks were improved, it was realized that four spikes (15mm) in a sprint shoe offered the world's fastest humans sufficient traction on implant with less resistance at withdrawal. To aid forefoot stability and decrease dirt adherence to the sole, a nylon foreplate replaced the

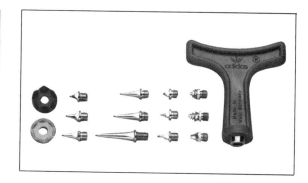

12-1. *Top left:* Evelyn Ashford—world record holder in the women's 100 meter sprint.   12-2. *Top right:* Spike variations, with spike wrench shown at right.   12-3. *Bottom left:* A track spike shoe used for a steeplechase event.   12-4. *Bottom right:* Renaldo Nehemiah—world record 110 meter hurdles from 1979–84.

traditional leather sole to create a more supple and tight-fitting track shoe. In the late 1950s came the invention of the replaceable spike, a major breakthrough. Shoes could then be used even after the original spikes had worn down. It took only a new set, easily inserted.

All track spike shoes must conform to certain specifications but these may vary for different events.

A maximum of six sole and two heel spikes is permitted; spikes must not project more than 25mm (1 inch) or exceed 4mm (0.16 inch) in diameter. Grooves, ridges and appendages are permitted on sole and heel. Soles must not exceed 13mm (½ inch) in thickness. Heel thickness must not exceed sole thickness by more than 13mm (½ inch) for walking events or 6mm (¼ inch) for all other events.

If there are more than six spike recepticles in the sole or more than two in the heel this is for optional adjustment; the spare holes should be filled with flat screws to prevent dirt from entering the tread receptacle.

With the advent of the synthetic or rubberized tracks in the mid-1960s, track spikes shortened to around 9mm and reverted to six spikes for better traction. The IAAF had to stipulate a maximum number and length of metal spikes mainly to prevent damage to synthetic tracks. With this ruling, and with shorter spikes in use, the few specialized track shoe manufacturers invented removable plastic "claws," which in conjunction with replaceable variable length spikes, give today's track shoes total versatility and adaptability for modern track surfaces.

The sprint shoe last is semi-pointed to prevent toe spread and the waist and heel are form fitting for a glove-like fit.

Full-length or two-piece nylon sole plates house the seven replaceable spike receptacles. These are often covered with pimpled rubber for added traction. For curve running (200–400 meter races) an adequate waist or shank torsion is advisable. Lightweight MCR, PU or EVA foams are used to give some padding, particularly in the heel area.

MIDDLE AND LONG DISTANCE TRACK SPIKES

Following the same pattern as sprint shoes, middle distance shoes vary only in the midsole area. Most middle distance runners land to the forepart area of the foot. A thin wedge or "shank" aids to prevent overpronation and less torque in bend running.

Spikeless track shoes, essentially one with a thin rubber traction outsole covering a midsole/wedge (maximum heel height—½", 13 mm) may be preferred if the track surface is exceptionally hard (e.g., Asphalt).

INTERVAL TRAINING SPIKES

These are used by many track athletes to prevent Achilles tendon strain while training. These track spikes have substantial heel wedges and midsoles, raising the heel and reducing pressure and stretch on the Achilles tendon. The normal asymmetric spike pattern in the forepart of the spike plate is preferred.

INDOOR TRACK SPIKES

With the beginning of modern indoor track and field competition in the 1950s (previously there were few indoor cinder or dirt tracks), a demand was created for short (pin) spiked running shoes. These shoes were produced in small quantities featuring a seven-spike asymmetric sole pattern and adequately padded heel for board running. These fixed spiked shoes, although proving highly successful for the elite specialist, became obsolete with the invention of the replaceable spike system, which enabled athletes to interchange spikes as the track and situation demanded. On modern track surfaces regular track spikes are used.

HURDLES AND STEEPLECHASE

The short and long hurdles require sprint shoes. However, in this age of specialization, hurdle athletes prefer wider toe lasts and shorter front spikes to avoid clipping the hurdle with the lead foot. For landing and forepart stability, slight modifications have been made to the modern sprint shoe. Also, a more heavily padded heel is desirable to cushion shock on landing.

In the steeplechase with its water jump, athletes prefer nylon or perforated uppers for comfort and quick drying of the uppers during the race. Good midsole and heel padding is desirable for landing and for barrier push-off.

THROWING EVENTS

SHOT PUT SHOES

Most throwing events have at least one thing in common: The athletes are big. Consequently, shoes for throwing events are still made primarily of leather or suede for maximum support and durability. The shot put shoe includes reinforced leather uppers with a sturdy heel counter, extra toe boxing and reinforcement in the quarter for lateral support. An extra Velcro strap may be incorporated for additional upper support. A good gripping gum rubber sole with substantial midsole and wedge shank provides adequate control of both anterior and lateral movements across the circle. Nylon tape lining helps limit stretch and adds support to lateral and longitudinal stresses placed on the upper.

DISCUS SHOES

Similar to the shot put shoe, discus shoes are made more flexible in the forepart with wrap-up sole to aid turning motion in the circle. Different soling materials are preferred on cement surfaces as compared with synthetic circle surfaces. Gum or gristle rubber are the best outer soling materials.

HAMMER SHOES

The uppers are similar to shot and discus shoes; however, the complete soles are constructed to be flexible in the forepart, midsole and heel areas to gain maximum traction in turning quickly in the circle. Flexible wrap-up traction rubber soles (often with no tread) are preferred. Gum or gristle rubber outer soles are popular.

JAVELIN BOOTS

These specialized shoes are the only throwing event shoes produced with spikes for run-up and plant traction before delivery. The shoes are made from lightweight leathers or nylon mesh with reinforced girth and lace eyestays. Soles have a heavy duty forepart and heel spike plates containing six front and two back spikes, which may be as long as 25mm for competitions on grass runways. A buckle or strap across the girth provides additional support.

JUMPING EVENTS

LONG JUMP

The uppers are generally fully lined nylon or high grade lightweight leathers such as kangaroo skin with adequate reinforcement in the girth. A jumper at take-off exerts about 600–800 pounds of pressure on the board, so it's essential that nylon tape linings and outside reinforced leather strips cradle the foot securely to avoid overpronation or toe spread, reactions that would reduce impact thrust. Moccasin construction or tubular-cut uppers, which wrap the leather completely under the foot, are most successful at accomplishing this.

Spike placement is changed from the asymmetric pattern to give more emphasis across the metatarsal joints at take-off (see figure 12-8) with two spikes in front for stability (by IAAF ruling, the maximum number of forepart spikes is six and two in the heel). Most long jumpers do not prefer heel spikes. The forepart spike plate is more sturdy to give extra support to the foot. Heel cushioning is emphasized to reduce shock absorption due to excessive pounding during the run-up and take-off. Heel cups inside shoes are allowed.

TRIPLE JUMP

These soles are very similar to long jump shoes but vary in the midsole area where a sturdier wedge provides better support for landing during the mid-stance and toe-off stresses of this event. Shoe support can be improved with velcro-fastened leather support straps. Maximum heel elevation is 26mm. Heel cups may be used inside shoe. Heel spikes are preferred in the event.

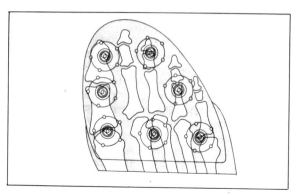

12-5. *Top left:* Leather discus shoes as worn by four-time gold medal winner Al Oerter.   12-6. *Top right:* Willie Banks, international track and field star. (Photo by Jeff Johnson)   12-7. *Bottom left:* A track spike boot used for a javelin event.   12-8. *Bottom right:* A typical spike placement pattern.

HIGH JUMP

In the world of specialized performance shoes, the high jump shoe has to be one of the most specific. Regardless of their chosen style of ascent over the bar, jumpers use a one-foot take-off. Because foot plant and take-off are so crucial to success in this event, design emphasis has concentrated on the "jump foot" shoe.

This jump foot or take-off shoe must be produced in both right foot and left foot versions, since jumpers may propel themselves with either. When the backwards ascent ("Fosbury

Flop") style of jumping became popular in the early 1970s, shoe companies had to adapt quickly, paying particular attention to the injury consequences of the flop. The result was a special high jump shoe with a different gradient on the sole to compensate for the abnormal twisting deformation of the take-off foot. Flop and forward ascent style shoes have different spike placement. The flop shoe has a thinner platform.

As with other spiked shoes, a limited number of spikes may be used in each high jump shoe: six in the forepart and two in the heel. The spike formation is designed biomechanically to give jumpers maximum traction and push at take-off. "Trailing foot" shoes, if used at all, vary considerably. Most companies now produce specific counterpart trail foot shoes that are lighter, contain fewer spikes and have more flexibility to assist the run-up.

To aid lift-off, jump shoes can be built up to a maximum elevation of 10mm in the forepart.

POLE VAULT

Due to the variety of jumping shoes and track spikes available today, most vaulters choose one or the other. However, a few prototype or limited production shoes have been termed "pole vaulting shoes" by one or two companies. These shoes are a combination of triple jump and interval type shoes, with shorter front spikes to reduce the possibility of clipping the bar.

WALKS

In the road walks, there are two internationally recognized competitive distances, 20 kilometers and 50 kilometers. Unlike leisure walking or hiking, international race walking has strict regulations governing the manner in which the walkers may proceed. They must maintain an unbroken link with the ground all the time. In other words, race walkers cannot lift their rear foot until the lead foot has made contact with the ground.

There is no "float" period when both feet are off the ground at once, as with running. Also, the leg must lock or straighten completely while the foot is on the ground. The soles of walking shoes may be as thick as 13mm (½"), while the heels must not exceed the forepart sole thickness by more than 13mm.

Prior to 1968, many different shoes were used for race walking, including just about everything from lightweight canvas rubber shoes to army type boots. Since the leading Mexican walkers revolutionized walking style in 1968, a more standard shoe has been preferred.

Sole construction is lightweight (EVA, MCR or PU) forepart, midsole and heel wedge with a harder compound than is used in running shoes. The outsole is made of hard-wearing gum rubber or carbon rubber. Training shoes may have a thicker outsole for better wear. Racing shoes, on the other hand, are as lightweight as possible, with a thinner outsole.

The shoe's toe area is wrapped-up and the walker uses this in the toe-off motion. The heel area is only slightly bias because the landing area is directly on the heel. A continuous one-piece heel is popular. The upper construction is of lightweight Kangaroo leather in a back tubular moccasin construction, which provides excellent heel support. A rigid non-collapsible heel counter is essential, generally supported by an extra outside leather counter.

The forepart usually incorporates cement construction with an insole board as a platform in the toe-off position. The upper cut is usually U-throat design with a normal lacing system. An apron cut or wingtip toe pattern is preferable; nylon tape lining in length and girth is used to prevent stretch. Some nylon materials have been introduced recently in uppers.

CONSTRUCTION

Certain construction features, particularly lightness and support, are desirable in many events. Often the best construction is the moccasin, or fake moccasin (tubular construction), on a slip-lasting (California lasting) system with U-throat design. This shoemaking method wraps the upper material completely around the foot, joining under the sole. This provides maximum tensile strength, wrapping the foot as if in a bandage and containing but one or two pieces of material, hence minimizing joining or sewing. Lacing systems have been standardized on the traditional eyelet and lace method, although speed lacing and velcro lacing have been used quite successfully.

UPPER MATERIALS

Uppers used in today's spiked shoes are made from the strongest and lightest suitable materials known to man. Kangaroo leather is preferred for its great tensile strength, thinness and light weight. Pigskin makes a good substitute. Synthetic substrate suedes from Japan, known as Nash suedes, are also very strong and lightweight. Nylon taffetas and meshes are used in conjunction with high-tech components to give maximum support and alignment to the shoe upper.

In addition to being made of more substantial material (usually suede or Nubock leather), field shoe uppers are usually constructed with extra support around the girth because of the tremendous stresses applied to the medial and lateral portions of the shoe. Weight is important but generally sacrificed for extra support or traction where necessary.

Linings are crucial in all track and field shoes, again mainly for extra support. Lightweight nylon tape is used both laterally and lengthwise in the shoe. This also helps prevent stretching of the uppers.

SOLING: SPIKED SHOES

Spike plates are made of nylon containing molded-in metal receptacles for spike or nylon appendage replacements. The replaceable spike system with its successor, the nylon append-age and spike combination, offers multiple selection to suit weather conditions and track surface. Various spike plate combinations are produced according to IAAF regulations. Although only six forepart metal spikes may be used in competition, manufacturers usually place seven spike receptacles, allowing the athlete flexibility to use a blank spike in the seventh position. Some have thinner areas at the joint for easier flex along with pressure-free zones to reduce creasing. The rest of the sole—namely the waist and heel sections—are usually soled with a lightweight traction or rubber suction sheeting upswept in the posterior and lateral areas. Extra padding or support is usually incorporated between the outsole and closed upper, depending on the event. Substantial heel padding or wedges are desirable to prevent bruising of the calcaneous (heel bone). Heel cups are used for additional protection in jumping shoes. One-piece nylon plates from sole through heel have been introduced for better torsional rigidity.

SOLING: FIELD SHOES

Spike plates are used in jumping shoes and javelin boots. Often heel spikes are necessary in these events.

Throwing shoes are soled with a variety of rubber composition soling materials. These are updated and improved depending on the circle surfaces most in use. Substantial foxing and toe cap rubbers are added to give durability. Rigid heel counters are important to prevent heel drift and give adequate support to the normally robust physique of the thrower.

"Footwork is the most important aspect of the game of tennis." Dennis Ralston, World Tennis

COURT SPORT SHOES

One of the largest categories in athletic footwear is the court shoe. In their early form the traditional "sneaker" or "plimsoll" canvas-upper shoes were used for all court sports. This type of shoe was of the simplest construction: basically a gum-rubber sole, with vulcanized or glued foxing adhered to a canvas duck upper. Amazingly, this shoe, in its basic form, has survived longer than most other forms of "traditional" athletic shoes. The rubber built-up canvas court shoe, in a perhaps more sophisticated form, is still a standard in the industry.

As a category, court shoes covers many sports, indoor and outdoor. Let's look at the different types of motion found in the various sports.

RACQUET SPORTS
Requires movement from side-to-side as well as forward and backwards. The center of gravity must be moved in all directions quickly and with control.

In the "ready" position the racquet player adopts a stance which distributes the body weight equally on both feet and legs, usually on the metatarsals and phalanges (balls of feet and toes).

In play the joints, muscles and tendons of the foot are subjected to stretching, pronation, supination, plantarflexion and dorsiflexion, pressure from stopping and starting as well as considerable lateral and medial rolling. From the wear patterns produced in even a short period of play it can be seen that court shoes used in racquet sports are subjected to more abuse than any other type of athletic shoe.

13-1. Little changed since the peak days of the sneaker era, the classic high-cut (foreground) and the later introduced low-cut versions (background) of Chuck Taylor's vulcanized rubber, canvas basketball shoes.

TEAM COURT SPORTS

Sports such as basketball, netball, volleyball and European team handball require quick reactions, jumping, sprinting and lateral/medial mechanics. Study of the kinesiology and biomechanics of the foot during these activities have shown that the foot is required to maneuver through the planes of plantarflexion, dorsiflexion, eversion and abduction, supination and pronation. Many court players assess the difficulties and strain on their lower extremities, and then add padding, insoles or orthotic devices to prevent injuries and improve performance. Strapping or taping of ankles, knees and feet is frequently used by competitive players.

Athletic shoe manufacturers have made many improvements to their court shoes using trial and error, biomechanical testing and by soliciting help and advice from leading players in testing prototypes. New materials in the upper and in the construction of the sole have also added new dimensions to performance and the prevention of injuries. However, the variety of lasts used for court sports such as widths, curved or straight, seem somewhat limited for their large volume area.

The remainder of this chapter will offer a brief overview of the various materials used in the construction of court shoes and an assessment of their comparative advantages and disadvantages.

COURT SHOE UPPERS

Heavy Duck Canvas. In both loose-lined and unlined form, cotton canvas material, in a simple one-on-one weave, has remained ever popular for court shoe use. Twills and synthetics have been added over the years to give additional strength to the natural cotton canvas. Heavy-weight duck canvas is usually preferred to give the required support in a court shoe. Loose linings or taped reinforcements also add support.

Being a woven material, canvas breathes well, and, given the friction and heat generated in most court shoes, breathability is extremely important in helping the feet stay cool and comfortable on the court. Air holes are often added in canvas shoes for extra breathability. Although not the lightest of materials, canvas comes in several weights (such as 8 oz. and 12 oz. duck) which can be used as an adequate and inexpensive upper material. Canvas uppers can be successfully combined with direct injection polyurethane soling, which is extremely light, and this has given the canvas upper a new lease on life.

OVERALL ADVANTAGES	DISADVANTAGES
Less expensive	Comfort factor
Breathable	Cheaper appearance
Good support	Frays easily
Washable	
Medium weight factor	
Easy drying	

Polyester canvas is a new generation of superior, stronger, easily washable, woven fabrics classified as canvas (VISA).

Canvas Mesh.

Canvas mesh has recently been introduced as a material suitable for court shoe uppers. It combines a thick canvas weave with either laminated foam or tricot. This mesh weave is also used unlined to give breathability and adequate support. It is priced similar to canvas.

OVERALL ADVANTAGES	DISADVANTAGES
Excellent breathability	Too porous (lets in grit and dirt)
Washable	Comfort factor (rough texture)
Medium weight	Tendency to "yellow"
Good support	Tendency to stretch
Easy drying	

NOTE: This material makes an excellent "vent" if used in conjunction with leather or suede uppers.

Nylon Mesh.

Nylon material started to be used in sports footwear in the early 1970s for court sports. Mainly due to the support necessary, stiffer knitted mesh nylons laminated with a soft tricot (skinfit) were introduced. This material has proven to be highly successful when reinforced with suede or leather in the friction or stress areas. Armoured mesh has many of the qualities of canvas and leather, and usually is priced between the two.

OVERALL ADVANTAGES	DISADVANTAGES
Breathable	Friction burns
Washable	
Lightweight	
Good support	
Easy drying	

Softer taffeta nylons, such as those used in running shoes, may offer a slight weight advantage and a lustrous look but they have the distinct disadvantage of giving less support and inadequate durability in court shoes.

13-2. Tennis shoe concept with double mesh and suede uppers. The radical two-piece sole idea is based on separate motions of rear and forefoot movement.

Leather Uppers. Leather upper court shoes rose to prominence in the late 1960s, although leather had been used previously with limited success. Leather and suede (less frequently used) added instant comfort and excellent support as well as natural breathing qualities to court shoe uppers. Leather can also be perforated, with no loss of strength, to add more breathability. Leather is durable, light, and it molds to the foot, bending and stretching just enough to give firm support with excellent comfort. Top grain cowhide and other lightweight full grains are most popular, as is Nubock leather for its suppleness and properties of adhesion to soling compounds.

OVERALL ADVANTAGES	DISADVANTAGES
Breathable	Friction burns
Easy to clean	Scuffing of finish
Lightweight	Careful drying
Good support	
Adapt to foot shape	

Poromeric Materials (Man-made, Breathable). These technically advanced PU or substrate materials (cangoran is the best known) have been recently introduced. They have found the greatest success in the court shoe area. They are leather-like in appearance and have breathable qualities not found in either the older PU or PVC. Poromeric materials are very lightweight and, backed with textile, offer adequate support to the foot. Presently priced about the same as leather.

OVERALL ADVANTAGES	DISADVANTAGES
Lightweight	Usually heavily reinforced
Some breathability	with leather or suede
Adequate support	Little cost advantage over
Easy drying	leather
	Tensile strength support

NOTE: Thinner poromeric materials with perforation holes have recently been introduced.

PVC Materials. Not well received in North America or Europe, PVC uppers have gained popularity in other parts of the world, particularly in Asia. Their biggest advantage is lack of transpiration. PVC uppers should be ventilated or perforated; otherwise they build up heat inside the shoe.

OVERALL ADVANTAGES	DISADVANTAGES
Easy to wipe clean	Excessive heat build-up
Cost	Comfort factor
Bond easily to most soling materials	Cheaper appearance
Medium weight	
Adequate support	

13-3. Mesh/leather basketball high-cut with shell sole. Puma was the first sport shoe company to pioneer the Velcro closure in 1968.

SOLING MATERIALS AND CONSTRUCTION

Rubber Built-up. This method usually combined with canvas or leather uppers after lasting. Resin based rubber or gum rubber slab outsole is combined with layers of rubber, and vulcanized by using a rubber foxing around the sole.

This construction method gives good lateral and medial support to the shoe, which is the main requirement of a court shoe. In leather, a sewn tape under the foxing helps adhesion to the upper and at the same time adds further support to the sides of the shoe at the sole line. Normally used on less expensive shoes. Only disadvantage is weight.

Unit Shell Sole. The last upper is placed inside a unit sole with walls or foxing cradling the upper. Often the unit shell sole is stitched either in the forepart or all round for added strength in addition to cementing. This type of sole gained much acceptance in the late 60s. It gives excellent side support with a considerable savings in weight. This type of soling has been most commonly used in combination with leather or suede uppers. Unit soles usually have honeycombed cushioned cells on the inside of the sole shell. Soles can be either rubber or PU units.

13-4. Canvas and suede upper with direct vulcanized rubber sole.

Direct Vulcanized Rubber Soles. This method of soling combines the upper with a rubber slab or shell sole by direct vulcanization. The main difference from built-up construction is the elimination of a separate foxing and several layers of rubber under the outsole. Vulcanization is excellent for bonding to the upper and gives good lateral and medial support as well as superb traction. Different densities and colors of rubber can be combined for a variety of cushioning and traction features.

PU Injection. This modern method of soling court shoes uses the direct injection of polyurethane, either as a single com-

13-5. Leather tennis shoe in classical lace-to-toe design. Directly injected dual-density polyurethane (PU) sole.

13-6. Tennis shoe—triple mesh and suede upper with direct injected polyurethane (PU) midsole/wedge and rubber outsole with raised toe bumper.

13-7. Tennis shoe—full-grain leather upper with a dual-density rubber outsole and stitched toe bumper. The mid-sole features dual-density EVA. A higher density u-shaped piece surrounds the outer heel to provide rear-foot stability, while the lower density provides cushioning.

13-8. Half-cup sole with cut-away waist and EVA midsole. All-leather upper for tennis.

pound, or as a dual density combination of soft expanded polyurethane midsole, heel wedge and foxing, with a much more abrasive resistant elastomer PU density outsole. This is the lightest type of soling available. Several manufacturers have added either leather wear strips or plugs into the molds to give additional wear, by diffusing the heat build-up which can melt PU under friction. These additional soling combinations tend to give polyurethane soling better wearing properties, especially where it's most needed—in the toe drag area.

For many years PU had the reputation of being "slippery" on the court. This problem is caused largely by a silicone film or skin that is used to obtain a clean release from the mold. It is easily corrected by scuffing the soles on pavement or some other abrasive surface for a few seconds. However, PU soling is not recommended for use on wood court surfaces.

PU Rubber Combination Soles. New innovations have recently produced this "ultimate" court sole. This is comprised of injected PU mid-sole, wedge and foxing with a high compression rubber traction outsole. Several athletic shoe companies are now producing versions of this process on high grade models. The type of soling combination has previously been technically difficult to produce due to adhesion problems between rubber and injected PU in the mold. This newly perfected soling process offers the athlete the superior shock absorbency, lightness and bonding to the upper of PU injected material and the advantages in traction and abrasion resistance of a high compression rubber compound outsole.

Prefabricated Soles. This is used primarily in running shoe construction. The mid-sole and heel wedge is made of soft MCR, EVA or PU and the outsole is of gum rubber, wrapped up at the heel and toe foxing. Although still used in volleyball, badminton and squash shoes, this soling construction does not give the same medial and lateral support as other constructions. The upper is usually heavily reinforced with suede to compensate for this disadvantage. Also, in contrast to the shell sole concept, this type of construction raises the heel up, rather than cradling the foot close to the ground for quick lateral mechanics. A combination of cut-away shell sole with microcellular inserts is the latest modification to this form of soling.

Open Shank Or Half-Shell Soles. In the 1980s a combination of rubber shell sole and soft prefabricated or unit inserts was successfully introduced for court shoe soles. This type sole is adapted from the original full rubber shell sole with the honeycomb cells replaced by EVA or PU as a midsole and wedge. The foxing is cut away in the shank area to reduce weight and allow visibility of the midsole material in the waist. The advantages are better shock absorbency, lighter weight and sufficient bonding and protection at the toe and heel.

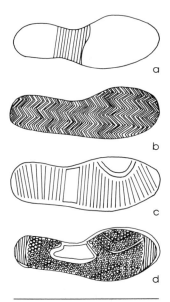

13-9. Traction Outsoles: (a) smooth—best for indoor carpet or astro turf surfaces; (b) herringbone—best for hard court or wood; (c) radial/ribbed—best for hard court; (d) pillared/nubbed multi-level—best for soft court.

Traction Outsoles.

Due to the exaggerated amount of stopping, starting and lateral motion, traction is all important in court sports. Ironically, that does not mean the more traction the better. If increasing traction were the major consideration suction cups could easily be employed on a sole. But besides the obvious lift-off problem, landing or planting the foot with the shoe locked to the floor would transmit tremendous pressures to the ankles and knees and cause many injuries. The quest for traction involves balancing many considerations.

The standard traction sole for court sports has been the herringbone pattern. This is probably still the most popular design. A flat or suction pivot feature at the ball of the foot unquestionably aids pivoting or turning and reduces wear on the tread directly under the ball of the foot.

Another "standard" court sole is the bi-level pillar tread introduced by Adi Dassler in the 1960s. The principle of this tread pattern is to carry the weight of the body on the top pillar layer until stopping pressure is applied to the sole, which brings the second or recessed layer into contact with the playing surface.

Some shoes feature two or three distinct designs on the same sole. The reasoning behind this is that the anterior, posterior, medial and lateral portions of the sole all play different roles in improving performance. The "radial tire" principle at the edge of the sole has been used, because as the subtalar joints, ankle and heel move medially or laterally it is better to have a levelled or rolled edge to avoid the foot rolling over a distinct edge.

Friction usually causes abrasion that affects sole wear in a manner similar to an eraser on paper. Non-marking sole compounds are thus required for all court sports.

Most soles tend to be wider for court sports, for flat-footed play, and they incorporate a bevelled edge at the toe and heel. A deep tread pattern on court shoes tends to grip better on loose surfaces, such as clay, whereas a shallow tread is preferred on smooth playing surfaces. Indoor court shoe soles, especially for smooth wooden playing surfaces, often use softer, more flexible compounds, such as gum rubber, to aid grip.

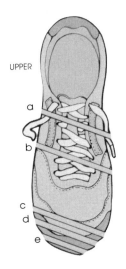

UPPER

a

b

c

d

e

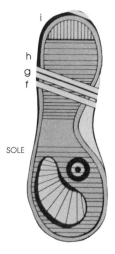

i

h

g

f

SOLE

13-10. Types of materials used for tennis shoe uppers—(a) leather, 53%; (b) nylon mesh, 38%; (c) other, 10%; (d) canvas, 7%; (e) don't know, 3%; and soles—(f) polyurethane, 35%; (g) natural rubber, 33%; (h) don't know, 32%; (i) other, 1%.

SPORT-BY-SPORT ANALYSIS

The remainder of this chapter will consider individual court sports. It will analyze the foot and leg mechanics and note the special shoe requirement associated with each one.

Tennis: Lawn Tennis (Longue Paume) **Origin:** England 1874
FOOT AND LEG MECHANICS: side to side; quick mechanics; center of gravity control; sprinting, jumping, stretching.
SURFACES: varied (lawn, clay, asphalt, synthetic, rubberized)
SHOE REQUIREMENTS: good lateral support; light to medium weight (max. wt. for size 9 is 13 oz.); flat sole with adequate heel lift; good cushioning in insole; adequate toe box; firm heel counter; good ventilation; non-slip traction; pivot-point and toe-drag reinforcement.

Tennis is unique because it is played on a wide variety of court surfaces. Selection of a suitable sole is most important. On grass, a traction sole that grips the surface is best (such as a deep herringbone or nub sole). On grass courts, up until recent times, small metal spiked shoes were commonly worn by many leading players, With the introduction of bi-level traction profiles on rubber soles and the less frequent use of grass as a playing surface, spiked tennis shoes have largely been elimianted. On clay, most courts prohibit soles with too deep a tread pattern, even though most players would prefer them, because of excessive court maintenance caused by wear. A smooth sole will pick up less clay or dirt on the tread. On artificial or synthetic surfaces, the harder soles are preferred for longer wear. High rubber content, rubber composition soles or dual-density polyurethane wear best. Soles with special rubber or leather inserts molded into polyurethane add extra life to heavily worn areas (such as toe-drag and pivot points).

Upper quarter patterns for tennis shoes are usually cut sufficiently high to give good lateral and ankle support to the foot. A wide variety of upper pattern designs are used. The most popular for men being the lace-to-toe cut, which allows for width adjustment. For women with a narrower foot the U-throat or extended eyestay cut is used. The apron toe box cut is also becoming widely used. High cut tennis shoe uppers are not popular but are used by players with a tendency towards ankle problems. Mid-cut (over the ankle line) court models have been introduced to promote better ankle stability. The top-line (ankle) must be well padded, especially along the medial ankle bone, to ensure comfort in shoes of this design.

Squash: (Squash Racquets) **Origin:** Harrow, England 1850
FOOT AND LEG MECHANICS: side to side; quick movement;

13-11. *Left:* Tennis great Martina Navratilova on the court.   13-12. *Right:* One athletic shoe company's version of tennis "whites." Ann White at Wimbledon, 1985.

quick stops; low center of gravity; control; stretching.

SURFACES: normally wood.

SHOE REQUIREMENTS: good lateral support; light weight; flat sole; slight or no heel lift; good cushioned insole; adequate toe box; firm heel counter; ventilation; non-slip traction; (gum rubber) pivot point; toe-drag and vamp reinforcement.

Court Tennis: (Royal Tennis, Jeu de Paume) **Origin:** France 14th Century

FOOT AND LEG MECHANICS: same as tennis.

SURFACES: cement or concrete composition floor.

SHOE REQUIREMENTS: same as lawn tennis.

Hard Rackets: Origin: England 1760

FOOT AND LEG MECHANICS: same as squash.

SURFACES: polished cement or slate.

SHOE REQUIREMENTS: same as squash.

Platform Tennis: Origin: USA 1928

FOOT AND LEG MECHANICS: same as tennis.

SURFACE: hardwood.

SHOE REQUIREMENTS: same as squash.

Paddle Ball: (Four wall, and one wall)   **Origin:** USA 1920's
FOOT AND LEG MECHANICS: same as squash.
SURFACES: indoor - wood and various compositions; outdoor - wood, cement.
SHOE REQUIREMENTS: same as squash.

Frontenis: (Fronton)   **Origin:** Spain (popular in Central and South America)
FOOT AND LEG MECHANICS: same as squash.
SURFACE: cement.
SHOE REQUIREMENTS: same as squash.

Soft Tennis: Origin: Asia
FOOT AND LEG MECHANICS: combination of tennis and squash mechanics.
SURFACE: tennis court surface (usually soft type).
SHOE REQUIREMENTS: tennis shoes are normally worn but squash/racquetball uppers are preferable if combined with suitable soling materials.

Racquet Ball: Origin: USA 1940s
FOOT AND LEG MECHANICS: same as squash.
SURFACES: normally wood.
SHOE REQUIREMENTS: same as squash.

Paddle Tennis: (Deck Tennis)   **Origin:** 1898
FOOT AND LEG MECHANICS: same as tennis.
SURFACES: various.
SHOE REQUIREMENTS: same as squash.

Badminton: Origin: Poona, India/England 1860
FOOT AND LEG MECHANICS: emphasis on front and back as well as side-to-side motion; quick movement; quick stops; low center of gravity; control; stretching.
SURFACES: normally wood.
SHOE REQUIREMENTS: some lateral support; light weight (11 oz. or less); flat sole; slight or no heel lift; well-cushioned insole; adequate toe box; firm heel counter; ventilation; non-slip traction (gum rubber) pivot point; toe-drag and vamp reinforcement.

Table Tennis: Origin: late 19th century
FOOT AND LEG MECHANICS: side to side; quick movement; stretching; center of gravity.
SURFACES: various (mainly wood).
SHOE REQUIREMENTS: same as badminton.

Jai Alai: (Pelota, Pelote Basque) **Origin:** Spain
FOOT AND LEG MECHANICS: same as for squash and jumping.
SURFACES: wood.
SHOE REQUIREMENTS: same as squash.

TEAM COURT SPORTS
Basketball: Origin: USA 1892
FOOT AND LEG MECHANICS: continuous forward or backward
   accelerations; quick side to side mechanics; quick stops;
   jumping.
SURFACES: usually wood (maybe synthetic or rubberized surface)
SHOE REQUIREMENTS: good lateral and medial support; light
   to medium weight (max. 13 oz. for men's size 9); flat sole;
   slight heel lift; good cushioning in insole; large, firm heel
   counter; toe box with drag protection; ventilation; pivot point
   sole; non-slip traction.

13-13. All-leather, high-cut
basketball models with fully
stitched 3/4 shell rubber sole.

NOTE: soles made with gum rubber or high rubber content are
excellent. Polyurethane is lighter and offers less traction. Soles
with multiple-edge patterns, such as circles, squares or dia-
monds offer better traction than herringbone pattern (which is
excellent for forward stop, but not as good for lateral stops).

   Uppers used in basketball still tend to favor highcut designs
for full ankle support. Preprioceptor straps to warn of ankle
misalignment have become popular since their introduction in
1983. In addition to offering added ankle support, highcut
uppers must not restrict ankle flex to a great degree. Lowcut
uppers are preferred for better ankle flexibility, as well as their
obvious weight saving advantage. A firm heel counter is advisable.

Netball:
FOOT AND LEG MECHANICS: same as basketball.
SURFACES: wood, synthetics.
SHOE REQUIREMENTS: same as basketball.

Volleyball:
FOOT AND LEG MECHANICS: quick movement; jumping; side
   to side; quick stops.
SURFACES: usually wood, various.
SHOE REQUIREMENTS: lateral support; lightweight; flat herringbone or deep ripple sole (gum rubber); good cushioning
   insole, especially at heel; firm heel counter; leather toe-drag
   protection; ventilation; nylon or cotton mesh canvas.

13-14. High-cut basketball model featuring 3/4 open waist dish sole and unique application of a TPR/nylon ankle stabilizing component part. Suitable for box lacrosse.

Indoor Handball: (European, Team Handball)
FOOT AND LEG MECHANICS: same as basketball.
SURFACES: usually wood, various.
SHOE REQUIREMENTS: same as basketball, with additional toe-drag and medial vamp protection. Lowcut models are preferred.

Box or Court Lacrosse: This sport is the indoor version of field lacrosse.
FOOT AND LEG MECHANICS: forward and backward running; lateral mechanics; throwing.
SURFACES: cement, wood, and court floorings.
SHOE REQUIREMENTS: same as for basketball. Good toe drag protection is advisable.

Sepak Takraw (Bola Sepak): A five-a-side volleyball-type game also using the feet. Played in Malaysia, Singapore and Indonesia.
FOOT AND LEG MECHANICS: similar to volleyball but also using kicking techniques.
SURFACE: same as badminton court.
SHOE REQUIREMENTS: same as for volleyball/badminton.

"On average, the soccer player is only in contact with the ball during two percent of his playing time." Field Sports survey, 1969

C H A P T E R 14

FIELD SPORT SHOES

Along with "athletics," swimming and war-related ballistic sports (karate, boxing, etc.), some field sports trace their origins to man's earliest form of society. Field shoes derived from regular high-cut boots have long been a popular style for rugged field use. In the early 1900s the semi-cut and three-quarter models became popular and were found to be better for performance. Low-cut quarters on field shoes followed, some 20–30 years later, allowing the foot and ankle more mobility and lighter weight, but at the cost of some ankle support.

The materials used were almost exclusively leather, and soles were attached mainly by tacks, and later by the Goodyear Welt system. In the later nineteenth century early forms of studded soles appeared. The earliest form of studs consisted of strips of thick leather nailed to flat soles to aid traction. Later, studs made of glued-up sole leather were nailed to heel and sole. The first metal cleats were used in the early 1920s, and the first one-piece fiber cleat appeared in the same period. American football brought the interchangeable cleat system into use in the 1920s and 30s, but interchangeable studs for soccer boots were not perfected until the late 1950s.

In both the earliest and the most recent field shoe designs, only leather uppers have been considered serviceable for use in rugged field sports. Many varieties of leathers have been used over the years. Generally the trend has been towards using the lighter, high tensile strength leathers. Kangaroo leather is regarded as the best leather available for the field shoe upper.

FIELD SHOE CONSTRUCTION

UPPERS

Leather is used almost exclusively as the upper material on field shoes. The leathers have become more refined, evolving from thick cow or ox hide to lighter and more supple leathers, such as calf, gazelle, goat and deer hide. Kangaroo leather, due to its high tensile strength and resistance to stretching, is considered the best leather available for field shoes. Split leathers are used in cheaper grade shoes, but for performance footwear only top grade leathers are used.

Mesh and soft nylons have been introduced on less rugged field models, and vinyl, usually backed with cloth, is used in some lower priced models.

LINING MATERIALS

Good quality field shoes should be lined, or at least reinforced, to retain shape and to absorb perspiration. Nylon, textile, nylon tricot (skinfit) are all acceptable linings. Leather is not much used for linings today. Soft PVC and PU are popularly used for collar and heel counter linings.

HEEL COUNTER MATERIAL

A firm heel counter is essential for field sports use. Heel counters prevent heel drift and hold the heel firm in the side-to-side motions required in most field sports. Inside heel counter materials include fiberboard, polyethylene and thermal plastic material. In addition to the inside counters, outside plastic or leather heel counters are used to give extra support and protection.

INSOLE SOCK LINING MATERIALS

Most field shoes are not well cushioned. On grass fields extensive cushioning has not been necessary. With the advent of artificial turf, however, better sock linings are becoming popular. Sponge or foam-cushioned liners, either duck or terry-cloth covered, have been used. Leather insoles are still considered the best for wear and perspiration absorption, but are rarely used, due to cost factors.

SOLE MATERIALS

Almost all replaceable or detachable cleats, studs or spikes are affixed or screwed into nylon unit soles which are in turn glued and riveted to the upper. Harder forms of nylon soles, such as

14-1. "One turn" cleat system development introduced at the Mexican Soccer World Cup, 1986.

hytrel and surlyn, can also be directly injected, with the cleat or stud system molded into the sole. Leather soles are used only infrequently. The replaceable stud system, which permits the interchange of different stud materials for different field conditions, was perfected in the 1960s. Replaceable studs vary from one sport to another, but leather, rubber, aluminum, nylon, PU and steel-tipped nylon are all in use. American football continues to use the female stud system, while soccer and rugby use the male stud system (see figure 14-2). More flexible nylon units with a wider stud base formation have been introduced recently, and they represent a further refinement of the screw-in stud system. Slight wedges and heel lifts are also used between the nylon sole plate and the upper to give some additional shock absorbency on harder playing surfaces.

For multi-studded soles several types of material are used, in both unit and injected forms. Rubber, PVC and PU nylon combinations are the most frequently used. Gum rubber and rubber combination unit soles are usually glued and stitched (sometimes riveted). PVC and hard PU soles are usually injected.

Spike and stud formations vary greatly from sport to sport, so we will deal with these separately later. In general it has been shown that a smaller stud in a denser formation helps to prevent ankle and knee injuries, due to the shallower stud penetration into the playing surface.

Screw-in studs and metal cleats are not advisable for use by pre-teenage players. The weight distribution is better in multi-studs and the fatigue factor less.

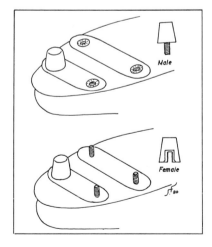

14-2. *Left:* Stud attachments.   14-3. *Right:* Soccer superstar Pelé from Brazil.

FIELD SPORTS: ANALYSIS OF FOOT AND LEG MOTION

All field sports contain a greater or lesser degree of bodily contact. The most rugged contact sports are probably American football and rugby. At the other end of the scale, softball and baseball involve relatively little body contact. All other sports played on turf, including soccer, Australian football, field hockey, field lacrosse, hurley and team handball, fall somewhere between these two extremes.

Field sports combine many types of motion. In baseball and lacrosse we find the ballistic motion of throwing. Soccer and Australian football involve kicking and forward running. American football stresses side-to-side motion, bodily contact, sprint starts and quick turns. But basic to all these sports is running. Many of the sports discussed in this section have modified running motions, especially sprinting and quick changes of direction while moving at close to top speed. The basic biomechanics of these motions are explained in the chapter on "Foot and Leg Movements", but relating them to specific considerations of field shoe design will require a sport-by-sport analysis.

SOCCER

FOOT AND LEG MECHANICS—mainly running, kicking, and some jumping, sliding and stretching. Multi-directional movement.

SURFACES—mainly natural grass, some artificial turf.

SHOE REQUIREMENTS—leather upper; light weight; good traction; heel support; soft or semi-soft toe; protection features; adequate torsional stability.

Soccer has more regular participants than any other sport in the world. This sport dates back many centuries, at least to Roman times, when a leather "bag" ball was kicked between two teams for recreation. Soccer is popular today on every continent, due to its low equipment cost, inherent appeal, and professional image.

The kicking style in soccer is varied. The ball is most often kicked with the medial, lateral or dorsal areas of the foot. In the example of the right footed kicker, the left foot is planted to the left of the ball. The kicking foot is lined up with the foot supined. The hip is used as a hinge or pivot and the foot and leg follow through after contact is made with the ball.

Uppers. A soccer shoe should fit like a glove for the foot. Soccer is the only ball sport played entirely with the feet (except for limited contact with head and shoulders). Hence the last

14-4. Leather soccer shoes with multi-studded sole.

should be tight fitting with a narrow toe. European lasts tend to be somewhat narrower than American lasts, to fit the European foot (which also has a high arch). An asymmetic pattern with higher medial quarter is preferable. One piece toe caps, extended eyestay patterns or reinforced apron toe box cuts (competition toe) are popular designs for soccer boot uppers. It is important that the player "feel" the ball on the foot. Softer thinner leathers, such as kangaroo or calf-skin, are preferred. Cowhide, split cowhide and man-made materials are used on lower-grade models. Side logos or reinforcing stripes from the eyestay to the sole on the medial and lateral sides of the shoe add lateral support. Inside bandages and thin nylon linings prevent stretching of thin leather uppers.

An adequately padded high tongue to reduce lace pressure and cushion the dorsal kicking area of the foot should be balanced with as thin a material as possible for "feel" of the ball. Many players impart considerable spin and control of the ball with the use of the tongue and lace area of the shoe.

Soles. There are three basic types of soles. Screw-in studded soles are used on softer grounds and multi-studded soles on harder grounds. Indoor soccer is played with a flat-soled shoe with unit shell, one piece sole or combination half shell with microcellular midsole/wedge for extra shock absorbency.

There are many sole patterns. Some use multi-directional bars in conjunction with studs as traction aids. Small grooves at the toe and heel may be inserted into the molds for stability and maneuverability under extreme surface conditions. Soles should have relatively flexible foreparts for running, balanced weight distribution, good torsional rigidity and support in the shank area. Reinforced sole profiles are designed to keep the sole from bending too much when contacting the ball in the "driving" position. Soles should be flush or recessed from the upper (featherline) to allow better foot contact with the ball.

Composition

Screw-in stud systems—studs made of rubber, leather, nylon or PU. Sole plates made of nylon, surlyn, hytrel or PU may be glued and riveted in unit form or direct injected with metal screw receptacles. Leather soles are still used. Maximum number of screw-in studs is six (F.I.F.A.) Diameter is ⅜" or 10mm.

Multi-studded soles—rubber, rubber composition, PVC, PU nylon combination (hytrel, surlyn). Can be either unit or direct injection. Minimum number of studs is 10. Diameter ⅜" or 10mm.

14-5. "World Class"—the shoe for the World Cup in Mexico features new screw-in studs. The first time screw-in studs have been successfully equipped with extremely robust ceramic heads. Advantages: absolutely wear resistant; studs maintain their original length; maximum grip and traction; stud heads always remain rounded: reduced risk of injuries.

14-6. Miami Dolphins' highly visible quarterback, Dan Marino.

Astro-turf soles for soccer have a great number of studs and traction bars. Astro-turf multi-studded soles have numerous low cleats to reduce friction. The consistent length of the turf and constant hardness (unlike real turf, which varies with climate and condition) enable the sole designs to be optimized for the surface. Synthetic turf is notoriously hard wearing on shoe soles. The astro-turf soccer shoe is produced on a normal soccer last.

AMERICAN FOOTBALL

Derived from the European sport of rugby, the indigenous North American game of football originated in the 1870s. Like rugby, football is a contact sport, and its primary movement is running. Protective equipment has seen increased use over the years, especially headgear. In this injury-related sport (which commands North America's largest sports viewing television audience) footwear has also undergone a critical evaulation with a view to preventing injuries.

The lower extremities of the body are particularly prone to injury in playing football, due to the quick lateral movements, and especially to the great forces brought to bear through contact with the upper and lower body in blocking and hitting. In recent years much research and many rulings from football's governing bodies have resulted in many changes and restrictions in football footwear. Knee injuries in particular have been shown in many cases to have been caused by excessive cleat or stud stability. Knee or ankle damage results when the foot plantar surface has no movement due to long cleats digging too far into the turf. The following ruling was introduced in 1985: Maximum diameter of cleat or stud tip—$7/16''$, maximum overall length—$\frac{1}{2}''$ on a maximum platform of $5/32''$. Experimentation with different cleat shapes and formations, including swivel plates and bar cleats, continues. Three different types of positionally specialized footwear are used in football:

1. For players in the protective positions (offensive and defensive linemen).
2. For backs (defensive and offensive).
3. For kickers.

FOOT AND LEG MOVEMENT:
1. **Linemen**—running; lateral movements; sprint starts; balance.
2. **Backs**—running; lateral movements; quick turns; spins; low center of gravity; balance.
3. **Kickers**—three styles of kicking are used in football:
   1) *Straight-on place kicking*: These kickers prefer a special hard or block toed shoe with square toe box. Unlike soccer-style

kicking, straight-on kickers contact the ball with the toe of the shoe, and thus require special protection.

2) *Soccer or side-on place kicking*: the same as the conventional soccer kick with the medial and dorsal part of the foot. Usually soccer shoes are preferred.

3) *Punting*: a movement where the kicker kicks the ball as it drops from his hands. The non-kicking foot is planted and the kicking leg swung through from the hip. The foot is in the supine position and the ball is contacted with the dorsal foot to about the shoulder level.

14-7. Mid-high grass cleat features a padded collar which rises above the ankle. It also has 3/8 inch squared cleats that extend off the sole. A good shoe for a football lineman.

SURFACES—natural and artifical turf.

SHOE REQUIREMENTS—(Widths from D to EEE are made by some manufacturers.)

1. **Linemen:** Uppers must be supportive and protective. Often high-cut or semi-cut boot designs are preferred. Ankle taping is typical. Good quality full-grain leathers of cowhide are most common. Recently, durable mesh nylon quarters reinforced with leather toe caps, counters and eyestays have been used, particularly on astro-turf shoes. Leather or nylon vamp linings are preferable in order to prevent stretching. Although shoe weight is an important factor due to the anatomical structure of the average lineman (average 6'3", 245 lbs.) support and protection are most important in these shoes. A good toe box and hard heel counter should be standard.

On natural grass the traditional seven-stud formation is still preferred. Stud length is restricted by many associations to 12 studs minimum, ½" in length, 3/16" in diameter, or optional for professional players. The additional polyurethane or nylon stud (the steel-tipped cleat is almost obsolete) is used at the tip for the sprint start position (three point stance). Nylon glued and riveted soles are preferred as they shed dirt and mud easily and prevent "caking" between the studs. Multi-studded rubber soles are also common on natural grass and are preferred in the shell or dish sole unit glued and stitched for additional lateral support. Astro-turf linesmen's shoes are the same as multi-stud for grass with shorter, more numerous studs for better traction and stability.

2. **Backs:** Uppers are much the same as for linesmen's shoes in construction. The low-cut asymmetric pattern is preferred, however, for extra mobility. Weight is more of a factor for the backs so kangaroo or lightweight cowhide is used.

Lightweight astro-turf shoes with nylon or cotton mesh uppers (reinforced completely with suede footbed, counter,

14-8. Leather upper, rubber-cup sole for synthetic turf use. Originally designed for American football.

14-9. Grass football cleat features a patent pending one-half inch cleat arrangement which extends off the sidewall to create heel stability. Features full-grain leather upper for ankle support.

14-10. Leather upper nylon sole plate with seven removable studs. The standard for natural turf American football.

toe cap and eyestay) have become popular since the late 70s. These shoes are extensions of the nylon style running shoe and usually have EVA or MCR midsoles and heel wedges with rubber "waffle" traction soles completely wrapped-up at the toe and front quarter for better lateral support. New sole pattern and innovations are constantly sought by manufacturers in astro shoes. Taping of ankles is common.

Soling is much the same as for the linesmen's shoes. In the multi-studded and astro soles, however, regular unit soles are common as they tend to be lighter. Materials are rubber or injected PVC/PU combinations (hytrel, surlyn). Leather soles are almost obsolete.

3. **Kickers:** For straight-on placekickers the square box toe is a very specialized shoe. It is usually hand made for the kicking foot and a conventional shoe is worn on the non-kicking foot. The shoe is usually modified for the individual kicker, at the professional levels of the sport.

For soccer style placekickers a soccer shoe is usually preferred. Some players kick in a traditional football back's shoe model. For punting, either a soccer or back's shoe is used.

BASEBALL

Baseball is a totally American derivative of the little-played English game of rounders. The game evolved about the end of the eighteenth century; as early as 1786. Baseball shoes have followed the same evolutionary pattern as American football shoes. No high-cut or semi-cut uppers are used today. The asymmetric low-cut pattern, with U-throat and conventional lacing system, has proven to be the ultimate design.

Today, baseball is not as exclusive to the U.S. as football. Countries such as Japan, Korea, Mexico, Canada and Cuba have professional teams, and baseball is a popular minor sport in many other parts of the world. Since the U.S. is still regarded as the home of baseball (the "World" Series is still contested by U.S. teams only and takes place in the U.S.), all innovations in baseball shoes, if not necessarily designed in the U.S., are tested and endorsed at the U.S. pro level.

FOOT AND LEG MECHANICS—sprinting; throwing; complex movements involved in batting.

The only movements that have not been adequately covered as a part of other field sports are the complex movement sequences involved in batting and throwing. Both motions involve weight transference to achieve maximum force and balance when swinging the arms to hit with the bat, and in throwing the ball (especially in pitching). The lower anatomy plays a major role in weight transference: the feet remain in a neutral position to give a better base of stability to the legs, thus compensating for the force exerted by the upper body.

SURFACES—natural or artificial turf (outfield only); dirt or clay on infield basepaths.

SHOE REQUIREMENTS—

1. **Upper:** top quality shoes of kangaroo or fine quality chrome-tanned cowhide leather. Nylon or other vamp linings to prevent stretch, and normal padded collar and tongue for comfort. A soft or semi-soft toe cap is preferred since there is very little body contact. Rigid heel counter, U-throat asymmetric low-cut pattern. Some lightweight nylon uppers completely reinforced with leather are being introduced. In less expensive models, split leather or nylon reinforced uppers are common. Traditionally, baseball shoes have the long turned-over "kilty" tongue to cover the laces. Lasts are similar to American football, with perhaps slightly more pointed toe.

2. **Soling:** Because natural turf is still most common (even on astro-turf fields the diamond is laid in dirt) the traditional steel split cleat with three front cleats and two heel cleats is used almost exclusively today, in both professional and amateur baseball. Minor leagues have ruled out the metal cleat for safety reasons. Removeable versions of this cleat system have been introduced recently in both steel and PU or nylon cleat materials.

   Although the basic function has not changed, the traditional Goodyear or lock-stitch design, leather sole and riveted split cleat has been largely superceded by the cement and rivet, nylon, molded metal cleat unit. These soles pick up less dirt and offer less pressure under the foot on harder surfaces.

   Many manufacturers offer a composition or rubber molded astro-turf studded shoe for the outfielders. This is very similar to the American football back's shoe, with a lightweight upper.

   For pitchers, pitching toes are often added as toe drag protection on the toecap of conventional shoes. This adds longer life to the pitcher's shoe, which undergoes considerable wear and tear on the pitcher's mound. For hitters it has been found that a circular track cleat formation prevents cleat drag and also aids in turning and base running (see figure 14-11).

SOFTBALL

Softball was originally derived as an indoor version of baseball in Chicago in 1887. It has since become a recognized outdoor game played by both men and women.

14-11. Inexpensive baseball shoe with PVC/nylon uppers. Molded in nylon sole and cleats.

FOOT AND LEG MECHANICS—same as baseball; underhand
pitching.
SURFACES—same as baseball.
SHOE REQUIREMENTS—same as baseball. Narrower women's
models are available. As the majority of softball is played at
the minor league level, molded multi-studded models are
more popular than metal baseball cleats. In many leagues
metal cleats are not allowed.

Shoes made specially for softball tend to be lighter in
weight than baseball shoes. Many use nylon reinforced uppers. Function and style of softball shoes are identical to
baseball. However, as the category is large in North America,
a lightweight multi-studded baseball shoe can be termed a
softball shoe.

PESAPALLO
COUNTRY OF ORIGIN—Finland

FOOT AND LEG MECHANICS—same as baseball
SURFACES—natural turf; hard packed earth or cinder.
SHOE REQUIREMENTS—same as baseball.

RUGBY
The father of all the body contact ball sports, rugby derives its
name from the famous English public school where it was first
played. Very little protective equipment is used, although most
players prefer footwear with a hard toe box for protection,
especially in the "scrum". Due to the strong influence of the
British Empire rugby is popular in New Zealand, Australia, South
Africa (as well as in France). In most other countries where it is
played it is considered a minor sport.
FOOT AND LEG MECHANICS—combination of American football lineman and back's movements. The drop-kick is essentially the same as the punt in American football, except that in
rugby the ball must touch the ground before it is kicked.
SURFACES—natural grass.
SHOE REQUIREMENTS—rugby boots use the same basic design
and construction as soccer shoes and the American football
back's shoe. The stud formation is similar to soccer, with four
front studs and two heel studs. Rugby still allows metal
(aluminum) studs in most levels of play. The semi-cut or three-
quarter cut style is preferred in rugby boots, for ankle protection.

For linemen, as well as for a large percentage of wing
quarter-backs, a hard square box toe is required. Multi-

studded versions of rugby boot models are also made, mainly for harder playing surfaces.

FIELD HOCKEY

Earliest references to field hockey date over 4,000 years ago to a drawing on a tomb at Beni-Hasan in Egypt's Nile Valley. European and South American records make reference to a similar sport dating from the middle ages. Although considered a minor sport in most countries, field hockey is very popular in many parts of the world. The game is played with a hard round ball, similar to a baseball or cricket ball, and wooden sticks. This is the traditional field sport from which ice hockey derived its fundamentals.

14-12. Ladies' soccer or field hockey grass shoe. Features all-leather uppers with cemented multi-studded rubber soles.

Field hockey footwear generally resembles that used in soccer, as the requirements are similar, except that the goalie requires special toe protection (as well as other body padding). The foot is not often brought into contact with the ball.

FOOT AND LEG MECHANICS—mainly forward running; lateral movements.
SURFACES—natural and artificial turf.
SHOE REQUIREMENTS—soccer shoes of the screw-in or multi-studded type are used for field hockey. Canvas uppers with direct vulcanized rubber studs are also popular. If a player requires more protection, the rugby style boot, with higher cut and box toe, is available. No metal studs or cleats are permitted. Special toe protectors are used by goalies to kick out the ball.

FIELD LACROSSE

Primarily a Canadian sport, it is similar to field hockey, except that the ball is thrown and caught with a stick that has a built-in pocket of webbing. The game is of American Indian origin, derived from the inter-tribal game baggataway before 1492.

FOOT AND LEG MECHANICS—mainly forward running; stick movements; throwing.
SURFACES—grass pitch.
SHOE REQUIREMENTS—same as for field hockey.

HURLING

The traditional Irish field game, which is a combination of field hockey and lacrosse.

FOOT AND LEG MECHANICS—same as field hockey and lacrosse.

SURFACE—natural turf.
SHOE REQUIREMENTS—same as field hockey and lacrosse.

AUSTRALIAN FOOTBALL
Basically played only in Australia. Very similar to rugby, with only slight variations. A heavy body contact sport.

FOOT AND LEG MECHANICS—same as in rugby.
SURFACES—grass pitch.
SHOE REQUIREMENTS—same as for rugby, although soccer boots are sometimes preferred.

GAELIC FOOTBALL
Perhaps the roughest of all the football-type games, this traditional Irish sport features teams of 15 that try to punch, dribble or kick the ball into or over the goal-net.

FOOT AND LEG MECHANICS—same as in rugby.
SURFACES—grass pitch.
SHOE REQUIREMENTS—same as rugby. Soccer boots may be preferred.

TEAM HANDBALL
A European team sport similar to soccer but played with the hands, using a smaller inflated ball.

FOOT AND LEG MECHANICS—mainly running, throwing and jumping.
SURFACES—grass, hard dirt or cinder pitch.
SHOE REQUIREMENTS—same as soccer.

CRICKET
The traditional English field sport dating back to c. 1250. Played in many parts of the world, including Australia, South Africa, New Zealand, Caribbean, India, Pakistan and the British Isles. Played with a hard ball and a bat. The antecedent of American baseball. The three types of players are batsmen, bowlers and fielders, who use the following foot and leg mechanics:

1. Bowlers—throwing; running.
2. Fielders—running; throwing.
3. Batsmen—bat strokes (hitting); running.

SURFACES—grass pitch.

SHOE REQUIREMENTS—Like the golf shoe, the cricket shoe has remained a hard toed shoe or boot with heel and metal spikes since the early 1900s. The cricket shoe does not undergo heavy stress although both batsmen and bowlers run and toe drag constantly. It is usually made of a good quality chrome-tanned cowhide, in white, with a girth support strap, rigid counter and box toe.

As with many sports shoes in the past 20 years, more modern materials and designs are now being used, such as nylon soles and low-cut uppers for more flexibility.

Wedge soles (as opposed to heels) are now common. As in other field sports, ripple design and astro-turf studded shoes are becoming popular in some countries. Tennis shoes are sometimes substituted at lower levels of he sport, but they do not offer either adequate traction or protection. Low or semi-cut uppers are both popular.

KORFBALL

Similar to netball or basketball, played on grass. Played in Europe.

FOOT AND LEG MECHANICS—same as in handball.
SURFACES—grass pitch.
SHOE REQUIREMENTS—multi-studded soccer, or screw-in soccer style. Studs no longer than 4 mm. No heavy-duty style shoes, such as rugby boots, baseball shoes or football shoes, are used.

SPEEDBALL

Combines elements of several team sports such as soccer and basketball. Carrying the ball and physical contact are not allowed.

FOOT AND LEG MECHANICS—same as soccer and basketball.
SURFACES—grass or dirt pitch.
SHOE REQUIREMENTS—same as for soccer.

SHINTY

A Gaelic field game similar to hurling and field hockey.

FOOT AND LEG MECHANICS—same as hurling and field hockey.
SURFACES—grass pitch.
SHOE REQUIREMENTS—same as for hurling and field hockey.

"Winter sports leave calories out in the cold."
Gerald Donaldson

15

WINTER SPORT SHOES

Winter sports originated centuries ago from the basic need for mobility on ice and snow. The earliest skis found in Scandinavia have been dated to 2500 B.C. and the earliest references to ice skating belong to Scandinavian literature dating back to the second century, when skates were made of bone and were fastened to the feet with leather thonging.

References to winter sports began to appear by the mid 1700s, when a skating club was formed in Scotland, and in the mid 1800s in Norway a ski club was formed by military personnel. The first artificial ice rink in the world was built in Chelsea, London in 1876. The International Skating Union was founded in 1892.

Early skates for sports, from the eighteenth century, consisted of metal blades riveted to high-cut leather soled boots (which were the fashion trend of the era). Early ski boots were adapted forms of mountain hiking boots made from heavy grade leather, usually in a lockstitch construction with heavily lugged soles. Boots used for speed skating originally had wooden soles.

We will deal with four major sports categories in this chapter. They are skating sports, ski sports, curling and tobogganing.

SPORT—BY—SPORT ANALYSIS

SKATING SPORTS

Skating is one of the most difficult motions humans have mastered. All of the body weight is transferred through the legs and feet and balanced on one or two thin metal blades attached to the soles of the boots. Skating motions are similar in all skating sports, although the footwear and blades are specialized for each sport.

In skating, performance is directly related to ankle movement. Although support for the ankle is essential, the subtalar joint must have some freedom to allow the foot to position the blade on the ice at various plantar-flexed and dorsal-flexed positions. This helps the skates grip the ice and lessens the possibility of knee and ankle strain when making turns and jumps.

There are two main types of construction in skating boots: the traditional leather boot and the newer injection-molded boot. The traditional leather boot has suitable ankle support, firm heel counter with elongated medial side and molded rigid plastic sole (plastic has totally replaced leather as a soling material since the mid-60s). Skate boots are cement and tack lasted. Soles are cemented and riveted or sewn to the uppers. Uppers are made from a thick grade leather or split leather with leather or textile lining, which give the foot and ankle adequate support but still allow some flexibility. Leather also transpires well and molds well to the foot. Metal eyelets are preferred in the lower portion of the throat, and metal hooks for ease of lacing above the ankle. Uppers are conventionally stitched.

First developed in 1957, the injection molded plastic boot was introduced into the market in 1971 for ice hockey. It was an offshoot of the molded boot used in alpine skiing. It was largely developed by the Lange Company in the U.S.A. Injection molding technology is the most revolutionary development in shoe making in the past 50 years. The process involves chemistry, engineering and plastics technology. Viscous plastic is injected into molds, under pressure, to form the upper and lower halves of the boot. The two halves are then joined together in a hinge form to complete the outer shell. Different thicknesses of plastic can be used in certain parts of the mold, allowing the boot to conform exactly to the sole or upper thickness required. A soft foam liner (recently orthopedically improved, with better support) completes the boot design

Liners are turnshoe lasted and stitched or thermo-heat sealed. Either a regular lacing system or a molded-in lace holder (with traditional lace) is used. Buckle or velcro systems are also available on the market.

Unlike the ski boot, ice skates must have some lateral ankle flexibility. To accommodate this action, a hinged two piece outer molding gives the boot some flexibility. Although the fit of the molded boot was originally questionable, since its introduction in the early 70s much improvement has been made, especially in the liners (which are now available in a variety of grades). The molded boot does offer advantages in retaining support, unlike leather boots which tend to become more flexible with time.

Molded skates are streamlined, have no seams and appear futuristic in style and design. They do not show scuff marks or creases. Perhaps their biggest advantage is that they are light. When coupled with a lightweight plastic blade they afford the skater greater maneuverability. Manufacturers also claim that they are warmer for outdoor use.

One-piece injection-molded PU boots, with the blade holder an integral part of the boot shell, are presently being contemplated for the figure skating market. These experimental "phase III" injected boots feature adjustable Velcro or strap and buckle closures (similar to downhill ski boots) and metal blades with recessed stop/start forward picks.

FIGURE SKATING
Olympic and World Championship figure skating events include ice dancing, figures, freestyle, single skating and pairs skating.

FOOT AND LEG MOVEMENT—skating; jumping; balance; spins; dance steps; lifting.

SURFACES—ice, artificial or natural rink.

SHOE REQUIREMENTS—(see also Roller Skate Boot, Chapter 16) The upper is either full or top grain cowhide. A substantial grade of leather and lining (2.5–3 mm) is used to give adequate support. Better quality boots are leather lined with either top grain or split suede. Medium grade boots are made from split leather and have textile or foam insulated liners for warmth and comfort. Inexpensive boots may have vinyl uppers lined with suede or synthetic materials. There are also PU injection molded boots available with separate flexible two-piece high ankle supports.

15-1. Monobloc injected figure skates with Velcro closure straps.

A substantial heel counter, usually elongated on the medial side for arch support is important in skating. A shanked insole is also critical for support. Soles are PVC or PU molded units with heels.

Leather soles may also be used in some top grain boots with screw-in blades, to enable the skater to change the position of the blade (this is not practical with riveted blades). Sole is approximately 8mm. thick. Figure skate lasts are semi-pointed with a narrow shank and heel shape to keep the foot in a contained position.

The quality of the overall skate unit is very much determined by the quality and grade of the blades. Blades are

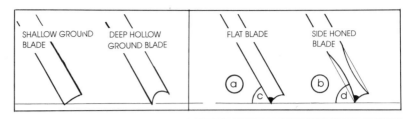

15-2. *Left:* A figure skate blade must possess a shallow precision hollow grind so as to minimize the problem of double tracking. A shallow ground blade does not penetrate the ice as much as a deep hollow ground blade. A deep hollow ground blade edge not in use can mark easier with greater ice penetration of edge in use. 15-3. *Right:* A blade is side honed both to reduce weight and give better blade edge. The illustration shows how side honing increases ice grip at pronounced angles as opposed to a flat blade. (B edge is much sharper than A and D° is greater than C°.)

tubular steel or plastic track with high tempered steel, hollow ground to give two skating edges to the blade. They are usually nickel or chrome plated.

Figures are skated on the inside or outside blade edge, which is approximately 3mm. wide. Lower grades may not be tempered or only surface hardened. This makes it difficult to retain an edge when sharpening. The edge is important in obtaining the correct forward thrust when skating.

Blades used for figure or free-style have a curvature from front to back called a radius or rocker. Blades are usually placed slightly towards the medial side of the sole midline.

A toe rake or pick is used in free-style for jumps or spins. Picks also help stop the blade sliding sideways on forward thrusts. A different set of skates, having no pick and less sharply ground blades, is often preferred for figures.

ICE HOCKEY

Earliest references of hockey being played on ice date to the seventeenth century in the Netherlands. However, Canada claims the origination of the game from 1855. A body contact team sport, using sticks and a hard rubber puck. Protective equipment is mandatory.

15-4. Ice hockey skate—Ballistic nylon mesh and full-grain leather uppers. Cement and rivet nylon/PU sole with plastic blade holder.

FOOT AND LEG MOVEMENTS—skating; quick stops; quick turns; balance.

SURFACES—ice, artificial or natural rink.

SHOE REQUIREMENTS—high-cut leather or ballistic nylon, with leather reinforcement at heel, eyestay, etc. Hard fiber or polyethylene toe box for protection and sturdy construction with padding at ankle for protection and comfort. Lining on the tendon guard and tongue is usually ballistic nylon cloth.

Leather lining on better grade boots. Nylon sole molded boot with hinged upper offers excellent durability and protection from puck and stick impact. High-cut at Achilles tendon for support and protection.

Lasts used in hockey boots have a broad, high toe box, a high waist and a narrow seat. Blade frame is either tubular or plastic with safety tips, carbon steel blades 3/32″ wide. Hollow ground. Skates must be of an approved design; speed or figure skates are prohibited for reasons of safety.

Goalie's skate—a special version is available for goalies, in either a fully-molded or leather boot, with molded protection casing. It is lowcut at the ankle to allow more flexibility and to accommodate goalie pads. This skate also has a much thicker reinforced blade, with no rocker, and with more surface on the ice to block shots at the goal.

15-5. Goalie's ice hockey skate with protective casing.

BANDY
Related to ice hockey, but played with a ball instead of a puck. Similar to field hockey.

FOOT AND LEG MOVEMENTS—same as hockey.
SURFACES—natural outside rink.
SHOE REQUIREMENTS—same as ice hockey.

SPEED SKATING
Olympic and world speed skating events cover distances from 500m to 10,000m for men and 500m to 3,000m for women.

FOOT AND LEG MOVEMENTS—forward skating; low center of gravity; balance. Racers often compete barefooted in their skate boots.
SURFACES—artificial or natural ice track.
SHOE REQUIREMENTS—uppers are deep-cut U-throat more full length lace-to-toe design, with D-ring or eyelet closure for maximum girth fitting on narrow facing last. Semi-cut (¾ cut) ankle boots are preferred. Rigid heel counter with elongated medial support. Leather or textile linking. Boots are light-to-medium weight, kangaroo box calf or full-grain leather. Padded ankle for comfort. Long, thin (app. 1/16″ wide) straight blades, either tubular steel or plastic frames for lightness. The blade, 30–45cm in length, is made somewhat distal from the boot by means of a higher frame or cones to allow lower angle lean between the boot and ice surface. Better quality blades are chrome plated. Unlike with figure skates, hockey skate blades are usually stone ground not hollow ground. In indoor

racing, where the athlete must compensate for the body's center of gravity around turns, the blade on the left boot is positioned slightly to the lateral side and the blade on the right boot to the medial side.

SKIING SPORTS

The earliest formal races and organized competition took place in Switzerland in 1911. The International Ski Federation (F.I.S.) and Winter Olympic Games were founded in 1924. Skiing sports are grouped into three distinct categories:

1. Alpine, or downhill, skiing
2. Ski jumping
3. Cross-country skiing.

ALPINE SKIING

Alpine skiing is one of the biggest recreational winter activities. There are three subcategories of downhill skiing: downhill, slalom, and giant slalom. All alpine skis have quick-release toe and heel bindings.

Downhill—Downhill skis are made from fiberglass and plastic materials. Some wood or metal may still be used. Metal edges are incorporated. These are the heaviest of the three types of downhill skis.

Slalom—same materials as for downhill, but skis are shorter and narrower. Welded metal edges.

Giant Slalom—same materials as for downhill, but with more flexibility. Narrower width than downhill skis.

FOOT AND LEG MOVEMENTS—heel and ankle retention (little or no lateral movement); ankle and knee flex; forward lean (anterior and posterior); hip and leg muscles; balance.

In this sport, the modern rigid polyurethane boot plays a major part in technique and movement. The skier should have a relaxed balanced stance, good reflexes, and maintain a constant, evenly distributed pressure between the anterior and posterior of the body.

SURFACES—snow-covered hill or mountain terrain.

SHOE REQUIREMENTS—hinged or one-piece injection molded plastic outer shell, with high-cut upper supporting lower leg. Rigid ankle and foot support. Forward ankle flex or canting, adjustable buckle, dial type device closure or straps for instep support and fitting. Shock-absorbing outside heels, made from rubber or polyurethane, are designed to give a more consistent interface with the ski binding.

Inner boot is of leather, padded PVC or PU (sewn or high frequency welded). Slip or turn lasted. Inner liners can contain

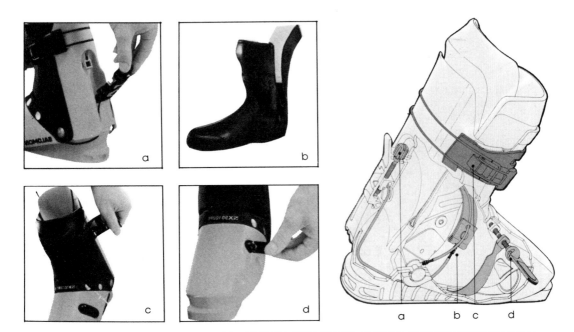

15-6. Adjustments on a typical ski boot: (a) By adjusting the micro-screw and closing the rear clip one can get a better fit at the heel of the boot. (b) The inner casing of the boot is a pre-formed, heat insulated material that fits snugly around the foot. (c) The inner casing of the boot can be adjusted once, without having to change with every use. This system works independently from the two outer buckles, which merely open and close the boot. (d) This mechanism on the outside of the boot adjusts the front.

footbed, various wedges, or adjustable canting devices for maximum damping effect. Molding foam or adjustable pressure flo-bags can also be inserted to relieve pressure. Heavily padded contour fitting tongue. Some boots may still have an inserted liner which is glued into the inner side of the shell. Virgin wool is frequently used for heat retention and moisture absorption.

Although ski boots are perhaps the most intricate and technical form of footwear in any sport not all innovations are long lasting. A concept introduced in 1980 took the ski market by storm in 1982. Rigid plastic knee-high support shell boots were claimed in principle to give better leverage, tibia protection and maximize edging ability. However, enthusiasm for the boots has declined since it has been found that their rigidity would not allow skiers to bend their ankles.

Many binding and ski boot manufacturers are working together in order to produce an integrated boot and binding combination, in which part of the binding would be molded or attached to the boot. The complete assembly would then be locked into a counterpart on the ski. This type of sole can be removed from the boot or left in the binding to provide the skier with a separate walking sole on the boot.

Rear-Entry or Mid-Entry Boots. Continuous technological advances in PU molded shells with inner liners have yielded yet another radical change in downhill-ski boots—the rear entry-boot. First introduced in the early 1980s by Hanson, rear and mid-entry boots have largely eliminated conventional buckles and overlaps on the vamp, instep and ankle regions to reduce pressure. Rear-entry systems have certain design features that differ from conventional top-entry boots. These may be summerized as follows:

POSSIBLE ADVANTAGES	POSSIBLE DISADVANTAGES
• Simple to use—ease of entry.	• Inability to secure the foot precisely inside the shell.
• Constant fit setting.	
• More natural forward flex design feature.	• Foot "centered" in the shell.
• Reduction of buckles to reduce pressure.	• Inadequate support and control for expert skiiers and racers.

In order to overcome the acknowledged objections to the rear-entry boot systems, manufacturers have devised varying solutions. In general they take two forms: Fitting cables that wrap elaborately around the foot to apply pressure from all sides and double shells in which the internal layer tightens down around the foot similar to more conventional closure systems.

The trend towards more streamlined simplicity of the exterior is being made possible by more complex adjustments and features inside the boot. Recent sales statistics (Winter 1985–86) indicate 82 percent of ski boots sold now are rear-entry design.

Electrically Heated Boots. Although an auxilliary boot-warmer pack has been commercially available since the 1970s, some of the larger manufacturers of molded ski boots are building a heating system directly into selected models. This comfort feature is also helpful in alleviating numb cold feet on the hills. A battery pack (Standard Alkaline or NiCad rechargeable) attached to the boot is wired to a printed-circuit heater under the toes and sole of the foot. There is usually enough power to supply several hours of continuous heating, however manufacturers recommend that heat is used intermittantly or as required. (An offswitch is built into the device.)

A simple neoprene thermal boot wrap may also help seal in

warmth. Made with Velcro closures for easy access to boot buckles, boot wraps are made in several sizes to fit over most boots.

One of the last categories of athletic footwear to accommodate the female leg and foot, some boot manufacturers are designing footwear to better complement the woman skiers style. Differences to look for in a woman's boot are an easier forward flex, an elevated heel (to compensate for a shorter Achilles tendon) and a more flared cuff. When added to skis and bindings right for a woman the combination results in more comfortable, enjoyable skiing.

SKI JUMPING

Credited as a Nordic/Scandinavian sport originally, ski jumping calls for special courage and for balancing skills in addition to natural skiing ability. Ski jumpers have travelled distances of 150–170 meters in the air. Hills are normally 70–90 meters.

15-7. Specially angled ski jumping boot. Goodyear welt construction.

FOOT AND LEG MOVEMENTS—ski crouch position; no lateral ankle movement; knee flex and lock position; balanced forward lean; flexible landing knee flex; hips bent into telemart position for counter force from landing; normal parallel downhill ski position.

SURFACE—specially constructed hill; compact snow surfaces.

SHOE REQUIREMENTS—lightweight leather boot, similar to hiking boot with same flex at ball. Rigid lateral ankle support. Rigid boot construction (Goodyear welt or lockstitch construction). Padded PVC or leather lined. Specially constructed with a forward lean angle of about 18 degrees. High-cut lower leg support. Rigid wedge sole (sometimes fiberglass-strengthened) with wide flared heel for stable landing platform. U-throat, D-ring lacing system.

CROSS-COUNTRY SKIING

Has probably become the largest recreational skiing sport. Competition races over 10,15,30 and 50 km. for men and 5 or 10 km. for women. Credited as a Nordic/Scandinavian sport, cross-country skiing is now popular in all snow climates.

Skis are long and narrow, made of lightweight fiberglass, plastic or wood (waxed and waxless). Toe bindings only. Heel or forepart stabilizers are optional.

Boots and binding systems should be considered together for compatibility, as there are several exclusive systems available.

FOOT AND LEG MOVEMENTS—fast walking motion; jog running; downhill skiing; balance. Boot and binding work like a

15-8. High shafted monobloc injected ski boot. They were the rage in 1981–82.

hinge between foot and ski.

SURFACES—snow covered cross-country terrain; "in-track" and trail skiing.

SHOE REQUIREMENTS—uppers are leather, high-tech nylon or poromeric materials. Monobloc PU or rubber one-piece upper/sole boots are also available. Linings may be leather, fleece or other synthetic materials. Although fleece is very popular it is not necessarily warmer. Fleece tends to compact and when wet, from perspiration or water, it cools the foot. This is why leather or thinner materials may be preferred for lining cross-country ski boots.

Leather and materials like Gore-tex breathe, which allows the air to transpire and circulate around the foot. Many man-made upper materials do not breathe, trapping perspiration and causing the foot to become colder.

Boots should be waterproof, as seam free as possible with rigid heel counters. Good flex in the forepart is essential.

Soles are made from PU, thermal plastic rubber or unit rubber. Rubber soles are preferred for walking on snow and ice when boot is used without ski. Soles may be injected, cemented and stitched or riveted. Some welted construction is still used in Europe. Soles should be torsionally rigid. Soles normally have metal or plastic toe plates in the extended forward edge of the sole or "snout" as guides for the toe binding pins (Norms). Cable bindings are also used in conjunction with Nordic Norm pins, with a grooved heel notch molded into the heel.

CONSTRUCTION—cement, tack or string lasting. Non-corrosive metal or blind eyelets. Shank in heel. Bellows tongue.

As already noted, soles and bindings on cross-country boots must be compatible. There are several norms that fit industry standard bindings as well as exclusive patented systems that require matched boot/binding couplings.

The Norms are:

1. Nordic Norm 71,75 and 79 mm (75 is the standard)—asymmetric.
2. Racing/Touring Norm 50 mm—symmetric.

The largest exclusive systems are:

• Adidas 38 mm Norm
• Lin System (Dynafit) 38 mm
• Salomon System

(These exclusive sole/binding attachments are further refinements to save weight and aid maximum toe-off leverage.)

Touring boots (Nordic Norm 75 mm x 12 mm (½")). Used for touring and recreation, normally on open trails. These boots are

BOOT-BINDING SYSTEMS

SYSTEM	FEATURES	WIDTH OF SOLE AND BINDING AT ATTACHMENT POINT	BOOT SOLE THICKNESS, MATERIAL	INTENDED USE	COMMENTS
Nordic Norm	Binding clamps welt ahead of boot upper. Asymmetrical; has right and left.	71, 75, 79 mm depending on boot size, type, 75 mm by far most common	12 mm, rubber, softer plastic	light touring, touring, Nordic downhill	Widespread, older standard products from many makers
Norm 38	Binding holds "snout" extension of boot sole. Symmetrical, no right or left.	38 mm	7 mm, hard plastic	racing, light touring	Adidas exclusive, some licensees also producing
Racing Norm	Binding holds tapered "snout" extension of boot sole. Symmetrical.	50 mm	7 mm, hard plastic	racing, light touring, touring	Widespread standard, products from many makers
Touring Norm	As for Racing Norm; has same profile, differs only in thicker boot sole. Symmetrical.	50 mm	12 mm, rubber, softer plastic	light touring, touring	Standard, products from several makers
System LIN	Springlike catch on rounded sole extension locks into mating binding. Symmetrical.	55 mm	7 mm, hard plastic	racing, light touring	Dynafit exclusive, no other makers
Salomon	Rectangular metal eye on sole toe mates tongue latch on binding. Symmetrical.	30 mm	7 mm, hard plastic	racing, light touring	Salomon exclusive, some boot licensees

either high or semi-cut with well padded ankle cuff or low-cut with ankle cuffs or skree used in deep snow. Touring boots are heavier and warmer than racing models. Leather is predominantly used becuase of its superior breathability. Construction can be either direct-injected PU, T.P.R. or cemented rubber unit sole. Some welted constructions are also popular in Europe. Thicker 12 mm soles are preferred for insulation against the cold. All PU or all-rubber molded boots can be used for extremely cold or wet conditions. 75 mm soles are preferred in open country for stability and comfort when less speed is required. 50 mm soles may be preferred if less "drag" is required in "breaking trail" with the wider bindings overlapping the narrow ski.

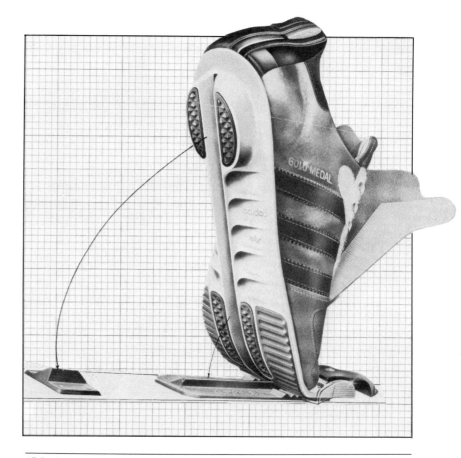

15-9. Adidas' integral 38mm cross-country ski system.

Racing or competition boots (Racing Norm 50 mm x 7 mm (¼")) (Norm 38 x 7 mm (¼")) (Other Exclusive Systems). These boots and binding systems are generally used for in-track racing and competitive skiers seeking the utmost in performance. The boots or shoes resemble track spike shoes with a protruding "snout" extension in front. They are low-cut oxford style, U-throat construction, leather or combination high-tech nylon with leather reinforcement, with conventional or speed lacing. Bellows tongue or Velcro apron lace cover.

Soles are thinner 7 mm (¼") nylon (or nylon with rubber inserts) cement and rivet construction or hard PU direct injection. Flexible lightweight soles are either 50 mm or less in width for in-track skiing with less overlap drag on the toe.

CURLING

Two teams of four players deliver round stones or "rocks" across a measured length of ice to a marked target area or "house." This sport is popularly played in most cold climate countries. The origins of curling date to the early eighteenth century in Scotland. Dress for curling is informal, except for the shoes, which have become a specialty item.

15-10. A typical shoe used for curling.

FOOT AND LEG MOVEMENTS—two types of movement are involved:
1.) *Delivery of the Rock*—The rock is delivered out of a "hack" position with front leg in a flex position at the knee, the back leg in a trail position for balance, and legs split far apart. Hip, knee, ankle joints, and anterior leg muscles are used. Foot is either in a fully planted ankle flexed position (flat delivery) or toe-flexed position if delivery is made off the toe. The back foot or trail foot is often turned to the side for better balance.
2.) *Sweeping Movements*—To make the rock slide more smoothly, team members move down the ice in a slide stepping action, while sweeping in front of the rock. This sweeping action can be performed quite vigorously; therefore, shoes should have good lateral and heel support.

SURFACES—indoor or outdoor curling rink.
SHOE REQUIREMENTS—leather uppers of various designs, semi-cut or oxford-cut for ankle flexibility. Well lined for warmth. Insulated insole. Sole can be either heel or wedge, usually MCR rubber or crepe rubber unit. Firm heel counter. Attachable slider on front of foot can vary from tip-slider to complete sole for flat footed delivery in the hack. Conventional eyelet or speed eyelet lacing system. Velcro closures have also been used. Padded collars (for comfort), right or left slider kits of vinyl or teflon are available options. Rubber overshoe may be used to cover slider when curler is sweeping.

BOBSLEDDING
An Olympic sport, probably adapted from recreational snow sledding in Finland. Modern competition started in 1924. Bobsledding with either single, pairs or four-man teams is done in a covered car. The rider or riders must push the car from a standing position before seating themselves in the sled and negotiating a specially constructed course of graded icy curves.

15-11. Special "Bobsledding" competition shoe with "brush" forepart spikes.

FOOT AND LEG MOVEMENTS—sprinting; pushing with upper body.
SURFACES—ice; hard-packed snow.

SHOE REQUIREMENTS—as this movement is basically sprinting on ice the shoes used for bobsledding are modified sprinter's shoes (Track). They are form-fitting, with a pointed last. Soft leather uppers with nylon tape lining, and light rigid heel counter. Toe foxing. Front toe plate with strips of metal brush spikes. Wrap-up heel and outer sole for additional lateral support.

LUGE

The luge is a one-man sled with the rider lying flat on his back, legs front. Although this sport is performed entirely in the lying position, a competition shoe has been developed to help improve performance. This shoe has been made similarly to a wet boot used for skin diving. The upper is made from Neoprene or latex foam with a PU coating for less wind resistance. This boot is a high-cut ankle length with front zipper. It has a lightweight curved sole specially designed to be more aerodynamically efficient. The boot is smooth with no creases to trap air. It has an anchored insert at the ball and heel. This shoe is wind tunnel tested.

"Let each step be whole, conscious and clear."
The Backpacker, Albert Saijo

OUTDOOR SPORT SHOES

In this chapter all of the outdoor specialty "activities" are listed. Most of the recreational activities in this section are non-competitive, but are classified as recreational sports in order to encompass the vast range of footwear types sold under the broad category of sports footwear.

The shoes discussed in this section are produced specifically for the intended sport. Should they overlap or be used for another purpose, this will be disregarded. As we have noted in "The Street Shoe Phenomenon", athletic footwear, produced for performance or functional sports use, has often been put to other use than that originally intended.

One thing that all athletic shoes have in common is that they are designed for a specific function. Design for functionality is the criteria used to select some of the footwear in the outdoor activities here classified as "sport".

Many of the sports listed in this section, such as walking, fishing and camping are among the top participation sports in the world.

HIKING

Hiking may be defined as a long walk over natural outdoor terrain. The boots now used have been adapted from those traditionally found in mountainous European regions, such as the Alps, where farmers required a sturdy shoe when tending their cattle or sheep in the high pastures, or when a trip to the nearest village meant at least a three to four hour hike.

16-1. Depending on whether you're out for a Sunday stroll in the woods behind your house...a day trip at a nearby state park...a weekend camping trip in a National Forest preserve...or a strenuous mountain climbing expedition, your footwear will vary with the length of your trip, the terrain and weather, your endurance and experience.

The average hiking boot weighs approximately three pounds, and a hiker will take over 2,000 paces in a mile. Boots with uppers of advanced technology fabrics have made considerable headway in the market against traditional leather styles, because of the weight advantage and the factors of comfort and breathability. Most of these advantages accrued from advances in running shoe technology in the 1970s.

Today this type of footwear can be divided into two categories:

1. a trail shoe or boot—used for backpacking and general mountaineering purposes
2. various weights of hiking boots.

FOOT AND LEG MECHANICS—see walking.

SURFACES—various outdoor terrains; usually woods, fields, hills and mountainous regions.

SHOE REQUIREMENTS—

1) *Trail shoe*—can be either oxford or ankle high-cut. Upper of full-grain cowhide (2.0–2.5 mm.) lined or unlined. Moccasin or plain vamp, derby cut, leather thong or heavy lacing. Metal eyelets, padded collar or topline. Rigid heel counter and reinforced toe. Good flex point across metatarsal area. Lug sole should be thick, semi-flexible and lightweight, with heel for traction and protection from

16-2. One of the first lightweight hiking boots on the market with Cordura fabric and leather uppers. EVA rubber sole combination.

rough terrain and rocks. Should be of rubber or composition PVC (Elvaloy). Short steel shank. Construction is usually cement or injection molded. Weight, 1½ to 2 pounds.

2) *Hiking boot*—full-grain oxhide or cowhide leather uppers (smooth or rough cut), over-ankle cut (6″), padded topline, leather or suede lined (combined thickness is 4 to 4.5 mm.) with additional inside ankle padding for comfort. Padded tongue, D-ring or hooks with flat laces. Rigid heel counter, reinforced toe box, wrap over ski vamp tongue (also called a French tongue). Semi-flexible sole is of thick rubber or PVC (Elvaloy), heavily lugged for traction.

Sole should be curved, with good toe pitch for walking action. The heel with short steel shank support assures good sole flex at the proper point.

16-3. Mountain hiking boot. Full-grain leather. French tongue lacing system. Waterproof Gore-Tex lining, EVA midsole. Vibram Kletter-lift outsole.

This type of shoe traditionally is either Goodyear welt with leather welt or stitched sole method. Other types of boots often referred to as hiking boots are: army boots, field shoes, buckle-style combat boots, paratroop boots and canvas jungle boots. These can be of various types of construction, not necessarily stitched, weighing 2½ to 4 pounds each. Some bend in forepart.

Another form of lightweight cement construction hiking boot has been introduced in the athletic footwear industry. This boot features woven coarse nylon uppers (Cordura) with leather or suede trim, often backed with waterproof "Gore-tex" material or insulating material such as "Thinsulate." Sole construction is of a firmer MCR; midsole and wedge type, with shallow lugging rubber outsoles. Weight of these models is about half that of more traditional hiking boots.

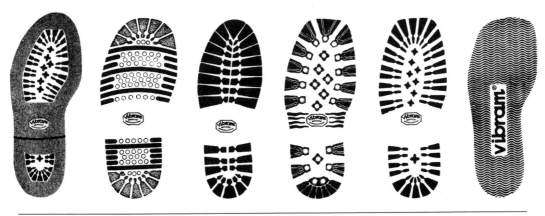

16-4. A wide range of soles are available for hiking boots.

Soles for outdoor terrain are available in a wide variety of weights, designs and thicknesses. Most are made of rubber, although polyurethane is becoming increasingly popular. The important issue in selecting sole designs is to consider the types of terrain to be encountered. Deep lug soles are not intended primarily for use on level smooth trails or gently sloping terrain, unless the weather has worsened its condition. Shallow lug soles or textured pattern designs are suitable on such trails. Deep lug soles are appropriate for rougher, colder territory.

WALKING

There are three basic classifications of walking as a sport:

1. Race, or competitive walking (covered under Track and Field Sports).
2. Hiking (covered above).
3. Exercise walking.

It is the third category, exercise walking, that has developed recently as an offshoot of the jogging and fitness boom of the late 1970s.

16-5. *Left:* The traditional "Vibram" lug sole made from wear-resistant high-quality rubber compound.
16-6. *Right:* Rockport "ProWalker" series in leather and leather/suede and mesh models with stitchdown construction.

FOOT AND LEG MECHANICS—see walking.

SURFACES—roadway; sidewalk; pavement; grass and parkland.

SHOE REQUIREMENTS—(see chapter on *Walking*). Very similar to long-distance running shoes. Lightweight leather or nylon (soft or mesh) uppers reinforced at toe, eyestay and heel with suede. U-throat design with apron cut or similar minimal seam variation. Padded or rolled collar, padded tongue. A three-quarter or mid-cut boot is available with supplemental ankle support. Good flex path. Rigid heel counter. Sole of either polyurethane, EVA or MCR wedge heel with firm heel density. Cushioned midsole. Wrap-up toe, gum rubber or carbon rubber outsole, low profile sole (adequate toe spring for better wear), minimal bias at heel for positive landing. Weight 11–13 ounces.

16-7. Rock climbing boots with high rubber foxing and leather soles.

MOUNTAIN CLIMBING

FOOT AND LEG MECHANICS—platform, balance and precise edging and Jam-crack techniques.

SURFACES—various rock and mountain terrain.

SHOE REQUIREMENTS—there are two types of boots made for climbing, rock-climbing boots and mountaineering boots.

16-8. Combination mountain and rock climbing boots with suede uppers, rubber foxing and outsole.

Rock-climbing boots offer maximum traction and grip for the foot on the rock face. The climber must feel his position and have some flexibility in the ankle. Boots should allow some friction and smear on granite yet still allow the climber to edge sharply on limestone holds. Soles are flexible but thick enough to platform the foot and they have hard smooth surfaces, not suitable for walking. They should be snug-fitting with semi-pointed toes for delicate footwork on rock face. Quarters should be flush with sole. These boots are lightweight compared to hiking or mountaineering boots (2–3 lbs.), and are specifically made for rock climbing, not mountaineering. It is important to break in these shoes on easy climbs to allow the sole to "scallop" and mold to the foot in order to allow the rubber sole and foxing to attain their maximum frictional properties. They have an above-ankle upper construction of leather, suede, canvas, or Cordura nylon. Leather or suede lined, with a thickness of 2.5 to 3.5 mm. Padded tongue, metal eyelets or eyelet hooks. Wrap-over vamp closure or full lace-to-toe cut. Rigid mid-sole, gristle or gum rubber outsole with lightweight smooth or shallow profile. Wide (2") rubber foxing around boot for abrasion and grip. Cement construction.

16-9. Modern styled hiking boots featuring monobloc injected uppers with leather shaft and liner. Rubber cemented outsoles for traction.

16-10. *Top left:* A variety of top Maine hunting boots in various heights. Insulated vulcanized waterproof rubber bottoms. Water-resistant full-grain cowhide leather tops. 16-11. *Top right:* Hunting boots in leather and camouflage Cordura nylon shaft. Direct PVC injected lug sole. 16-12. *Bottom:* Rocky Boots' selection of hiking and hunting boots showing a variety of constructions and materials.

Cold weather mountaineering boots are the heavyweight versions of the hiking boot (5–7 lbs.). These boots are suitable for ice and mountain climbing. They are extremely stiff and allow the foot very little flexibility. They do, however, offer maximum support so that the boots can act as platforms for better stability. In addition to a full-length shank, leather or wooden midsoles are attached between the welt and the outsole to obtain more stability. Ice spikes or crampons are attached as over shoes on ice or glacier climbs. These boots are ideal for extended cross-country travel where maximum protection is necessary, but they are not recommended for ordinary hiking activities.

Construction is basically the same as for heavy-duty hiking boots using Goodyear welt method or polyurethane outershell with soft leather inner liner. (Same construction as the monobloc injected ski boot.)

HUNTING

There are a wide variety of outdoor and hunting boots on the market today. They vary considerably, from 6″ high-cut non-lined uppers with injected soles to 9″ high-cut insulated and lined Goodyear welt with waterproofed leather uppers. It will suffice to describe the most common or popular boot designed and sold in this category.

FOOT AND LEG MECHANICS—see walking.

SURFACES—wood; stream; marsh; various types of outdoor terrain.

SHOE REQUIREMENTS—high-cut full-grain leather boots. Heights of these silicone-tanned or water resistant boots are 6″, 8″ or 9″. Unlined or lined and insulated. Derby cut, sealed and waterproofed seams, brass eyelets and D-rings. Padded topline or collar, looped, backstay cushion insole with arch support. Full bellows stock gusset. Taslon laces. Injected oil-resistant PVC lug sole or Goodyear welted nailless construction. Full-breasted or half-wedge heel. Steel shank. Plain or plug vamp. Maine hunting boots are leather uppers with rubber vulcanized soles, also known as bottom pacs. Cordura camouflage nylon with full leather footbed and trim is an alternative upper material.

16-13. Waterproof insulated hunting boot. Thinsulate lined leather upper. Gore-Tex waterproof sock lining, steel shank EVA midsole, Vibram unisole.

16-14. Hunting boot with innovative PU shell vamp and removable Gore-Tex bootie liner. Soles are expanded SBR and EVA.

SNOWSHOES

North American Indians devised the earliest form of footwear for mobility on deep snow. It consisted of wooden boughs strapped onto the feet with leather thongs. This eventually evolved into a wooden frame interlaced with rawhide.

FOOT AND LEG MECHANICS—see walking or jogging. Also note that the narrow heel section of the snowshoe contacts the ground first.

SURFACES—snow or ice.

SHOE REQUIREMENTS—the principle of the snowshoe is to distribute the body weight over a large area, thus lessening the tendency to sink into the snow with each step.

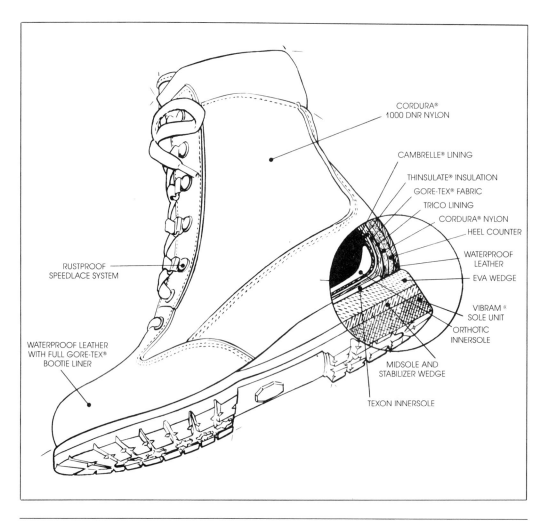

CORDURA®
1000 DNR NYLON

CAMBRELLE® LINING

THINSULATE® INSULATION
GORE-TEX® FABRIC
TRICO LINING
CORDURA® NYLON
HEEL COUNTER
WATERPROOF
LEATHER
EVA WEDGE
VIBRAM®
SOLE UNIT
ORTHOTIC
INNERSOLE

RUSTPROOF
SPEEDLACE SYSTEM

WATERPROOF LEATHER
WITH FULL GORE-TEX®
BOOTIE LINER

MIDSOLE AND
STABILIZER WEDGE

TEXON INNERSOLE

16-15. Drawing showing features of Rocky Boots' "stalker" hunting model.

Snowshoes today are made on a light wooden frame with an oval shape. They are approximately 3 feet long and 18 inches wide and weigh approximately 3½ pounds per pair. Suitable snowshoes for racing or training measure somewhat less in length and around 10 inches in width. They are attached to the boot in one of several ways:

1. with leather thonging or strap tied around the foot as a harness or Velcro straps, which attaches to the wooden snowshoe frame by a hinge under the ball of the foot.
2. by using the traditional 75 mm. cross-country ski boot and binding attachment, screwed directly to the cross strut of the snowshoe frame.

3. by a new rubber device which has a foot opening that stretches around the boot and clasps at the toe.

Lapp boots or mukluks without heels (heels wear through the webbing) can be used with the snowshoe. For serious snow training or racing, snowshoes can be worn with a flat soled running shoe, preferably with a studded grip type for additional traction.

One-piece polyurethane injected units incorporating frame and webbing are advertised to be lighter and stronger than the traditional snowshoe.

SNOWMOBILING

This motorized recreational sport has gained popularity since the 1960s, mainly in North America.

FOOT AND LEG MECHANICS—balance and grip on the machine. Some walking.

SURFACES—snow covered terrain; snow mobile running boards.

SHOE REQUIREMENTS—The boots designed for snowmobiling are vulcanized rubber soles with coarse nylon shaft uppers. Felt lined, zippered with straps and buckles. Draw string top. One-piece builtup calendered sole with traction tread. As there is a minimum of foot movement, good insulation is desirable.

Safety-tip: There are many lower-priced versions of this type of shoe available offering a minimal amount of insulation and protection. If you are stranded in heavy snow country you will need a boot offering excellent insulation, traction and protection for a possible long hike for help.

CAMPING

When manufacturers designate a boot specifically for camping it is normally a semi-cut or less expensive version of a hunting boot. Camping is basically a recreation and therefore requires fewer features than either a hiking, walking or hunting boot.

FOOT AND LEG MECHANICS—same as walking and hiking.

SURFACES—various outdoor terrains.

SHOE REQUIREMENTS—semi-cut leather or coarse nylon uppers. Derby cut. Leather uppers with plain or full moccasin stitched vamp. Coarse nylon uppers with suede or leather reinforced eyestay, heel counter pocket and toe cap. Rigid heel counter and boxtoe, padded topline collar and tongue, looped backstay. Leather or textile lining. Brass eyelets of D-rings, taslon laces. Low profile sole, to avoid carrying dirt into

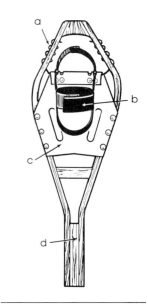

16-16. This racing snowshoe, designed by Barney Klecker, is 34" long and 10½" wide with: (a) adjustable tension master cord; (b) binding; (c) snowshoe insert; (d) frame.

the tent. Wedge or heel with steel shank. Goodyear welt construction or fake welt cement construction.

It is also advisable to take along a lightweight canvas rubber vulcanized deck shoe for water activities or for inside the tent.

FISHING

Fishing is another recreational activity that enjoys huge popularity. In North America it is one of the top recreational activities. U.S. statistics show that in the summer of 1979 fishing was fifth-ranked in participation (male and female) behind swimming, general exercise, camping and running/jogging. For the discussion of footwear needs, fishing can be divided into four categories:

1. **Waders**—hip or chest waders are used by the serious angler who wishes to gain better access to the fish, as when surf-casting or fly-fishing in narrow streams. These extended boots are made of sheet rubber or PVC coated nylon in one piece from the boot shaft up to the hips or the chest.

   The boot itself is of vulcanized rubber with lugged or rippled tread on the sole. Rigid (sometimes metal) heel plates may be added to keep the body weight down on the stream or riverbed. Rugged profiled soles for traction. The tops are secured with braces over the shoulders and are belted around the waist. Some chest waders have inflatable tops for buoyancy and maneuverability, and for safety in deeper water. Waders are available in full sizes only, and measurements are taken from inside leg seam and outside seam under arm.

2. **Salt or Open Sea Fishing**—canvas deck shoes are most popular in this type of fishing. Rubber built-up gum boots are also used extensively on fishing boats. Another preference is for neoprene socks or booties covered with plastic sandals.

3. **Ice Fishing**—hunting or hiking boots are the most popular, along with rubber built-up gum boots. Insulated or felt lined boots are preferred. A deep lugged sole or loggers calked sole with hob nailed edges give the best grip on ice. Snow shoes are also used.

4. **General Fishing**—on boats, canvas deck shoes are most popular. Many other forms of rubber and canvas footwear are also used. Leather and suede are not recommended for water sports where shoes are likely to receive constant soaking. For on-shore fishing, a nylon mesh

upper with rubber built-up vulcanized sole is popular. The shoe is a lightweight camper-style derby cut, with wedge heel and calendered sole. Many varieties (or combinations) of the above categories are used when little chance of water contact is anticipated.

WIND SURFING (SAIL BOARDING)

A relatively new sport which combines features of sailing and surfing. Started in the U.S.A. in the 1960s and rapidly became popular there and in Europe.

FOOT AND LEG MECHANICS—similar to water skiing and downhill skiing. Balance; agility; center of gravity.
SURFACES—high-impact plastic board with or without foot
  straps.
SHOE REQUIREMENTS—a lightweight nylon mesh suede
  footbed. Ankle height upper with U-throat and speed lacing.
  Suction sheet rubber tread sole, with wrap-up foxing. Heel
  counter, ankle and heel padding. (Similar to a ski boot liner
  but completely flexible.) Lateral support and protection, as
  well as traction and warmth, are desirable features. A form of
  modified nylon backed (neoprene) latex foam rubber wet sock
  with either a vulcanized or cemented rubber sole is also used.
  These types of shoes are not necessarily required in warm
  weather and light winds. In competition, cold weather and
  stiffer breezes, however, shoes are essential. The last shape is
  similar to a boxing or wrestling shoe.

16-17. Special shoes are used for sail boarding.

PARACHUTING

Parachuting is a modern sport. It became an international event in 1951.

FOOT AND LEG MECHANICS—landing with bent knees, ankle
  support.
SURFACES—various outdoor terrains.
SHOE REQUIREMENTS—high-top oxhide leather or coarse nylon boot (reinforced with suede at heel, toe and ankle). Fully
  padded and lined. U-throat, wing-tip cut, conventional lacing
  (12–14 eyelets). Padded tongue. Rigid heel counter. Cement
  and tack lasted. Cement construction sole, of thick MCR,
  midsole and wedge. Rubber ripple outsole with foxing at the
  toe. Pneumatic air-cushion soles for shock absorbency are
  also used. Blind eyelets are used to avoid snagging lines. The
  lacing system is also covered with tape for the same reason.

ORIENTEERING

A sport for individuals or teams. Involves a cross-country run, usually through heavily wooded areas, negotiating a preset course with map and compass. Popular in Scandinavia and England.

FOOT AND LEG MECHANICS—similar to cross-country running
   (see *Running section*).
SURFACES—rugged outdoor terrain (wooded, water, etc.).
SHOE REQUIREMENTS—due to the nature of the terrain a
   rugged durable shoe is required. Both competition and racing
   models are available. Racing models are lighter. Specialized
   orienteering shoes are a cross between a track shoe and a
   multi-studded soccer shoe.

   Upper of soft nylon or polyurethane coated rubber substrate material. Suede reinforced at toe, heel counter and
   eyestay. Another popular upper material is a PVC coated
   nylon, which is extremely durable and waterproof. Rolled and
   bound collars are preferred over simple padded collars for
   less water absorbency. Track or training shoe last is used. U-
   throat, strap over toe, tubular moccasin or cement construction, some with foxing. Conventional lacing. Uppers with
   padded collar and tongues are often perforated for easy
   expulsion of water (running through streams, etc.). Sole is of
   rubber, multi-studded (15–20 nubs), or rippled cement and/or
   rivet construction. Some ripple soles, combination studs for
   lateral movement (down hills) are manufactured in Europe.
   Slight heel wedges are popular for shock absorbency.

``The multiplicity of life styles are a constant
challenge to creativity.''
Epilogue, The Art & Science of Footwear Manufacturing

C H A P T E R 　 **17**

SPECIALTY SPORT SHOES

A thletic footwear is diverse. The encyclopedia of sports and games lists over 400 national or international sports activities. Many of these sports use shoes classified under another major area (e.g., field hockey players usually wear soccer shoes). In this chapter we will see just how diversified and specialized sport shoes have become in the past quarter century. In the category of *Specialty Sport Shoes* we will discuss all competitive sports not covered in the broad classifications of track, field, outdoor court or winter sport. Many of the sports dealt with in this chapter are major participation sports in their own right. As we stated in the discussion of marketing and advertising, there are two business criteria that justify making a certain shoe for a sport. They are:

1. Sales volume in the sport (mass participation)

2. Major advertising value

One could consider the athletic shoe industry as a devoted group striving for innovation and perfection in sports. Many of the sports for which shoes are produced do not fall under the criteria of mass participation or of advertising value. Yet these shoes are demanded by the world's best in the sport and somewhere in the world there are a few manufacturers prepared to meet this demand. Such is the nature of the athletic footwear business.

Due to the widely varying nature of sports classified as "specialized" the following subcategories will be discussed individually:

17-1. Shoes for gymnastics—nappa upper leather, stretching compensation, durable elastic rubber boarding, stuffing-cover-sole, combined Cosy rubber walking-sole.

17-2. Light shoes for gymnastics—stretch upper, elastic bordering, instep buckle, stuffing-cover-sole, prominent fit.

- GYMNASTICS
- COMBAT
- TARGET
- TARGET BALL
- EQUESTRIAN
- WHEELS
- WATER

GYMNASTICS

Gymnastics, like the other ancient sports of track and field and swimming, dates back to the Greek era. It is one of the foundation sports in the Olympic Games.

FOOT AND LEG MECHANICS—running; jumping; stretching; balance. Gymnastics is performed either free style on mats or on apparatus of different kinds. As gymnastic maneuvers combine many types of motion, only those involving the lower extremity are considered.

SURFACES—floor mats; gym/wood or synthetic flooring.

SHOE REQUIREMENTS—gymnasts must be able to feel the floor, or apparatus, with as little interference as possible. Thus, lightweight gymnastic slippers are used. These are of synthetic, canvas, nylon or a soft glove leather upper, simply stitched with an elastic vent or tape strap to hug the foot. The soling is usually a lightweight thin reinforced gum rubber and leather nonslip sole.

This type of shoe is of the simplest construction. It is made by simply stitching the upper and sole together and turning the slipper inside out. There are no special features to the shoe other than its lightness and a glove-like fit to feel as natural as possible on the gymnasts foot.

WEIGHTLIFTING

Weightlifting was not recognized as a true sport until late in the nineteenth century in England and in France, although lifting weights of some kind in competition dates to prehistoric times. Weightlifting is now an Olympic event. There are nine official weight classes for contestants, from flyweight to super heavyweight. The competition consists of two separate lifts—snatch and jerk. The total weight of the two lifts is added to arrive at the score for each contestant.

FOOT AND LEG MOVEMENT—lifting; balance; leg splits or bends; locking of knees.

SURFACE—specially prepared sprung wood flooring.

SHOE REQUIREMENTS—a true specialty shoe with only a limited number of companies making a few thousand pairs per year and distributing them on a global basis. Due to the stress placed on the lower anatomy weightlifting boots or shoes are of a sturdy leather or suede upper (2.5–4 mm thickness). Lined and reinforced with extra-strong heel counter and medial arch support. For additional support across the instep or waist of the shoe a thick leather strap with buckle is added. For maximum width fitting a lace-to-toe cut is usually preferred. Shoes must not be unnaturally widened. Soles are either thick composition rubber or leather, with regular lifted heels or wedges. A shank is used for added sole strength on heel models. Heels should not exceed 4 cm. in width. Construction is either a lockstitch Goodyear welt method, or tack and cement construction of the sturdy boot type. Because the feet are planted during the lifting of the bar, the weight of the boot is not particularly a factor in this event.

17-3. Shoes for weightlifting—derby-cut velour suede upper with supporting leather strap. Leather midsole with special wood shank and heel.

AEROBIC EXERCISE/DANCING

Although not considered a sport, the popularity of organized exercise to either an aerobic schedule or to music has rapidly increased. Primarily a woman's fitness activity.

FOOT AND LEG MECHANICS—stationary running; jumping; skipping; stretching; multi-directional dancing; emphasis on forefoot movement.

SURFACES—aerobic exercise is usually performed on indoor wood or hard composition surfaces (such as linoleum). Aerobic dancing is usually performed on carpet or covered surfaces.

SHOE REQUIREMENTS—the generally accepted aerobic exercise shoe has evolved into a cross between a lightweight running shoe with adequate shock absorbency, and a modified indoor court shoe with some medial and lateral support as well as wrap-up toe and heel protection.

Uppers of soft smooth garment leather or nylon taffeta with leather or suede trim. U-throat or strap-over-toe designs. Narrow fitting for women.

Sole of gum or SBR rubber with wrap-up toe and EVA wedge and midsole for slight elevation and adequate shock absorbency.

A pure aerobic dance shoe tends to be much closer to a gymnastic slipper or dancing pump than to a running shoe. Canvas or nylon taffeta upper, pointed or close fitting last.

17-4. The aerobic shoe "look" that became a new category for athletic footwear in the 1980s and the latest "street shoe" phenomenon.

17-5. Dancing shoes—ideal for all modern dances like Rock 'n Roll, Jazzgymnastics—nappa upper leather, soft chromleather walking sole.

17-6. Larry Holmes (left) and Mohammed Ali (right), two heavyweight shoe endorsees.

17-7. A typical boxing shoe.

17-8. Mesh/suede boxing shoes with McKay stitched rubber soles.

Wrap-up rubber foxing at toe and heel for drag protection and extra support. Thin, built-up vulcanized sole with shallow tread pattern.

The aerobics exercise shoe now incorporates many technical features such as forefoot stabilizer straps and forefoot shock attenuating products. Different hardnesses and densities of EVA and PU are used as shock absorbing forefoot pads as well as viscollastic polymer pads incorporated into the sockliner. Flexibility in the forepart is important. Some shoes have outside heel stabilizers.

COMBAT SPORTS

BOXING

Boxing as a sport dates to the ancient Greeks. Modern boxing rules were formulated in England in the middle of the eighteenth century. There are 12 weight categories. The sport is not only a popular amateur and Olympic sport, but a much publicized professional sport as well.

FOOT AND LEG MECHANICS—balance; stretching; lunging; lateral movement; skipping. In boxing, the legs are used for balance and movement, to support the upper body, as well as weight transference into the punch.

SURFACES—specially prepared wood and canvas surface, with felt or rubber underpadding.

SHOE REQUIREMENTS—requires a lightweight leather or nylon high-cut boot, normally up to the calf (10″ high-cut). This gives the boxer adequate ankle and lateral support.

Materials used are usually soft calf or cowhide, suede and kidskin leathers. Nylon mesh reinforced with suede, as well as cheaper lined vinyls, can be used on lower-priced models. The cut is form fitting in both the foot and the shaft of the boot, which is usually peg-topped for snug fit. Traditional lace-to-toe design is preferred with 13–19 eyelets according to the height of the cut.

Soling is usually flat (zero heel) or slight heel wedge to keep the weight on the balls of the feet. Split leather soling material, or rubber non-slip inserts, are popular for top-grade boots. Composition gristle or rubber soles are used on other grades of boots. Lightweight cement and stitched constructions are preferred to the more traditional lockstitch methods.

WRESTLING

Wrestling is one of the ancient combat sports. It dates back at least to Egyptian times. Free-style wrestling is the most common modern form, and is the form used in International and Olympic competition. Greco-Roman style wrestling is a similar form. There are many other ancient forms of wrestling. In one of them, Japanese Sumo wrestling, shoes are not even worn!

FOOT AND LEG MECHANICS—Due to the complex leg mechanics in wrestling, both standing and on the mat as part of hold positions, only body balance and center of gravity are listed as main movements.

SURFACES—smooth rubber padded mat 12 m square, often on a wooden platform.

SHOE REQUIREMENTS—uppers are over the ankle (8–9 inch) highcuts in leather, soft reinforced nylon or canvas. Conventional lacing 8–12 eyelets. Reinforced toe and outside heel counter.

Soles are split leather with smooth or textured rubber inserts for flexibility in mat-work cemented and stitched construction, no heels, no buckles or nails are allowed. Greco-Roman boots are usually higher than freestyle, and have a more rigid nonslip sole.

FENCING

Fencing as a sport was begun in Britain in the middle of the sixteenth century. There are three weapons, the foil, epee, and sabre. It is an Olympic sport.

FOOT AND LEG MECHANICS—balance; stance; lunging; forward and backward movements.

SURFACES—various: wood, rubber, metal mesh, synthetic. The area is called the "piste" and has a minimum length of 13 meters.

SHOE REQUIREMENTS—upper is of leather or nylon mesh oxford cut, strongly reinforced in heavy wear or drag areas (toe, medial vamp and quarter), medial heel with rubber foxing. Cement or moccasin rearpart construction. Rigid heel counter, conventional or speed lacing. Nylon or textile lined for extra strength. Arch support and padded collar for comfort.

Sole is made from lightweight MCR with slight heel wedge. Traction holes in sole with herringbone or symmetrical smooth patterned tread.

TARGET SPORTS

ARCHERY

It is claimed by the *Guinness Book of Sports Records* that archery has the earliest origins of any sport. Target archery is an Olympic event for men and women. Arrows are shot from a standing position from prescribed distances from a target. Field and crossbow archery also use targets, with varying rules under different courses.

FOOT AND LEG MECHANICS—standing position; balance and stability.

SURFACES—grass; field; artificial or indoor surfaces.

SHOE REQUIREMENTS—there are no footwear restrictions specified in the rules of either target or field archery. Therefore a variety of high, mid, and low-cut boots and shoes are worn. Recently a company has produced a shoe called "Archer," which is a basic low-cut leather general training shoe. It has a U-throat, wing-tip cut, with a multi-studded traction rubber shell sole giving extra stability on grass or artificial turf. It is also recommended by the manufacturer for indoor shooting ranges. Being a general purpose sport shoe it is cement and tack lasted with a cemented unit shell sole.

SHOOTING

As a sport, target shooting dates back to the fifteenth century in Switzerland. As an Olympic event, there are three categories. These are rifle shooting (small bore, big bore and air rifle), pistol shooting (rapid fire) and clay pigeon shooting (Olympic trench, down-the-line and skeet).

For the kneeling and standing positions in rifle and pistol shooting a rigid boot is found to be advantageous. Regulations specify the maximum upper height, thickness and sole dimensions. These specifications, drawn up by the "International Shooting Union," are the most exact for any sport shoe.

The following are the specifications for the specialized shooting boots manufactured to the I.S.U. guidelines:

Normal street type or light athletic shoes not exceeding the following specifications are permitted.

1) The upper part (above the line of the sole) material must be soft, flexible, pliable, not thicker than 2 mm. including all lining, when measured on any flat surface, such as point D in *figure*.

2) The sole must be flexible at the ball of the foot as in a normal street shoe.

3) The height of the shoe from the floor to the highest point (dimension C) may not exceed 2/3's of the length (dimension B). (For instance if the shoe length is 30 cm., the height may not be more than 20 cm.)

4) The shoes which are worn must be a matched pair.

The shooting shoe upper consists of any over-the-ankle boot

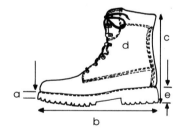

17-9. Regulation dimensions for a shooting shoe—(a) maximum thickness of sole at the toe, 10 millimeters; (b) overall length of shoe according to size of wearer's foot; (c) maximum height of shoe not to exceed two-thirds (2/3) length of B; (d) upper part of shoe material, maximum thickness 4 millimeters; (e) heel, maximum 30 millimeters.

with padded collar. 12 to 13 D-rings lace to toe cut. It is usually made of a smooth calf leather and has a padded tongue, rigid heel counter, slanted heel and extra stiff wedge sole for maximum stability. The toe is angled as an additional flat support in the kneeling position. It is a highly specialized shoe.

Shooters in other disciplines, such as skeet shooting, trench shooting, or down-the-line shooting, usually wear a shoe or boot having a flat sole, but allowing some ankle movement. Flat soled training shoes with wedge soles are popular.

Another regulation governs the dimensions of a cylindrical kneeling pad which may be used. These dimensions are: max. length = 20 cm., diameter = 12—18 cm.

BOWLING (PINS)
The present form of bowling with pins dates to the sixteenth century in Central Europe and Scotland. Mechanized indoor 5 and 10 pin bowling enjoys popularity today in North America and Europe. 9 pin bowling is also played in other parts of the world.

FOOT AND LEG MECHANICS—balance; step; lunge; slide.
SURFACES—wood or synthetic lanes.
SHOE REQUIREMENTS—this specialized sport has seen the development of specialized shoes for each foot. For the right-handed bowler the sole of the left (or delivery) shoe is all leather with white rubber heel. The right (or trailing) shoe has a rubber sole tipped with leather and a white rubber heel. This enables the bowler to slide on the front foot and to brake, push-off or balance with the back foot.

Uppers are either leather, suede or nylon (reinforced with suede) oxford low-cuts. Traditional lacing extends to the toe for total width adjustment. Construction is either cement and stitch or stitchdown welt/lockstitch. The sport is mainly recreational, however, and many different cuts and designs are available.

Soles are of split leather or more expensive vegetable-tanned leathers, such as nubock or buckskin. Holes may be perforated in the outsole to control the amount of slide. Less expensive models may have a composition leather/board sole.

LAWN BOWLS (FLAT OR CROWN GREEN)
The sport of outside target bowls has been traced as far as ancient Egyptian civilization. It is played either singly or in teams of up to four per side.

FOOT AND LEG MECHANICS—same as bowling delivery but without the approach steps. Delivery is made from a rubber mat called a footer. Back foot must be on or above the mat at the moment of release.

SURFACES—rectangular or square grass greens. The green is surrounded by a ditch or bank.

SHOE REQUIREMENTS—shoes may be of any upper material (usually leather), with smooth unit or prefabricated rubber soles. Wedges are allowed but no heels. Construction is either cement, Goodyear welt or lockstitch. There is usually a padded collar for comfort, rigid heel counter and good flex point. As the shoe is not subjected to great strain, many regular shoe designs are used (e.g., blucher). Canvas shoes with flat vulcanized-rubber soles are also used.

BOCCIE (BOULES) GORODKA, KEGELN

A form of bowls that is popular in Europe. Played between two players or teams.

FOOT AND LEG MECHANICS—same as for bowling.

SURFACES—pitch and various surfaces.

SHOE REQUIREMENTS—same as for lawn bowls (no formal regulations).

CROQUET

A seventeenth century game popularized in England. The original rubber and canvas "sneaker" was developed for this sport. It was called a croquet sandal. Played by two or four players.

FOOT AND LEG MECHANICS—similar to bowls, but using a wooden mallet to strike the ball.

SURFACE—rectangular grass lawn.

SHOE REQUIREMENTS—same as for lawn bowls.

GOLF

Golf has the largest participation of all the specialty sports and draws the most interest internationally. Many countries have claimed to have originated this sport, which in some form dates back before Christ. The recognized formal origin of golf must rest, however, with the royal and ancient golf club of St. Andrews, near Fife, Scotland, in the year 1754.

The game is extremely popular in many parts of the world, particularly Britain, Japan and North America. It is played by men and women of all ages from 10 to 12 years old and up. Part of the appeal of the game is due to its prestigious reputation, but it is a challenging mental (self-improvement) sport as well as an easy and relaxing form of exercise. As competitive as the sport itself is, the average golfer is somewhat unique in the sports world in as much as he or she seems to value the features of comfort, waterproofing, lightness and ease of cleaning, before actual performance on the links.

Different players, and different playing conditions, require different shoes. If you have a hard driving game or usually walk a hilly course, you may feel and play better in shoes that give you firm support. But, if you usually ride a cart or play a more relaxed game, you could be happier with a construction and materials offering a softer more comfortable shoe.

17-10. All-leather golf shoe uppers with traditional Kilty tongue.

FOOT AND LEG MECHANICS—walking; stance; balance. The golf swing or stroke is a complex, coordinated side-to-side motion which involves the hips, knees, ankles, subtalar and foot joints. The forward leg acts as a brace or anchor while the rear leg flexes and pivots to complete the follow through.

SURFACES—grass fairway; rough unprepared areas; sand bunkers; water traps; smooth grass putting greens.

SHOE REQUIREMENTS—leather or man-made PVC upper, stitched or flow-molded one-piece finish. Leather or textile lined for comfort, with a well-cushioned or orthopedic footbed insole for support, regular lacing system, U-throat design. The covering over the laces is called a "kilty", or apron, and it protects the laces from snagging in the sole cleats.

There are a variety of cuts, including U-throat, lace-to-toe, blucher and balmoral designs. Regular shoe styling is often incorporated into golf shoe designs. Moccasin, brogue and derby patterns are popular. As with regular footwear, the designs or patterns don't affect the shoe function.

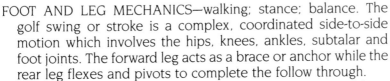

17-11. Spikeless golf shoe model derived from the Astroturf football sole.

Soling can be of PVC, MCR, EVA or leather, with a traditional heel. Polyurethane wedge unit or direct injected soles are becoming more popular as they are light and waterproof. Golf soles are equipped with a removable cleat system (usually six or seven forepart and four heel spikes). Spiked shoes are preferred (with spike receptacles embedded in the sole individually or in the form of plates) for grip on grass and rough terrain.

Traditional golf shoes developed from street footwear have remained similar in construction as well as styling. Construction is normally cement and tack lasting with heel counters, and substantial thickness in upper materials. Waterproof injected soles are functional for wet weather golfing. Microcellular rubber soles are lighter and more flexible. Polyurethane soles combine flexibility, lightness and waterproofing.

17-12. Golf shoe with soft PVC upper and direct injected PVC outsole.

EQUESTRIAN

Men began riding horses during a time when hunting and self-preservation were a way of survival. As a competitive sport, horse racing was one of man's earliest sports activities. The other areas of related equestrian sports can be categorized as follows:

- HUNTING, OR STEEPLE CHASING
- SHOW JUMPING
- DRESSAGE
- POLO
- RODEO
- HARNESS RACING
- THREE-DAY EVENT

FOOT AND LEG MECHANICS—Leg and footwork in riding play a different role than in most other sports. As the body is seated or haunched, the legs and feet play balancing, gripping and guiding roles in the mounted position. In harness racing the riders place their feet into stirrups mounted to the sulky. In rodeo the rider is sometimes required to dismount and perform certain activities on the ground.

SHOE REQUIREMENTS—With the exception of harness racing and rodeo riding, riding boots for all other events and sports are similar. Uppers are made from cowhide, calf or other sturdy fullgrain leather, chrome tanned. Softer leathers are leather lined. The boot extends over the calf and often has contrasting topleather as in hunting habit. The boot and shaft are form-fitting to the foot, ankle and calf, so as to allow the rider to be in contact with his or her mount. Spurs are metal attachments to the heels which the rider uses to prod the horse indicating different movements.

Riding boots have definite heels that can be used as stirrup stops when necessary. Heel counters are smooth so as to give the riders maximum contact with the horse's flanks. Particular attention should be paid to the ''pass line'' in riding boots, due to the tight fitting requirement to give optimal fit. (The pass line is the long heel measurement on the last between the seat to instep point).

Soles are either leather or unit rubber. Construction is either cement or lockstitch. Tack lasting is also still used in the heel. The shaft is sewn to the boot before attachment to the sole. Rubber or PVC molded boots of the same shape and design are popular in the lower price points.

In harness racing the rider's boots play practically no role in performance. No specific boot has been designed. Usually a semi or highcut leather boot with heel is preferred with some form of fleece or leather lining.

Rodeo boots, or cowboy boots with pointed toes and high heels, are used for rodeo events. These boots are full-grain leather, often leather lined and are of lower calf length. It is not clear whether rodeo boots have been traditionally worn and found to be suitable, or were functionally designed.

WHEEL SPORTS

ROLLER SKATING

First devised in Belgium in the mid-1700s possibly as a training method for ice skating, roller skating survived on its own as a warm weather activity. Present-day roller skates were introduced and patented in the U.S. in 1863.

The first models consisted of wooden spools fitted to adapted ice skates. The next improvement was small boxwood wheels with cushioned rubber pads. The introduction of ball bearings and metal wheels didn't take place until the end of the nineteenth century. Rubber wheels appeared during the boom period of the mid-1950s. A current boom in roller skating was largely prompted by the introduction of polyurethane wheels, which, combined with free or precision ball bearings, make roller skating an up-and-coming outdoor as well as indoor sport.

Trucks, plates and axles.
Ice skating and rollerskating boots are usually very similar. The main difference is that a lower cut boot may be used for roller skating if required, due to a more stable four-wheel base, as opposed to a 3mm blade that requires complete ankle support. The attachments to the sole in roller skating consist of a plate or truck chassis made of either polished one-piece aluminum or a recently introduced nylon material called zytel. The wheels are suspended or hung on rubber cushioned hangers at the front and rear (king pin) of the truck and attached to an axle with lock nuts. The truck is secured to the sole with two rivets or screws and bolts in the forepart and heel.

There are two types of plates:
1. 3/32″ diameter precision axle (suitable for 2½″ rink wheels)
2. 5/16″ diameter axle (suitable for both smaller rink wheels or 60–70mm outdoor wheels).

As upper quality varies in grades of skates, the main difference in quality of performance depends on the bearings and wheels themselves. Bearings used today are either loose bearings or precision bearings. Precision bearings are two sets of eight bearings self contained in metal rings, pressed into the wheel, which rotate around each other. Regular or semi-precision ball bearings have two sets of eight bearings, which are slipped on the axle on each side of the wheel. Precision bearings are smoother and more efficient and are used for all competition skating.

Lower grade skates may have a system of loose bearings contained by a metal retainer or core.

Wheels. Hard rubber wheels have been largely replaced by polyurethane wheels that have more resilience and "memory." Wheels can be of varying diameter and circumference, the preference being 55–70 mm. Urethane wheels are either injected or poured. Cast or poured are preferable.

The five primary types of roller skate wheels can be described as follows:

Indoor—smaller, harder rubber composition or PU.

Outdoor—softer PU or composition with high degree of resiliency or "rebound."

Artistic—hard wheel for fast roll with excellent gripping qualities.

Speed—wooden wheels were banned in 1977–78. Wheels are now PVC, PU or nylon compound.

Hockey—outdoor wheels are metal or PU. Indoor wheels are PU.

Stops. A replaceable rubber stop pad at the toe of the boot helps the skater stop and push off for traction. Leather or plastic protective toe guard stripes attach to the bottom eyestay row and extend over the tip of the boot to secure under the stop. They are designed to protect the toe area from excessive wear and drag.

As in ice skating there are several forms of roller sports as well as the popular recreational pastime and exercise. These include: figure and dance skating, speed roller skating, roller hockey and roller derby.

Figure and dance skating. This sport, similar to its ice skating counterparts, includes both national and international competitions.

FOOT AND LEG MECHANICS—the same as in figure and dance ice skating, including push-off, glide, balance, jumps and turns.

SURFACES—hardwood, cement, asphalt, asbestos and synthetic rubbers.

SHOE REQUIREMENTS—Boots for roller skates have an upper identical to ice skate boots. Men's boots are traditionally black, and ladies, white; however, other colors are available in better grades. The finest boots are made from full-grain calf in elk leather with soft or split leather linings. Thickness is important for adequate support. The combined outer and lining materials should be a minimum of 2.3–2.7 mm thick. This also prevents stretching.

On lower grade boots, varying grades of leather, split leather and vinyl, PVC and man-made materials are used. Uppers are highcut 13–17 eyelets with the higher eyelets usually hooks for easier lacing. Soles are either hard PVC or rubber unit soles or thick leather tack, cement or lockstitch construction. Soles must be substantial to anchor skate plates adequately. Steel, wooden or polypropylene shanks are used to support the plantar fascia and underfoot in the waist of the shoe.

A strong heel counter with elongated medial arch support is essential for firm control. A tight, form-fitting, semi-pointed last is preferred. Due to the pressures applied to boots in both ice and roller skating, custom fitting, support and extra padding features are offered by specialty boot makers.

Speed roller skates.
Speed skating events consist of from two to six skaters racing on an oval wooden track about 20 feet wide. Top skaters achieve speeds in excess of 25 mph.

FOOT AND LEG MECHANICS—same as in ice skating.
SURFACES—hardwood oval tracks, sometimes banked, approximately 167 feet long by 66 feet across.
SHOE REQUIREMENTS—same as ice speed skates. Soles must be adequate to anchor skate tracks. Wheel base is longer and lower than figure skates, and weight is very important.

Roller derby.
Sport of American origins, roller derby involves teams of five skating for team supremacy. Body contact and blocking are an integral part of the sport.

FOOT AND LEG MECHANICS—same as in speed skating with some variations due to the amount of unusual body contact in the sport.
SURFACES—same as for speed skating. Highcut figure skates are also used.

Roller hockey. First introduced in England in the late-1870s, this game is played by teams of five to a side and is similar to ice hockey, including the body contact. However, the stick is more like a field hockey stick and a hard ball is used.

FOOT AND LEG MECHANICS—same as in ice hockey.

SURFACES—Indoor rinks are cement or hardwood, while outdoor rinks may be asphalt or cement.

SHOE REQUIREMENTS—same as for ice hockey with roller skates. Since an ice hockey boot with hard toes and achilles tendon protection is used, roller wheels are attached instead of a blade. Steel wheels may be preferred on outdoor rinks.

CYCLING

Cycling has been a major method of transportation for almost 150 years. Cycles may be made with one or more wheels; however, the bicycle (two wheel) vehicle is by far the most common.

In terms of footwear, cycling presently has two distinct categories: 1) cleated "racing" shoes and 2) non-cleated "touring" shoes. Both have stiff soles to transmit foot power more comfortably and efficiently to the pedals. Each of these shoe categories is functionally and cosmetically different. Cleated or racing shoes are used specifically by those riders who rarely dismount while travelling. Non-cleated or touring shoes are more functionally suited for riders planning to regularly dismount, such as in the city, mountains or leisure riding where you may need to touch ground often.

Racing. Bicycle racing started in Great Britain or France in the 1860s. Top bikers have reached speeds of over 150 mph behind an automobile in timed speed trials and maximum distances covered may exceed 500 miles in a 24 hour time span.

Cycle racing can be categorized into two major segments: 1) road racing and 2) track racing. Other competitive cycle races include: cyclocross, time trials, hill climbs and stationary roller races.

Road races normally consist of tours over a set distance in a certain number of stages or shorter, one-day circuit races consisting of numerous repeated laps.

Track racing has many disciplines. A steeply banked track is used for pursuit and handicap races, as well as for point-to-point, scratch and madison races.

FOOT AND LEG MECHANICS—Propulsion of the cycle is achieved by using the gluteus, quadriceps, hamstrings and

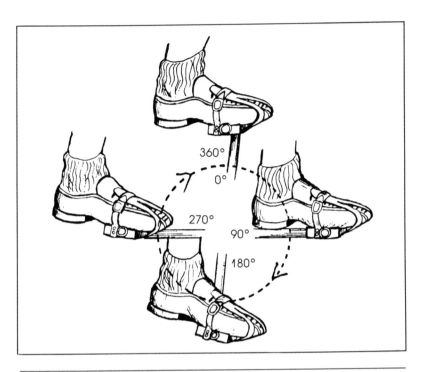

17-13. Cycling pedal movements with toe clips.

calf muscles to generate a thrusting force through the forefoot or ball of the foot. The majority of power is generated during the downward thrust; a lesser amount occurs during the up-stroke. With training however, useful power occurs over most of the pedal circle. This technique is called "ankling" or simply pedaling style. Coaches and riders frequently debate the merits of pedaling style. It seems to be a varying value, depending upon whether the rider is more a "spinner" or a "pusher". Spinners prefer lower gears at higher rpm's and pushers use higher gears at lower rpm's. Most advisors encourage a natural action of the foot, as in walking. Many cyclists place pressure on the lateral or medial sides of the foot, thus causing the foot to cant in a varus or valgus position. Pedals and cleat attachments on shoes can be adjusted to compensate for this canting.

SURFACES—Cycle shoes act on metal or nylon pedals with either smooth surfaces or two parallel cage plates. Pedals may have steel clip and leather or nylon strap (traps) cinching foot to pedal. These act on the shoe upper.

SHOE REQUIREMENTS—Cycling racing shoes are made on specific lasts with a shape similar to a sprinters running track shoe; semi-pointed toe, wide girth, narrow waist and narrow

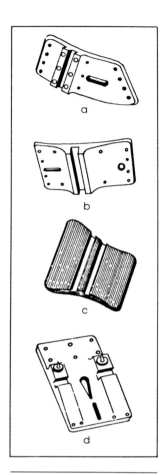

17-14. Shoe cleats, for use only with road- or track-racing shoes made for this purpose. Cleats fit into rattrap pedals, permit you to pull pedals up and push them down, and keep feet from sliding off pedals. (a) a road cleat; (b) a track cleat; (c) a leather model used for touring; (d) a cleat for cyclo-cross racing.

heel. They also require considerable toe spring and a high toe box for more efficient toe movement.

As cycling shoes originated in France and Italy they tend to be built on narrow lasts. Wider shoes are now available for other market areas such as North America, where the foot width is generally wider.

Upper materials used are mainly smooth, supple calf or kid leather with perforated holes for lightness and ventilation. Combination uppers of leather-reinforced armoured (ballistic) mesh nylon are also popular, again for lightness and ventilation. The U-throat cut or full lace-to-toe design (often called the bicycle cut) are preferred for cycling. Most racing shoes are unlined and therefore tend to stretch, so it is recommended to buy leather shoes tight. Lace closure systems are most common but Velcro fastening is also popular with additional girth cinch straps to ensure firm and comfortable fit. Many models include extended eyestay strap design or reinforced toecap; rigid heel counter, rolled or paddled topline collar and lightly padded tongue and insoles for added comfort.

Soles are either steel or wood reinforced, or rigid unit nylon or PU. Holes are bored through the sole so that cleats may be affixed and water expelled rapidly. Rubber heel and toe pads prevent slipping when walking. Shoe construction methods are conventional lasting with cement and rivot or cemented soles. A few models have directly injected high density synthetic soles.

Cycle shoes are positioned and/or clamped to the pedals (depending on the system) by means of cycle cleats. These cleats allow optimum efficiency in cycling because, along with clip and strap, they lock the foot to the pedal, permitting the foot to pull up on the pedal and to attain a locked position when pushing down. Rattrap pedals with straps and toe clips increase cycling efficiency by as much as 40 percent. Toe clips come in four sizes: (American shoe sizes) small (6–8), medium (8½–10), large (10½–12) and extra large (13–14).

Rigid sole plates prevent bruising of the metatarsal bones from pedal pressure and allow more even pressure on the pedal. There are several different cleat attachments specialized for cycle cross-racing, touring, track and roads. Most shoes made for cleats use an adjustable cleat which bolts or screws to the sole and allows angular and fore or aft adjustment.

Racing Style Cleat Attachments and Clipless Systems. This is a fast evolving, innovative area of sport shoe

technology. Since the late 1970s many different adjustable molded-in and screw-on cleat systems have been introduced into the market. Many require exclusive integral shoe-binding-pedal systems that are not interchangeable with other components.

Innovative sole/cleat systems *that fit standard pedal attachments* include Puma's molded-in, rotating 3-option disk-cleat that has adjustable grooves to achieve the correct angle and exact anterior ball pressure point on the pedal. Le Coq has a similar system with a notched cog disc to prevent slippage. Patrick's molded-in cleat is adjustable and included with the shoe, as is the Power shoe from Bata.

Vittoria has an innovative cleat system with an anchor nut which moves in a slotted track underneath the cleat.

The Cinelli system was the first clipless binding on the market. This system, adaptable to conventional cleated shoes, locked the shoe to a standard pedal with a nylon cleat screwed to the shoe that dovetails into a metal trough attached to the pedal. The shoe is locked to the pedal with a metal pin that is lever driven into the cleat. This system has largely been superseded by the integral clipless systems.

An innovative *clipless integral shoe/pedal system* called the *Look system* pioneered that clipless revolution. Using a special Aerolite pedal, which is a single light-weight sleeved spindal, a nylon cleat with a hemispherical cut-out pushes on and rolls off the pedal. The special Look system cleat fits all standard cleated shoes that have Look compatible drill holes for attachment. *Adidas* also market their own integral quick release system, which uses a shoe with slots in the side of its sole that engage ridges on the pedals. A tab in the center keeps the shoe in place. Release is achieved by using a lever on the side of the pedal.

Howell cycle binding uses a system with a spring-loaded bar on the pedal which locks into place inside a recess in the shoe's sole. Twisting the foot disengages the shoe from the pedal which leaves a non-cleated sole surface for walking.

Velcro straps have gained importance with the advent of new clipless shoe/pedal systems. The straps prevent the upper from separating from the sole by acting as a surrogate toe strap during the upstroke. They also serve the purpose of a more snug tie fit to secure the shoe to the new style pedals.

Touring Shoes.
Touring cycle shoes are designed for recreational cyclists who prefer a combination shoe made for both cycling and walking. They are created as dual purpose products. Touring shoes, unless adapted to take cleats, are not as efficient on the cycle, but are more convenient and comfortable for off cycle purposes. Walking in conventional cleats will damage the

17-15. Traditionally styled rubber Vulcanized cycle touring shoe with canvas upper.

cleats and soles of shoes, as well as being uncomfortable. A good touring shoe is stiff enough to transmit sufficient power to the pedal, yet flexes enough at the break point for comfortable, efficient ground contact.

Last shapes used for cycle touring models resemble running shoe (training) lasts. Some may have modified characteristics of both cycling racing and running shapes. Uppers are made from durable, breathable fabrics such as: ballistic nylon mesh, canvas or softer nylons with leather, suede or synthetic reinforcements at the high abrasion toe clip and strap contact points. Comfortable amenities, such as padded tongues, padded collars and back tabs, linings and cushioned sock liners, as in running shoes, are common standard features in touring models. Specifically designed running shoe features such as variable lacing and notched achilles back tabs are also appearing now on cycle models. Many have high visibility reflective trim which is an obvious plus feature for the safety conscious cyclist.

Touring shoe soles require a rigid forepart as a platform for pedalling, however, they must flex in an upward direction to allow walking comfort. Most touring models also have a slight to medium heel wedge for added shock absorbency and comfort. Soling materials are predominently made from SBR rubber or PU to provide necessary traction on the ground and grip on the pedals. Heel wedges may be in the form of a unit, one-piece construction or prefabricated EVA, similar to a running shoe sole. Toe bumpers and side foxing give added reinforcement to pedal contact areas. Sole tread patterns vary considerably from a slotted channel forepart or "sawtooth" ridged block arrangement, to a flat wide channel forepart covered with gum or non-slip rubber. There is usually enough play in these tread designs for satisfactory foot positioning for most riders. Most common construction is cemented soles. Older styles, but still functional, may be vulcanized rubber.

A cycle *mountain touring shoe* has recently been developed as a hybrid hiking/walking/cycle touring model suitable for all-terrain activities. This shoe has a better reinforced upper and deeper treads to accommodate larger pedals used on mountain bikes.

Triathlon Shoe. Triathlon is the modern-day "Iron Man" event consisting of consecutive long-distance swimming (2 miles), cycling (100 miles) and running (Marathon) events. (Distances may vary per event.) Usually specialized cycle racing and marathon running shoes are changed between events with the clock ticking. However, in order to save time spent on changing shoes the ever-innovative athletic shoe makers have introduced a combination running/cycling shoe for this sport.

The shoe differs from a cycle-touring model in that it is primarily made for running with adequate shock absorbing midsole and heel wedge. The upper is similar to a racing/trainer made of lightweight mesh and suede or leather with enough added reinforcement for pedal trap use. The innovative sole application is in the form of an attachable nylon or high-density PU outsole plate. The hard plate covering the forepart of the sole and extending into the shank provides the necessary rigidity for pedal use. The removable outsole plate may be ridged as in most touring models or contain a form of adjustable universal cycle cleat as used in cycle racing.

17-16. Speed bike champion, George Morin, wearing specialized track or road motorcycle boots.

MOTORCYCLING

Motorcycle racing began in England at the end of the nineteenth century. The fastest speeds on a circuit track exceed 160 mph. The fastest speed ever clocked on a motorcycle is over 300 mph. Competitions are varied. Some of them are:

- ROAD RACING
- SIDECAR COMBINATIONS
- DRAG RACING
- SPEEDWAY (dirt track)
- SPRINT RACES
- ICE RACING
- MOTOCROSS (scrambles)
- TRIALS
- GRASSTRACK RACING

FOOT AND LEG MECHANICS—the lower anatomy plays a balancing and gripping role in most motorcycle races. In some forms, such as speedway racing, the leg and foot are used as a "prop" while cornering. Comfort, protection and durability of the shoe are important considerations in this sport.

SURFACES—asphalt road; cinder tracks; grass terrain; ice.

SHOE REQUIREMENTS—boots for motorcycling can be classified in four categories:

1) *Racing*—boots are mid-calf length, semi-soft leather. Leather lined gusset. Zippered. Rigid counter, reinforced toe box. Soles are either a single thickness of leather (cement and stitch) or unit rubber sole (cement) with heel and inside ankle padding. Rubber, oil-resistant soles with some tread are preferred for push starts.

2) *Enduro*—boots are highcut (over calf), sturdy full-grain leather with leather or vinyl lining (2.5–2.8 mm.). Zipper and buckle fasteners. Rigid heel counter, toe shank. Outsole should be a lugged traction tread, for rugged terrain.

17-17. Custom-made motorcycle dirt-track racing boot. Steel helps protect a rider's outrigger foot.

3) *Motocross*—boots are highcut, made of thick leather, un-lined or with leather lining (2.7–3 mm.). Zipper and five to seven regular or speed buckles. Elasticized cuffs to keep out dirt. Rigid heel counter. Hardened box toe. Thick leather or rubber composition soles, Goodyear welt vul-canized rubber or unit rubber construction. Metal shin plates and front steel toe caps are riveted for protection and drag reinforcement. Steel overshoes can also be added for drag protection and as reinforcement for soles and medial side. These steel reinforcing plates are used in speedway as well as motocross. Soles are flat, with little or no tread.

4) *Touring*—boots are used as a general purpose riding boot in several disciplines. Its features are: comfort, protection and durability. It is lighter than the enduro, or motocross variety, but sturdier than the lighter racing boot. It is calf length with medial skin and ankle padding and pull-on straps. Zippered and gusseted to keep out wind and water, with one to three buckles. Rigid heel counter, hardened box toe. Oil-resistant soles, Goodyear welt, unit rubber or composition cement construction. Some fea-ture pockets on side for keys, etc.

Recently a rigid polyurethane molded boot, hinged at the ankle (similar to a ski boot) has been introduced. This is a full calf-length boot offering lighter weight and good protection from stones and dirt. Some boots have air vents at the front and back and come in enduro and motocross versions with either lugged or flat soles.

MOTOR RACING (AUTO RACING)

The first auto race was held in France in 1891. Like motorcycle racing, auto racing features many different disciplines. These may be classified as:

- CIRCUIT RACING
- STOCK CAR RACING
- TOURING RACES (RALLYING)
- DRAG RACES
- HILLCLIMB
- SLALOM
- AUTOCROSS
- RALLYCROSS
- HILL TRIALS
- HIGH SPEED TRIALS

FOOT AND LEG MECHANICS—since the driver is in a seated position, only limited motion is required within the usually cramped cockpit. Feet must be moved quickly and surely between brake, clutch and gas pedals.

SURFACES—various rubber or metal pedals and levers.

SHOE REQUIREMENTS—there are two principal types of auto racing shoes made, although a variety of regular footwear is also used.

The first is a moccasin slipper with lightweight flexible uppers and a plug vamp. The sole has a series of holes punched through and a rubber nubbed sole plate is pushed through so that the ends of the nubs appear at the bottom or outsole. This shoe is extremely flexible and allows for foot expansion as well as sure traction on the pedals.

The second type, a recent development, is a safety shoe for auto racing drivers. This shoe conforms to International Clothing Regulations for circuit racing and is flame-proof for a period of 3-3½ minutes. The uppers are high-cut or semi-cut boot style with U-throat or lace-to-toe design. Regular lacing with Velcro strap top closure. Upper materials are either suede with fireproof Nomex or Kynol lining or Nomex outer material fully reinforced in toe, heel and sides with leather or suede to help resist wear and for better adhesion with the sole. Special up-swept back heel and Achilles padding for comfort. High-cut styles incorporate an extended Velcro secured flop for wrapping around multi-layered suits.

Sole may be non-slip rubber material or rubber midsole/ wedge covered with split leather outsole for pedal control. The shape of the last allows a narrow fitting upper to assure optimum performance and less leg and ankle fatigue. The shoes are lightweight (12–13 ozs.) to permit quick footwork.

A more protective high shafted boot is also available for drivers such as stunt or drag racers with additional layers to conform to SFI 3–2 standards. These overboot styles have a leather outsole and side zippers.

GO CART/RALLY RACING

A modern automobile sport popular in North America, South America, Hong Kong, Japan and Western Europe. There are two classifications:

- SPRINT (driver in upright position)
- ENDURA (driver in prone position)

FOOT AND LEG MECHANICS—as distinct from auto racing, the Go-cart driver requires protection from wheel burns and an aerodynamically designed sole (similar to that for luge racing, see *Winter Sports section*). The feet are exposed in a forward position in the cart.

SURFACES—rubber or metal pedals and levers.

SHOE REQUIREMENTS—uppers are made of Cordura nylon or fireproof Nomex material, with suede or leather reinforcement. High-cut design for protection. Sole is of wedge design, with wrap-up SBR or gum rubber outsole. Soft forepart is required for throttle control. Extended wrap-up heel.

At least one specialized manufacturer makes a boot with an angled shaft (approximately 18 degrees backward) for better comfort in the seated prone position.

WATER SPORTS

SCULLING AND ROWING
Dates to the early eighteenth century in England as a competitive sport. It has been an Olympic event since 1936. Rowing is divided into two broad categories, regatta events and head-of-the-river races, which are basically timed events with boats setting off at measured intervals. All international rowing events are of the regatta variety, and include both sculling and rowing. There are three types of sculling events and five rowing events.

Footwear for rowing and sculling must be carefully chosen because of the possibility of accidents on the water.

FOOT AND LEG MECHANICS—Rowers and scullers are seated on a sliding seat. The feet are placed in a "cradle", and secured, to enhance grip and leverage during the rowing motion. With the feet secured the main thrust comes from the quadriceps and hamstrings, with some assistance from the gluteous and calf muscles. Knee flex is the most important joint movement. The feet are mainly used to push against the foot boards.

SURFACES—wooden, rubber or plastic surfaces on the foot board.

SHOE REQUIREMENTS—rowing shoes are like cycling shoes. Uppers are of perforated leather on a track shoe last, U-throat, with regular or speed lacing. Soles are rubber or nylon units or leather (stitch-and-cement). Some shoes have screw plate attachments in the forepart, to secure the shoe directly to the footboards. In case of accident, a special Velcro fastener on the heel permits easy release without unlacing the shoe. An extended heel padding and rigid heel counter are added for comfort and protection. A variety of nonspecialized flat soled shoes are used in conjunction with leather or nylon holding straps attached to the foot board.

17-18. Rowing shoes with quick release Velcro heel feature.

WATER SKIING

Originated in plank gliding and aquaplaning in the early 1900s. The present day form of water skiing began in the U.S.A. around 1920. In addition to being a popular leisure sport, water skiing is a competitive sport. Competitions are divided into three events: jumping, slalom and trick skiing. The combined total of points in all three events determines the winner of a championship.

FOOT AND LEG MECHANICS—flexing; bending; torsion; balance and stability. Rigid ankle support is required for most movements. Jumping is done on two skis, slalom uses only one (with the free leg held behind the other). Trick skiing involves various movements, especially balancing.

SURFACES—smooth water (lake, reservoir or river).

SHOE REQUIREMENTS—various types of skis are used, but none can exceed 25 cm. in width or 100 cm. in length. Any type of "foot binding" or boot may be affixed to the ski. Recreational skiers usually wear a latex or neoprene toe and heel harness, with some reinforcement at the toe strap and an extended heel.

Competition skiers use a more sophisticated piece of footwear which can be classed as a "boot". Heel and toe pieces are foam-lined neoprene, overlaid with rubber reinforcing straps. These tension-adjustment bindings provide ankle sup-

17-19. Typical horseshoe type binding

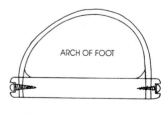

17-20. H.O. ski boot type binding

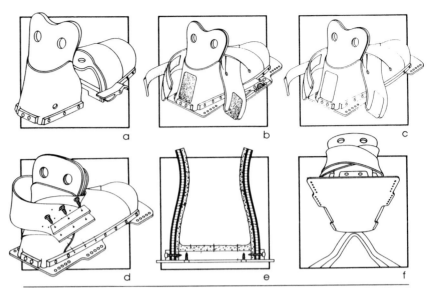

17-21. (a) Neoprene Adjustable Ski Boot—adjustable ski boot features a fixed heel and removable front toe. (b) Adjustable Ski Boot with Velcro Wrap—adjustable ski boot features a fixed heel and a removable adjustable front toe with Velcro wrap. (c) Low Wrap Ski Boot with Velcro Wrap—patterned after High Wrap Competition Ski Boot, the low wrap offers a high degree of custom fit. (d) High Wrap Competition Ski Boot—the high wrap is a plate-mounted fixed ski boot made for an individual's own shoe size. It should be used only by the stronger and more advanced skier. (e) The ski boot replaces the traditional "horse-shoe" design with a foot shaped design. The result has been one of the biggest revolutions in water skiing equipment. (f) Ski Boot Interchangeability—by utilizing the same hole pattern on plate bindings the customer has the option of upgrading his equipment.

port similar to the hard-shelled boots used by snow skiers. The front foot is placed in the plate-mounted support binding. The back foot is slipped into an elevated-heel/toe-strap harness.

YACHTING

The origin of yacht racing can be traced to England in the middle of the eighteenth century. There are currently six Olympic events in yacht racing. Three types of footwear are used. They are:

1. Leather upper, stitched unit sole—oil or silicone impregnated leather to repel water, stay soft and dry quickly. Moccasin style slip-on, with rolled or padded top line. Another popular design is the three-eyelet moccasin with leather thong lacing. A Gore-Tex water resistant liner or bootie is available on some models.

   Soles are cement-and-stitch with an overlapping welt. Usually a unit sole construction of white SBR rubber, with good flex and squeegee-type traction tread. Yachtsman Paul Sperry designed this sole in 1935.

2. **Canvas duck**—canvas is recommended for boating or yachting. The material dries quickly and is not greatly affected by water (in terms of cracking, finish or stiffness). Upper patterns are traditionally plain vamp blucher cut. Construction is usually string-lasted. Built-up rubber, vulcanized gum or rubber composition soles, with non-slip tread. Circular vamp design cut is popular and functional for boating.

   A unique tread is available for yachting (or boating). It is a siped (or calendered) slab sole that rejects water when the shoe is returned to a flat position. This sole is manufactured by stretching the rubber and cutting the sole with special knives. When released the rubber slab contracts into a smooth flush sole. When flexed, the cuts or treads open up for traction and squeeze out water at the same time. As in all built-up models, a rubber foxing is applied around the sole. This serves as a water repelling bumper on a deck shoe. Other traction outsoles are available featuring saw-toothed angled tread and radial side foxing to help prevent hydroplaning.

3. **Yachting boot**—a high (over the calf) rubber boot with non-slip gum rubber sole. A nylon waterproof cuff is attached to the top of the boot. The boot is normally of lightweight, built-up vulcanized rubber construction.

All three types should fulfill the following criteria:
1. traction on wet surfaces
2. protection from cuts, cold and wetness
3. non-damaging to deck surface
4. quick-drying
5. light and comfortable
6. easily removed in water (for swimming)
7. won't pick up sand or pebbles in tread
8. won't corrode in salt water or stain hose and feet

SPECIALIZED CATEGORY

COACHES' AND OFFICIALS' SHOES
These basically fall into two broad categories: flat court shoes and field shoes. Coaches and especially officials have traditionally worn the same or similar shoes to the competitors in their particular sport. The performance needs for officials and coaches are somewhat less than for the players, except perhaps in ice hockey refereeing. Another criteria, amended in many sports in the past decade, stipulated black or neutral shoes for the officials' uniform.

B I B L I O G R A P H Y

BOOKS:

Brooke, Iris. *Footwear: A Short History of European & American Shoes*. New York: Theatre Arts Books, 1971.

Cavanagh, Dr. Peter R. *The Running Shoe Book*. Mountain View, California: World Publications, 1980.

Clerici, Gianni. *The Ultimate Tennis Book*. Chicago, Illinois: Follett Pub. Co., 1975.

Cohn, Walter E. *Modern Footwear Materials & Processes*. New York: Fairchild Publications, 1969.

Complete Buying Guide: Fishing Equipment. New York: Pocket Books.

The Diagram Group. *Rules of the Game*. New York: Paddington Press, 1974.

Donaldson, Gerald. *The Walking Book*. New York: Holt, Rinehart & Winston, 1979.

Dorland's Illustrated Medical Dictionary, 25th ed., Philadelphia, Pennsylvania: W.B. Saunders Co., 1980.

Hlavac, Dr. Harry F. *The Foot Book: Advice for Athletes*. Mountain View, California: World Publications, 1977.

Lund, Morton. *Ski Technique.* New York: Harper & Row, 1975.

McWhirter, Norris. *Guinness Sports Record Book.* New York: Bantam Books, 1980.

Rinaldi, Robert R. and Michael L. Sabia, Jr. *Sports Medicine.* Mount Kisco, New York: Futura Publishing Co. Inc., 1980.

Samitz, M.H., and Alan S. Dara, Jr. *Cutaneous Lesions of the Lower Extremities.* Philadelphia, Pennsylvania: J.B. Lippincott Co., 1971

Sheehan, George. *Dr. Sheehan on Running.* Mountain View, California: World Publications, 1975.

Sloane, Eugene A. *The All New Complete Handbook of Bicycling.* New York: Simon & Schuster, 1980.

Squires, Dick. *The Other Racquet Sports.* New York: McGraw-Hill Inc., 1978.

Subotnick, Steven I. *Podiatric Sports Medicine.* New York: Futura Publishing Co., 1975.

_____. *The Running Foot Doctor.* Mountain View, California: World Publications, 1977.

Sweetgall, Robert. *Rockport's Fitness Walking.* New York: The Putnam Publishing Group Inc., 1985.

Yanker, Gary D. *Rockport's Exercisewalking.* Chicago, Illinois: Contemporary Books Inc., 1983.

Walker, Samuel Americus. *Sneakers.* New York: Workman Publishing Co., 1978.

PERIODICALS:

Athlete's Feet. Mountain View, California: World Publications (from the editors of *Runner's World*).

Canadian Footwear Journal. Toronto, Canada: Southam Business Publications Ltd.

Footwear News. New York: Fairchild Publications.

Golf Digest. Norwalk, Connecticut: Golf Digest/Tennis Inc.

Golf Magazine. New York: Times-Mirror Magazines.

The Runner. New York: CBS Magazines.

Runner's World. Mountain View, California: World Publications.

Running Times Magazine. Woodbridge, Virginia: Running Times Inc.

Ski. New York: Times-Mirror Magazines.

Sport & Mode. Wiesbaden, West Germany.

Sporting Goods Business. New York: Gralla Publications.

The Sporting Goods Dealer. St. Louis, Missouri: The Sports News Publishing Co.

The Sporting News. St. Louis, Missouri: The Sporting News Publishing Co./Times-Mirror Magazines.

Sports Illustrated. New York: Time Inc.

Sports Magazine. New York: Sports Media Corp.

Sports Merchandiser. Atlanta, Georgia: WRC Smith Publishing Co.

SportStyle. New York: Fairchild Publications.

Tennis. Norwalk, Connecticut: Golf Digest/Tennis Inc.

World Tennis. Norwalk, Connecticut: Golf Digest/Tennis Inc.

PAMPHLETS & BULLETINS:

ABC Publishing/Los Angeles Magazine—*Official Olympic Guide to Los Angeles.*

Adidas U.S.A. Inc.—*Adidas Science of Sport.*

National Walking Council—Herz, C.K. *Walk for Pleasure.*

New Balance Publications—Macik, John. *The Proper Fit.*

Nike Inc., Oregon.—*Nike Tech-togs*.

N.S.G.A., Chicago, Illinois—Somer, John. N.S.G.A. *Product Information*.

Poron, Division of Roger Corp.—*Shoe & Foot Comfort*.

Pony Sports & Leisure, Inc.—Bush, Jim. *The Running Report*.

SATRA U.K. and Canada.—*Shoe & Allied Trades Research Association Publications*.

Scholl Inc., Memphis, Tennessee.—Dr. *Scholl Publications*.